CHILD SEXUAL ABUSE AND PROTECTION LAWS IN INDIA

CHILD SEXUAL ABUSE AND PROTECTION LAWS IN INDIA

DEBARATI HALDER

Los Angeles | London | New Delhi
Singapore | Washington DC | Melbourne

First published in 2018 by

SAGE Publications India Pvt Ltd
B1/I-1 Mohan Cooperative Industrial Area
Mathura Road, New Delhi 110 044, India
www.sagepub.in

SAGE Publications Inc
2455 Teller Road
Thousand Oaks, California 91320, USA

SAGE Publications Ltd
1 Oliver's Yard, 55 City Road
London EC1Y 1SP, United Kingdom

SAGE Publications Asia-Pacific Pte Ltd
3 Church Street
#10-04 Samsung Hub
Singapore 049483

Published by Vivek Mehra for SAGE Publications India Pvt Ltd, typeset in 10.5/13 pts Adobe Caslon Pro by Zaza Eunice, Hosur, Tamil Nadu, India and printed at Chaman Enterprises, New Delhi.

Library of Congress Cataloging-in-Publication Data

Name: Halder, Debarati, author.
Title: Child sexual abuse and protection laws in India / Debarati Halder.
Description: New Delhi, India: SAGE Publications, 2018. | Includes
  bibliographical references and index.
Identifiers: LCCN 2018013184 (print) | LCCN 2018013289 (ebook) | ISBN
  9789352806867 (Web PDF) | ISBN 9789352806850 (E pub 2.0) | ISBN
  9789352806843 (hardback: alk. paper)
Subjects: LCSH: Child sexual abuse—Law and legislation—India. |
  Children—Crimes against—India. | Children—Legal status, laws,
  etc.—India. | India. Protection of Children from Sexual Offences Act,
  2012.
Classification: LCC KNS4190 (ebook) | LCC KNS4190 .H35 2018 (print) | DDC
  345.54/025554—dc23
LC record available at https://lccn.loc.gov/2018013184

ISBN: 978-93-528-0684-3 (HB)

SAGE Team: Rajesh Dey, Sandhya Gola, Shaonli Deb and Rajinder Kaur

Dedicated to my mother, who gave me a secured childhood and my husband, who ensures a safe childhood for our daughter.

Thank you for choosing a SAGE product!
If you have any comment, observation or feedback,
I would like to personally hear from you.

Please write to me at **contactceo@sagepub.in**

Vivek Mehra, Managing Director and CEO, SAGE India.

Bulk Sales

SAGE India offers special discounts
for purchase of books in bulk.
We also make available special imprints
and excerpts from our books on demand.

For orders and enquiries, write to us at

Marketing Department
SAGE Publications India Pvt Ltd
B1/I-1, Mohan Cooperative Industrial Area
Mathura Road, Post Bag 7
New Delhi 110044, India

E-mail us at **marketing@sagepub.in**

Get to know more about SAGE

Be invited to SAGE events, get on our mailing list.
Write today to **marketing@sagepub.in**

This book is also available as an e-book.

Contents

Part IV: Sentencing and Rehabilitation

List of Abbreviations

AD&MS	adult dating and matrimonial sites
AICTE	All India Council for Technical Education
CIF	Childline India Foundation
CRC	Convention on the Rights of the Child
CrPC	Code of Criminal Procedure
CWC	Child Welfare Committee
DCPU	District Child Protection Unit
FIR	First Information Report
IPC	Indian Penal Code
ISLR	Indian Student Law Review
ITPA	Immoral Traffic (Prevention) Act
JJ	Juvenile Justice
JJB	Juvenile Justice Board
MPSNS	multipurpose social networking sites
NCRB	National Crime Records Bureau
NSPCC	National Society for the Prevention of Cruelty to Children
POCSO	Protection of Children from Sexual Offences
SJPU	special juvenile police unit
TJ	therapeutic jurisprudence

List of Abbreviations

Foreword

It gives me great pleasure to write a brief foreword for this book titled *Child Sexual Abuse and Protection Laws in India* by Dr Debarati Halder. It has the potential to be a very important contribution, not only at a scholarly level in relation to legal studies in India but also to raising awareness regarding sexual offence in general.

The book sets out the legal provisions in great detail and also lists important case laws to put flesh on the jurisprudential bones. In doing so, it is clear throughout that the author has emphasized the therapeutic and anti-therapeutic nature of the law. Sexual offences, by their nature, evoke very strong emotional reactions and, in some respects, highlight the need to have an awareness of therapeutic issues more than other areas of law. Debarati has very aptly covered this in this book.

In this book, the author has rightly commented on 'how' the law is applied and not just 'what' the law is stated to be. A basic tenet of therapeutic jurisprudence is that how the law is applied which is fundamental to how it is perceived by victims of abuse, in particular. The sensitivity, or otherwise, of the police in investigating allegations is also crucial to the level of confidence or mistrust that complainants have in reporting abuse.

Sexual violence is a worldwide phenomenon that causes great harm. The situation in India needs to be seen in this context. The book includes chapters on the nature of sexual offence theories that explain why it occurs and the laws for regulating the same. It is also interesting to note how the author has addressed the issue of cybercrime, especially sexual crime targeting children. The author has very finely discussed how terms such as 'sexual grooming' and 'paedophilia' apply to sexual attraction to pre-pubertal children and not just to minors. The book offers an excellent conclusion and suggests some very innovative reporting mechanism for younger children.

I want to congratulate Dr Debarati Halder for her tremendous work and commitment to promoting more therapeutic approaches in legal circles to sexual violence in India and beyond. The high-profile cases she has referred to at the start of this book made headlines around the world; thus, there is great interest to see how the law (and attitudes) has changed in India.

I am sure that this book will be valuable to lawyers, the judiciary, law students and academic staff as well as some within the general public.

Kieran McGrath
Director, Irish Child and Family Institute

Preface

Prior to 2012, India had a very limited legal understanding about crimes against children. The Protection of Children from Sexual Offences (POCSO) Act, 2012 introduced new arenas of child rights whereby the law meant for prevention of sexual offences also recognized a child's right for gender orientation. POCSO Act, 2012 thereby recognized rights of *all* children irrespective of gender and gender orientation to be protected against sexual abuse perpetrated by *anyone* including adults and children, irrespective of gender and gender orientation. This provision recognized various forms of child sexual abuse including offences involving online child sexual abuse and using children for pornographic purposes. The POCSO Act also recognized certain offences which were either considered as less severe or were not recognized as offences by existing laws; these included stalking, grooming and enticing for sexual gratification, showing offensive contents and so on. The POCSO Act also presented a set of procedural provisions which are therapeutic in nature when seen from therapeutic jurisprudential perspective. At any rate, this Act was not properly implemented by the police, the child welfare committees and the judiciary. The rehabilitation of juvenile offenders posed another issue since POCSO Act did not touch upon either the rehabilitation of the victims or the offenders. Resultant victims and their families did not feel encouraged to report the offences in spite of the best efforts of the government and non-government stakeholders. The situation was slightly improved with the introduction of the amended Juvenile Justice (JJ) (Care and Protection of Children) Act, 2015, which further categorized three types of offences depending upon the nature of the punishments prescribed by the Indian Penal Code and the POCSO Act. This categorization was made specifically for administering juvenile justice system. However, neither this could be properly implemented. After the recent incidents of child rape cases in northern regions in India, the government has decided to amend the provisions for punishments: the Criminal Law Amendment Ordinance, 2018 has amended Indian Penal Code, Criminal Procedure Code, Indian Evidence Act and the POCSO Act to prescribe death penalty for rape of children below 12 years of age. It is hoped that the laws thus amended may be properly implemented.

The recent National Crime Records Bureau (NCRB) report, 2016 show a steep escalation of the statistics of crimes against children in India. However, on the other hand, some recent judgements of the Supreme Court of India have shown remarkable development in the understanding of child rights in the backdrop of child sexual abuse. However, this does not give a full picture of the developed under-standing from the grass-root levels. The reason for this diversity could be lacunas in the laws, lack of understanding of the provisions by the stakeholders including the police, criminal justice machinery (especially, lower judiciary), child welfare committees, lack of proper infrastructure and so on. The author further feels that time has come when the judiciary and the other stakeholders must understand POCSO Act and the JJ Act, 2015 from therapeutic jurisprudential aspect as well. This book therefore explains the provisions of POCSO Act and JJ Act, 2015 in the backdrop of forms of child sexual abuse from the perspective of therapeutic jurisprudence.

This book also emphasizes upon certain innovative mechanisms to sensitize children about offensive behaviours that should be reported. While the awareness mechanism of 'bad touch and good touch' is being used to sensitize children for reporting sexual abuse, the author also highlights another issue of awareness, namely, 'bad talk and good talk', in this book. This kind of awareness would sensitize the children as to what should be understood as normal, non-offensive speech and what should be construed as offensive, misogynist, discriminatory, threaten-ing, sexual bullying, sexually explicit and sexually enticing speech that should be avoided and that should also be reported in case the same is used by anyone against a child.

Further, this book introduces an innovative mechanism for report-ing sexual abuse by way of showing dance *mudras* (hand movements) that can symbolize types of offence such as sexual penetration, specific body parts that may have been violated or even may help the traumatized child to express the identity of the harasser if the same is a known person or a family member such as the father, a brother or any other male or female members of the family.

It is expected that this book would help not only the lawyers, judges, police officers, child-welfare committee members, and child right activists and related stakeholders, but may also be a good resource for law students, researchers and people in general.

Debarati Halder

Acknowledgements

When we speak about child rights, it is imperative to discuss certain forms of abuses and exploitation of children. As a practitioner, I had the opportunity to visit different child welfare committees, courts and especially, offices of district legal services authorities (DLSAs) to understand what the new forms of child sexual abuse are, why child victims do not wish to report, where the lacuna in laws lies and why good laws like the POCSO Act or the JJ Act, 2015 fail. There is a long list of authorities and individuals who deserve my sincere thanks for helping me conceptualize this book and finally write it.

At the outset, I must thank Professor David Wexler, proponent of modern therapeutic jurisprudence (TJ), for guiding me about TJ principles and how courts should function as problem-solving courts. I also express my thanks to Mr Kieran McGrath and the esteemed members of International Society of Therapeutic Jurisprudence for constantly guiding me.

I must thank Mr Ritesh Hada, Chairman, Karnavati University, Gandhinagar, Gujarat; Dr Deepak Shishoo, Hon'ble Provost of Karnavati University; and Dr Akanksha Singh, Director–Administration, Unitedworld School of Law, Karnavati University, for extending support to write this book.

I thank the honourable secretaries of DLSAs of Tamil Nadu, Kerala, West Bengal and Manipur for helping me understand how the DLSAs function in reality to extend support to child victims including rehabilitation of the victims and offenders. I also thank members of child welfare committees of Tirunelveli, Tamil Nadu and other states for helping me understand the positive and negative points of POCSO Act and JJ Act, 2015 and the execution of these laws by the police officers in practice.

I extend my thanks to my esteemed friend Mr Raghul Sudheesh for initial editing of the content of this book. I must also extend my thanks to my wonderful colleagues at Unitedworld School of Law, Karnavati University, for motivating me.

This book would not have been possible without the moral support of my husband, Dr K. Jaishankar, Professor and Head of the Department of Criminology, Raksha Shakti University, Gujarat, and President of South Asian Society of Criminology and Victimology. I thank him for constantly encouraging and motivating me to write this book. I also thank him for being a wonderful and caring father who took care of our daughter, Mriganayani, when I was busy working on this book.

I have no words to express my thanks to my mother, Mrs Dipika Haldar, without whose help this book would not have finished within due time.

My special thanks to our daughter, Mriganayani, for extending her support to all my endeavours. She is my main inspiration to do more research on this very issue.

Part I

Introduction

CHAPTER 1

Background

The gang rape of a paramedic female student on 16 December 2012 at Delhi shook the whole of India.

The impact was so huge that the Parliament decided to revamp the criminal laws meant for punishing the sexual offences targeting women. In this process, the Criminal Laws Amendment Act, 2013 was born which introduced many new measures to curb offences against women including acid attack, stalking, voyeurism and so on. This further amended specific provisions of Criminal Procedure Code (CrPC) and also the Indian Evidence Act, 1872 to suit the needs. Near about the same time when this heinous rape happened in Delhi, on 21 December 2012, a 12-year-old girl was murdered by a 36-year-old man in Tuticorin, Tamil Nadu. The girl was strangled with her own dupatta when she started to scream due to molestation and attempt to rape by the accused. This case created furore among the residents. The accused, who was found to be a habitual offender already booked for rape and murder in earlier cases, was subsequently arrested under charges of attempt to murder.[1] This case was one of the first sensitive cases relating to sexual offences targeted at children after the Nirbhaya

---

[1] PTI, '35-Year-Old Held for Attempted Rape, Murder of Teenaged Girl', *The Hindu*, 22 December 2012. Available at: http://www.thehindu.com/news/national/tamil-nadu/35yearold-held-for-attempted-rape-murder-of-teenaged-girl/article4229117.ece (accessed on 17 January 2018).

case[2] which attracted large-scale media attention.[3] Since then, umpteen numbers of cases of sexual offences targeting children have surfaced. In January 2015, in a Bengaluru school, a minor girl was allegedly sexually molested by her physical instructor within the school premises.[4] In February 2015, in Thane, Maharashtra, a 9-year-old boy was sexually assaulted by a 14-year-old boy, who took the victim to a secluded place, showed him porn clippings in his mobile before sexually assaulting him.[5] In the same month, in Bengaluru city again, an 8-year-old girl was allured by her rapist who, on the pretext of playing with her, took her to a secluded place to eventually rape and then kill her.[6] In July 2015, in Tuticorin, Tamil Nadu, a minor girl, aged about 9 years, was sexually assaulted by an 80-year-old man, who was the grandfather of a friend of the victim.[7] In May 2015, Yadava Manikanta was arrested for creating a Facebook page to upload and share images of children reportedly for sexual gratification. He was arrested under Protection of Children from Sexual Offences (POCSO) Act, 2012 and also under Tamil Nadu Prevention of Dangerous Activities of Bootleggers, Drug Offenders, Goondas, Immoral Traffic Offenders and Slum-Grabbers

[2] The case of gang rape of the paramedic student at Delhi is also known as 'Nirbhaya Case'.

[3] The author was also interviewed by the television media including Puthiya Thalaimurai, a Tamil news media channel, in relation to this case, wherein she expressed that POCSO, 2012 must be used in such cases.

[4] Sudipto Mondal, 'Minor Girl Raped in School in Central Bangalore', *The Hindustan Times*, 8 January 2015. Available at: http://www.hindustantimes.com/india-news/violence-in-central-bangalore-after-minor-is-molested/article1-1304217.aspx (accessed on 17 January 2018).

[5] Manoj Badgeri, 'Nine-Year-Old Boy Sexually Assaulted by Minor at Kalwa', *The Times of India*, 3 February 2015. Available at: http://timesofindia.indiatimes.com/city/thane/Nine-year-old-boy-sexually-assaulted-by-minor-at-Kalwa/articleshow/46099741.cms (accessed on 17 January 2018).

[6] Maya Sharma, 'Local Worker Arrested for Allegedly Raping, Killing 8-Year-Old in Bengaluru', *NDTV*, 8 February 2015. http://www.ndtv.com/bangalorenews/localworkerarrestedforallegedlyrapingkilling8yearoldinbengaluru73792 (accessed on 1 March 2015).

[7] Staff reporter, 'Octogenarian Gets RI for Sexual Assault on Minor Girl', *The Hindu*, 17 July 2015. Available at: http://www.thehindu.com/news/national/tamilnadu/octogenariangetsriforsexualassaultonminorgirl/article7432683.ece (accessed on 18 July 2015).

Act, 1982 (also known as Tamil Nadu Goondas Act, 1982) for creating/distributing child porn materials in the electronic media.[8] In August 2015, a 19-year-old boy from Pollachi, Coimbatore was arrested on charges of creating a similar page on Facebook with images of girl children and sexually explicit comments.[9] In 2017, a 4-year-old girl was sexually assaulted in a reputed school in south Kolkata by two school PT teachers. The men were reportedly arrested under Section (S.) 4 and S.6 of POCSO Act, which indicates that she had been subjected to penetrative sexual assault and aggravated penetrative sexual assault within an institutional care system by multiple perpetrators.[10] Each of the aforementioned cases presents different forms of and different understandings of sexual offence against children. As it may be seen, it was not the girls only who were victimized, or it was not the adults only who were perpetrators. Similarly, again as it may be seen, victimization may take place through digital communication technology even if the victim is unaware of his/her perpetrator's actions. Some of the aforementioned cases were booked under POCSO Act, 2012, some were booked under different penal provisions. But all of the aforementioned cases show the various forms of sexual offences against children that are now being reported in India. However, it is necessary to mention that even though POCSO, 2012 was introduced by the Parliament in June 2012, the use of this law by the police in booking cases for sexual offences targeting children has remained comparatively poor. As per the recent statistics released by the National Crime Records Bureau (NCRB) of India, in 2014, among the total 89,423 cases that were registered as crimes against children, the total numbers

---

[8] TNN, 'Man Held for Creating FB Page with Paedophilic Content', *The Times of India*, 12 May 2015. Available at: http://timesofindia.indiatimes.com/city/chennai/Man-held-for-creating-FB-page-with-paedophilic-content/articleshow/47241605.cms (accessed on 17 January 2018).

[9] Express News Service, 'Child Porn on FB Lands Tamil Nadu Youth in Net', *The New Indian Express*, 7 August 2015. Available at: http://www.newindianexpress.com/states/tamil_nadu/Child-Porn-on-FB-lands-Tamil-Nadu-Youth-in-Net/2015/08/07/article2961424.ece (accessed on 17 January 2018).

[10] Monideepa Banerjie, '2 Teachers Arrested for Assaulting 4-Year-Old Student in Kolkata', *NDTV*, 2 December 2017. Available at: https://www.ndtv.com/kolkata-news/gd-birla-rape-case-2-teachers-arrested-for-assaulting-4-year-old-student-in-kolkata-1782612 (accessed on 17 January 2018).

of cases registered under POCSO Act is only 8,904. However, in reality every day numerous incidences of sexual offences targeting children occur in cities and villages, schools, shelter homes, public places and even in the child's own home. While many parents feel reluctant to report the crimes in fear of further harm to the children as well as to their families, majority of the victims and their families feel demotivated to report the incidences to the police because they may have come across such incidences occurring to others or heard about police apathy to the victims of sexual crimes and their reluctance of registering any case. This is because in some such incidences the officers may not be aware of the new legal developments. Further, prolonged trial periods and traumatizing experiences of the children as well as their parents in the court, at home, school and in the victim's own locality may also demotivate victims and their families to report crimes. Consider the case of the sexual assault and rape cases where the alleged accused Asaram Bapu, a self-styled godman, was charged with rape and sexual assault of several women including minor girls. A 16-year-old girl was the first to file a Zero FIR[11] through her parents in 2013 for the charge of rape. Following this, some other women also came up to lodge reports of sexual assault by the godman. As of now, several witnesses have allegedly been killed. Asaram was arrested and put in jail, charged with provisions including S.342 (punishment for wrongful confinement), S.354 A (sexual harassment and punishment for the same), S.370(4) (trafficking of minor and punishment for the same), S.376(2)(f) (punishment for rape being a relative, guardian, teacher and the like), S.376D (gang rape and punishment for the same), S.506 (punishment for criminal intimidation), S.509/34 (punishment for harming the modesty of women, read with acts done by several persons in furtherance of common intention) and S.120(B) (punishment for criminal conspiracy) of Indian Penal Code (IPC)

---

[11] Zero FIR refers to FIR lodged by the victim or victim's kin in different jurisdiction than that where the crime had occurred. In many cases where victims are women or children, courts have encouraged the filing of Zero FIR since it may not have been possible for the victim to register complaint with the police in the same jurisdiction where the crime may have occurred. For example, see Gulab Bothra v. State, CRL.M.C. 50/2015 in the High Court of Delhi at New Delhi, decided on 11 March 2015.

and S.23 (punishment for cruelty to juvenile or child) and S.26 (exploitation of juvenile or child employee) of Juvenile Justice (Care and Protection) Act (JJ Act), 2000 and S.5(f)/6 (penetrated sexual assault by management of educational or religious institution, read with punishment for the same), S.5(g)/6 (gang penetrative sexual assault read with punishment for the same) and S.7/8 (sexual assault read with punishment for the same) of POCSO Act. The minor victim, who was the first complainant in this case, felt scared to lead her normal life apparently due to the assumption that she or her family members may have similar fate as that of other witnesses who were killed or attacked.[12] As per the latest update, Asaram Bapu has been convicted with life imprisonment by the trial court. While this became a celebrity case due to the involvement of influential people as accused, we may get to see numerous cases such as this where victims' families have been threatened to not to lodge police reports, or the case has been settled out of court with the victim being persuaded to accept a lump sum (which may be lesser than the actual compensation amount as has been fixed by laws meant for victim compensation).[13] Such a pathetic condition prevails largely due to poor understanding of the laws meant for child protection including POCSO Act, 2012 on the part of the criminal justice machinery, organizations meant for child protection including NGOs, educational institutes as well as parents.

Need of This Book, Aim and Scope

Existing Legislative Lacunas for Dealing with Child Sexual Abuse in India

In many instances, it can be seen that when a child complains about a particular 'uncomfortable' incidence that may have happened with him/her, elders or caregivers may refuse to take it as a serious matter.

---

[12] Express News Service, 'Sunday Story: Asaram Bapu Rape Case—In Godman They Fear', *The Indian Express*, 19 July 2015. Available at: http://indianexpress.com/article/india/india-others/sunday-story-asaram-bapu-rape-case-in-godman-they-fear/#sthash.fAUGCD5C.dpuf (accessed on 17 January 2018).

[13] The author got to know of such incidences from her experiences as a panel advocate to the Child Welfare Committee in Tamil Nadu.

Consider the cases of verbal bullying or teasing in schools or on the Internet where fellow children or even seniors schoolmates, teachers, relatives, and the like may use derogatory, sexist comments; or consider uncomfortable physical touch that the child may experience from his/her own friends, strangers or elders at home. In the first case, the parents may either tell the children to not to feel bothered with such comments or get back to the bully or the teaser with similar derogatory words. In the second case as well, unless the parents are aware about the psychological as well as physical effect of 'bad touch' on the children, the later may continue to suffer and may grow up as extremely complicated teenagers who may either be violent in nature or may suffer from withdrawal symptoms. It is because laws in India for long had avoided fulfilling the need to criminalize 'bad talk'[14] as well as 'bad touch' meted out to children. In India, the concept of crimes against children was to an extent trapped in the understanding of child labour and trafficking, denial of basic fundamental rights including right to shelter, care and protection for the child, right to get education, right to healthy life and so on. Most of the laws relating to these were enacted according to the various provisions as well as guidelines of UN child rights convention, 1989. These laws, including provisions from IPC, JJ Act, 2000 (amended in 2006); Immoral Traffic (Prevention) Act (ITPA), 1956; Prohibition of Child Marriage Act, 2006; Information Technology (IT) Act, 2000 (amended in 2008) and the like did touch upon sexual offences against children exclusively. It was only with the POCSO Act, 2012 that sexual offences against children received a holistic approach from the Indian Parliament.

POCSO Act, 2012 and the New Changes

POCSO Act, 2012 and the rules made thereunder have several unique specialities which are essential for ensuring healthy development of

---

[14] D. Halder, 'A Retrospective Analysis of S.66 A: Could S.66 A of the Information Technology Act be Reconsidered for Regulating "Bad Talk" in the Internet?', accepted for publication in the forthcoming volume of *Indian Student Law Review* (ISLR), published by School of Excellence in Law, Dr Ambedkar Law University, Chennai, 2015.

the child: these include recognition of gender orientation of the child, segregation of sexual offences meted out to the children and the punishments for the same, establishments of special courts, special juvenile police unit and special prosecutorial guidelines for dealing with offences as well as child victims under this Act and overriding effects on traditional criminal laws including IPC which may prove extremely beneficial for cases including those of marital rape involving children.[15] Further, with the introduction of the JJ Act, 2015,[16] the POCSO Act, 2012 has fulfilled the long awaited need for a regulatory provision which provides equal rights to children irrespective of their caste, creed, language, gender and gender orientation and so on to seek justice for sexual offences. However, the legislation needs to be explained further in the light of the JJ Act, 2015[17] for better execution by the criminal justice machinery.[18] It has fulfilled the long awaited need for a regulatory provision which provides equal rights to children irrespective of all discriminatory factors, as stated earlier, to seek justice for sexual offences.

Need and Scope of This Book

POCSO Act, 2012, read with amended JJ Act, 2015, provides an excellent child-right jurisprudence. This author argues that this revised form of child-right jurisprudence also affirms the concept of therapeutic jurisprudence (TJ), which speaks about the healing power of law. TJ relates to victims' rights and mental and physical well-being of individuals including victims by using law as a therapeutic agent.

---

[15] CCL-NLSIU, 'Child Marriage and the Protection of Children from Sexual Offences Act, 2012'. Available at: https://www.nls.ac.in/ccl/justicetochildren/poscoact.pdf (accessed on 1 August 2015).

[16] JJ Act, 2015 was an amended version of the then existing JJ Act, 2000 and introduced specific provisions including those related to administration of juvenile justice where juvenile offenders may have been apprehended for various sorts of crimes.

[17] Ibid.

[18] Human Rights Watch, 'Breaking the Silence: Child Sexual Abuse in India', 7 February 2013. Available at: http://www.hrw.org/report/2013/02/07/breaking-silence/ (accessed on 1 August 2015).

In India, presently no literature offers holistic explanation of child sexual abuse and the revised preventive laws, that is, POCSO Act, 2012 read with JJ Act, 2015 considered from the aspect of TJ. POCSO Act, 2012 and JJ Act, 2015 offer an improved method of dealing with the victims of child sexual abuse and also with the juvenile perpetrators. Using doctrinal methodology and depending upon secondary data including books, peer-reviewed articles, case laws and, in some cases, personal observations of this author, this book explains the revised categorization of the offences of child sexual abuse including online abuse of children and the preventive mechanisms as has been offered by POCSO and JJ Acts and offers suggestion for rehabilitation including counselling of the victims and the juvenile perpetrators from the perspective of TJ. As this book addresses the issues from a novel perspective, that is, the perspective of TJ, with latest case laws and critical explanations of the same, it will enlighten the law-school students, legal researchers, legal practitioners, police officers and other stakeholders dealing with child abuse about new forms of offences and crimes, restorative sentencing policies and innovative rehabilitation mechanisms.

Aim of the Book

In the recent judgement in Independent Thought v. Union of India and Another,[19] the Supreme Court of India has reversed the traditional understanding of sexual intercourse and sexual acts with child brides by their husbands. Criminalizing such sexual acts with child bride as rape, the court observed that '… but in our opinion sexual intercourse with a girl below 18 years of age is rape regardless of whether she is married or not'. This very statement of the court shows the shifting paradigm of child sexual abuses by courts. Judicial activism is expanding in regard to child sexual abuse cases in India. This book aims to research upon such ever-expanding judicial activism on child right jurisprudence in

---

[19] Independent Thought v. Union of India and Another, WP (Civil) no. 382 of 2013. Available at: http://supremecourtofindia.nic.in/supreme-court/2013/17790/17790_2013_Judgement_11-Oct-2017.pdf (accessed on 11 October 2017).

modern India. This book also aims to develop a model sentencing and rehabilitation mechanism in line with TJ principles. Last but not the least; the book aims to become an essential handbook for practitioners, police officers, child protection officers and judges and law students for understanding and dealing with child sexual abuse cases by using the laws in a therapeutic way.

Division of the Chapters

This book addresses child sexual abuses and the protective laws from Indian contexts. It becomes essential therefore to look into the historical aspects which motivated the creation of new laws. It is also essential to analyse the typology of sexual offences that have been introduced by POCSO Act. Discussions about protective laws should also include discussions on procedural aspects as how the criminal justice machinery should deal with such cases without breaching the privacy of the victimized children. Similarly, this discussion must also include discussions related to rehabilitation and sentencing of the victims and the offenders. These have been carried out in four parts in this book, namely, (i) 'Introduction', (ii) 'Types of the Offences and Punishments', (iii) 'Procedural Practices for Reporting, Investigation, Prosecution and Trials' and (iv) 'Sentencing and Rehabilitation'. Each part is further divided into separate chapters to deal with the subject. As such, Part I, that is, 'Introduction', is divided into two chapters, namely, 'Background' and 'Impact of Child Rights Convention and Its Optional Protocol on Development of Child Sexual Abuse Preventive Laws in India'. As the title of the first chapter suggests, this chapter will discuss in detail the existing situation which demanded a change in law dealing with sexual offences targeted at children and committed by children. The existing JJ Act, 2000 did not specifically focus on sexual offences targeted at children. It rather holistically covered the subject of child abuse with the help of provisions from the IPC. This created a procedural lacuna in addressing different types of sexual offences including cyber sexual offences. Further, the first chapter also indicates the need for therapeutic jurisprudential approach on the part of the criminal justice machinery for addressing cases of child sexual abuse. The second chapter critically analyses the role of

UN Convention on the Rights of the Child (CRC) and its optional protocols on child sexual abuse in creation of exclusive laws including the POCSO Act and the JJ Act, 2015 for addressing child sexual abuse in the Indian context.

Part II titled 'Types of the Offences and Punishments' discusses about the typology of sexual offences targeted against children. This typology is provided by the POCSO Act and each of the four chapters under this part discusses about specific typology of offence. As such, Chapter 3 deals with penetrative sexual assaults and the punishments thereof as has been stated in the POCSO Act, 2012. This chapter also discusses as how penetrative sexual assaults are dealt with in specific countries such as the United Kingdom, the United States and the like; Chapter 4 deals with sexual assault and sexual harassment and the punishments thereof and also discusses laws relating to this in various other jurisdictions; Chapter 5 deals with cyber sexual crimes targeting children. With the advent of technology, Internet and digital communication mediums are being used to commit sexual offences against children. It is unfortunate to note that the perception among the criminal justice machinery as well as many other stakeholders, including parents and teachers, regarding cyber sexual crimes targeting children has remained restricted to usage of children for creation of pornographic contents only. In reality, there can be instances where the child may him/herself be involved in his/her own victimization. Many children and their parents may feel extremely reluctant to report offences of this nature anticipating secondary harassment in the hands of the police because of their own involvements. However, this should not be the proper way to deal with cyber sexual crime victims, especially when they are minors. Chapter 5 therefore explains various types of cyber sexual offences that may happen through Internet and the existing laws that must be availed by the police and the practitioners. Chapter 6, the last one in this part, discusses about criminal motives and punishments for the same. This chapter also showcases how this issue has been dealt with under laws in various jurisdictions.

Procedural practices for reporting, investigation and prosecution in cases relating to sexual offences targeting children are dealt with under Part III. This part is further divided into three chapters. Chapter 7 deals with reporting of crimes, investigation and victim/witness protection. As such, this chapter explains the procedures which must be availed of as per the POCSO Act, the rules made thereunder, the JJ Act, 2015 and the other policy guidelines that have been framed for the welfare of the children in such cases. This chapter also speaks as why and how the procedural aspects must adhere to therapeutic jurisprudential aspects. It also throws light on how law students, practitioners, police officers and child line workers may encourage more reporting by the children as well as the parents without disturbing the privacy of the victims. Chapter 8 speaks about juvenile offenders. Chapter 9 speaks about prosecution and trial and speaks about the special courts set-up under POCSO Act, its powers and duties and so on. Discussions on protective laws for preventing child sexual abuse and protecting children from primary and secondary victimization must necessarily include discussions on sentencing and rehabilitation related to sexual offence cases targeting children. Part IV discusses this in two chapters, namely, Chapter 10 and the concluding chapter. It needs to be understood that children may not only be victims, they may be perpetrators as well. While sentencing the courts must therefore be careful not only about the welfare of the children who are victims of sexual offences done by adults as well as by juvenile offenders, but also about the juvenile offenders themselves. Further, courts must also need to pay attention to the psychological well-being of the child victims. What are the measures that can be taken to ensure physical as well as psychological well-being of the child victims? Which are the possible ways by which the judiciary can motivate the child to come out of the trauma? What would be the role of the judiciary and criminal justice machinery as a whole to prevent social ostracism for the child victim and his/her family? What are the civil right mechanisms by which the child victim may be brought back to normal life again? This chapter answers all these questions. Further, this chapter also showcases various sentencing policies of laws of different jurisdictions.

CHAPTER 2

Impact of Child Rights Convention and Its Optional Protocol on Development of Child Sexual Abuse Preventive Laws in India

Introduction

Rights of child for care and social protection were first recognized under Article 25(2) of the Universal Declaration of Human Rights in 1948. However, this was a rather narrower approach to child rights compared to the UN CRC which was created in 1989. Further, the later created a legally binding responsibility for the State parties to implement it through their domestic laws. However, it was not until 2012 that the CRC, along with its optional protocol on sale of children, child prostitution and child pornography, 2002, was implemented by the Indian Parliament through the POCSO Act, 2012. The Preamble to the POCSO Act may show adherence to the principles of CRC and its optional protocol. It says:

> An Act to protect children from offences of sexual assault, sexual harassment and pornography and provide for establishment of Special Courts for trial of such offences and for matters connected therewith or incidental thereto. WHEREAS Clause (3) of Article 15 of the Constitution, inter alia, empowers the State to make special provision for children,
>
> AND WHEREAS, the Government of India has acceded on the 11th December, 1992 to the Convention on the Rights of the Child, adopted by the General Assembly of the United Nations, which has prescribed a set of standards to be followed by all State parties in securing the best interest of the child;
>
> AND WHEREAS it is necessary for the proper development of the child that his or her right to privacy and confidentiality be protected and respected by every person by all means and through all stages of a judicial process involving the child;
>
> AND WHEREAS it is imperative that the law operates in a manner that the best interest and well-being of the child are regarded as being of paramount importance at every stage, to ensure the healthy, physical, emotional, intellectual and social development of the child;
>
> AND WHEREAS the State parties to the Convention on the Rights of the Child are required to undertake all appropriate national, bilateral and multilateral measures to prevent: a. the inducement or coercion of a child to engage in any unlawful sexual activity; b. the exploitative use of children in prostitution or other unlawful sexual practices; c. the exploitative use of children in pornographic performances and materials;
>
> AND WHEREAS sexual exploitation and sexual abuse of children are heinous crimes and need to be effectively addressed
>
> BE it enacted by Parliament in the Sixty-third Year of the Republic of India as follows:

It can be seen that the aforementioned Preamble lays down the purpose and need of the Act along with the title of the Act. In brief, the needs of the Act are stated as follows:

(a) To protect children from sexual assault, sexual harassment and pornography
(b) To provide for establishment of special court for trial of such offences and for matters connected therewith or incidental thereto

The purposes that this Act aims to serve are the following:

(i) To execute the State's power to make some provisions for children as has been empowered by Article 15(3) of the Constitution of India
(ii) To frame a set of standard rules, legal principles and policies for the best interest of the child as has been urged to all State parties by the UN CRC, to which India has acceded on 11 December 1992
(iii) To provide adequate socio-legal infrastructure for development of the child
(iv) To protect and respect his/her right to privacy and confidentiality in all means by everyone and also in sorts of judicial proceedings involving the child
(v) To achieve the goal of ensuring healthy, physical, emotional, social and intellectual development of the child by operating the law for the best interest of the child
(vi) To undertake all appropriate national, bilateral, multilateral measures to prevent the inducement and coercion of a child to engage in any unlawful sexual activity, the exploitative use of children in prostitution or other unlawful sexual practices and the exploitative use of children in making pornographic performances and materials

Prior to the coming into force of the POCSO Act, 2012, no law in India had such specific object and focus on child protection issues from the aspect of sexual offences. While IPC and JJ Act are to be considered as two specific laws from which many child right-related guidelines, rules and policy guidelines have stemmed out, they failed to cover certain aspects of child sexual harassments that were finally taken up by POCSO Act. This chapter discusses the needs and the purposes for which this Act has been enacted and the scope of this Act. This chapter is divided into three parts including the introduction. The second part would discuss about the UN CRC and additional protocols to it, which is the main guiding principle for the POCSO Act. The third part would discuss about the impact of CRC and its optional protocol on the development of POCSO Act, 2012, and JJ Act, 2015.

Brief Analysis of Convention of Child Rights and the Optional Protocol Regarding Sexual Abuse of Children

As may be seen from the foregoing discussions, the concept of child rights was rather confined to the idea of special care and assistance to the child for a healthy e growth. The Universal Declaration of Human Rights, 1948 and the international covenants on civil, political, economic, social and cultural rights were more concerned for a holistic, peaceful and safe growth of the human society (inclusive of children), which was hugely affected due to the World Wars. Much emphasis was given in all these international documents on the necessity of safe family environment for children. This concern was born mainly because the World Wars orphaned several children. Simultaneously, several children were also subjected to torture due to their parents' status as subjects of enemy State. However, these documents were not necessarily legally binding on State parties. Further, these documents including the Declaration of the Rights of the Child, adopted by the General Assembly in 1958, did not explain the rights of the child as well as duties of the stakeholders including that of the State and family against any exploitation broadly. This was addressed by the CRC, 1989.[1] CRC recognized the inherent dignity of children and advocated for equal and inalienable rights of all human beings including children.

[1] 'Convention on the Rights of the Child', G.A. Res. 25, U.N. GAOR, 44th Sess., Supp. No. 49, at 171, U.N. Doc. A/44/49, 1989.

This Convention also recognized the special needs of childhood care and protection, healthy family environment for a child and the rights of the child against any sort of exploitation, which is necessary for the healthy development of human society. The concept of exploitation in this Convention was highlighted mainly from the perspective of child labour, which includes not only working in hazardous condition, but also sexual slavery. Due to immaturity in children, they may often fail to understand the sexual exploitation done to them by elders. Sexual exploitation may take place either within a family or by way of illegal profit-making whereby children are trafficked for sexual gratification in lieu of money.[2] The Convention also noted the need to protect the interest of the child in the background of traditional and cultural background of each individual including the child. Nonetheless, this Convention made a pathway for developing domestic laws for protection of child rights and preventing exploitation of children by way of labour, including hazardous labour.

A brief overview would show different rights of children and different duties of the State parties that were recognized by the CRC: As such, Part I of the Convention speaks about the general rights of the children. The Convention in Article 1 expands its scope to cover every human being below the age of 18 years with an exception clause which specifies that the scope of the Convention and the definition of the term 'child' would be applicable to any other human being of any age unless the member State of that particular person recognizes the age of majority at an early age. Article 2 states that each State party must respect the rights of the child within its jurisdiction irrespective of the child's parentage, nationality, gender, race and so on. It may be noted that in this particular Article the Convention extends the responsibility of the State parties to recognize and respect the rights of the child even if he/she does not belong to the same State party, but resides within its jurisdiction. The second paragraph of Article 2 directs the State parties to take appropriate measures to protect the child against any form of discrimination or punishment basing upon the status of

---

[2] Sara A. Dillon, 'What Human Rights Law Obscures: Global Sex Trafficking and the Demand for Children' (Research Paper No. 08–4, 117 U.C.L.A. Women's L.J. 121, Suffolk University Law School, 2008).

the child, his/her opinion, parentage, beliefs of the parents and so on. A unique point to be noted here is the recognition of child's right to express opinion and his/her right against any kind of oppression in this regard. Article 3 directs the State parties to ensure best interest of the child in all endeavours taken by everyone irrespective of public or private social welfare institutions, government administrations, courts of laws, parents, guardians and so on who are responsible for the well-being of the child; the second paragraph of Article 3 directs State parties to ensure proper care and protection of the child through legal and administrative endeavours taking in account the rights and duties of persons and institutions responsible for the well-being of the child. The third paragraph directs the State parties to ensure that all stake-holders responsible for the care and protection of the children shall conform to proper standard in regard to safety, health and suitability and numbers of the staff in supervision of the care and protection of children. Article 4 directs the State parties to take special measure for ensuring economic, social and cultural rights of children with the help of available resources of the State parties, and within the framework of international cooperation when needed.

Articles 5 to 9 of the Convention emphasize on the importance of recognizing the child's identity and the role of family in the overall development of the child. Article 5 thus directs the State parties to respect and recognize the rights and duties of the parents or legal guardians and extended families as has been framed and nurtured by the local customs. Such rights and duties must be recognized for the best interest of the child and for further recognition of the rights of the child as has been enshrined in the Convention. Article 6 directs the State parties to recognize the right to life and survival as inherent rights of the child. Article 7 emphasizes on the duty of the State parties to register the birth of every child within their jurisdiction and provide nationality to the same so that the child inherits the rights as per the national laws of the same country. It directs the State parties to ensure that no child is stateless. Article 8 directs the State parties to respect the right of the child to retain his nationality, identity and family relationship without unnecessary interference. This Article also directs the State parties to assist the child in regaining his/her nationality or identity in case he/she has been deprived of the same.

Article 9 directs the State parties to ensure that the child is not severed from his/her family or parents unless the severance is needed for the best interest of the child, for example, in cases of abuse or negligence. It also directs the State parties to provide opportunity for the child or his family members to get information about any of the parents or other family members who may have been severed by the State, for the welfare of the child. In case the child is separated from any one of the parents, this Article also directs the State parties to provide opportunity for the child and the estranged parent to get connected as per the laws of the country of the child concerned, unless the same is against the best interest of the child. Article 10, in furtherance of the directions stated in Article 9, states that applications from the child or his/her parents to visit each other for reunification of the family must be dealt with expeditiously by the State parties and without causing humiliation to the applicant. It further directs the State parties to provide the child assistance to keep regular relationship and meet parent/s who may stay in different States and allow the child and his/her parents to enter or leave the countries for the best interest of the child, unless the same is not possible for any emergent situation which may also deter the welfare of the child. However, Article 11 of the Convention puts a restriction to the movement of the child from one State to another or one place to another within the jurisdiction of the same State. This Article builds the core concept of child trafficking and directs the State parties to take adequate steps to prevent such illicit transfer and non-return of the children and also to promote bilateral or multilateral agreements to end such illicit transfer of children.

Articles 12 to 17 of the Convention speak about child's rights to express his/her opinion, gain information, freedom of association and right to privacy. Each of such rights, however, may be restricted on several grounds on the best interest of the child primarily. As such, Article 12 directs the State parties to take measures to assure the child to express his opinion in matters affecting him/her, especially when he/she has the maturity to form an opinion and express the same in matters related to his well-being in any judicial or administrative proceedings. The State parties are also directed to ensure that the child is provided adequate help in such proceedings as well. Article 13 directs the State parties to ensure that the child can exercise his right to gain and impart information through all mediums including through writing, orally or any other medium. This Article mentions that even though the State parties can have their own restrictive rules in this regard, which should be for the best interest of the child, the rules should be on the basis of two probable reasons: (a) possibility of harm to the reputation of others and (b) protection of national security, public order, health or morale. It must be noted that this Article constitutes the basis of anti-harassment (including bullying by or targeting at children) and pornography and obscenity laws. Article 14 directs the State parties to ensure freedom of thought, conscience and religion but only with restrictions which must be based on concepts of public safety, public order, health and morale and when such exercise disrupts fundamental rights of others. Article 15 directs the State parties to ensure the child's right to freedom of association but the same again is restricted on the grounds of public safety, order, health and morale and also for the best interest of the child, especially where he may get exploited by deviant individuals including children. Article 16 may be said to be one of the core component parts of the POCSO Act, since it directs the State parties to ensure right to privacy and reputation of the child and right against unlawful invasion to his family, home or correspondence. Article 17 emphasizes on the importance of mass media with regard to the positive growth and development of the child. It therefore directs the State parties to encourage the development of mass media as disseminator of information for the sociocultural, linguistic and overall psychological growth and development of the child. Also, this Article directs the State parties to encourage the mass media to develop certain policies and the like to prohibit misuse of the same which may be detrimental to the emotional and psychological growth of the child. Article 18 further focuses on the duties and responsibilities of the parents and legal guardians towards the upbringing of the children and directs the State parties to extend all sorts of assistance in child-rearing for the best interest of the child. Also, the Article emphasizes upon well-being of working parents, their right to better child-care facilities and so on.

Articles 19 to 33 of the Convention speak about preventive measures in regard to physical and mental abuse of children. Article 19 directs the State parties to take appropriate legislative, social and administrative measures to protect the children from all sorts of abuse including physical, psychological and sexual abuse, negligence, etc. and also take adequate measures for reporting, creation of social programmes, etc. when such abuse happens in the care of parents or legal guardians or any other institution which is entrusted to provide care and protection to the child. Articles 20 and 21 of the Convention direct the State parties to create laws for ensuring proper care and protection for the child who is deprived of his family environment, and for recognizing the proper process of adoption of such children in accordance with the need of the child and the best interest of the child. Article 22, on the other hand, directs the State parties to ensure safety and protection for any child who is seeking refugee status and also to extend all sorts of help for reuniting him with his family unless the same is not possible. In the latter case, the Article further directs the State parties to extend all sort of care and protection and ensure creation of family environment by arranging for shelter. Article 23 speaks about rights of disabled children against abuse, negligence and their right to health, equality and proper care. Article 24 speaks about right to health care for every child and directs the State parties to ensure measures to prevent infant mortality and medical negligence. Article 25 speaks about right of the child placed in institutional care for periodic review of physical and mental health treatment. Article 26 on the other hand directs the State parties to take measures for social security and social insurance schemes for the benefit of the children. Article 27 speaks about living condition of the children and directs the State parties to ensure better and healthy living condition for all children irrespective of their socio-economic and religious background. Articles 28 to 31 emphasize upon mental development of the child, including development of laws, policy guidelines to prevent mental abuse of the child by way of discrimination to right to education, leisure activities and so on. Article 28 therefore directs State parties to create laws and policy guidelines for providing compulsory and free education for the overall development of the child. Article 29 directs the State parties to ensure that the education policy must be goal-oriented towards development of the child as a responsible citizen of free society and it should also encourage setting up of educational institutions by private bodies. Article 30 further directs the State parties to ensure that a child belonging to special ethnic, religious or linguistic group should not be discriminated and should get equal rights to education, health and social association. Article 31 speaks about the right of the child to leisure activities and participation in cultural activities irrespective of the ethnicity, language, religion and so on. Article 32 speaks about economic exploitation of children. While the rest of the provisions in this group focused on certain positive rights, this particular provision highlights right against child labour and also directs the State parties to fix minimum age standard and time period for employment for children. Article 33 emphasizes upon narcotic and substance abuse of children and directs the State parties to create laws and policy guidelines and to execute multilateral treaties and the like for prevention of such abuse as well as trafficking of narcotic substances.

Articles 34 to 36 of the Convention speak about sexual exploitation of children. Article 34 directs the State parties to undertake to protect children from all kinds of sexual exploitation and sexual abuse including inducing the child to participate in any sexual practice, exploitative use of children in prostitution and in pornographic materials. Article 35 directs the State parties to take appropriate action by way of creating domestic laws as well as ratifying bilateral or multilateral treaties to prevent child trafficking. Article 36, again, directs the State parties to protect the children from any other form of exploitation prejudicial to the welfare of the child. It may be understood here that sexual exploitation may also be a particular form of economic exploitation or a form of child labour. The Convention, therefore, urges the State parties to perceive the matters individually depending upon each form of exploitation, as well as holistically.

Articles 37 to 40 of the Convention emphasize upon punishment of children. Article 37 directs the State parties to ensure that no child accused should be subjected to harsh punishment including capital punishment or rigorous imprisonment and such child must be dealt with without harming his dignity and self-respect. The Article also directs the State parties to ensure that such children may be put in proper living condition and child-friendly atmosphere if separated from parents or families for the best interest of the child, and they should have right to easy access to legal representation. Article 38 speaks about children in armed conflict and directs the State parties to ensure proper protection for such children. This Article also directs the State parties to ensure that children under the age of 15 must not be exposed to hostilities and must not be enrolled in any armed forces. For children above 15 years of age and below 18 years, priority must be given to older children for such enrolment. Article 39 emphasizes upon therapeutic approach of the State parties to child victims as well as child offenders who may have had to undergo punishment of any sort. It therefore directs the State parties to undertake all sorts of legislative, administrative and social approaches to promote physical and psychological recovery of such children for reintegration of such children. Article 40, again, speaks about child offenders and their rights. It directs the State parties to ensure that such children who are in conflict with law must be given adequate legal assistance without harming their inherent fundamental rights as children, as has been stated in the present Convention.

Article 41 of the Convention concludes Part I of the Convention by stating that nothing in the Convention shall affect any provisions which are more conducive to the realization of the rights of the children and which may be contained in the domestic laws of the State parties or international law in force for the States. Part II of the Convention containing Articles 42 to 45 directs the State parties to take measure to publicize the Convention and creation of committee for child rights, and other specialized agencies to take care of the well-being of the children. Part III of the Convention speaks about ratification of the Convention, signature and amendment to the same by the State parties.

Optional Protocol and Special Emphasis on Sexual Exploitation of Children

As it may be seen from the aforementioned, while Articles 34 to 36 specifically focused on sexual exploitation of children and Article 34 emphasized upon exploitative use of children for illicit sexual gratification, Part I of the Convention as a whole must be considered to understand the rights of the children in the background of any sort of exploitation of children including sexual exploitation. The

Preamble to the POCSO Act also indicates the same. However, it can be said that Articles 34 to 36 of the Convention form the heart of POCSO Act. But discussion on international measures to direct State parties to frame rules and regulations to prevent sexual exploitation of children would remain incomplete without the discussion on the optional protocols to the CRC on the sale of children, child prostitution and child pornography, which is the baseline of the POCSO Act.

Optional protocol to the CRC on the sale of children, child prostitution and child pornography[3] in Articles 1 to 12 directs the State parties to take up legislative, administrative and social measures to prohibit sexual exploitation of children. Article 1 directs State parties to prohibit sale of children, child prostitution and child pornography. Article 2 provides definition of the aforementioned three issues; according to this Article,

(a) Sale of children means any act or transaction whereby a child is transferred by any person or group of persons to another for remuneration or any other consideration;

(b) Child prostitution means the use of a child in sexual activities for remuneration or any other form of consideration;

(c) Child pornography means any representation, by whatever means, of a child engaged in real or simulated explicit sexual activities or any representation of the sexual parts of a child for primarily sexual purposes.

The meaning and scope of the three terms are further expanded in Article 3. In the context of sale of children, the article expands the definition to include (i) the offering, delivering or accepting, by whatever means, a child for the purpose of: (a) sexual exploitation of the child, (b) transfer of organs of the child for profit and (c) engagement of the child in forced labour and (ii) improperly inducing consent, as an intermediary, for the adoption of a child in violation of applicable international legal instruments on adoption. In the context of

---

[3] 'Optional Protocol to the Convention on the Rights of the Child on the Involvement of Children in Armed Conflict', General Assembly Resolution A/RES/54/263 of 25 May 2000.

child prostitution, the Article expands its scope to include offering, obtaining, procuring or providing a child for child prostitution. In the context of child pornography, the Article expands the scope of the definition to include producing, distributing, disseminating, importing, exporting, offering, selling or possessing for the aforementioned purposes child pornography. This Article also directs the State parties to make appropriate laws in this regard to recognize these three issues as penal offences and take appropriate measures to enforce these provisions especially to prevent any anomalies in this regard in cases of adoption laws and procedures. Articles 4 and 5 emphasize upon jurisdiction issues. Article 4 directs the State parties to enact laws in regard to jurisdiction and power of the States to try the cases. Article 5, on the other hand, speaks about bilateral and multilateral treaties for resolving extradition issues involving child sexual abuse including sale of minors, prostitution and child pornography. Articles 6 and 7, in furtherance of the aim mentioned in Article 5, directs the State parties to extend fullest cooperation to each other in matters of investigation and other legal procedures in accordance with each State party's domestic laws. Article 8 emphasizes on the rights of the child victim. It directs the State parties to ensure that different types of victimization targeting the child are given proper legal recognition, the child is provided adequate protection as a victim as well as a witness, due care to be taken to execute justice to the child victim without harming his/her self-respect, dignity, physical and mental health and assisting the child for legal representation for a speedy judicial procedure. This Article also directs the State parties to impart training to stakeholders working on child safety issues and to enact child-friendly policies to carry on investigation even if there are issues regarding uncertainty of age of the victims. Article 9, on the other hand, directs the State parties to enact child-friendly law in this regard and to ensure equal right to justice to all children without discrimination. It also speaks about victim compensation and prohibitory measures to penalize production and dissemination of materials advertising the offences. Article 10 directs the State parties to increase internal cooperation, ratify treaties and create multilateral agreements for proper investigation, execution of judicial procedures and so on for penalizing and prohibiting child trafficking, child prostitution, child sex tourism and child pornography. Article 11 announces that the present protocol shall not affect any domestic or international law which is more conducive towards welfare of the child in this regard. Article 12 urges State parties upon ratification of the protocol by it, to submit a report to the committee on the rights of the child and comprehensive reports on the measures taken by it to give effect to the protocol in its jurisdiction.

As may be seen from the aforementioned discussion, the CRC and the additional optional protocols to it created the baseline for creation of child-friendly laws for prohibiting three main types of sexual offences targeting children: sale of children for sexual gratification, child prostitution and child pornography. All of these three types of offences include sexual exploitation and sexual slavery of children irrespective of their gender. The Convention and the protocol emphasized on the need for proper criminal justice mechanism to deal with such issues which may save the victims from becoming physically and mentally disturbed for their whole lives. The aim of the Convention and the protocol is to prevent sexual abuse of the victims which, if not taken care at young age, may result in creation of more offenders and victims in future. Even though India already had several laws addressing child trafficking or anti-child pornography laws, there was a need for a law from the perspective of POCSO Act, created on the basis of this Convention and the corresponding protocols, aims to suit this need.

Impact of CRC and Its Optional Protocol on Development of Child Sexual Abuse Preventive Laws in India

The international developments in the understanding of child rights and the responsibilities of the State have been implemented in India through different legislations. The IPC was the first to criminalize sexual victimization of girl children through several provisions under Chapter XVI of the code. These provisions include the following:

1. S.366A speaks about procuration of minor girl and states that

> Whoever, by any means whatsoever, induces any minor girl under the age of eighteen years to go from any place or to

do any act with intent that such girl may be, or knowing that it is likely that she will be, forced or seduced to illicit intercourse with another person shall be punishable with imprisonment which may extend to ten years, and shall also be liable to fine.

2. S.366B of the IPC speaks about importation of girl from foreign country and states that

> Whoever imports into India from any country outside India or from the State of Jammu and Kashmir any girl under the age of twenty-one years with intent that she may be, or knowing it to be likely that she will be, forced or seduced to illicit intercourse with another person, shall be punishable with imprisonment which may extend to ten years and shall also be liable to fine.

3. S.370A, IPC (inserted via Criminal Law Amendment Act, 2013) speaks about exploitation of a trafficked person and states that

> (i) Whoever knowingly or has a reason to believe that a minor has been trafficked, engages such minor for sexual exploitation in any manner, shall be punished for a rigorous imprisonment for term which shall be not less than five years, but may extend to seven years, and shall also be liable to fine.

Further, in subsection (ii) it states that

> Whoever knowing by or having reason to believe that a person has been trafficked engages such person for sexual exploitation, in any manner, shall punished with a rigorous imprisonment for term which shall not be less than three years, but which may extend to five years and shall also be liable to fine.

4. S.372 of the IPC which speaks about selling minors for purposes of prostitution and the like states that

> Whoever sells, lets to hire, or otherwise disposes of any person under the age of eighteen years with intent that such

person shall at any age be employed or used for the purpose of prostitution or illicit intercourse with any person or for any unlawful and immoral purpose, or knowing it to be likely that such person will at any age be employed or used for any such purpose, shall be punished with imprisonment of either description for a term which may extend to ten years, and shall be liable to fine.[4]

5. S.373, IPC speaks about buying any minor for purposes of prostitution and the like and states that

Whoever buys, hires or otherwise obtains possession of any person under the age of eighteen years with intent that such person shall at any age be employed or used for the purpose of prostitution or illicit intercourse with any person or for any unlawful and immoral purpose, or knowing it to be likely that such person will at any age be employed or used for any purpose, shall be punished with imprisonment of either description for a term which may extend to ten years, and shall also be liable to fine.[5]

[4] Explanation 1 attached to this Section states:

When a female under the age of eighteen years is sold, let for hire, or otherwise disposed of to a prostitute or to any person who keeps or manages a brothel, the person so disposing of such female shall, until the contrary is proved, be presumed to have disposed of her with the intent that she shall be used for the purpose of prostitution.

Explanation 2 attached to this Section states:

For the purposes of this section 'illicit intercourse' means sexual intercourse between persons not united by marriage or by any union or tie which, though not amounting to a marriage, is recognized by the personal law or custom of the community to which they belong or, where they belong to different communities, of both such communities, as constituting between them a quasi-marital relation.

[5] Explanation 1 attached to this Section states:

Any prostitute or any person keeping or managing a brothel, who buys, hires or otherwise obtains possession of a female under the age of eighteen years shall, until the contrary is proved, be presumed to have obtained possession of such female with the intent that she shall be used for the purpose of prostitution.

While these provisions are generally used as preventive mechanisms against physically transferring children (especially girl children) from protective custody of their lawful guardians and sexually exploiting them after such removal, it may be noticed that there were no separate provisions for dealing with sexual harassment with children or rape of minors. However, S.375 (which defines rape) had been traditionally extended to cover rape of minors as the provision states:

> A man is said to commit 'rape' who, except in the case hereinafter excepted, has sexual intercourse with a woman under circumstances falling under any of the six following descriptions: First—against her will; secondly, without her consent; thirdly—with her consent, when her consent has been obtained by putting her or any person in whom she is interested in fear of death or of hurt; fourthly—with her consent, when the man knows that he is not her husband, and that her consent is given because she believes that he is another man to whom she is or believes herself to be lawfully married; fifthly—with her consent, when, at the time of giving such consent, by reason of unsoundness of mind or intoxication or the administration by him personally or through another of any stupefying or unwholesome substance, she is unable to understand the nature and consequences of that to which she gives consent; sixthly—with or without her consent, when she is under sixteen years of age.[6]

Explanation 2 attached to this Section states that "'Illicit intercourse" has the same meaning as in Section 372'.

[6] However, this definition of rape has been amended vide the Criminal Law (Amendment) Act, 2013. The new provision under S.375 presently defines rape as follows:

A man is said to commit 'rape' if he

a. penetrates his penis, to any extent, into the vagina, mouth, urethra or anus of a woman or makes her to do so with him or any other person; or

b. inserts, to any extent, any object or a part of the body, not being the penis, into the vagina, the urethra or anus of a woman or makes her to do so with him or any other person; or

c. manipulates any part of the body of a woman so as to cause penetration into the vagina, urethra, anus or any part of body of such woman or makes her to do so with him or any other person; or

d. applies his mouth to the vagina, anus, urethra of a woman or makes her to do so with him or any other person,

It may be seen that this development in regard to the question of age of consent in cases of rape was reached after the famous case of Tuka Ram and Another v. State of Maharashtra,[7] also known as Mathura rape case, which involved a minor. Further, S.377 of the IPC which speaks about unnatural offences[8] had been traditionally used to cover

---

under the circumstances falling under any of the following seven descriptions:

First.—Against her will.

Secondly.—Without her consent.

Thirdly.—With her consent, when her consent has been obtained by putting her or any person in whom she is interested, in fear of death or of hurt.

Fourthly.—With her consent, when the man knows that he is not her husband and that her consent is given because she believes that he is another man to whom she is or believes herself to be lawfully married.

Fifthly.—With her consent when, at the time of giving such consent, by reason of unsoundness of mind or intoxication or the administration by him personally or through another of any stupefying or unwholesome substance, she is unable to understand the nature and consequences of that to which she gives consent.

Sixthly.—With or without her consent, when she is under eighteen years of age.

Seventhly.—When she is unable to communicate consent.

Explanation 1.—For the purposes of this section, 'vagina' shall also include labia majora.

Explanation 2.—Consent means an unequivocal voluntary agreement when the woman by words, gestures or any form of verbal or non-verbal communication, communicates willingness to participate in the specific sexual act:

Provided that a woman who does not physically resist to the act of penetration shall not by the reason only of that fact, be regarded as consenting to the sexual activity.

Exception 1.—A medical procedure or intervention shall not constitute rape.

Exception 2.—Sexual intercourse or sexual acts by a man with his own wife, the wife not being under fifteen years of age, is not rape.

[7] 1979 AIR 185.

[8] S.377 IPC states that

Whoever voluntarily has carnal intercourse against the order of nature with any man, woman or animal, shall be punished with imprisonment for life, or with

offences targeting children of both sexes. One example of usage of this provision in such cases is Childline India Foundation & Anr. v. Alan John Waters & Ors.[9] The explanation attached to it says, penetration is sufficient to constitute the carnal intercourse necessary to the offence described in this section.

Apart from the aforementioned provisions of the IPC, the ITPA also provided remedies for sexual abuse of children especially in cases where such children were trafficked for prostitution and related sexual abuse. The uniqueness of ITPA lies in the fact that it extends to whole of India (S.1(2)) and it extends its restorative jurisprudential scope to both male and female children. In this Act, the issue of sexual abuse of children is seen from two perspectives:

(i) Child labour by way of earnings from the child prostitution and supporting any adult: S.4 of the ITPA prescribes punishment for living on the earnings of prostitution. In S.1, it states:

> Any person over the age of eighteen years who knowingly lives, wholly or in part, on the earnings of the prostitution of any other person shall be punishable with imprisonment for a term which may extend to two years, or with fine which may extend to one thousand rupees, or with both, and where such earnings relate to the prostitution of a child, shall be punishable with imprisonment for a term of not less than seven years and not more than ten years.

The Supreme Court in the case of Gaurav Jain v. Union of India and Others[10] observed that child prostitutes constitute 12 per cent to 15 per cent of the prostitutes of any area. These children may be compelled to pay for day-to-day living of adults as well as other small children in the family especially when there is a financial scarcity in the family. In other cases, such children may be used by prostitution kingpins or pimps to earn money by way of engaging

---

imprisonment of either description for a term which may extend to ten years, and shall also be liable to fine

9 (2011)6 SCC 261.
10 AIR 1997 SC 3021.

them in prostitution. In this regard, mention must be made of the case of Bachpan Bachao Andolan v. Union of India and Others[11] where it was observed that sex tourism involving children is growing alarmingly in India and there are huge numbers of prostitution agencies who illegally supply minor girls for this purpose. In this case, it was also observed that sex trafficking involving child prostitutes and creation, production and distribution of child pornography are related issues and both can form a typical type of hazardous labour for children.

(ii) Trafficking for sexual abuse: While S.4 of the ITPA prescribed punishment for living upon the earnings by way of prostitution, including child prostitution, S.5 of the ITPA expands its scope to cover trafficking for sexual abuse including prostitution. It prescribes punishment for procuring, inducing or taking person for the sake of prostitution. It segregates the offences into four categories and penalizes all of them whether done separately or together; it thus says in Subsection (1):

> Any person who—(a) procures or attempts to procure a person whether with or without his/her consent, for the purpose of prostitution; or (b) induces a person to go from any place, with the intent that he/she may for the purpose of prostitution become the inmate of, or frequent, a brothel; or (c) takes or attempts to take a person or causes a person to be taken, from one place to another with a view to his/her carrying on, or being brought up to carry on prostitution; or (d) causes or induces a person to carry on prostitution; shall be punishable on conviction with rigorous imprisonment for a term of not less than three years and not more than seven years and also with fine which may extend to two thousand rupees, and if any offence under this sub-section is committed against the will of any person, the punishment of imprisonment for a term of seven years shall extend to imprisonment for a term of fourteen years.

Proviso added to this Subsection specifically mentions about trafficking children for the purpose of prostitution and states that

[11] (2011)5 SCC 1.

If the person in respect of whom an offence committed under this sub-section, is a child, the punishment provided under this sub-section shall extend to rigorous imprisonment for a term of not less than seven years but may extend to life.

Subsection (3) explains the jurisdictional issues in such cases and states:

An offence under this section shall be triable,—(a) in the place from which a person is procured, induced to go, taken or caused to be taken or from which an attempt to procure or taken such persons made; or (b) in the place to which she may have gone as a result of the inducement or to which he/she is taken or caused to be taken or an attempt to take him/her is made.

Ss.5A, B and C further penalize related activities in this regard. As such, S.5A expands the meaning of trafficking by including recruiting, transporting, transferring, harbouring or receiving a person for the purpose of prostitution by means of, (a) threat or use of force or coercion, abduction, fraud, deception; (b) abuse of power or a position of vulnerability; or (c) giving or receiving of payments or benefits to achieve the consent of such person having control over another person.[12] S.5B penalize trafficking on first conviction with rigorous imprisonment for a term which shall not be less than seven years and in the event of a second or subsequent conviction with imprisonment for life. (S.5B(1)), S.5B(2) penalize attempts to commit or abetment to commit trafficking and elevates such offences to the standard of committing actual trafficking. When courts consider cases of child trafficking, it has been seen that both Ss.4 and 5 (including 5A and B) may be given equal importance. This is evident from the observations made in the Bachpan Bachao Andolan case,[13] where it was noted:

[12] Explanation added to it further says

where any person recruits, transports, transfers, harbours or receives a person for the purposes of prostitution, such person shall, until the contrary is proved, be presumed to have recruited, transported, transferred, harboured or received the person with the intent that the person shall be used for the purpose of prostitution.

[13] Bachpan Bachao Andolan v. Union of India & Others; See Supra n. 8.

Three significant elements constitute trafficking: (a) the action involving recruitment and transportation, (b) the means employed such as force, coercion, fraud or deception including abuse of power and bribes; and (c) the purpose being exploitation including prostitution. It must be noted that to fulfil the third condition as has been mentioned above, S.5C of ITPA must also be considered which criminalises visiting brothels for sexual exploitation of trafficked victims. Ss.6, 9 and 10A further criminalise detention for prostitution especially in custody (S.9) and correctional institutes (S.10A).

However, as may be understood from the aforementioned discussions, ITPA is specifically meant for criminalizing prostitution including child prostitution when the victim is trafficked, engaged forcefully in the prostitution without his/her consent.

Similarly, JJ Act also provided solace to the children who are victims of sexual abuse or who may be potential victims of sexual abuse by expanding the definition of 'child in need of care and protection' under S.2(d) to cover children who are or who may likely be sexually abused, trafficked or used for unconscionable gains (S.2(d)(vi, vii, viii)). But the erstwhile JJ Act's scope in regard to sexual abuse of children was limited towards providing care and protection by ensuring rehabilitation and reintegration of the victim. While Indian criminal laws recognize rape as a heinous crime, other forms of sexual offences targeted to children including sexual assault, aggravated assault, non-penetrative sexual harassment, child pornography, stalking and so on were not recognized by any law. Such lack of specific legislation was also noted by the Ministry of Women and Child Development which, in order to support for stringent punishment for such offences, championed the POCSO Act, 2012.[14] Incidentally, even though JJ Act Bill, 2014[15] was introduced in the Lok Sabha in 2014 to amend the existing JJ Act, 2000, the Bill did not get presidential assent till

---

[14] NCPCR, 'POCSO Introduction', 2014, Available at: http://ncpcr.gov.in/index1.php?lang=1&level=1&&sublinkid=14&lid=607 (accessed on 6 October 2015).

[15] Bill No. 99 of 2014.

January 2016. As the opening paragraph of the JJ Act Bill stated, the Bill was brought in to

> consolidate and amend the law relating to children alleged and found to be in conflict with law and children in need of care and protection by catering to their basic needs through proper care, protection, development, treatment, social reintegration, by adopting a child-friendly approach in the adjudication and disposal of matters in the best interest of children and for their rehabilitation through processes provided, and institutions and bodies established, hereinunder and for matters connected therewith or incidental thereto.

The introductory paragraph further stated the purpose for introducing the amended Act in the following lines:

> WHEREAS, the provisions of the Constitution confer powers and impose duties, under clause (3) of article 15, clauses (e) and (f) of article 39, article 45 and article 47, on the State to ensure that all the needs of children are met and that their basic human rights are fully protected; AND WHEREAS, the Government of India has acceded on the 11th December, 1992 to the Convention on the Rights of the Child, adopted by the General Assembly of United Nations, which has prescribed a set of standards to be adhered to by all State parties in securing the best interest of the child; AND WHEREAS, it is expedient to re-enact the Juvenile Justice (Care and Protection of Children) Act, 2000 to make comprehensive provisions for children alleged and found to be in conflict with law and children in need of care and protection, taking into consideration the standards prescribed in the Convention on the Rights of the Child, the United Nations Standard Minimum Rules for the Administration of Juvenile Justice, 1985 (the Beijing Rules), the United Nations Rules for the Protection of Juveniles Deprived of their Liberty (1990), the Hague Convention on Protection of Children and Co-operation in Respect of Intercountry Adoption (1993) and other related international instruments.

It was only when the juvenile accused in the Nirbhaya gang-rape case got acquitted in December 2015, that the Bill got the assent of the president as the Supreme Court of India specifically emphasized upon government action towards revamping the juvenile justice administration, especially for heinous offences, including sexual offences committed by juvenile offenders, when the court was moved for considering the said juvenile offender at par with adult offenders for prosecution and sentencing him. As such, while the JJ Act, 2015 also covers other issues regarding adoption which were not covered by the earlier version, it is now functional for administering juvenile justice; the specific features of the amended law includes classification of the offences as per the seriousness and the periods of punishments as awarded by any penal law dealing with such offences; specific provisions for children in conflict with law, who may need care and protection and Juvenile Justice Board's (JJB) duty to transfer such cases to the child welfare committees; special power to the JJB to consider the mental maturity of the juvenile offenders not below the age of 16, so as to provide their opinions as whether such juveniles can be tried as adults for heinous and serious offences and the like. Nonetheless, the amended Act may be tremendously beneficial to regulate sexual offences targeting children and also those offences which are committed by children against children.

Part II

Types of the Offences and Punishments

CHAPTER 3

Penetrative Sexual Offences

Introduction

It may be interesting to note that in India while POCSO Act has been created to deal with sexual offences against children, it does not have any holistic definition of the term 'child sexual abuse'. Child sexual abuse can be defined as

> ... any activity with a child, before the age of legal consent, that is for the sexual gratification of an adult or a significantly older child. Sexual abuse includes oral-genital, genital-genital, genital-rectal, hand-genital, hand-rectal, or hand-breast contact; exposure of sexual anatomy; forced view of sexual anatomy; and showing pornography or using a child rt3 of pornography. Sexual intercourse includes vaginal, oral, or rectal penetration. Penetration is entry into an orifice with or without tissue injury.[1]

As can be seen from this definition, and also as has been stated in the Optional Protocol to the UN CRC (as discussed in the previous

[1] Emmanouil I. Sakelliadis, Chara A. Spiliopoulou and Stavroula A. Papadodima, 'Forensic Investigation of Child Victim with Sexual Abuse', *Indian Pediatrics* 46(2) (2009): 144–151.

chapter), child sexual abuse can be largely grouped into two categories: penetrative sexual offences and non-penetrative sexual offences. Considering the consequences of penetrative sexual offences, which may often result in unwanted pregnancy for young girls, death or grievous harm in the genitals due to forced penetration, violent fondling of the genitals, psychological trauma, etc., such offences need to be dealt with highest gravity. Prior to the implementation of the POCSO Act, penetrative sexual offences against children were largely limited to forceful vaginal penetration. As such, the gender of the victims was limited to that of minor girls and that of the offenders to males. The available laws that were used prior to the implementation of the POCSO Act for regulating penetrative sexual offences, included the traditional provisions of IPC relating to procuration of minor girls (S.366A), trafficking of girls to and from India for sexual slavery and buying and selling for prostitution (Ss.366B, 372, 373) and so on. However, necessity was felt to expand the scope of the laws relating to sexual offences, including penetrative sexual offences targeting children. This necessity was met through Chapter II (A and B) of the POCSO Act, which deals with the issue of penetrative sexual offences against children. This chapter of the book discusses about Chapter II (A and B) of the POCSO Act in detail. This chapter therefore provides a profile of penetrative sexual offences against children, the existing laws that were being used to regulate the issue and the present role of the POCSO Act in regulating the issue.

Profile of Penetrative Sexual Offences Against Children

Existing Legal Understanding

In the modern Indian legal understanding, the earliest available profile of penetrative sexual offence can be found in S.375 of the IPC (Rape). According to this provision, a man commits rape to a woman when sexual intercourse takes place under the following six circumstances: It is committed (i) against her will, (ii) without her consent, (iii) when her consent was obtained by putting her or any one in whom she has interest, in fear of death or hurt, (iv) when she consents thinking he is the man to whom she is legally married, but in reality, he is not the same, (v) her consent has been obtained in a state of mind, when she is unable to understand the nature and consequences of that to which she had given consent, due to unstableness of mind or intoxication or administering stupefying or unwholesome substance to her either by the person himself or by someone else, (vi) with or without consent when she is under the age of 16. Noticeably, the definition of rape was expanded and these six conditions were amended through the Criminal Law Amendment Act, 2013 which enhanced the age of consent (as specified in the sixth circumstance) to 18 years and added one more circumstance, which stated that sexual intercourse between a man and a woman would be considered as rape when she is unable to communicate the consent. The definition of 'rape' has been expanded to include (i) penetrating the penis to a woman's vagina, mouth, urethra, anus to any extent or making her to do so either with him or any other person, (ii) inserting any object to any body part mentioned previously or making her to do so with him or any other person, (iii) applying his mouth to any of the body parts of her as mentioned previously and making her to do so either with him or any other person under the aforementioned seven circumstances. The explanation added to this provision through Criminal Law Amendment Act, 2013 further clarified the meaning of the term 'vagina' as inclusive of labia majora (Explanation 1 to S.375, IPC), and the term 'consent' as 'unequivocal voluntary agreement for willingness to participate in the sexual act, which is communicated through any verbal or non-verbal communication, word, gesture, etc.' (Explanation 2 to S.375, IPC). The proviso to S.375, IPC further clarifies that a sexual intercourse committed in the aforementioned manner cannot be excused as an ordinary sexual intercourse and the victim cannot be said to have given consent just because the victim woman would not have resisted to the act of penetration. However, the exceptions to S.375 of the IPC provide that this provision would not be applicable to any medical procedure or intervention and neither to sexual intercourse or acts done by a man with his wife. The second exception further provides that the concerned act would not be considered as rape if the wife is not under 15 years of age. While this had been the traditional profile of penetrative sexual offence against women and girls (as per

S.375, IPC, amended through Criminal Law Amendment Act, 2013), S.377 (Punishment for Unnatural Offences) of the IPC was generally used to regulate sexual offences against boys.[2] As such, it may be seen that the two essential ingredients for terming a sexual intercourse or sexual behaviour as 'rape' are (a) penetration and /or activities as has been stated under S.375 of the IPC (as amended vide Criminal Law Amendment Act, 2013) and (b) lack of consent of the victim woman. Only when these requirements are met, a sexual intercourse may be termed as rape; otherwise, in the absence of these, sexual intercourse cannot be termed as rape even if the accused, being a male, is incapable to perform ordinary sexual intercourse as has been stated in the first circumstances of S.375 IPC, like an ordinary male, but may be able to fulfil other criteria of S.375, IPC.[3]

Profile of Penetrative Sexual Offence under POCSO Act

POCSO Act was implemented in 2012 with special understanding of sexual abuse of children, including penetrative sexual abuse. Ss.3, 4, 5 and 6 of the POCSO Act deals with penetrative sexual offences against children. According to the POCSO Act, penetrative sexual offence can be divided into two groups: penetrative sexual assaults and aggravated penetrative sexual assaults. S.3 in particular provides a detailed definition of penetrative sexual assault on children; according to this provision, penetrative sexual assault by any person irrespective of gender and age may mean:

---

[2] S.377 IPC states

Whoever voluntarily has carnal intercourse against the order of nature with any man, woman or animal, shall be punished with 152 [imprisonment for life], or with imprisonment of either description for a term which may extend to ten years, and shall also be liable to fine. Explanation— Penetration is sufficient to constitute the carnal intercourse necessary to the offence described in this section.

[3] Pinki Pramanik v. State of West Bengal & Anr., CRR 2848 of 2013 in the High Court of Calcutta.

(i) Penetrating by a man of his penis to any extent into the vagina, mouth, urethra or anus of a child, or making the child to do so with him, or any other person, or;

(ii) Inserting to any extent any part of the body, not being the penis, into the vagina, mouth, urethra or anus of a child, or making the child to do so with him, or any other person, or;

(iii) Inserting to any extent, any object into the vagina, mouth, urethra or anus of a child, or making the child to do so with him, or any other person, or;

(iv) Manipulating any part of the body so as to cause penetration into the vagina, mouth, urethra or anus of a child, or making the child to do so with him, or any other person, or;

(v) Applying mouth to the penis, vagina, urethra or anus of a child or making the child to do so with him or any other person.

S.4 of the POCSO Act pronounces punishment for penetrative sexual assault, which is imprisonment for a term not less than seven years and which may also extend to life. S.4 further makes the offender liable to pay fine along with the punishment for imprisonment.

S.5 further speaks about aggravated penetrative sexual assault on children if it is done by a caregiver of any institution where the child is kept for safe custody, police officers within the jurisdiction of the police office, or members of security forces, or if it is in the nature of gang rape. Further, the scope of S.5 also extends to cases where penetrative sexual assault has been caused by dangerous weapons and the like which may have caused damage to the internal organs of the child and also where the child is below 12 years of age, or when the child is pregnant or when such act has been committed knowing the mental condition of the child. S.5 thus lays down the following grounds where penetrative sexual assault can be said to be aggravated penetrative sexual assault:

(a) Whoever, being a police officer, commits penetrative sexual assault on a child

(i) within the limits of the police station or premises at which he is appointed; or

(ii) in the premises of any station house, whether or not situated in the police station, to which he is appointed; or

(iii) in the course of his duties or otherwise; or

(iv) where he is known as, or identified as, a police officer; or

(b) Whoever being a member of the armed forces or security forces commits penetrative sexual assault on a child

(i) within the limits of the area to which the person is deployed; or

(ii) in any areas under the command of the forces or armed forces; or

(iii) in the course of his duties or otherwise; or

(iv) where the said person is known or identified as a member of the security or armed forces; or

(c) Whoever being a public servant commits penetrative sexual assault on a child; or

(d) whoever being on the management or on the staff of a jail, remand home, protection home, observation home, or other place of custody, or care and protection established by or under any law for the time being in force, commits penetrative sexual assault on a child, being inmate of such jail, remand home, protection home, observation home, or other place of custody or care and protection; or

(e) whoever being on the management or staff of a hospital, whether Government or private, commits penetrative sexual assault on a child in that hospital; or

(f) whoever being on the management or staff of an educational institution or religious institution, commits penetrative sexual assault on a child in that institution; or

(g) whoever commits gang penetrative sexual assault on a child; or

(h) whoever commits penetrative sexual assault on a child using deadly weapons, fire, heated substance or corrosive substance; or

(i) whoever commits penetrative sexual assault causing grievous hurt or causing bodily harm and injury or injury to the sexual organs of the child; or

(j) whoever commits penetrative sexual assault on a child, which

(i) physically incapacitates the child or causes the child to become mentally ill as defined under clause (b) of section 2 of the Mental Health Act, 1987 (14 of 1987) or causes impairment of any kind so as to render the child unable to perform regular tasks, temporarily or permanently; or

(ii) in the case of female child, makes the child pregnant as a consequence of sexual assault; or

(iii) inflicts the child with Human Immunodeficiency Virus or any other life threatening disease or infection which may either temporarily or permanently impair the child by rendering him physically incapacitated, or mentally ill to perform regular tasks; or

(k) whoever, taking advantage of a child's mental or physically disability, commits penetrative sexual assault on the child; or

(l) whoever commits penetrative sexual assault on the child more than once or repeatedly; or

(m) whoever commits penetrative sexual assault on a child below twelve years; or

(n) whoever being a relative of the child through blood or adoption or marriage or guardianship or in foster care or having a domestic relationship with a parent of the child or who is living in the same or shared household with the child, commits penetrative sexual assault on such child; or

(o) whoever being, in the ownership, or management, or staff, or any institution providing services to the child, commits penetrative sexual assault on the child; or

(p) whoever being in a position of trust or authority of a child commits penetrative sexual assault on the child in an institution or home of the child or anywhere else; or

(q) whoever commits penetrative sexual assault on a child knowing the child is pregnant; or

(r) whoever commits penetrative sexual assault on a child and attempts to murder the child; or

(s) whoever commits penetrative sexual assault on a child in the course of communal or sectarian violence; or

(t) whoever commits penetrative sexual assault on a child and who has been previously convicted of having committed any offence under this Act or any sexual offence punishable under any other law for the time being in force; or

(u) whoever commits penetrative sexual assault on a child and makes the child to strip or parade naked in public, is said to commit aggravated penetrative sexual assault.

The explanation attached to S.5(g) of the POCSO Act further states:

> When a child is subjected to penetrative sexual assault by one or more persons in a group, in furtherance of common intention, each of such persons shall be deemed to have committed gang sexual assault within the meaning of this clause and each of such person shall be liable for that act in the same manner as if it was done by him alone.

S.6 of the POCSO Act prescribes punishment for aggravated penetrative sexual assault which is rigorous imprisonment for a term not less than ten years, but which may also extend to life, and pecuniary fine. The POCSO Act or the POCSO Rules, however, does not mention the amount of the pecuniary fine.

It may be seen that POCSO Act was implemented before the Criminal Law Amendment Act, 2013 was brought in to amend several provisions including S.375 of the IPC. As such, the profiling of penetrative sexual offence in S.375 of the IPC and S.3 of the POCSO are almost similar except the following basic distinctions which are shown in Table 3.1.

Table 3.1 **Basic Distinction between S.375, IPC and S.3 of the POCSO Act**

S.375 of the IPC	S.3 of the POCSO Act
S.375, IPC is specifically meant for victims who are adult women and also minor girls	S.3 of the POCSO Act is specifically meant for victims who are children irrespective of their gender
The offender is always male	The offender may be male, female or a third gender person
Penetrative sexual offence or rape is a combination of one or more than one or all seven circumstances of physical sexual behaviour as has been mentioned in S.375 and necessarily involves the question of consent of the victim	Consent of children is immaterial in this case

Source: Author.

The five characteristics of penetrative sexual assault as has been explained by S.3 of the POCSO Act are discussed in detail further:

(i) Penetration: Traditionally, it was understood that rape can be said to have been committed either to a woman or a child only when there is a penetration of the penis to the vagina of the victim without the wilful legal consent of the victim. As such, it has been a settled rule that 'Penetration is the sine qua non for an offence of rape', as it was held in the case of Aman Kumar v. State of Haryana.[4] However, it was in the case of Sakshi v. Union of India[5] that the Supreme Court of India acknowledged the necessity to expand this narrow definition. In this particular case, it was observed that insertion of any body part including the penis and any other object into the body parts of the victim/s including his/her private parts may be equally psychologically traumatizing and yield similar physical harm. However, rape by penetration of penis may still hold special place in the eyes of law because such unwanted and forceful sexual intercourse may develop in unwanted pregnancy for women and girls which may invite more risks especially if the victim is a minor. Sakshi v. Union of India further broke the myth that only girls can be victims of penetrative sexual offence within the meaning of S.375, read with S.376 of the IPC. It may be noted that S.377 of the IPC recognizes boys as victims of sexual assault only when they have been victimized by carnal intercourse. But this particular provision still attracts debates regarding its constitutionality and its narrow understanding of carnal intercourse. Further, making the child to do the act of penetration under the instruction of the perpetrator was not recognized as a crime in India until recently. As such, when a male child was forced to put his penis in the mouth of the perpetrator, the victim may had to often land in trouble due to his gender, as S.375 of the IPC recognized only women as victims. In such situations, there were almost always remained chances to make the boys forcefully push into the shoes

---

[4] Aman Kumar v. State of Haryana, (2004) 4 SCC 379.
[5] Sakshi v. Union of India, AIR 2004 SC 3566.

of the perpetrator because the actual perpetrator (especially if she was a woman), may often escape the clutches of laws by posing as a victim who had been penetrated in the mouth by the penis by the minor boy. S.3 of the POCSO Act laid the confusion at rest by expanding the meaning of penetration. S.3 (a) specifically lays down that to attract this provision and the penalties as mentioned in S.4, penetration done by penis to any extent into the vagina, mouth, anus or urethra of the child would be enough. Further, the provision can also be attracted if the child is made to do the same with the perpetrator or any other person.

It must also be noted that in some jurisdictions, rape has been shown as a separate offence than assault by penetration. Hence, in the United Kingdom, while S.5 of the Sexual Offences Act, 2003 (Rape of a Child Under 13) mentions that intentional penetration into the vagina, anus or mouth of the other person who is under 13 may constitute rape, S.6, dealing with the assault of a child under 13 years by penetration, mentions that such penetration must be sexual in nature.[6] But S.3 of the POCSO Act does not differentiate between rape and sexual assault by penetration and clubs up both the concepts under one heading, namely, 'penetrative sexual assault'. As has been mentioned previously, S.3(a) of the POCSO Act dealing with penetrative sexual assault by penis to any female child is given first importance in the provision meant for defining penetrative sexual offences to children because of the probable consequences on the victim, which may result in unwanted pregnancy and grave health risk for the minor mother and the baby. Understanding the gravity of the issue, the legislature further emphasized this in S.5 of the POCSO Act, which terms it as aggravated penetrative sexual assault when such penetration makes the female child pregnant (S.5(j)(ii) of the POCSO Act) or is made repeatedly (S.5(l)), or to a child under the age of 12 (S.5(m)) and such perpetrator/s is/are made liable to be punished under S.6 of the POCSO Act which prescribes rigorous imprisonment for not less than 10 years or for life and

---

[6] See Ss.5 and 6, Sexual Offences Act, 2003 (UK). Available at: http://www.legislation.gov.uk/ukpga/2003/42/part/1 (accessed on 25 January 2018).

also fine. In this regard, mention must be made of the case of Unknown v. State of Gujarat & Others[7] where the Gujarat High Court permitted a 14-year-old female rape survivor to undergo abortion of eight weeks old foetus, which was conceived due to the alleged rape to the victim, after ascertaining the necessary medical tests including the DNA test.

(ii) Inserting of any body part: 'Penetration', if taken in its medico-legal terms, may mean

> acts which include sexual intercourse, cunnilingus, fellatio, anal intercourse, or any other intrusion, however slight, of any part of a person's body or of any object into the genital or anal openings of the victim's, defendant's, or any other person's body. Emission of semen is not required.[8]

For long, this understanding of penetration in relation to sexual assault of women and children were ignored by the lawmakers as well as the courts in India.[9] It was only with Sakshi v. Union of India[10] that the need for amending laws to expand the meaning of sexual abuse including penetrative sexual abuse, which may include penetration by any other body part or any object other than the penis, was ascertained by the courts in India. But it was only with the implementation of the POCSO Act that such sort of penetrative sexual offence was recognized as a crime for the first time in India. Following POCSO Act, S.376 of the IPC was also amended vide the Criminal Law Amendment Act, 2013 to include such sort of penetration within the broader arena of penetrative sexual abuse. As per S.3(b) of the POCSO Act,

---

[7] Unknown v. State of Gujrat & Ors., (Special Criminal Application (Direction) No. 7737 of 2015. Available at: http://www.livelaw.in/gujarat-hc-allows-a-rape-survivor-to-abort-her-8-week-old-foetus/ (accessed on 20 February 2016).

[8] http://medical-dictionary.thefreedictionary.com/sexual+penetration (accessed on 25 January 2018).

[9] Tara Dutt v. The State, Cr. Rev. Petition No. 321 of 2008 in the High Court of Delhi. Available at: http://indiankanoon.org/doc/136220056/ (accessed on 18 January 2018).

[10] AIR 2004 SC 3566.

penetration for sexual gratification of the other on the children may include inserting any body part, not being the penis into the mouth, anus, urethra of the child or making the child to do so with other/s. In numerous instances, it had been seen by the courts that the victims may be abused by perpetrators, who may have inserted their finger/s inside the vagina of the girls.[11] It is neither abnormal to see minor boys being victimized by way of penetrative sexual assault wherein any other body part or other objects may have been inserted into the anus, urethra or mouth of the victims by the perpetrators.[12] In the first case, such aggressive sexual behaviours may fall squarely within the meaning of the sexual abuse of minor girls. Courts in many instances had come across such cases where the primary choice of the police had been S.375/376, IPC. Interestingly, even though S.3 (penetrative sexual assault), S.4 (punishment for penetrative sexual assault), S.5 (aggravated penetrative sexual assault) and S.6 (punishment for aggravated penetrative sexual assault) of the POCSO Act should be used as sufficient provisions in such instances, the police often tends to club the provisions of POCSO with Ss.375/376 of the IPC mainly because the victims are girls and these specific provisions in the IPC are meant only for women and girls.[13] However, the reason for showing first preference for the provisions of IPC for booking the offender may also lie in the fact that POCSO Act being a new provision implemented in 2012, either the police officers may not had been aware of the exclusive scope of this provision, or the cases may had been booked prior to the implementation of the POCSO Act and when the cases came up to the courts, at the instance of the courts, specifically under

[11] Ibid. Also, see Somar Nat v. State of Bihar & Others, Criminal Miscellaneous No. 13889 of 2014, Patna High Court. Available at: http://indiankanoon.org/doc/192514666/ (accessed on 21 January 2016).

[12] Kishan Lal v. State of Rajasthan, 1998 CriLJ 4508.

[13] In Re: State v. Sachinder, on 7 March 2014, Case ID No. 02403R0053532013. Available at: http://indiankanoon.org/doc/10139295/ (accessed on 22 January 2016); State v. Alam Khan on 24 November 2014, Sessions Case No. 38/14, Unique ID Case No. 02404R0053902014. Available at: http://indiankanoon.org/doc/147482301/ (accessed on 21 January 2016).

S.216 of the CrPC (court may alter charge), the provisions of POCSO Act may have been added later.[14] On the other hand, in the second case, when the victims are minor boys, it may often be seen that insertion of any other body parts including finger/s, etc. may be primarily booked under S.377 of the IPC especially when both the perpetrator as well as the victim are males.[15] This is because, for long, such sort of penetrative sexual assaults had been dealt with as unnatural offence and carnal intercourse. The same had been the situation when the victim and the perpetrator had been women. But S.3(b) of the POCSO Act has a better scope in such cases especially when seen from the aspect of sexual abuse of children irrespective of gender. It may be interesting to note that in case such sort of penetrative sexual assault is done by any woman to a male child, S.3(b) of the POCSO Act can be fittingly applied for such cases. Further, if such penetration including inserting any object or body part into the vagina, anus, etc. of the child is done repeatedly, under coercion or with a result that may permanently damage his/her internal organs, the same may be treated as aggravated penetrative sexual assault under S.5 of the POCSO Act.

(iii) Inserting of any object: The expanded meaning of penal-vaginal-anus penetration also includes insertion of any object other than body parts under S.3(b) of the POCSO Act. The severe impact of sexual penetration by way of inserting an object (an iron rod) in the case of Nirbhaya[16] is worth mentionable here. Even though Nirbhaya was an adult woman, it may be noted here that if such insertion of object is done to minors, irrespective of their gender, it may have severe physical and emotional consequences including

[14] Somar Nat v. State of Bihar & Others, Criminal Miscellaneous No. 13889 of 2014.

[15] State v. Ram Bhawan, on 20 May 2014, FIR No. 272/2011, In the Court of Sh. Ashok Kumar, Metropolitan Magistrate (South East)–07, Saket Courts, Delhi. Available at: http://indiankanoon.org/doc/183296595/ (accessed on 1 February 2016).

[16] State Through Reference v. Ram Singh & Others (2013), Death Sentence Reference No. 6/2013, CRL. APP. NOS. 1398/2013, 1399/2013 and 1414/2013 on 13 March 2014, in the High Court of Delhi.

death of the victim. It is for this reason that S.3(b) of the POCSO Act expanded the meaning of penetrative sexual assault by including insertion of any 'object' other than body part.

(iv) Manipulating any part of the body so as to cause penetration: This particular sexual behaviour was also brought in within the arena of penetrative sexual assault on children by S.3(c) of the POCSO Act. It may be interesting to note that S.3 of the POCSO Act uses the term 'or' after each Subsection only to indicate that even when the perpetrator has committed such particular offence and not the other offences as has been mentioned in S.3, the behaviour can fall within the meaning of penetrative sexual assault. Linguistically manipulating may mean 'to control something using the hands', or to control someone or something to the advantage of the manipulator unfairly or dishonestly, or 'to control something using hands', or 'to treat a part of the body, using the hands to push back bones into the correct position and put pressure on muscles'.[17] Child sexual exploitation prevention laws of several jurisdictions have used the term 'manipulation' in regard to child sexual exploitation within the scope of the first meaning as shown in the aforementioned lines. For example, a booklet titled *Stopping the Sexual Exploitation of Children and Youth*, published by the Ministry of Public Safety and Solicitor General of British Columbia, uses the term 'manipulation' to mean how children and young persons can be seduced and manipulated to participate in physical as well as online sexual harassment of themselves.[18] However, the later meaning provides a positive understanding of the term manipulating; but it also provides a wider idea as what may constitute manipulation. A combination of the meanings offered hereby may mean that manipulating may also mean unfair and coercive handling of the body parts for the manipulator's own

---

[17] See http://dictionary.cambridge.org/dictionary/english/manipulate (accessed on 20 January 2016).

[18] For more, see Ministry of Public Safety and Solicitor General, Victim Services and Crime Prevention, British Columbia (2011), Stopping the Sexual Exploitation of Children and Youth. Available at: http://www.pssg.gov.bc.ca/crimeprevention/shareddocs/pubs/crime-prev-series2-sexual-exploitation-children-youth.pdf (accessed on 10 July 2016).

advantage, which may include forceful pushing of the body parts, internal muscles, etc. A clear reading of S.3(c) of the POCSO Act may also show that manipulating of the body parts so as to cause penetration into the vagina, mouth, anus or urethras may mean using force on the body parts for the undue advantage of the manipulator for causing penetration. It may be pertinent to note that POCSO Act does not use the term 'rape' or 'attempt to rape' or 'sexual assault' to include the instances of child sexual abuses within its arena. As such, all of such sexually aggressive behaviours have been clubbed up to constitute the meaning of penetrative sexual assault on children. However, seeing from the perspective of its linguistic meaning, it needs to be noted that offences where sexual penetration had not taken place in reality, but where the perpetrator had manipulated any body part of the child in order to commit penetrative sexual offences, must also be brought in under the purview of S.3(c) of the POCSO Act and also under S.5 when the nature of the offence falls under the category of aggravated penetrative sexual assault.

(v) Applying mouth to the penis, vagina, urethra or anus of a child or making the child to do so with him or any other person: The expanded meaning of penal-vaginal-oral-anus penetrative sexual abuse in S.3 of the POCSO Act also includes applying mouth to the penis, vagina, urethra or anus of the child or making him/her to do so with the perpetrator or any other person. It may be pertinent to note that earlier S.375 of the IPC had provided an extremely restricted meaning of rape which did not include such sexual behaviour of the perpetrator. Further, when such sexual behaviours were meted out to victims by offenders of the same gender or to victims by offenders who were their own blood relatives, the case used to be tired under S.377, IPC, providing little scope for actual justice for the deeply traumatizing crime. This lacuna was noted by courts in several judgements including Smt. Sudesh Jhaku v. K.C.J. and Others,[19] where the six-year-old daughter of the accused was victimized by him by way of sexual

---

[19] Smt. Sudesh Jhaku v. K.C.J. and Others, 1998 CriLJ 2428, 62 (1996) DLT 563.

penetration as well as by making the child to apply mouth to the penis. Later with the introduction of the POCSO Act, this provision and also S.5 of the POCSO Act have been used by the police and also by the courts to provide deeper importance to the instance of penetrative sexual offence done by applying mouth to the penis, vagina, etc. of the child.[20]

Penetrative Sexual Offences for Child Brides

While the term 'penetrative sexual assault' as has been stated under S.3 and S.5 of the POCSO Act explained previously is now considered as a heinous and serious crime as per the JJ Act, 2015,[21] it becomes a critical question as whether the same can be considered in cases of child marriages, procuration of minor girls and teen dating and sexual intercourses. Child marriages are prohibited under the Prohibition of Child Marriage Act, 2006. As per this provision, no marriage can be performed unless the girl is above 18 years of age and the boy is above 21 years of age (S.2(a) of the Prohibition of Child Marriage Act, 2006). This provision further states that where marriages are made between two minors[22] the marriage may be voidable (S.3(i) of the Prohibition of Child Marriage Act, 2006). Further, such marriages can be null and void as per S.12 of this provision when the minor child (a) is taken or enticed out of the keeping of the lawful guardian; or (b) by force, compelled, or by any deceitful means induced to go from any place; or (c) is sold for the purpose of marriage; and made to go through a form

[20] Mr J.S. Choudhary v. Mr Mahesh Bora, S.B.Criminal Revision Petition No. 192/2014, In The High Court of Judicature for Rajasthan at Jodhpur, Asharam @ Ashumalv. The State of Rajasthan & Ors., S.B. Criminal Revision Petition No. 192/2014.

[21] This has been discussed in Chapter 8 of this book.

[22] It may be pertinent to note that while S.2(a) of the Prohibition of Child Marriage Act, 2006 defines 'child' as a person who in case of a male, who has not completed 21 years of age and in case of a female, who has not completed the age of 18 years of age on the day of marriage, S.2(f) of this Act states that minors mean persons who under the Majority Act, 1875 has not attained the age of majority, that is, 18 years (S.3). This provision corroborates with the meaning and definition of 'child' as has been stated by S.2(12) of the JJ Act, 2015, which says any person who has not attained the age of 18 is a child.

of marriage, or (d) if the minor is married after which the minor is sold or trafficked or used for immoral purposes. In any case, as per S.10 of this provision, whoever performs, conducts, directs or abets any child marriage is liable to be punished for rigorous imprisonment for two years and also pay a fine of one lakh rupees. S.9 further prescribes the same punishment for an adult male above 18 years of age who performs child marriage with a minor girl. Child marriages are considered as one of the biggest threats to children, especially young girls in India because this may not only prevent a female children from enjoying a healthy childhood and right to education as has been enshrined in the Constitution of India under Article 39(f) and Article 21(A), it may also invite huge risks of health hazards due to penetrative sexual intercourse and consequently child pregnancy. Based on these understandings, the scopes of Ss.3, 4, 5 and 6 of the POCSO Act had been extended to cover any kind of penetrative sexual assault on children, especially when the child is below 12 years of age (S.5(m) of the POCSO Act). However, it needs to be understood that IPC takes a critical stand on the issue of marital rape or penetrative sexual assault on wives of lawful marriages. S.375 of the IPC in its second exception thus states that sexual intercourse or sexual acts by a man with his own wife, not being under the age of 15, cannot be termed as rape. However, this would not mean that S.375 may have an overriding effect on the Prohibition of Child Marriage Act, 2006 which makes such marriages voidable but pronounces punishment for the adult male partner in the marriage. The Courts in India have come across numerous such cases where they have to face the question of contradiction raised by S.375 IPC, Prohibition of Child Marriage Act and the POCSO Act. This becomes more critical in cases involving love marriages of girls aged 16 and above with men who are adults. In this regard, consideration must be made for inherent meaning of S.366A (Procuration of Minor Girl) of the IPC and S.363 (Kidnapping from Lawful Guardian) of the IPC and judicial understanding of the same. In Varadarajan v. State of Madras,[23] the Supreme Court laid down clear distinctions between taking and allowing a minor to accompany a person. The court held:

---

[23] AIR 1965 SC 942.

There is a distinction between 'taking' and allowing a minor to accompany a person. The two expressions are not synonymous though it cannot be laid down that in no conceivable circumstances can the two be regarded as meaning the same thing for the purposes of S.361. Where the minor leaves her father's protection, knowing and having capacity to know the full import of what she is doing, voluntarily joins the accused person, the accused cannot be said to have taken her away from the keeping of her lawful guardian.

This further, attracts the Sixth Clause of S.375 of the IPC which says that a man is said to commit rape if the action of committing rape falls within the ambit of any of the Subsections from S.375(a) to (d) and is done with or without the consent of the girl if she is under the age of 18 years.[24]

However, the confusion relating to the second exception of S.375, IPC was finally set at rest by the Supreme Court in the case of Independent Thought v. Union of India & Another,[25] where the court had read down this particular exception. The court held that sexual intercourse with child bride, that is, girls below the age of 18 is nothing but rape. This decision was reached on the understanding that sexual interaction with the child bride would cause health hazards to the 'victim wife'. The court also observed that Exception 2 of S.375 IPC is discretionary and arbitrary because it discriminated girls who are married. Justice Madanlokur's observation while reading down Exception 2 to S.375 IPC is noteworthy here. He stated:

> Whether sexual intercourse between a man and his wife being a girl between 15 and 18 years of age is rape? Exception 2 to Section 375 of the Indian Penal Code, 1860 (the IPC) answers this in the negative, but in our opinion sexual intercourse with a girl below 18 years of age is rape regardless of whether she is married or not. The

[24] The age of consent of the girl has been raised from 16 to 18 vide Criminal Law Amendment Act, 2013.

[25] Independent Thought v. Union of India & Another, WP (civil) no. 382 of 2013. Available at: http://supremecourtofindia.nic.in/supreme-court/2013/17790/17790_2013_Judgement_11-Oct-2017.pdf (accessed on 11 October 2017).

exception carved out in the IPC creates an unnecessary and artificial distinction between a married girl child and an unmarried girl child and has no rational nexus with any unclear objective sought to be achieved. The artificial distinction is arbitrary and discriminatory and is definitely not in the best interest of the girl child. The artificial distinction is contrary to the philosophy and ethos of Article 15(3) of the Constitution as well as contrary to Article 21 of the Constitution and our commitments in international conventions. It is also contrary to the philosophy behind some statutes, the bodily integrity of the girl child and her reproductive choice. What is equally dreadful, the artificial distinction turns a blind eye to trafficking of the girl child and surely each one of us must discourage trafficking which is such a horrible social evil.[26]

Further, the court also observed that sex with minor bride should be considered as offence by the husband just as beating may be considered as an offence. This judgement therefore made it clear that S.375(2) of the IPC cannot and should not override the POCSO Act and the scope of Ss.3, 4, 5 and 6 of the POCSO Act would extend to marital rape of minor brides. This author feels that this judgement is a fine example of application of TJ by the court for an issue which had been shrouded by long existing customs and a bad exception to a good law. As has been discussed earlier in this book, the modern concept of TJ embraces the concept of using law as a tool for ensuring mental as well as physical well-being of consumers of justice. TJ however excludes anti-therapeutic approaches of law. S.375(2) of the IPC indeed was anti-therapeutic as it discriminated married girl children from being treated at par with unmarried girl children because they were considered to be within the marriage institution and the penal law excluded such category of sexual intercourse from the definition of rape. As such, the decision of the court in this case has removed all doubts regarding marital rape including sexual penetration of child brides. Hence as per present judicial understanding child marriage is not only void, but also is criminalized especially since the girl would presumably be subjected to sexual penetration by the husband. However, the both the courts and the prevailing laws are silent about

---

[26] Ibid., 2.

under age bridegrooms. It is assumed that the provisions of POCSO Act would prevail both over male and female children who may have been married off due to social customs. However, this author feels that in cases where both the bride and the groom are minors and they are married due to societal and family pressure, they should not be pushed to the arena of POCSO Act but should rather considered as victims of circumstances who should be subjected to rehabilitation. In such cases, the families and individuals who may have conducted the marriage may be subjected to Prohibition of Child Marriage Act, 2006.

CHAPTER 4

Sexual Assault and Sexual Harassment of Children

Introduction

Sexual abuse of children also includes different sorts of unwanted touch on their body excluding penetrative sexual assaults. According to National Society for the Prevention of Cruelty to Children (NSPCC), England, there can be two different types of sexual abuse to children, namely, contact abuse and no-contact abuse. The earlier may include penetrative sexual abuse and unwanted sexual touching. The latter may include encouraging children to see or hear sexual acts, online abuse, grooming, making child abuse/porn images and so on.[1] The UNICEF document titled 'Sexual Violence Against Children in the Caribbean' also shows that sexual abuse may necessarily include unwanted sexual touch which does not amount to penetration.[2] Such different sorts of

---

[1] NSPCC, 'How Do You Define Child Sexual Abuse'. Available at: https://www.nspcc.org.uk/preventing-abuse/child-abuse-and-neglect/child-sexual-abuse/ (accessed on 23 January 2018).

[2] Glenford Howe, 'Sexual Violence Against Children in the Caribbean', Report 2012. Prepared for UNICEF by Barbados and Eastern Caribbean Office. Available at: http://www.unicef.org/easterncaribbean/ECAO_

unwanted touch may include fondling of the softer body parts including chest/breast, stomach, thighs, upper arms, palms, cheeks, lips and the like; touching or pressing with force the genital areas of child, kissing and so on. It is termed as 'unwanted' because such touch may not be gentle, may not be simple, loving, comforting and petting which may make the child feel loved or calm down; such touch may be made to actually create a sexual stimuli with which the child is not familiar or comfortable and which may essentially create a sexual stimuli to the perpetrator. Similarly, as has been shown by the NSPCC, sexual abuse of children also includes sexual harassment which is no-contact abuse. This may or may not include bodily touch, but may necessarily include certain physical activities, passing sexually tainted remarks, remarks following or monitoring the child with a sexual intent, making the child to sexually act as per the wish of the perpetrator, without even touching or penetrating, digitally recording the same and so on. These forms of child sexual abuse have been included in the POCSO Act. While contact-based sexual abuse has been grouped under the term 'sexual assault', no-contact based sexual abuse has been grouped under the term 'sexual harassment' in the POCSO Act. This unique feature of the POCSO Act has been included by the lawmakers considering the special place of children in families, including joint families, where caregivers may not always be the mother herself or both the parents, and also the orthodox societal mindset where children are taught to trust and respect their teachers or 'Guru' in the educational institutes in the similar fashion as should be done to parents. This distinctive societal set-up may bar children from understanding several sorts of unwanted touch or speech or activities of the perpetrators as sexually abusive; they may further be prevented from reporting any sorts of sexual abuse to the parents. Chapter II of the POCSO Act in Parts C, D and E provides an exhaustive elaboration of sexual assault and sexual harassment on children and the consequent punishments. This particular chapter of the book therefore discusses broadly about sexual assaults and harassment of children as per the POCSO Act, different types of such assaults and harassment and why these need to be seen from special perspectives.

Sexual_Violence_againstChildren_in_the_Caribbean.pdf (accessed on 12 March 2016).

Sexual Assault

The term 'sexual assault' has been defined by the US Department of Justice as

> ...any type of sexual contact or behavior that occurs without the explicit consent of the recipient. Falling under the definition of sexual assault are sexual activities such as forced sexual intercourse, forcible sodomy, child molestation, incest, fondling, and attempted rape.[3]

This definition provided by the US government is inclusive of forced sexual intercourse, which, under the POCSO Act, finds a separate legal recognition under S.3 (penetrative sexual assault) and S.5 (aggravated penetrative sexual assault). S.7 of the POCSO Act explains the term 'sexual assault' on children by stating:

> Whoever with sexual intent, touches the vagina, penis, anus or breast of the child or makes the child touch the vagina, penis, anus or breast of such person or any other person or does any other act with sexual intent, which involves physical contact without penetration, is said to commit sexual assault.

S.8 of the POCSO Act prescribes punishment for sexual assault on children by stating that 'whoever commits sexual assault, shall be punished with imprisonment for either description, which shall not be less than three years, but may extend to five years and is also liable to fine'. S.9 of the POCSO Act further speaks about aggravated sexual assault and lays down following 21 grounds where sexual assault committed upon a child may be termed as aggravated sexual assault:

(a) Whoever, being a police officer, commits sexual assault on a child

    (i) within the limits of the police station or premises at which he is appointed; or

---

[3] 'What Is Sexual Assault?' Available at: http://www.justice.gov/ovw/sexual-assault (accessed on 23 January 2018).

       (ii) in the premises of any station house, whether or not situated in the police station, to which he is appointed; or

     (iii) in the course of his duties or otherwise; or

     (iv) where he is known as, or identified as, a police officer; or

(b) Whoever being a member of the armed forces or security forces commits sexual assault on a child

       (i) within the limits of the area to which the person is .deployed; or

     (ii) in any areas under the command of the forces or armed forces; or

     (iii) in the course of his duties or otherwise; or

     (iv) where the said person is known or identified as a member of the security or armed forces; or

(c) Whoever being a public servant commits sexual assault on a child; or

(d) whoever being on the management or on the staff of a jail, remand home, protection home, observation home, or other place of custody, or care and protection established by or under any law for the time being in force, commits sexual assault on a child, being inmate of such jail, remand home, protection home, observation home, or other place of custody or care and protection; or

(e) whoever being on the management or staff of a hospital, whether Government or private, commits sexual assault on a child in that hospital; or

(f) whoever being on the management or staff of an educational institution or religious institution, commits sexual assault on a child in that institution; or

(g) whoever commits gang sexual assault on a child.

(h) whoever commits sexual assault on a child using deadly weapons, fire, heated substance or corrosive substance; or

(i) whoever commits sexual assault causing grievous hurt or causing bodily harm and injury or injury to the sexual organs of the child; or

(j) whoever commits sexual assault on a child, which

       (i) physically incapacitates the child or causes the child to become mentally ill as defined under clause(b) of section 2 of the Mental Health Act, 1987(14 of 1987) or causes impairment of any kind so as to render the child unable to perform regular tasks, temporarily or permanently; or

(ii) inflicts the child with Human Immunodeficiency Virus or any other life threatening disease or infection which may either temporarily or permanently impair the child by rendering him physically incapacitated, or mentally ill to perform regular tasks; or

(k) whoever, taking advantage of a child's mental or physically disability, commits sexual assault on the child; or

(l) whoever commits sexual assault on the child more than once or repeatedly; or

(m) whoever commits sexual assault on a child below twelve years; or

(n) whoever being a relative of the child through blood or adoption or marriage or guardianship or in foster care or having a domestic relationship with a parent of the child or who is living in the same or shared household with the child, commits sexual assault on such child; or

(o) whoever being in the ownership, or management, or staff, or any institution providing services to the child, commits sexual assault on the child; or

(p) whoever being in a position of trust or authority of a child commits sexual assault on the child in an institution or home of the child or anywhere else; or

(q) whoever commits sexual assault on a child knowing the child is pregnant; or

(r) whoever commits sexual assault on a child and attempts to murder the child; or

(s) whoever commits sexual assault on a child in the course of communal or sectarian violence; or

(t) whoever commits sexual assault on a child and who has been previously convicted of having committed any offence under this Act or any sexual offence punishable under any other law for the time being in force; or

(u) whoever commits sexual assault on a child and makes the child to strip or parade naked in public, is said to commit aggravated penetrative sexual assault.

Explanation to S.9(g) of the POCSO Act further states:

When a child is subjected to sexual assault by one or more persons in a group, in furtherance of common intention, each of such persons shall be deemed to have committed gang sexual assault within the meaning of this clause and each of such person shall be liable for that act in the same manner as if it was done by him alone.

It must be noted that the wordings of S.9 and S.6 of the POCSO Act (aggravated penetrative sexual assault) are same except that in the case of penetrative sexual assault, the term 'sexual assault' has been used in S.9. As such, in both the cases, the gravity of the offence has been established with the changing nature of the offender; in cases of penetrative assault (S.3) or sexual assault (S.7) not amounting to aggravated assaults, the nature of the offender is restricted to that of a stranger or any other individual in whom the child does not have trust, who is not known to the child or who is not having the custody of the child. S.10 of the POCSO Act prescribes punishment for aggravated sexual assault, which is imprisonment for either description and which shall not be less than five years but extend to seven years and also fine.

It may be interesting to note that the 2015 records of the NCRB showed that all over India 3,795 incidences of sexual assault on children under S.8 of the POCSO Act (punishment for sexual assault) were recorded by the police.[4] The NCRB data also showed that a total of 241 convictions under S.8 of POCSO Act in courts were recorded and a total of 4,694 cases booked under S.8 of the POCSO Act (punishment for sexual assault) were still pending as of 2015 in different courts in India.[5] As such, as per S.7 of the POCSO Act, sexual assault may be of three types: (i) touching the body parts of the child with sexual intent, (ii) making the child to touch the body parts of him/her or any person and (iii) doing any act involving physical contact without penetration. Considering these three types, it may be seen that the lawmakers in S.7 of the POCSO Act have carefully segregated touching with sexual intent from penetrative sexual assault, which also includes touching concluding in penetration. The two terms, namely, 'penetrative sexual assault' and 'sexual assault', have distinct meanings as per Ss.3, 5, 7 and 9 of the POCSO Act. These are shown in Table 4.1.

While many international researches have shown that sexual assault not amounting to penetration may happen more with the female

---

[4] Retrieved from http://ncrb.gov.in/StatPublications/CII/CII2015/FILES/Statistics-2015_rev1_1.pdf (accessed on 2 February 2016).
[5] Ibid.

Table 4.1 Distinctions Between Penetrative Sexual Assault Including Aggravated Penetrative Sexual Assault and Sexual Assault Including Aggravated Sexual Assault

Penetrative Sexual Assault Including Aggravated Penetrative Sexual Assault	Sexual Assault Including Aggravated Sexual Assault
Such offences are defined under S.3 (penetrative sexual assault) and S.5 (aggravated penetrative sexual assault).	Such offences are defined under S.7 (sexual assault) and S.9 (aggravated sexual assault).
It necessarily includes penetration of the penis or any body part/s into the vagina, anus, urethras, mouth of the child or making the child to do the same with the perpetrator or others.	It does not include penetration of any sort including penetration of any body part such as fingers into the vagina, urethras, anus and the like.
It may include touching of the body parts of the child which may fall within the meaning of sexual assault as per S.7 and S.9 and also penetration.	It includes only touching the body parts with sexual intent.
It also includes penetration with objects other than penis or body parts.	It may include activities limited to touching, pressing on the body parts of the child with harmful objects, heated substance, corrosive sustenance, deadly weapon and the like for sexual gratification of the perpetrator and not penetration.
It also includes applying mouth to the penis, vagina, urethras, anus of the child and making the child to do so with him or others.	It includes touching the said body parts by hands or any other body parts including fingers and toes but the scope of Ss.7 and 9 is limited to such touching only. When the perpetrators engage in physical activities such as applying mouth to the said body part/s the offence must be seen in the light of Ss.3 and 5.

(Continued)

Table 4.1 *(Continued)*

Penetrative Sexual Assault Including Aggravated Penetrative Sexual Assault	Sexual Assault Including Aggravated Sexual Assault
Punishment for penetrative sexual assault includes imprisonment which is not less than 7 years and which may also be even for life and pecuniaryfine in both the cases (S.4 of the POCSO Act). Punishment for aggravated penetrative sexual assault includes rigorous imprisonment for not less than 10 years, which may even extend for life and pecuniary fines in both the cases (S.6 of the POCSO Act).	Punishment for sexual assault not amounting to penetrative sexual assault includes imprisonment for a period of not less than three years, but which may extend to five years and also pecuniary fines in both the cases (S.8 of the POCSO Act). In cases of aggravated sexual assault, the punishment includes imprisonment for a term not less than five years and may extend to seven years and also pecuniary fine in both the cases (S.10 of the POCSO Act).

Source: Author.

children, closely followed by the ratio of male children,[6] in India, reports of sexual assault are made more for female victims compared to male victims. Further, it may be pertinent to note that in India the courts may still analyse the term 'sexual assault' in its widest connotation including sexual penetration.[7] However, this author came across very few court cases where the accused had been convicted within the meaning of Ss.7 and 9 of the POCSO Act and where the term 'sexual assault' was used by the courts (including the lower courts) to indicate sexual assault as within the meaning of only S.7 of the POCSO Act and not inclusive of penetrative sexual assault.[8] This is mainly because the inherent meaning of 'sexual assault' for the purpose of the POCSO Act, 2012 is derived mainly from S.354 of the IPC, which speaks about 'assault or criminal force to woman with intent to outrage her modesty' and states:

[6] Howard N. Snyder, 'Sexual Assault of Young Children as Reported to Law Enforcement: Victim, Incident, and Offender Characteristics'. Available at: http://files.eric.ed.gov/fulltext/ED446834.pdf (accessed on 2 January 2016).

[7] See Mallikarjuna Reddy v. State of Karnataka, Criminal Petition No. 6084/2013, Beeruv. State (NCT of Delhi), CRL.A. 1079/2010.

[8] See State v. Jagat Ram @ Pavva S/o Munna Lal, SC No. 113/13, FIR No. 224/13, Vikas Kumar Meskar v. Union of India & Ors., CWP No. 25186 of 2014.

Whoever assaults or uses criminal force to any woman, intending to outrage or knowing it to be likely that he will thereby outrage her modesty, shall be punished with imprisonment of either description for a term which shall not be less than one year, but may extend to five years, and shall also be liable to fine.

Even though S.354, IPC is meant for women at large, traditionally S.354 of the IPC has been used to punish accused for sexual assault not amounting to penetrative sexual assault or rape, but 'indecent assault' on children,[9] inappropriately touching body parts of children including bottoms, tearing the apparel of the victims,[10] pressing the breasts[11] or making them lie forcefully on the bed with intent to rape, but not actually committing any penetrative sexual assault which may amount to assault on women within the meaning of S.354 of the IPC. Since POCSO Act is relatively a new provision, courts which may be dealing with cases that have been charge sheeted or for which orders have been challenged prior to 2012, may have used the term 'sexual assault' within the broadest meaning as has been discussed previously and not within the meaning of Ss.7 and 9 of the POCSO Act.

Sexual Harassment

S.11 of the POCSO Act provides six characteristics of sexual harassment, any of which or more than one or all of them may constitute sexual harassment of children if committed with sexual intent by the perpetrator. These are as follows:

(i) Uttering any word or making any sound or making any gesture or exhibiting any object or any body part with intention that such word or sound may be heard or gesture or such object or body part may be seen by the child:

These characteristics are largely drawn from S.509, IPC which was traditionally used for punishing offenders for harming the modesty of women. S.509, IPC states:

[9] State of Punjab v. Major Singh, AIR 1967 SC 63.
[10] Ram Pratap v. State of Rajasthan, 2002 CriLJ 1430.
[11] Hari Mohapatra and Another v. State of Orissa and Others, 1996 CriLJ 2952.

Whoever, intending to insult the modesty of any woman, utters any word, makes any sound or gesture, or exhibits any object, intending that such word or sound shall be heard, or that such gesture or object shall be seen, by such woman, or intrudes upon the privacy of such woman, shall be punished with simple imprisonment for a term which may extend to three years and fine.

S.11(a) of the POCSO Act has adopted this particular provision for children of any gender and not necessarily females. Further, as the explanation to S.11 states, 'any question, which involves sexual intent, shall be a question of fact'. In this regard, it may be necessary to note that not all activities of uttering a word, making a gesture or showing something may be considered as within the scope of S.11(i) of the POCSO Act. It was observed in the case of State v. Ankit Duvey:[12]

Bare perusal of S.11 of POCSO Act indicates that there must be something on the part of wrongdoer which may annoy the victim in one way or another way. But when a friend or lover of a child do some activities or pass some comments, which do not hurt or annoy the child, [these] are not sufficient to attract the provisions of sexual harassment.

As such, such uttering of the words, making gestures and so on must be made with sexual intent, which is against the will of the child. This was very pertinently observed in the aforementioned case, where the honourable judge stated:

It is pertinent to state that provisions of POCSO Act do not prevent a child to have friendship or even love affair with opposite sex. It is pertinent to state that love always does not mean sexual relations. One may have even healthy love affair with his/her partner. To have a friendship is one of the basic human rights, and no child can be deprived from his/her said right. If any person exceeds the limits of friendship

---

[12] State v. Ankit Dubey on 26 May 2014, SC No. 95 of 2013, ID No.: 02401R0227562013.

with a child, sufficient provisions have been enacted to deal with such person. Mere fact that the conversation or activities between friends/lovers is not liked by other persons including their parents is not sufficient to invoke the provisions of POCSO Act. For instance, on the eve of one's birthday, two growing up opposite sex child hug and exchange kisses to each other. Their act may not be liked by other members of the society including their family members but their annoyance is not material to invoke the provisions of POCSO Act. The crucial point is there should be sexual intent on the part of wrongdoer and the same can be pointed out by the victim only. For instance, sometimes kissing may not have sexual intent whereas sometimes simple hands shake may have the element of sexual intent. It depends on numerous other factors. Similarly, if during friendship or love affair, if one partner proposed another for marriage, it may or may not be sufficient to attract penal provisions.[13]

If this limitation of the provision is kept in mind, it would be beneficial for the society as a whole especially when matured teenagers and their families may be often victimized in the name of moral policing for love affairs and caste-based violence.

(ii) Making a child to exhibit body or any part of the body so as to be seen by the perpetrator or any other person: While the previous clause of S.11 covered behaviours of the perpetrators including showing body parts to children with sexual intent, Clause (ii) of S.11 further includes perpetrator's behaviour of making the child to exhibit body part to him or anyone else. Such activities may typically include confining the child victim and forcing him/her to show his body parts to the perpetrator or any other person for visual sexual gratification. This may also include sexting whereby children may be groomed by perpetrators to send images of their private parts or semi-nude or naked images.[14] It may be noted that children of either gender may be sexually abused by adults or

---

[13] Ibid.
[14] More about this has been discussed in Chapter 5.

older children either at public places, privately or at educational institutions. It has been noted by this author that many adolescent children may be sexually harassed in this way at educational institutes or hostels whereby older teens or senior students may force them to remove clothes and show their body parts by way of ragging. In this connection, provisions relating to ragging must also be discussed. S.2 of the Tamil Nadu Ragging Prohibition Act defines the activity of ragging as

> ...display of noisy, disorderly conduct, doing any act which causes or is likely to cause physical or psychological harm or raise apprehension of fear or sense of embarrassment to a student of any educational institution and includes (a) teasing, abusing or playing practical jokes on or causing hurt to such student, or (b) asking the student to do any act or perform something, which such student will not in the course will be willing to do.[15]

Basing on this principle regulation and also the broader understanding of the Supreme Court in SLP No. 24295 of 2006 dated 16 May 2007 and Civil Appeal Number 887 of 2009 dated 8 May 2009, many institutions including All India Council for Technical Education (AICTE) have also made their respective anti-ragging preventive provisions. As such, the All India Council for Technical Education (Prevention and Prohibition of Ragging in Technical Institutions, Universities including deemed to be Universities imparting Technical Education) Regulations, 2009 had formed a constructive definition of ragging under S.4 which is worth mentioning here. S.4(g) of this regulation includes 'any acts of physical abuse, including all variants of it, sexual abuse, homosexual assaults, stripping, forcing obscene and lewd acts, gestures, causing bodily harm or any other danger to health or person' as ragging. It needs to be mentioned here that as the anti-ragging (prevention) law came into force in 1997, so long gender-neutral regulation regarding sexual harassment of children including such physical activities

---

[15] S.2, Tamil Nadu Prohibition of Ragging Act, 1997.

including stripping or making the child to show body parts were restricted only within the educational institutions. With the introduction of the POCSO Act, such activities carried on either privately or publicly at any place against any child by anyone can now be regulable.

(iii) Showing any object to any child in any form or media for porno-graphic purposes: S.11 of the POCSO Act also expands its scope to include such behaviour where the perpetrator may have shown any object to any child in any form or media for pornographic purposes. While detailed discussions in this regard has been held in Chapter 6 of this book, for the purpose of this chapter it may be said that sexual harassment of children may necessarily mean either all or any of the activities mentioned under S.11. 'Showing of any object' may mean pornographic clippings, still images of private parts including genitals, breasts or parts of the breasts and the like to the child and this can be included within the scope of S.11 only when it is done with sexual intent for pornographic purposes and not when it is shown as a part of educational purposes.

(iv) Repeatedly or constantly following the victim either physically or by digital or electronic mode: In general, such activity is also known as stalking. The Criminal Law Amendment Act, 2013 has recognized this particular activity as stalking under S.354D of the IPC, which prescribes punishment for stalking includ-ing cyber-stalking women. A unique factor of POCSO Act is to introduce stalking within the meaning of sexual harassment even though the term 'stalking' has not been used in S.11 or in any other provision in POCSO Act. While S.354D of the IPC restricts the gender of the victims to women and that of the per-petrators to men, S.11 makes stalking a gender-neutral offence which includes children of all genders as probable victims and includes perpetrators of all age groups and genders. However, it must be further noted that such 'repeatedly following' must be done with sexual intent. Courts in numerous occasions have held that repeatedly or constantly following any child and com-municating with him/her to pressurize for marriage or love affair by ways either to create threat or annoyance in the victim,[16] may fall within the meaning of S.11(iv) of the POCSO Act. However, simultaneously, it may not be used to attract penal provisions on the accused merely because the victim and the accused had love affair and it could not reach the ultimate destiny (i.e., marriage). The court hence rightly observed in the case of State v. Satvinder Singh @ Mohit,[17] that 'mere fact that accused refused to marry the victim is not sufficient to prove his guilt particularly when PW2 [complainant/victim] categorically admitted in her testimony that accused had not done any "galat harkat" with her at any point of time'.

(v) Threatening to use in any form of media a real or any form of fabricated depiction, through electronic, film, digital or any other mode, of any part of the body of the child or the involvement of the child in sexual act: Due to huge penetration of Internet and digital communication technology, children have open access to communicate with people who may not be known to them directly. Such communication may turn extremely dangerous for children especially when the person so communicating is given access to the private life of the child either by way of looking into the digital albums of the child or by way of gaining confidence of the child whereby the latter sends private images of him/her without knowing the consequences. Further, there are several instances where children, especially older teens, may opt for taking photographs in compromising position with others, including school friends or even lovers, who may be much older than they. There are also instances of voyeurism and photo morphing and misuse of the information of the children through digital media. However, when such images especially of the body parts of the children or their real or fabricated images are so captured and then used for threatening them or coercing them, it may fall squarely within the meaning of revenge porn or violation of privacy or voyeurism which have been discussed in detail

[16] See State v. Rajesh Sharma on 24 July 2014, Sessions Case No. 139/13, Unique ID No. 02404R0071802013.

[17] State v. Satvinder Singh @ Mohit on 11 December 2014, SC No. 186/13 ID No. 02401R0577772013.

in Chapter 6 of this book. S.11(v) of the POCSO Act includes such activities within the meaning of sexual harassment, especially when such activities are done with sexual intention and to harass the child victims sexually. This particular provision does not use the term 'revenge porn' to explain this behaviour. However, it may be noted that in many other jurisdictions such behaviour has been penalized under the term 'revenge porn'.[18]

(vi) Enticing the child for pornographic purposes or giving gratification thereof: This particular behaviour may be understood quite in the light of sexual grooming of children by paedophiles, who target pre-pubescent as well as post-pubescent children for their own sexual gratification. Similar to S.11(v), where the term 'revenge porn' is not used, S.11(v) does not use the term 'grooming' but keeps the scope of the clause wide enough to include any such activity which are done with sexual intent. A detailed discussion on this issue has been carried on in Chapter 6.

S.12 of the POCSO Act prescribes punishment for sexual harassment of children which is imprisonment for a term which may extend to three years and also fine. It needs to be remembered that as per S.41 of the POCSO Act, the activities mentioned in Ss.9 or 11 would not amount to sexual assault, aggravated sexual assault or sexual harassment if some of such activities such as pressing the body parts, photographing and recording certain body parts including private body parts, are done solely for the purpose of medical treatment. However, even in course of medical treatment, if the concerned doctor or medical staff sexually assault or harass the victim within the meaning of Ss.9, 10, 11 and 12 of the Act, the accused may not get the benefit of S.41. In this regard, the case of Dr L. Prakash, popularly known as 'Chennai sex doctor', must also be mentioned. The said Dr Prakash was apprehended in 2001 for creating and producing obscene and sexually explicit videos using minors and adults who used to come to his clinic for treatment. He was arrested under the IT Act, 2000 and Indecent Representation of Women (Prevention) Act, 1986 for using individuals, including his patients and his staff, for creating pornographic films

---

[18] For detailed discussion on this, see Chapter 5 of this book.

which were being sold to porn websites in the United States. He was later acquitted by Madras High Court after serving an imprisonment sentence for 13 years.[19] It needs to be mentioned that if this case would have happened after the POCSO Act came into force, the accused would not have got any benefit of S.41 of the POCSO Act, which is an Exception Clause.[20] Further, it may be pertinent to note that since Criminal Law Amendment Act, 2013 has introduced a fresh version of penal laws regarding violence against women, the criminal justice machinery, including the police, may tend to book the accused under both IPC as well as the POCSO Act provisions, especially when the victim is a female child. While this may not be necessary as POCSO Act is an exclusive, all-inclusive provision itself specifically meant for children, for the welfare of the children, S.42 of the POCSO Act must be considered, which has provided that

> Where an act or omission constitute an offence punishable under this act or any other law for the time being in force, then, notwith-standing anything contained in any law for the time being in force, the offender found guilty of such offence shall be liable to punishment under this Act or under the Indian Penal Code as provides for punishment which is greater in degree.

Hence if the accused is booked for sexual harassment or sexual assault under this Act as well as under the Ragging Prevention Act, 1997 or any law under the IPC meant for regulating violence against women, the court must take the philosophy of the law as mentioned in POCSO Act, but simultaneously pronounce the punishment under that law which provides heavier punishment.

[19] See Fatima Riswana v. State Rep. By A.C.P., Chennai & Ors on 11 January 2005, Appeal (Crl.) 61–62 of 2005, Arising out of SLP (Crl) Nos. 1518–1519 of 2004, Criminal Appeal Nos. 61–62 of 2005, Arising out of SLP (Crl.) Nos. 1518–1519 of 2004 with Criminal Appeal No. 63 OF 2005 (Arising out of SLP (Crl) No. 1606 of 2004).

[20] S.41 of the POCSO Act states: 'The provisions of Sections 3 to 13 shall not apply in case of medical examination or medical treatment of a child when such medical examination or medical treatment is undertaken with the consent of his parent or guardian.'

CHAPTER 5

Cyber Sexual Crimes

Introduction

While the sexual offences that POCSO, 2012 recognizes and criminalizes fall either in the category of physical touch or verbal communication with sexual advances, the uniqueness of POCSO Act lies in the fact that it also recognizes and criminalizes cyber sexual offences targeting children. According to Halder and Jaishankar,[1] cybercrimes are

> offences that are committed against individuals or group of individuals with a criminal motive to intentionally harm the reputation of the victim or cause physical or mental harm, or loss to the victim, directly or indirectly, using modern telecommunication networks such as internet (chat rooms, emails, notice boards and groups) and mobile phones (SMS/MMS).

Cybercrimes targeting individuals can be of various types. It may be sexual or non-sexual; may be of the nature of monetary crimes, hate crimes, privacy infringement and so on. Irrespective of the nature of the crimes, these may happen to children. Vice versa, children may be the offenders as well. Some of the crimes done on the Internet,

---

[1] D. Halder and K. Jaishankar, *Cyber Crime and the Victimization of Women: Laws, Rights, and Regulations* (Hershey, PA: IGI Global, 2011), 15.

which may be primarily non-sexual in nature and where children may be involved either as victims, offenders or both, may have some shades of sexual crimes. These may include privacy infringement, hate crimes and so on, whereby the child in question may unknowingly become a victim of Internet sex industry. Consider the case of Air Force Bal Bharti School of South Delhi in 2001,[2] where a student was arrested for creating porn website and posting vulgar remarks about teachers; he was agitated because of offline teasing by friends.[3] In 2001, children did not have the opportunity to access social media or digital communication medium such as WhatsApp to communicate with others. However, since 2004 onwards, social media such as Orkut, Myspace and Facebook became popular with adults as well as children. There are numerous examples where children may have felt offended by simple teasing remarks by fellow classmates on social media and as repercussion have created contents to take revenge on the other, which may be sexually explicit in nature. The content creator/publisher may never know how such contents may land in porn sites due to viral nature of the Internet and how it may change his/her position from being a victim of school bullying on Internet to an offender of cyber sexual crimes. In some cases, however, the child knowingly publishes such contents to make his/her victim suffer mental trauma or agony in the similar fashion as he/she (the content publisher) may have gone through due to the behaviour of his/her victim. Cases of revenge porn are ideal examples of this. Again, consider the cases of job scam or dating scam. Young people under the age of 18 may be allured to send their photographs as part of prospective job application or for building up emotional relationship virtually. Such images of the children may be misused by perpetrators. They can be morphed or may be used as it is for online sexual gratification of others. Besides, the perpetrators may also make money by selling these images to porn sites. It is often seen that in such cases where criminal activities and motives may lead to different facts, the investigators, lawyers and judges may often fail

---

[2] Basharat Peer, 'Student Accused in Porn Website Case Secures Bail', 30 April 2001. Available at: http://www.rediff.com/news/2001/apr/30porn.htm (accessed on 23 January 2018).
[3] Ibid.

to provide due justice to actual victim/s. The first injustice on the child victim may be borne by the school itself wherein he may be suspended from the school. His/her family may even restrict his/her right to access information through Internet and digital communication technology. Next, he/she may face graver harassment for his/her own involvement in the occurrence of the victimization from the police, who may be unaware of the nature of the cybercrimes as well as present legal developments in this regard. It is for this very reason that stakeholders such as students of law, criminology, sociology, information communication technology and so on; legal practitioners; judges; police officers; and, most importantly, the teachers as well as parents must learn about varied forms of cybercrimes against children, especially cyber sexual crimes targeting children and the related laws, which can be found primarily under different provisions of POCSO Act, IPC and those of the IT Act.

However, the term 'cyber sexual offences' does not restrict the scope of the concept of cybercrimes targeting children only to acts or contents that are generated on the Internet targeting children. The term 'cyber sexual offences' extends its scope to cover illegal activities whereby perpetrators may victimize the children by showing sexually explicit or obscene contents which are neither generated by the perpetrators nor received by them or the victims in their own devices. As such, there are numerous instances of such illegal activities where children have been shown porn clippings in the mobile phones by adults or older minors. How do such activities harm children? What are the legal provisions available under the POCSO Act as well as in other legal provisions in India to deal with such issues? This chapter will answer these issues as well.

Profiles of Sexual Crimes Targeting Children on Internet and Related Laws

The Present Legal Understanding

When we speak about profiles of cyber sexual crimes targeting children on the Internet, we need to know the history of legislations that has finally shaped the present governing laws in this regard in India. The issue of regulating cyber sexual crimes targeting children has become extremely important because this is directly linked with the sexual exploitation of children. Eminent legal luminary Yaman Akdeniz was one of the first academics to note this. In the opening paragraph in the introductory chapter of his book *Internet Child Pornography and the Law: National and International Responses*, he stated:

> The availability and distribution of child pornography through the Internet has become a social concern for the society since mid-1990s, when paedophiles started using this medium to share sexually explicit content. These activities take place within a 'subculture [that] operates beyond the boundaries of any particular state or legal jurisdiction and represents a new pattern of globalized crime and deviance'.[4] At the time of *Operation First-Out* in April 1994 it was acknowledged that the police in England and Wales knew 'nothing about the internet or the strange world they were about to encounter'.[5] This personal ignorance was reinforced by the technological shortcoming that officers were only able to examine the UNIX computer machines confiscated in the operation with the help of US Customs officers. Following this 'enormous step into the unknown',[6] attempts at regulating the availability of child pornography on the Internet has taken the centre stage because of its sensitive nature and its links to the sexual exploitation of children.[7]

In the United Kingdom, the United States and Canada, some of the first legislations were created to criminalize production, creation and distribution of child porn contents. Subsequently, the problem of illegal harmful content on the Internet was addressed by various stakeholders including the European Commission in its European Commission Working Party Report, 1996 on illegal and harmful

---

[4] P. Jenkins, *Beyond Tolerance: Child Pornography on the Internet* (New York, NY: New York University Press, 2001), 5.

[5] *R v. Fellows and Arnold* [1997] 1 Cr App R 244; [1997] 2 All E.R. 548; [1997] *Crim. L.R.*, 524.

[6] D. David, *The Internet Detective: An Investigator's Guide* (London: Home Office, Police Research Group, 1998).

[7] Yaman Akdeniz, *Internet Child Pornography and the Law: National and International Responses* (New York: Routledge, 2016 [Ashgate Publishing, 2008]), 1.

content on the Internet[8] and Decision No. 276/1999/EC of the European Parliament and of the Council of 25 January 1999 adopting a multiannual community action plan on promoting safer use of the Internet by combating illegal and harmful content on global networks.[9] But it was only with the European Union Convention on Cyber Crimes, 2001 that the issue of child pornography was addressed which finally motivated many countries including India to develop laws regulating child pornography. The 11th and 12th paragraphs of the preamble of this convention are particularly noteworthy which are as follows: 'Mindful also of the right to the protection of personal data, as conferred, for example, by the 1981 Council of Europe Convention for the Protection of Individuals with regard to Automatic Processing of Personal Data' (Para 11) and 'Considering the 1989 United Nations Convention on the Rights of the Child and the 1999 International Labour Organization Worst Forms of Child Labour Convention' (Para 12). Hence, it may be understood that this particular convention threw light on engaging children in different forms of illegal and unethical profit making through Internet, namely, creation of harmful, sexually explicit contents by using the children as 'actors' for sexual gratification of adults and also older children. To prevent such sexploitation of children, the convention under Title 3 named 'Content-related Offences' and the one under Title 5 named 'Ancillary Liability and Sanctions' prepared five sorts of master plans:

(i) Directing member States and other States to criminalize the following conducts: (A) producing child pornography for the purpose of its distribution through a computer system; (B) offering or

---

[8] Resolution of the Council and of the representatives of the governments of the member states, meeting within the Council of 17 February 1997 on illegal and harmful content on the Internet. Official Journal C 070, 06/03/1997 P. 0001–0002. Available at: http://eur-lex.europa.eu/legal-content/EN/TXT/?uri=CELEX:41997X0306 (accessed on 23 January 2018).

[9] Decision No. 276/1999/EC of the European Parliament and of the Council of 25 January 1999 adopting a multiannual community action plan on promoting safer use of the Internet by combating illegal and harmful content on global networks, Official Journal C 070, 06/03/1997 P. 0001–0002. Available at: http://eur-lex.europa.eu/legal-content/EN/TXT/?uri=CELEX:31999D0276 (accessed on 23 January 2018).

making available child pornography through a computer system; (C) distributing or transmitting child pornography through a computer system; (D) procuring child pornography through a computer system for oneself or for another person; (E) possessing child pornography in a computer system or on a computer-data storage medium.

(ii) Creating a functional definition of 'child pornography' that may be adopted by all States to criminalize the same; the definition stated that 'the term "child pornography" shall include pornographic material that visually depicts: (a) a minor engaged in sexually explicit conduct; (b) a person appearing to be a minor engaged in sexually explicit conduct; (c) realistic images representing a minor engaged in sexually explicit conduct'.

(iii) Setting age limit for considering a person as minor by stating that 'the term "minor" shall include all persons under 18 years of age. A party may, however, require a lower age-limit, which shall be not less than 16 years'.

(iv) Directing member States and other States to create laws for criminalizing any intentional attempt and abetment of the offences including those related to child pornography.

(v) Directing member States and other States to take

> such legislative and other measures as may be necessary to ensure that legal persons can be held liable for a criminal offence established in accordance with this Convention, committed for their benefit by any natural person, acting either individually or as part of an organ of the legal person, who has a leading position within it, based on: a power of representation of the legal person; an authority to take decisions on behalf of the legal person; an authority to exercise control within the legal person.

Further, the convention also agreed for directing the member States and other States to establish laws for penalizing the negligence of 'legal person' for lack of supervision or control which may have prevented the crime.

While these guidelines of the EU convention had been the major motivation for many countries including India to create child pornography laws, India, unlike other countries, is a signatory to the UN CRC and Optional Protocols on the sale of children, child prostitution and child pornography dated 25 May 2000.[10] India ratified the Optional Protocol to the Convention on 16 August 2005. It may be necessary to note that the first version of IT Act, 2000 (Act no. 21 of 2000) which received the presidential assent on 9 June 2000 had included S.67 to criminalize obscene publications on the Internet under Chapter XI which dealt with such offences. This provision stated:

> Whoever publishes or transmits or causes to be published in the electronic form, any material which is lascivious or appeals to the prurient interest or if its effect is such as to tend to 'deprave and corrupt' persons who are likely, having regard to all relevant circumstances, to read, see or hear the matter contained or embodied in it, shall be punished on first conviction with imprisonment of either description for a term which may extend to five years and with fine which may extend to one lakh rupees and in the event of a second or subsequent conviction with imprisonment of either description for a term which may extend to ten years and also with fine which may extend to two lakh rupees.[11]

As may be seen from the text of this provision, it did not mention anything specific on production, creation or distribution of child porn materials. It rather holistically addressed Internet obscenity. Ironically, this provision did not prove fruitful to regulate child pornography in India; nor there is good precedence where the criminal justice machinery has used this provision to effectively book cases on child pornography. This is evident from the 2001 case of Air Force Bal Bharati School, where a boy was arrested under this provision (S.67 of the IT Act, 2000) for creating porn website with images of female classmates and teachers from his school with lewd remarks as a revenge mechanism. But this was not the only case where S.67 of the IT Act

---

[10] Details are available at: https://treaties.un.org/doc/Publication/CN/2000/CN.1032.2000-Eng.pdf (accessed on 26 January 2018).

[11] Text of the provision is available at: http://www.dot.gov.in/sites/default/files/itbill2000_0.pdf (accessed on 26 January 2018).

was used but failed to provide proper justice; in an earlier research by this author,[12] she has analysed this case in the following words:

> In 2001 when the 16-year-old student of Air Force Bal Bharti School created a porn website with the pictures of his female classmates and teachers, unlike the US, the police did not arrest the accused.[13] The case was handled by the juvenile welfare board after the father of one of the minor female victims lodged a complaint to the police. Even though the Indian Parliament had passed the Information Technology Bill, 2000 which was heavily influenced by the model law on electronic commerce adopted by the United Nations Commission on International Trade Law; adopted by the United Nations by resolution A/RES/51/162, dated 30th January 1997; the police was left much in awe of the nature of the crime as that was the first of its kind in India. The boy was released on bail by the juvenile court, Delhi.[14] Justice Sanjay Agarwal, who granted bail to the accused, noted that this is an 'example of tech graffiti' and it should 'not be taken seriously'.[15]

But he was proved very much wrong. Next, when the students of Delhi Public School were caught circulating clipping of their two classmates in compromising position in 2004 by the school authorities, and the clipping was even found on the Internet for a larger audience, the police immediately applied S.67 of the IT Act along with S.292 of the IPC to arrest the key person, a boy of 17, who had allegedly captured the sexual act along with the girl. The arrest was made after two more high-profile arrests, involving the CEO

---

[12] D. Halder and K. Jaishankar, 'Revenge Porn by Teens in the United States and India: A Socio-legal Analysis', *International Annals of Criminology* 51, nos. 1–2 (2013): 85–111.

[13] Basharat Peer, 'Student Accused in Porn Website Case Secures Bail', rediff. com, 30 April 2001. Available at: http://www.rediff.com/news/2001/apr/30porn. htm (accessed on 26 January 2018).

[14] Presently Juvenile Court is substituted by Juvenile Justice Board after coming into effect of the Juvenile Justice (Care and Protection) Act, 2000. For more details, see http://delhicourts.nic.in/JUVENILE_JUSTICE_BOARD.htm (accessed on 26 January 2018).

[15] These comments were published in the news report that covered the hearing. See Chapter 3, note 6.

of Bazee.com, Avinash Bajaj, who allegedly bought the clipping to circulate it through the website, and one Raviraj, a student of Indian Institute of Technology, Kharagpur, who allegedly sold the clippings to Bazee.com, an auction site. While S.67 of the erstwhile IT Act, 2000 dealt with publishing, transmitting and causing to be published any obscene material in the electronic form, S.292 of the IPC prescribes punishment for selling, publishing, distributing, importing or exporting, making a monetary profit of or advertising for obscene material;[16] S.294 prescribes punishment for obscene acts and songs in public.[17] Even though the CEO of Bazee.com (which was later sold to eBay) challenged the Delhi High Court judgement[18] that quashed the penal code provision against him, but permitted prosecution under the provisions of IT Act, on the ground of lack of clarity of S.67 in reference to his case and due diligence of the website,[19] there were no further news about the prosecution or the post-prosecution treatment of the main accused, the 17-year-old student, except that he was suspended from the school.

As it could be seen, in both these cases, and especially in the latter case, the court highlighted the monetary gain for adults out of the clipping that was made depicting private, sexual moments of two adolescent teens and later focused its attention more on the issue of distributing pornography by an adult, that is, Bajaj. In the earlier case, the judge waived off any 'seriousness' to the issue of the motive of the

---

[16] S.292(2), IPC prescribes punishment with imprisonment of either description for a term which may extend to two years and with fine which may extend to two thousand rupees and, in the event of a second or subsequent conviction, with imprisonment of either description for a term which may extend to five years and also with fine which may extend to five thousand rupees.

[17] S.294 of the IPC, 1860 prescribes punishment with imprisonment of either description for a term which may extend to three months, or with fine, or with both.

[18] Avinash Bajaj v. State, 2005, 3 Comp LJ 364 Del.

[19] *Business Standard*, 'DPS MMS Scandal: SC Stays Proceedings against eBay, Its Chief', 26 August 2008. Available at: http://www.business-standard.com/india/news/dps-mms-scandal-sc-stays-proceedings-against-ebay-its-chief/332573/ (accessed on 26 January 2018).

wrongdoer. Predominantly, that may have affected the legal treatment of the offender teen in the latter case.[20]

As it may be seen from the aforementioned excerpt, the concept of cyber sexual offences targeting children in India was trapped in the bizarre understanding of creation and sale of 'obscene contents', which often overlapped with the concept of 'child pornography'. There was no specific law to define the concept of child pornography or separate it from the concept of general obscenity or pornography on the Internet meant for adults. This situation was improved with the introduction of a set of amendments to the IT Act, 2000 in 2008. This amendment to the main Act split S.67 into three other provisions:

(i) S.67: This was amended vide IT Amendment Act, 2008. The header of this provision was changed from 'publishing of information which is obscene in electronic form' to 'punishment for publishing or transmitting obscene material in electronic form'. As such, the amended version changed the extent of punishment by stating that

> Whoever publishes or transmits or causes to be published in the electronic form, any material which is lascivious or appeals to the prurient interest or if its effect is such as to tend to deprave and corrupt persons who are likely, having regard to all relevant circumstances, to read, see or hear the matter contained or embodied in it, shall be punished on first conviction with imprisonment of either description for a term which may extend to three years and with fine which may extend to five lakh rupees and in the event of a second or subsequent conviction with imprisonment of either description for a term which may extend to five years and also with fine which may extend to ten lakh.

(ii) S.67A: This provision was inserted vide the IT Amendment Act, 2008 under the heading 'punishment for publishing or transmitting of material containing sexually explicit act, etc., in electronic form'. It stated that

---

[20] Supra note 2, pp. 99–101.

Whoever publishes or transmits or causes to be published or transmitted in the electronic form any material which contains sexually explicit act or conduct shall be punished on first conviction with imprisonment of either description for a term which may extend to five years and with fine which may extend to ten lakh rupees and in the event of second or subsequent conviction with imprisonment of either description for a term which may extend to seven years and also with fine which may extend to ten lakh rupees.

The Section further provided an exception clause which stated:

This section and S.67 does not extend to any book, pamphlet, paper, writing, drawing, painting, representation or figure in electronic form (i) the publication of which is proved to be justified as being for the public good on the ground that such book, pamphlet, paper, writing, drawing, painting, representation or figure is in the interest of science, literature, art, or learning or other objects of general concern; or (ii) which is kept or used bona fide for religious purposes.

(iii) S.67B: This provision was also inserted vide IT Amendment Act under the heading 'Punishment for publishing or transmitting of material depicting children in sexually explicit act, etc., in electronic form'. This was the only provision under Chapter XI of the amended Act which focused on cyber sexual crimes targeting children. It stated as follows: Whoever, (a) publishes or transmits or causes to be published or transmitted material in any electronic form which depicts children engaged in sexually explicit act or conduct or (b) creates text or digital images, collects, seeks, browses, downloads, advertises, promotes, exchanges or distributes material in any electronic form depicting children in obscene or indecent or sexually explicit manner, or (c) cultivates, entices or induces children to online relationship with one or more children for and on sexually explicit act or in a manner that may offend a reasonable adult on the computer resource, or (d) facilitates abusing children online, or (e) records in any electronic form own abuse or that of others pertaining to sexually explicit act with children, shall be punished on first conviction with imprisonment of either description for a term which may extend to five years and with a fine which may extend to ten lakh rupees and in the event of second or subsequent conviction with imprisonment of either description for a term which may extend to seven years and also with fine which may extend to ten lakh rupees. Provided that the provisions of S.67, S.67A and this section does not extend to any book, pamphlet, paper, writing, drawing, painting, representation or figure in electronic form (i) the publication of which is proved to be justified as being for the public good on the ground that such book, pamphlet, paper writing, drawing, painting, representation or figure is in the interest of science, literature, art or learning or other objects of general concern; or (ii) which is kept or used for bonafide heritage or religious purposes. Explanation added to this provision states that for the purposes of this section, the term 'children' means any person who has not completed the age of 18 years.

Along with these amendments, the IT Act, 2000 (amended in 2008) also inserted S.66E under the heading 'punishment for violation of privacy'. It states:

Whoever, intentionally or knowingly captures, publishes or transmits the image of a private area of any person without his or her consent, under circumstances violating the privacy of that person, shall be punished with imprisonment which may extend to three years or with fine not exceeding two lakh rupees, or with both.

Explanation added to this Section further provides the following:

(a) 'transmit' means to electronically send a visual image with the intent that it be viewed by a person or persons;

(b) 'capture', with respect to an image, means to videotape, photograph, film or record by any means;

(c) 'private area' means the naked or undergarment clad genitals, pubic area, buttocks or female breast;

(d) 'publishes' means reproduction in the printed or electronic form and making it available for public;

(e) 'under circumstances violating privacy' means circumstances in which a person can have a reasonable expectation that—

    (i) he or she could disrobe in privacy, without being concerned that an image of his private area was being captured; or

    (ii) any part of his or her private area would not be visible to the public, regardless of whether that person is in a public or private place.

Further, the IT Act also created S.77B under the heading 'offences with three years' imprisonment to be cognizable' to specify the cognizable and bailable offences under this Act. It stated that 'notwithstanding anything contained in CrPC, 1973, the offence punishable with imprisonment of three years and above shall be cognizable and the offence punishable with imprisonment of three years shall be bailable'. As such the sexual offences as have been shown in Ss.66E, 67, 67A and 67B are all cognizable offences since the minimum imprisonment sentence for all these have been fixed at three years. Further, except Ss.66E and 67, other sections mentioned previously may not be bailable if the imprisonment term is fixed for more than three years as has been provided in these sections. However, there was still no focused law on sexual offences targeting children and this vacuum was addressed in 2012 with the introduction of POCSO (Act no. 32 of 2012). Specific sections were introduced to address cyber sexual harassment targeting children under S.11 of the POCSO Act, 2012, which has been discussed in detail in the previous chapter of this book.[21] Along with S.11, other provisions including S.12 that prescribes punishment for the same, S.13 titled 'use of child for pornographic purposes', S.14, which prescribes punishment for the same, S.15 titled 'Punishment for Storage of Pornographic Materials Involving Child', S.16 titled 'Abetment of Offence', S.17 that prescribes punishment for the same and S.18 titled 'Punishment for Attempt to Commit an Offence' were also introduced.

[21] For more detail, see Chapter 4 of the book.

While POCSO Act was made specifically for children in 2013 vide Criminal Law Amendment Act, 2013, a set of new laws were introduced to IPC, among which S.354C, titled 'Voyeurism', is mentionable in this regard. It says,

> Any man who watches, or captures the image of a woman engaging in a private act in circumstances where she would usually have the expectation of not being observed either by the perpetrator or by any other person at the behest of the perpetrator or disseminates such image shall be punished on first conviction with imprisonment of either description for a term which shall not be less than one year, but which may extend to three years, and shall also be liable to fine, and be punished on a second or subsequent conviction, with imprisonment of either description for a term which shall not be less than three years, but which may extend to seven years, and shall also be liable to fine.

Explanations attached to this provision further says,

> For the purpose of this section, 'private act' includes an act of watching carried out in a place which, in the circumstances, would reasonably be expected to provide privacy and where the victim's genitals, posterior or breasts are exposed or covered only in underwear; or the victim is using a lavatory; or the victim is doing a sexual act that is not of a kind ordinarily done in public.

The second explanation attached to it further says, 'where the victim consents to the capture of the images or any act, but not to their dissemination to third persons and where such image or act is disseminated, such dissemination shall be considered an offence under this section'. It needs to be mentioned that even though S.66E of the Information Technology Act, 2000 (amended in 2008) addresses the same issue, unlike this particular provision, it is not gender specific. Again, even though S.67B of the IT Act, 2000 (amended in 2008) loosely covers this issue, there is no provision to address voyeurism under POCSO Act, 2012. However, the issue is touched over by S.13 of the POCSO Act which speaks about creation of child pornography.

Types of Cyber Sexual Offences Targeting Children in India

From the earlier discussion related to existing laws regarding cyber sexual offences targeting children, it may be understood that there are mainly three types of cyber sexual offences.

Showing of Offensive, Objectionable, Porn Contents to Children

Showing of porn clippings to children are increasingly becoming a dangerous trend among adults as well as teenagers.[22] It is ironical to note that not only adults and teenagers, who are not related to the victims, may commit such offences, but in several cases, this author has observed that relatives including fathers, uncles, brothers, etc., may also commit the same offences which may or not may be followed by sexual assault to the minor. In most of these cases, the child victims are threatened to not to divulge anything to the mothers or to the parents (in case the perpetrator is other than close relatives). The parents or guardians may come to know about such incidences only when the child victims start showing a change in their behaviour, or may undergo severe pain due to physical pain caused by sexual assault following showing of such clippings. In some cases, such trait may follow physical sexual assault of the victim. In other cases, the perpetrator may

---

[22] 'UP Teacher Held for Showing Pornographic Clip to Students', *News18.com*, 12 December 2014. Available at: http://www.ibnlive.com/news/india/up-teacher-held-for-showing-pornographic-clip-to-students-730865.html. Also see 'School Bus Driver, Helper Held for Forcing Kids to Watch Porn in Delhi', *Firstpost*, 10 May 2013. Available at: http://www.firstpost.com/delhi/school-bus-driver-helper-held-for-forcing-kids-to-watch-porn-in-delhi-769701.html (accessed on 29 January 2018); Eram Agha, 'School Van Driver Caught Showing Porn to Class II Students', *The Times of India*, 27 August 2015. Available at: http://timesofindia.indiatimes.com/city/agra/School-van-driver-caught-showing-porn-to-Class-II-students/articleshow/48702290.cms (accessed on 29 January 2018); Manoj Badgeri, 'Nine-year-old Boy Sexually Assaulted by Minor at Kalwa', *The Times of India*, 3 February 2015. Available at: http://timesofindia.indiatimes.com/city/thane/Nine-year-old-boy-sexually-assaulted-by-minor-at-Kalwa/articleshow/46099741.cms (accessed on 29 January 2018).

restrict himself/herself to showing the children the porn clippings. In all these cases, portable smart mobile devices like cell phones may be used. However, it would be wrong to say that showing of porn contents to the children happens only manually through mobile phones. There are numerous examples from all over the world to show that the child may be exposed to pornography even in the course of online communication by way of grooming.[23] There is no specific separate law addressing this sort of offences in either POCSO Act or the IT Act. But this is covered under S.11 of the POCSO Act under the broad term 'sexual harassment'. S.11(iii) is particularly applicable to all such cases which says, 'A person is said to commit sexual harassment upon a child when such person with sexual intent shows any object to a child in any form or media for pornographic purposes.' In cases when such act of the perpetrator is coupled with subsequent intention to allure the child for creation of porn contents, the officer concerned or the lawyer or the judges must also consider analysing the case from the perspective of S.11(vi) which says, 'A person is said to commit sexual harassment upon a child when such person with sexual intent entices a child for pornographic purposes or gives gratification there for.' S.12 of the POCSO Act, 2012 prescribes punishment for such offences which is imprisonment for a period of three years and also fine.

This genre of offences needs minute analysis for two basic reasons: (i) causes of the offence and (ii) effect on the child victim. When we speak about causes of the crime, it may be seen that there are numerous factors which may lead to occurrence of the crime. These may include pervert mindset of the offender, availability of the offensive contents in the Internet and easy accessibility of the same by smartphones especially with the help of 3G or 4G mobile telecommunication technologies, policies of organizations to allow the adult to keep such smartphones with him/her and use it during school hours/duty hours. When seen from the perspective of Ss.11 and 12 of the POCSO Act, 2012, there are two factors to consider when investigating the mindset

[23] D. Halder and K. Jaishankar. 'Patterns of Sexual Victimization of Children and Women in the Multipurpose Social Networking Sites', in *Social Networking as a Criminal Enterprise*, eds. C. Marcum and G. Higgins (Boca Raton, FL: CRC Press, Taylor and Francis Group, 2014), 129–143.

of the offender: sexual intent of the offender and intention to harm the child victim psychologically and physically. The questions which may come up here are: (i) Whether the adult watched the porn or made the child to watch the same with a sexual intention towards the child? (ii) Even if he was watching the porn clippings alone and if the child suddenly appeared and caught him watching the same, can he claim a right to watch porn clippings when he is alone? (iii) Considering that the phone device belonged to an adult, can the said adult store any objectionable content in his/her device? In this context, it becomes necessary to analyse the recent government decision to ban porn sites in India. In the case of Kamlesh Vaswani v. Union of India & Others,[24] which was filed in the nature of public interest litigation, among the prayers, the petitioner also prayed for creating a national policy in regard to circulation and watching of porn contents and also for declaring the act of watching porn videos and circulating the same as non-bailable and cognizable offence. Specifically notable in this regard is the oral observation of Chief Justice H. L. Dattu in the court proceedings of this case on 8 July 2015. When the petitioner submitted that no order has been passed so far to any government departments in regard to banning of porn websites, Chief Justice Dattu observed that

> Such interim orders cannot be passed by this court. Somebody can come to the court and say 'Look, I am an adult and how can you stop me from watching it within the four walls of my room? It is a violation of Article 21 [right to life and personal liberty] of the Constitution'. Yes, the issue is serious and some steps need to be taken…the Centre has to take a stand… let us see what stand the Centre will take.[25]

Subsequently, the Ministry of Communication and Information Technology, Department of Telecommunication, Government of India vide order dated 31 July 2015 blocked 857 websites which were

---

[24] Kamlesh Vaswani v. Union of India & Others, 2014, 6 SCC 705.

[25] Serish Nanisetti, 'Is Watching Porn a Fundamental Right?', *The New Indian Express*, 10 July 2015. Available at: http://www.newindianexpress.com/cities/hyderabad/Is-Watching-Porn-a-Fundamental-Right/2015/07/10/article2911541.ece (accessed on 29 January 2018).

stated to be sites showcasing or containing pornographic materials.[26] This order actually called for disablement of the sites under the power conferred under S.79(3) of the IT Act, 2000 (amended in 2008) (exceptions to the exemption from liability). But there was a huge uproar against such blanket ban. Later the ban was relaxed and it was made applicable only to websites which cater child pornographic contents. Now, let us consider the case of school staff watching porn and showing the same to the children.[27] Even though the news report did not reveal the subsequent investigation report, or case details, in the background of the observation made by Chief Justice Dattu, it can be said that even if the adult may have watched the clippings in private but not in his own room and may be in any place like school where he may be working as a teacher, he may still be pleaded guilty because he was not watching the contents in private in his own room. As such, the said adult may not avail the defence of right to privacy for watching the porn contents in the school building. Next, even if the students appeared when he did not actually expect them, it may be presumed that students could get the glimpse of what he was watching. In his designation as a teacher on duty, he may neither avail the defence of any exceptions provided in the proviso to S.67B which states:

> Provided that the provisions of S.67, S.67A and this section does not extend to any book, pamphlet, paper, writing, drawing, painting, representation or figure in electronic form (i) The publication of which is proved to be justified as being for the public good on the ground that such book, pamphlet, paper writing, drawing, painting, representation or figure is in the interest of science, literature, art or learning or other objects of general concern; or (ii) which is kept or used for bonafide heritage or religious purposes.

Explanation: For the purposes of this section, the term 'children' means a person who has not completed the age of 18 years. This is

---

[26] The copy of the order can be accessed at 2015-07-31_DoT-block-order-decency.pdf uploaded in the website of The Centre for Internet & Society. Available at: http://cis-india.org/internet-governance/resources/dot-morality-block-order-2015-07-31/view (accessed on 29 January 2018).

[27] For more detail, see Chapter 4 of the book.

because his course of action (of watching it in another teacher's mobile phone, who may have deleted the contents later) may not support his plea in this regard. Further, for establishing his innocence, he may need to establish his defence by stating that he did not watch the clippings 'with any sexual intent', which is the prime constituting element of sexual harassment in relation to such cases as per S.11 of the POCSO Act, 2012. But contrary to this example, in cases where a person may be accused to have sexually assaulted the child victim after showing the porn clippings to him, there may exist a clear chain of events whereby it can be said that the accused had allured the victim to see the 'prohibited stuff' which he generally cannot see at home or at school, and then had sexually assaulted him. As may be seen, in such cases, the accused would have done the act of showing the porn content with a sexual intention towards the victim and also with an intention to physically and sexually exploit the victim.

Coming to the issue of effects of showing porn to the children, the worldwide ongoing researches have shown varied results: as such, children may feel shocked, surprised and may also undergo unnecessary sexual excitement. Boys and girls may have different aftereffects; boys may feel sexually excited and girls may feel ashamed, guilty or disgusted. It may also happen vice versa.[28] It is also noted that when such contents contain highly sexually explicit materials including sexually abusive contents projecting especially women, and they are showed by adults to the children, the latter may feel shocked, sick and disgusted. In some cases, older children may also try to practise several sexual conducts shown in such contents either with themselves (e.g., masturbation) or with other children or adults.[29] Further, children may also turn into regular consumers of such porn clippings. From this discussion, it can be seen that there can be three different types of effects of showing porn contents to children: (i) emotional trauma

---

[28] Chiara Sabina, Janis Wolak and David Finkelhor, 'The Nature and Dynamics of Internet Pornography Exposure for Youth', *Cyber Psychology & Behavior* 11, no. 6 (December 2008): 691–693. Available at: http://www.unh.edu/ccrc/pdf/CV169.pdf (accessed on 17 August 2016).

[29] M. Flood, The harms of pornography exposure among children and young people, *Child Abuse Review*, 18 (2009): 384–400.

and physical uncomfortableness of the child, which may or may not be sadistically enjoyed by the perpetrators, (ii) psychological grooming of the child to be involved in sexual exploitation by the perpetrator and (iii) changing the child to a consumer of porn contents whereby the perpetrator can build up a profit-making relationship with the child as a supplier of such contents. All these constitute sexual abuse of the child and the law's primary goal should be to prevent such sexual abuse in the course of harassment. S.12 of the POCSO Act, 2012 prescribes punishment for such acts which is imprisonment for a term which may extend to three years and with fine. However, in the case of an act of showing of pornography to children in the course of online communication and grooming, S.67B (c) of the IT Act, 2000 (amended in 2008) must be read with Ss.11 and 12 of POCSO Act, 2012. S.67B(c) of the IT Act, 2000 (amended in 2008) which states that whoever cultivates, entices or induces children to online relationship with one or more children for and on sexually explicit act or in a manner that may offend a reasonable adult on the computer resource shall be punished on first conviction with imprisonment of either description for a term which may extend to five years and with a fine which may extend to ten lakh rupees and in the event of second or subsequent conviction with imprisonment of either description for a term which may extend to seven years and also with fine which may extend to ten lakh rupees.

Creation, Production, Distribution of Child Porn Materials by Virtual Data Mining

While in the earlier case, the perpetrator may not use the child to create, produce or distribute any child porn materials but may only restrict himself/herself with exposing the child to porn materials either manually or in the course of online communication, this particular genre of offence may include various types of other offensive activities including data mining for the purpose of creation, production and distribution of child porn materials. For better understanding, let us analyse the following two examples:

(a) As per this news report published on 12 May 2015, Yadava Manikanta, a Tirupati-based man, was arrested for creating child pornographic materials in Facebook pages. The news report states that he used to randomly shoot photographs of individuals, especially of young girls, and circulate them to his associates in closed groups in Facebook. He also used to collect photographs of girls from Facebook profiles. These images of girls gathered by him by such data mining were used to create Facebook pages which also used to have vulgar words describing these girls. Civil society members reported Manikanta especially after one of such pages named 'Chinna Ponnu Veriyargal' started getting noticed by Facebook users due to its huge fan following. He was arrested under IT Act, 2000 (amended in 2008) and also POCSO Act. The news report did not provide any specific provisions under these laws.[30] However, the latest news report suggested that he was tracked down in Tamil Nadu and detained in a prison in Tamil Nadu. With further investigation and framing of charges, he was also slapped with Tamil Nadu Prevention of Dangerous Activities of Bootleggers, Drug-offenders, Forest-offenders, Goondas, Immoral Traffic offenders, Sand offenders, Slum-grabbers and Video Pirates Act, 1982 (also known as Gundas Act), which was amended with effect from 13 October 2014 vide S.3 of the TN Act of 19 of 2014.

(b) On August 2015, another 19-year-old youth was arrested for charges of creating Facebook pages containing images of girl children accompanied by sexually explicit words. These pages were also noticed by an NGO who reported the matter to the Facebook as well as to the police. After due investigation, it was found that the said page or creator of the same had no connection with Yadava Manikanta, even though the facts of the case are similar. The youth was arrested under IT Act, 2000 (amended in 2008) and also under POCSO Act. The news reports did not provide any particular section of these provisions under which the accused may have been booked.

---

[30] TNN, 'Man Held for Creating FB Page with Paedophilic Content', *The Times of India*, 12 May 2015. Available at: http://timesofindia.indiatimes.com/city/chennai/Man-held-for-creating-FB-page-with-paedophilic-content/articleshow/47241605.cms (accessed on 29 January 2018).

As may be seen from these two examples, the act of creation, production and circulation of paedophilic contents by virtual data mining has two patterns depending upon the procedure and motive of the wrongdoer; these two patterns are discussed in the following paragraphs:

In the first pattern, the creation, production and circulation of paedophilic contents may occur by the perpetrator's act of random data collection and data mining. The motive may be self-sexual gratification by way of creating the contents in the form of single content, which may be a fake avatar[31] of the victim, a porn website, a page in social media such as Facebook, a mashed video containing all the still or audio–visual images of children as well as adults and so on. The motive may also include profit making by circulating of such paedophilic contents. The two examples provided earlier may be categorized as offence done in this pattern. The wrongdoers generally may not know the victims directly, may neither interact with them after collecting the images of them. As it may be seen from the two examples, in this pattern, the victims need not be victimized directly in the same way as may happen when they are contacted by the perpetrator directly either through online communication technology or by direct interaction in the real life. The victims may not undergo the feeling of shock, uncomfortableness, feeling of disgust, shame and the like in the course of creation or production of such contents, because they may be unaware of such misuse of their information and images. But they may develop such traumatizing feelings when the contents are being circulated and they come to know of it. In such cases, the wrong doer may be booked under Ss.14(1) and 15 of the POCSO Act

---

[31] The author in her earlier publication had defined the term Fake Avatar as

a false representation of the victim which is created by the perpetrator through digital technology with or without the visual images of the victim and which carry verbal information about the victim which may or may not be fully true and it is created and floated in the internet to intentionally malign the character of the victim and to mislead the viewers about the victim's original identity. See p. 197 in D. Halder, 'Examining the Scope of Indecent Representation of Women (Prevention) Act, 1986 in the Light of Cyber Victimization of Women in India', *National Law School Journal* 11 (25 May 2013): 188–218.

read with S.13 of the same. The latter criminalizes use of child for pornographic purposes. It says:

> Whoever uses a child in any form of media (including programmes or advertisements telecast by television channels or internet or any other electronic form or printed form, whether or not such programme or advertisement is intended for personal use or for distribution) for the purposes of sexual gratification, which includes (a) representation of a sexual organ of a child, (b) usage of child engaged in real or stimulated sexual acts (with or without penetration), (c) the indecent or obscene representation of a child, shall be guilty of the offence of using child for the pornographic purposes.

Now note the last category of the sexual gratification. The aforementioned two examples show similar traits, where the images of the children were noticed accompanied with sexually explicit and obscene words. The Explanation attached to these sections states:

> For the purpose of this section, the expression 'use a child' shall include involving of a child through any medium like print, electronic, computer or any other technology for perpetration, production, offering, transmitting, publishing, felicitation and distribution of the pornographic materials.

S.14(1) of the POCSO Act, 2012 prescribes the punishment for such offences by stating that

> Whoever uses a child or children for pornographic purposes shall be punished with imprisonment of either description which may extend to five years and shall also be liable to fine and in the event of second or subsequent conviction, with imprisonment for either description for a term which may extend to seven years and also be liable to fine.

The offender must also be booked under S.67B—(a) and (b) specifically—of the IT Act, 2000 (amended in 2008). The provisions state:

> Whoever, (a) publishes or transmits or causes to be published or transmitted material in any electronic form which depicts children

engaged in sexually explicit act or conduct, or (b) creates text or digital images, collects, seeks, browses, downloads, advertises, promotes, exchanges or distributes material in any electronic form depicting children in obscene or indecent or sexually explicit manner, shall be punished on first conviction with imprisonment of either description for a term which may extend to five years and with a fine which may extend to ten lakh rupees and in the event of second or subsequent conviction with imprisonment of either description for a term which may extend to seven years and also with fine which may extend to ten lakh rupees.

It may be noted that S.15 of the POCSO Act, 2012 prescribes punishment for storage of pornographic material involving child for commercial purposes and states that 'any person who stores for commercial purposes any pornographic material in any form involving a child, shall be punished with imprisonment of either description which may extend to three years or with fine, or with both'. It may be further noted that while POCSO Act does not specifically criminalize storing of child porn materials for any non-commercial purpose, S.67B(b) of the IT Act, 2000 (amended in 2008) fills up this lacuna. However, when such act of creation, production, circulation of the child porn materials is done with intent to gain profit by selling the materials to children, the offender must also be booked under S.293 of the IPC which states:

> Whoever sells, lets to hire, distributes, exhibits or circulates to any person under the age of twenty years any such obscene object as is referred to in the last preceding section, or offers or attempts so to do, shall be punished on first conviction with imprisonment of either description for a term which may extend to three years, and with fine which may extend to two thousand rupees, and, in the event of a second or subsequent conviction, with imprisonment of either description for a term which may extend to seven years, and also with fine which may extend to five thousand rupees.

In the second pattern, the creation, production, distribution of child porn materials may include prior online communication between the perpetrator and the victim. Such communication may be done for the purpose of grooming the child victim not only to cooperate with the perpetrator for creation of such paedophilic contents but also for consuming the contents. In this regard, this author's observations with regard to uniqueness of multipurpose social networking sites (MPSNSs) such as Facebook and the like and the risks involved therein could be noted, which are as follows:

> The uniqueness of the MPSNSs lies in the fact that persons from the age group of 13 can become members/users. This has given wide opportunity for teenagers to discover a completely new world through the MPSNSs. The teenage users not only get to show off their latest profile pictures but also can choose their own friends. The platform is basically a home without any strong adult supervision for teenage users. Paradoxically, unsupervised teenagers tend to fall prey for a number of unsocial 'games', and MPSNS teen habitats are no exception. In case of sexual crimes targeting children in the MPSNSs, two distinct types of contributors can be found: (1) child user himself or herself who posts his or her detailed personal information and personal pictures through his or her own profile pages or school groups and (2) adult perpetrator who may create an alluring profile for trapping the target victim.[32] He or she may also create child pornographic materials with the contents that he or she may have collected from the MPSNSs for wider consumption by other adults as well as young adults either in the MPSNSs or in adult dating and matrimonial sites (AD&MSs) or interactive vlogging sites (IVSs). With these two types of contributors, MPSNSs may witness a number of forms of sexual crimes, which are listed as follows:

> 1. Creation of fake profiles by the adult perpetrator for alluring the victim: Even though perpetrators can carry on with the sexual victimization of children with their original profiles, professional contributors to paedophilia may do this through their fake identities created especially to befriend the children.[33] Such fake

[32] J. Savarimuthu, *Online Child Safety: Law, Technology and Governance* (Basingstoke, Hampshire: Palgrave Macmillan, 2012).

[33] R. Broadhurst and K. Jayawardhena, 'Online Social Networking and Paedophilia: An Experimental Research "Sting"', in *Cyber Criminology: Exploring Internet Crimes and Criminal Behavior*, ed. K. Jaishankar (Boca Raton, FL: CRC Press, Taylor and Francis Group, 2011), 79–103.

identities can be that of a teenager or a young adult or a friendly adult male/female. These fake identities use fictitious names and personal information, and they may prefer to opt for 'customs settings' which would make their privacy settings look like 'open only to close friends' or 'open only to friends'. It may be noted that MPSNSs such as Facebook or Twitter in their policy guidelines clearly mention that no individual can create an account with false information. But such rules are grossly violated. It can further be noted that even though these MPSNSs have special safety regulations for preventing child sexual victimization, due to less monitoring of the contents filled in by the users, such profiles continue to harass children.

2. Grooming and trapping children: Grooming and trapping children can be done by many ways, including simple chatting in the MPSNSs. The adult perpetrators, through either their original profiles or their fake profiles, approach profiles of the children who are open to strangers.[34] If the victim accepts the groomer as 'friend', it becomes easier for the groomer to acquire information about the maturity status of the victim. This is mainly acquired from the status messages that are shared by the victim, unclaimed pictures with messages embossed on them, which may be shared from other friend's collections, and so on. In case the child has an open profile, it becomes even easier for the perpetrator to trap him or her. The perpetrator groomer finds emotionally disturbed children as an easy catch. The grooming session may begin with sympathetic chats or motivating chats whereby the groomer may show himself or herself as equally disturbed or someone who has already gone through a similar situation.

The communication may progress on a period-to-period or hour-to-hour or even day-to-day basis, slowly introducing the victim to sexually erotic speeches. Mostly when the victim is a younger teen, he or she may be asked about the types of underwear he or she is wearing and then the speeches slowly move on to removing the clothes and orally representing private body parts. In the case of older and matured teens, the groomer may directly ask him or her to show his or her private body parts using webcams. In this process, the groomer may also transform the victim to a

---

[34] Broadhurst and Jayawardhena, 'Online Social Networking and Paedophilia'.

contributor to paedophilia, as well as also turn him or her into a consumer of the same.

3. Data mining from the profiles of children: In the process of grooming of the victims, the perpetrator also gathers data about the victim himself or herself, his/her friends and acquaintances and the victim's potential to contribute towards the victimization. Such data may be revealed by the victim himself or herself in the course of a grooming session, in his/her own profile or in the status messages. The perpetrator may also accumulate data from the acquaintances' profiles. Such data can speak about the victim's day-to-day activities, his/her likes and dislikes and also sexual orientation. Data mining also extends to still and audio–visual images that may be available in the friends' or acquaintances' albums. It has also been seen that such predators may target visual images of the victim, especially girls where they are seen bikini clad, in swimsuits, underwear or revealing dresses.

4. Converting children into contributors to and consumers of paedophilic materials: The most deplorable issue is the conversion of children into contributors to and consumers of paedophilic materials in the MPSNSs. In the first case, children may get involved without awareness. Some children who may be unaware of social networking dangers may reveal much information about their activities online, including their present and future geographic locations. Along with this, they may also post personal pictures in their albums that may not have sufficient safety settings to prevent outsiders from looking at them. Such activities testify to the routine activities theory whereby such child users become chosen targets of the perpetrators.[35] MPSNSs such as Facebook also provide options to download pictures from friends' albums. This makes the situation more vulnerable as the perpetrator may access and acquire the paedophilic material without actually asking the victim to contribute the same.

---

[35] K. Choi, 'Cyber-routine Activities: Empirical Examination of Online Lifestyle Digital Guardians and Computer Crime Victimization', in *Cyber Criminology: Exploring Internet Crimes and Criminal Behavior*, ed. K. Jaishankar (Boca Raton, FL: CRC Press, Taylor and Francis Group, 2012), 229–252.

Even though children as contributors may have attracted researchers' interests lately, the present behavioural pattern of child users of the internet definitely demands thorough research on the adolescent sexual fantasies of children. Such fantasies may be revealed by children's dress and preference to watch visual images of adult men and women showing much skin. In Facebook, Twitter and YouTube, such sexual fantasies can be exercised by posting pictures whereby adolescent teens dress up in revealing dresses like adults or share unclaimed pictures that depict such visual images. YouTube, on the other hand, provides excellent opportunities to upload sexual fantasy videos. Such videos can be posted by the matured teens by way of sharing sexted images, playing adult games such as imitating adult sexual activities in the video or acting like pregnant women and so forth. Child contributors are further encouraged by internet games such as The Sims. These games encourage subscribers to create live images through cartoon-like figures and such images can be made to act as per the wishes of the users/subscribers.

Children turn into consumers of the paedophilic materials especially when the perpetrator starts satisfying their adolescent sexual fantasies. This can happen either through chatting and introducing the victim to paedophilic materials or through directly sharing the content with the victim. Directly sharing the content involves a number of related issues, including peer-to-peer file sharing, sending the material to the victim's email free of cost on a trial basis, forwarding the content through the victim's online acquaintances and so on. If the victim is convinced to buy the material, it may further involve secret usage of adult net banking facilities or credit card facilities. However, it must also be noted that what generates in the MPSNSs as guidance for ways to consume the paedophilic material may end in the victim actually accessing the material on YouTube and related sites. At YouTube, varieties of videos may be available, including personal amateur videos covering sexual activities and movie clips showing sex scenes. While in some such videos YouTube may ask users to verify their age or restrict the user based upon the preliminary information supplied to it through the account information, many videos are open to the public, including children. This broadens the risk of introducing the child victim to sexually explicit materials, and they gradually get addicted to view more real-life images of such nature.[36]

In such cases, the offender must be booked under Ss.13 and 14(1) of the POCSO Act and also under S.11(ii) and (vi) of the POCSO Act, read with S.12 of the same (punishment for sexual harassment). These provisions broadly touches upon the issue of grooming by stating that

A person is said to commit sexual harassment upon a child when such person with sexual intent makes a child exhibit his body or any part of his body so as it is seen by such person or any other person (S.11(ii)) or entices a child for pornographic purposes or gives gratification therefor (S.11(iv)).

Along with these, S.67B of the IT Act, 2000 (amended in 2008) must also be applied to book the offender. This Section in Subsection (C) speaks about grooming and criminalizes the act of cultivating, enticing or inducing children to online relationship with one or more children for and on sexually explicit act or in a manner that may offend a reasonable adult on the computer resource. Further in Subsection (D) this Section criminalizes facilitating abuse of children online and in Subsection (E) criminalizes recording, in any electronic form, own abuse or that of others pertaining to sexually explicit act with children, which may be a component part of creation, production and distribution of child porn materials by virtual data mining including grooming and enticing of children.

Creation, Production and Distribution of Pornographic Materials by Using Children in Physical Space

Among the various types of cyber pornography or paedophilia, this particular type is the most severe one because it may involve physical

---

[36] Halder and Jaishankar, 'Patterns of Sexual Victimization of Children and Women in the Multipurpose Social Networking Sites', 129–133.

as well as psychological permanent harm to the children who may be used for creation, production and distribution of paedophilic materials. The following example of the Swiss couple may best explain the issue:

In 2003, the sessions court in Mumbai created a landmark in child paedophilia cases by sentencing a Swiss couple, Wilheim Marti, 62, and his wife, Mary Lily Marti, 59, a rigorous 7 years imprisonment for alluring minor girls for performing sexual activities and photographing them. It may be noted that when the couple were arrested, the courts had to rely on S.67 of the IT Act, 2000. As the reports suggest, on their appeal against this order, the Mumbai High Court released them after they had agreed to pay compensation to the victims and serving a jail term for 39 months.[37] There was uproar against this judgement as it made the perpetrators to escape the full sentences in lieu of monetary compensation, which according to several activists were unethical, against the judicial principles and against the child rights. Unfortunately, the Supreme Court stayed the judgement of the Bombay High Court but the couple availed bail. As per the latest available news report, the couple was absconding as of 2011.[38]

Both S.67B of the IT Act, 2000 (amended in 2008) and POCSO Act vide S.13 criminalize the creation, production, distribution of child porn materials by using children in physical space. Depending upon the facts of the case, if it is seen that the child has undergone some sorts of harassment as has been stated in S.11(ii), (v) and (vi) before or while in the course of making such porn contents, the police must also book the offender under S.12 of the POCSO Act which prescribes punishment for sexual harassment. S.11(ii) of the POCSO Act states that a person is said to commit sexual harassment upon a child when such a person with sexual intent makes a child to exhibit his body or any part of his body so as to be seen by him or any other person. S.11(v) of the POCSO Act may be applied when the child is threatened to be used for creation of porn contents; this provision

---

[37] 'The Price of Rape', *The Telegraph*, Calcutta, 23 March 2011. Available at: http://www.telegraphindia.com/1110323/jsp/opinion/story_13752053.jsp (accessed on 29 January 2018).

[38] Ibid.

states that a person is said to commit sexual harassment upon a child when such a person with sexual intent threatens to use, in any form of media, a real or electronic depiction through electronic, film or digital or any other mode of any part of the body of the child or the involvement of the child in a sexual act. S.11(vi) may be applied when such a child is enticed to take part in such kind of creation, production and so on of the paedophilic contents. It may be seen that if the case of the Swiss couple would have been tried at present state, the offender may also be booked under S.12 of the Act which prescribes punishment for sexual harassment, especially if the case was seen in the background of this particular provision, that is, S.11(vi). It must also be noted that even in 2011 when the perpetrator availed the bail, there were no proper regulations available to regulate such activities from the perspective of the benefit and welfare of the child except S.67B of the IT Act. Presently, such cases can be regulated by POCSO Act, especially S.14, which categorically prescribes punishments for types of involvements and abuse meted out by the perpetrator to the victim.

While speaking of regulating creation, production and distribution of child pornographic contents created by physically abusing children, mention must be made of child rape videos. Of late it has been seen that many perpetrators are recording rape incidences in their smartphones and subsequently they are being floated in the digital communication medium either through message service technologies such as WhatsApp, Viber or through social media such as Facebook or even through web portals of news channels. This author has also noticed that many civil society stakeholders including NGOs may float such videos to get widespread awareness about the victimization and also ask the receiver to identify the perpetrators if they have come across the accused. Such actions, even if done for the benefit of the victim, must be avoided. It must be understood that S.23 of the POCSO Act, 2012 provides strict prohibitory guidelines for media-reporting procedure. It does not specifically prohibit circulation of rape videos which shows the accused in the course of rape, sexual assault or molestation, but consider the prohibitory guidelines stated in Subsection (1); it states that 'no person shall make any reports or present comments on any child from any form of media or studio or photographic facilities without having complete and authentic information which may have the effect of lowering his reputation or infringing upon his privacy'. Nonetheless, when such videos or images are floated on the Internet, they may stay afloat for a long time. This may become extremely disturbing for the victims even if their faces are not shown. Consider if the victims happen to see the images in the Internet themselves, they may feel re-traumatized since they may feel that the incidence of victimization has been witnessed by many. S.23(2) has further made provisions for restricting the publication of the names or any other identity disclosing information including residential area, school and neighbourhood. It says, 'no reports in any media shall disclose the identity of the child including his name, address, photograph, family details, school, neighbourhood or any other particulars which may lead to disclosure of the identity of the child'. The exception clause to this Subsection however provides that such disclosure may be permitted only for the best interest of the child under the permission of the Special Court, which may be fit to try the offence. As it may be seen, when such videos or images surface, it is always better to report the matter to the nearest police station or to the court rather than circulating it again to others. Subsection (3) of S.23 holds both the publisher and the owner of the media or studio, etc., jointly liable and Subsection (4) prescribes punishment therefor. As such, if such images are circulated, not only the person who is circulating or publishing the images may be prosecuted but also the service provider may be prosecuted if it fails to exercise due diligence as has been stated in S.79(3) of the IT Act, 2000 (amended in 2008).

Sexting

Discussions of cyber sexual offences targeting children must also include discussion of sexting.[39] This author had earlier defined the term 'sexting' in the following words:

[39] The following part of this chapter is the reproduction of this author's earlier publication titled 'Teen Sexting: A Critical Analysis on the Criminalization vis-à-vis Victimization Conundrums' (co-authored with Dr K. Jaishankar), which was published by Korean Institute of Criminology in *The Virtual Forum Against Cybercrime (VFAC) Review* 1, no. 6 (July/August 2014): 26–43. This is

In a word, sexting means sending and consequently receiving text messages carrying sexual expressions and sexual images through mobile phones. Even though technically sexting may mean any such electronically communicated text message which can include email message as well as mobile phone message, the term sexting is popularly used for indicating mobile phone text messages only. Such sexually explicit communications existed since the beginning of web era, where communicating partners can be (i) only adults, or (ii) adult/s–children or (iii) only adolescent teens or (iv) adult–teens.[40]

Sexting may include the following:

1. Sending nude selfies to others
2. Self-capturing images of private parts including genitals, breasts, cleavages and sending these images to others
3. Taking selfies while in compromising position and sending it to the other partner or other individuals

Can Sexting be Considered as Child Pornographic Material?

Sexting may necessarily be a behaviour of pre-teens and teenagers. But nonetheless sexting is that grey area in the eyes of law which needs a special attention from the legal fraternity including the courts. This is because in sexting a child may not only capture his/her own nude or semi-nude images, he/she may disseminate the same to others including adults or younger children. Ironically, the child who may be doing sexting may never know that he/she may be prosecuted for generating child pornography images. This is mainly because of certain specific Subclauses of S.67B of the IT Act, 2000 (amended in 2008), which categorically explains what may be considered as offensive child pornography under the Indian laws; these are stated as follows:

---

reproduced with slight modifications with prior permission from the publisher/editor of the *VFAC Review*.

[40] D. Halder and K. Jaishankar, *Cyber Crime against Women in India* (New Delhi: SAGE Publications, 2017), 126–127.

67B. Punishment for publishing or transmitting of material depicting children in sexually explicit act, etc. in electronic form. Whoever, (a) publishes or transmits or causes to be published or transmitted material in any electronic form which depicts children engaged in sexually explicit act or conduct or (b) creates text or digital images, collects, seeks, browses, downloads, advertises, promotes, exchanges or distributes material in any electronic form depicting children in obscene or indecent or sexually explicit manner or ... shall be punished on first conviction with imprisonment of either description for a term which may extend to five years and with a fine which may extend to ten lakh rupees and in the event of second or subsequent conviction with imprisonment of either description for a term which may extend to seven years and also with fine which may extend to ten lakh rupees.

As may be seen from the earlier discussion, the word 'whoever' must be given widest connotation to include children, male or female. Analysed in this broad light, the inherent meaning of sexting, that is, conveying nude selfies, may loosely come within the purview of Subclauses (a) and (b) of the aforementioned provision. But seen from the perspective of adolescent behaviour, we may further raise a few questions: whether the act of sexting can be considered as indecent? Whether the nude selfie that has been captured by a child unknowing of its consequences may be considered as sexually explicit content or obscene content generated by the child? This author feels that while there arises a clash between questions relating to punishing a child for ignorance of law as well as ignorance about the consequences of the act and the rules of law which criminalize certain behaviours for all for the social rule, this question, that is, whether sexting can be considered as child pornographic material or not, must also be analysed in the light of S.11(ii) and (iii) (sexual harassment) and S.15 of the POCSO Act (using children for pornographic purposes). The later provision speaks of using the child for pornographic purposes, which gives clear indication that it may not include a child's fancy dreams of spreading his/her nude selfies to other children for simple ego boosting. But S.11 may be further analysed to examine the question whether sexting can be penalized in the light of child pornography laws. S.11(ii) of the POCSO Act states, 'a person is said to commit sexual harassment upon a child when such person with sexual intent makes a child exhibit his body or any part of his body so as it is seen by such person or any other person'. S.11(iii) further states, 'a person is said to commit sexual harassment upon a child when such person with sexual intent shows any object to a child in any form or media for pornographic purposes'. S.11 in its explanation clause further states, 'any question which involves sexual intent, shall be a question of fact'. As may be seen earlier, S.11 (ii) and (iii) do not speak about sexting or self-generated nude images directly. But whether the meaning of the words 'for pornographic purposes' in Clause (iii) of S.11 may be broadened to include sexual intention of the child who may have sexted his/her nude images to other child/children, is again a question which must be analysed in the light of the meaning of 'child pornography'. Para 8 of 18 US Code § 2256 defines 'child pornography' as

> any visual depiction, including any photograph, film, video, picture, or computer or computer-generated image or picture, whether made or produced by electronic, mechanical, or other means, of sexually explicit conduct, where
>
> (A)   the production of such visual depiction involves the use of a minor engaging in sexually explicit conduct;
>
> (B)   such visual depiction is a digital image, computer image, or computer-generated image, that is, or is indistinguishable from, that of a minor engaging in sexually explicit conduct; or
>
> (C)   such visual depiction has been created, adapted, or modified to appear that an identifiable minor is engaging in sexually explicit conduct.[41]

Further, the term 'sexually explicit conduct' for the purpose of Internet child pornography has been defined by Para 2B of 18 US Code § 2256, which is as follows:

> 'Sexually explicit conduct' means
>
> (i)   graphic sexual intercourse, including genital-genital, oral-genital, anal-genital, or oral-anal, whether between persons of the same or opposite sex, or lascivious simulated sexual

---

[41] Para 8 of 18 US Code § 2256.

      intercourse where the genitals, breast, or pubic area of any person is exhibited;

(ii) graphic or lascivious simulated;

    (I) bestiality;

    (II) masturbation; or

    (III) sadistic or masochistic abuse; or

(iii) graphic or simulated lascivious exhibition of the genitals or pubic area of any person;

Seeing from the earlier discussion, this author feels that child pornography laws may not be used for sexting cases, because sexting may be an adolescent behaviour which may not fall in the strict category of child pornography in the absence of malicious intentions of the child. Further, if the adolescent is charged and subsequently arrested for sexting, it may prove more dangerous. The children of digital era are well versed with practical as well as theoretical usage of electronic technology. This author in her previous publication *Revenge Porn by Teens in the United States and India: A Socio-legal Analysis* (co-authored with K. Jaishankar) has shown several case studies from the US where the 'offender' has been sentenced to be in probation or even termed as juvenile delinquent. In certain cases, they have also been ordered to stay without mobile phones for days and do community services.[42] But can this prevent the adolescent from being an offender again? Even if he is kept in juvenile home in case of serious charge, in probation, or he is secluded from other children including his mobile devices, he can always teach other children to do such 'mischief'. The child can become sort of a hi-tech guru who will spread the message of how not to be caught while sexting. In such case, the aim of the law and the judicial decision regarding the offending child will hopelessly fail. For example, consider the case of the first teenager who spread the computer virus way back in the 1980s. He set an example to other kids of how quickly to become famous. Similarly, the newspaper reports, media highlights and even hundreds of Internet researches of

---

[42] For more information, see Halder and Jaishankar, 'Revenge Porn by Teens in the United States and India'.

the offending sexter may motivate other children to follow the same mischievous way to get 'sudden fame'.

Revenge Porn

Cyber sexual offences targeting children must also include discussions on revenge porn. Even though the terms 'revenge' and 'revenge porn' have been used with reference to cyber victimization of adult women by way of interpersonal victimization,[43] revenge porn also claims its victims in teenagers. This author in her earlier publication titled *Revenge Porn by Teens in the United States and India: A Socio-legal Analysis* has defined the term revenge porn as follows:

> An act whereby the perpetrator satisfies his anger and frustration for a broken relationship through publicizing false, sexually provocative portrayal of his/her victim, by misusing the information that he may have known naturally and that he may have stored in his personal computer, or may have been conveyed to his electronic device by the victim herself, or may have been stored in the device with the consent of the victim herself; and which may essentially have been done to publicly defame the victim.[44]

While reported cases on revenge porn among the teens are plenty in the Western countries, including the United States, in India, judicial decisions regarding revenge porn-related cases for children are very rare. The cases such as Bazee.com or DPS Bal Bharati of early

---

[43] Halder and Jaishankar, *Cyber Crime and the Victimization of Women*, 24, 27, 32, 42, 47 and 48; also see Mary Anne Franks, 'Unwilling Avatars: Idealism and Discrimination in Cyberspace', *Columbia Journal of Gender and Law* 20 (2011): 224. Available at: http://ssrn.com/abstract=1374533; Ann Bartow, 'Pornography, Coercion, and Copyright Law 2.0', *Vanderbilt Journal of Entertainment and Technology Law* 10, no. 4 (2008): 101–142. Available at: http://works.bepress.com/cgi/viewcontent.cgi?article=1030&context=ann_bartow (accessed on 29 January 2018).

[44] Halder and Jaishankar, 'Revenge Porn by Teens in the United States and India', 90.

2000–2002[45] may show that the concept of revenge porn was never understood properly. Instead, the courts may have analysed it in the light of unethical monetary gain by using child for pornographic purposes.[46] Further, we also need to remember that in cases of revenge porn, sexting may play an important role: the victim may unknowingly become a contributor to his/her own victimization in case the image is supplied to the offender by him/herself by way of sexting.

The generation of web 2.0 had literally outsmarted the older generation and created this peculiar trend which was later followed by many adults to execute their revenge. This is evident from the search results in the Internet with key words as 'revenge porn', 'porn India', 'India teen porn' and the like. The numerous results may also include various porn websites created under categories such as 'Indian Desi Girl', 'South Indian Mallu' and the like apart from YouTube videos with similar tag words. Nonetheless, the case sets precedence for many other teens to execute their revenge through various websites which can be accessed by teens below 16 years, predominantly through the popular social networking sites. However, before discussing the legal treatment of these issues, an analysis on the Indian socio-economic condition with regard to sexting is essential here.

Sexting or consensually digital capturing of the private moments of two teens of different sexes, or sending pictures of oneself with scanty attires through video chats, etc., are new-age behaviours for Indian teens. The social culture of average Indian societies predominantly barred the parents to allow the children to wear revealing 'Western dresses' which may show too much of the skin. However, the situation rapidly changed since the introduction of new-age movies, huge display of usage of electronic devices such as mobile phones, desktop and laptops in the popular movies and TV serials meant for teens and young adults and the gradual lowering of the prices and easy availability of these devices for household purposes and easily available

---

[45] This author has elaborately discussed about these cases in her book Cyber Crimes against Women in India in pp. 139–148. For more information, see Halder and Jaishankar, '*Cyber Crime against Women in India*'.

[46] Ibid.

broadband services. The web 2.0 era children are now used to see both the parents occupied with their digital devices for their own professional and personal purposes. The Internet accessibility changed the orthodox mindset of Indians and this resulted in change in formal dress code to exclusive teen hangouts, to even the approach towards the sex education at homes and also at schools. This had further encouraged the younger generation to ape the Western culture to dress 'sexily' to attract the opposite sex and even conveying self-captured images to impress Internet-savvy high-school sweethearts and dating partners, and also consensual capturing of the sexual performances (excluding penetration) with the partner by the partner himself or by automatic devices that would finally store the 'moments' in the partner's device. Even though this new teen sexual behaviour has gained a highlight due to the infamous Delhi DPS school case, where a 16-year-old boy allegedly circulated a video clipping of his sexual acts along with his classmate, another 16-year-old girl,[47] there are hardly any Indian study with reference to the usage of such clipping for teen revenge and legal treatment of the same from the perspective of pornography and privacy laws. The reason could be highly attributed to the stringent juvenile justice laws prevailing in India which prevent detailed publishing of ongoing cases involving minors as offenders and confused state of laws when it comes to victim-aided offences in the cyber space like that of Delhi DPS school case.

Even though neither the IT Act nor the POCSO Act has any dedicated provision to prohibit revenge porn, this author feels that S.66E of the IT Act, 2000 (amended in 2008) (violation of privacy) may be read with S.67B of the Information Technology Act and Ss.11, 13 and 15 of the POCSO Act as has been discussed in the previous paragraph about sexting. S.66E of the IT Act is emphasized here especially because this provision prohibits creation, production and dissemination of content against the consent of the individual whose images are being captured. Further, S.15 of the POCSO Act may also be considered to prosecute revenge porn cases. This provision

[47] 'Sex Scandal: Boy Who Shot MMS Clip Held', *Express India*, 19 December 2004. Available at: http://www.expressindia.com/news/fullstory. php?newsid=39787 (accessed on 2 February 2015).

prescribes punishment for storing child porn images for commercial purposes and states, 'any person, who stores, for commercial purposes any pornographic material in any form involving a child shall be punished with imprisonment of either description which may extend to three years or with fine or with both'.

Even though cyber sexual offences targeting children had been addressed by various laws including the IT Act, 2000 (amended in 2008), Immoral Trafficking Prevention Act and the IPC, the POCSO Act, 2012 provided more specialized approach to the issue from the perspective of rights of the child. But POCSO Act still needs to be developed in this regard. The law is still silent about storing child porn images for private viewing. Further, as has been discussed earlier, there is no clear provision dealing with revenge porn or sexting which are growing dangerously. The law also needs to be developed for dealing with virtual data mining for creation of paedophilic contents. It is unfortunate to note that there are few reported cases of cyber sexual offences where POCSO Act has been used by police. This is mainly because the children may not be encouraged to report such cases unless they are severely victimized; also, the police may be unaware of the proper provisions that may be used for specific incidences of cyber sexual offences as has been shown here. It is hoped that if these lacunas are cared for, POCSO Act, 2012 can create a wonderful example for the world.

CHAPTER 6

Abetments, Attempts and Criminal Motives in Sexual Abuse of Children

Introduction

In the earlier chapters, several types of sexual offences against children have been discussed. Each attracts various degrees of punishment according to the gravity of the offence. However, the goal of criminal justice system may fail if the criminal law is restricted to offences already committed and not for the act of planning to commit the offences or helping others to commit the offences. It becomes more important to consider these issues when the victim is a child. As we have seen in the earlier chapters, all forms of penetrative sexual assaults and sexual assaults including aggravated forms of the same may even cause death of the child, may permanently make him/her disabled and physically and emotionally traumatized. Similarly, sexual harassment, including cyber sexual harassment, may turn the child withdrawn, may also push him/her to commit suicide due to the shame. Attempt to cause the same may also bring acute emotional trauma to the child victims. Similarly, abetment to commit an offence may push anyone who may have no prior criminal records, to commit a crime; such individual may be a juvenile himself. Could attempt to commit any sexual offence targeting children attract any penal provision? How may abetting of an offence be seen as an offence itself? This chapter discusses these.

What Is Abetment?

Abetment was traditionally defined in the IPC as follows:

A person abets the doing of a thing, who

Firstly—instigates any person to do that thing; or

Secondly—engages with one or more other person or persons in any conspiracy for the doing of that thing, if an act or illegal omission takes place in pursuance of that conspiracy and in order to the doing of that thing; or

Thirdly—intentionally aids, by any act or illegal omission, the doing of that thing. Explanation 1—a person who, by wilful misrepresentation or by wilful concealment of a material fact which he is bound to disclose, voluntarily causes or procures, or attempts to cause or procure, a thing to be done, is said to instigate the doing of that thing. Explanation 2—whoever, either prior to or at the time of the commission of an act, does anything in order to facilitate the commission of that act, and thereby facilitate the commission thereof, is said to aid the doing of that act. (S.107, IPC)

This meaning of abetment has been adopted by several child-related laws in India, including the JJ Act, 2015, which in S.87 states that 'Whoever abets any offence under this Act, if the act abetted is committed in consequence of the abetment, shall be punished with the punishment provided for that offence.' Explanation attached to this provision states that 'An act or offence is said to be committed in consequence of abetment when it is committed in consequence of the instigation or in pursuance of the conspiracy or with the aid, which constitutes the abetment.' Similarly, S.20 of the ITPA, 1956 says, 'Whoever abets any offence punishable under this Act shall, whether or not the offence abetted is committed, be punishable with the same punishment as is provided for the offence which has been abetted.' Explanation attached to this provision further states that 'For the purpose of this Act, abetment has the meaning assigned to it in the Indian Penal Code' (45 of 1860). S.16 of the POCSO Act has adopted the same meaning of abetment as has been stated in S.107 of the IPC, only with a slight difference, that is, adding the term 'offence' in place of the term 'thing' as has been used in the IPC. Further, S.16 includes an extra explanation for the purpose of the POCSO Act. This explanation reads as follows:

> Explanation III.—Whoever employ, harbours, receives or transports a child, by means of threat or use of force, or other forms of coercion, abduction, fraud, deception, abuse of power, or of a position, vulnerability, or the giving or receiving of payments, or benefits to achieve the consent of a person having control over another person, for the purpose of any offence under this Act, is said to aid the doing of that Act. (S.16 of the POCSO Act)

S.17 of the POCSO Act prescribes punishment for abetment by stating that whoever abets any offence under this Act, if the act abetted in consequences of the abetment, shall be punished with punishment provided for in that offence. Explanation attached to S.17 further says that 'An act or offence is said to be committed in consequence of abetment, when it is committed in consequence of instigation, or in pursuance of the conspiracy, or with the aid, which constitutes the abetment.' It needs to be understood that S.16 impliedly includes the philosophy of other provisions relating to abetment including Ss.108 (abettor), 108A (abetment in India of offences outside India), punishment of abetment, if the act abetted, is committed in consequence and where no express provision is made for its punishment. As the traditional law suggests and S.16 of the POCSO Act also agrees with the traditional suggestions, abetment is constituted by any or all of the three factors:

(i) Instigating a person to commit an offence: This means either actively suggesting to do the act or stimulating, hinting, directing by any means of languages either expressively or indirectly, to do the act.[1] Instigating or inciting an offence can become punishable when words or language used for instigating have reasonable certainty.[2] But the courts have also held that simple advising to commit a crime may not amount to abetment unless such advice results in actual committing of the crime.[3] Further, the courts have also held that where one person instigates another by letter sent by post, the first commits abetment as soon as the contents of the letter are read by the recipient.[4] However, in this age of digital technology, this particular view of the courts has to be seen in the light of electronic contract if the instigation is communicated via digital and electronic communication media.

(ii) Engaging in a conspiracy to commit the crime: Abetment may necessarily mean engaging in a conspiracy to commit a crime. As the courts have held, when the design to commit the crime rests with the intention only, which has neither been carried out nor communicated to result in actual crime, abetment may not be said to have been committed. But when two persons agree to carry on the plan, such action may attract the inherent meaning of S.107, IPC.[5]

(iii) Intentionally aiding a person to commit the crime: The third clause of S.107 states that aiding a person to commit a crime must be done intentionally, that is, with full knowledge of the consequences of the act for which he is aiding the actual offender.[6] But if a man aides in committing a crime without actual knowledge of the consequences of such aiding, would he be still indicted as abettor? This author came to know of several instances where innocent young teenagers may be employed to capture images of women and children taking bath in public

---

[1] Emperor v. Amiruddin Salebhoy Tyabjee, 1922, 24 Bom. L.R. 534, 542.
[2] Prem Narain v. State of UP, AIR 1957, All 177.
[3] Raghunath Dass v. Emperor, AIR 1920, Pat 502.
[4] Queen-Empress v. Sheo Dial Mal, 1894, ILR 16 All 389.
[5] Per Willes J. in Mulcahy v. Regina, 1868, L.R. 3 H.L. 306, 317.
[6] Shri Ram v. State of UP, 1975, Cr.L.J. 240 (SC).

ponds or beaches only to use such images for ulterior purposes including using them to create pornographic contents, including child pornographic contents.[7] Further, it has also been observed by this author that many social media subscribers including children may be used as aid stalkers or proxy stalkers to provide information to the main offender to carry on stalking either electronically or in real world. In such cases, what would be the stand of the law in indicting them? In such cases, once the innocence of the individual is proved, the law would indict the 'master' and not the 'agents'.

These inherent meanings of S.107 IPC and also S.16 of the POCSO Act may be considered for convicting people who may have instigated in committing child sexual abuse for fulfilling their own selfish gain including satisfying revenge and conspiring to execute sexual abuse of children by way of immoral trafficking of children for prostitution. It must also be understood that S.16 of the POCSO Act adds a third explanation to the provision for abetment. This provision would now be applicable in cases such as earlier, where children may be employed as agents of crime. The aforementioned principles stand true in cases of disturbing trends of filming sexual abuse, including child rape or molestation. It needs to be understood that as per S.67B of the IT Act, 2000 (amended in 2008) and also S.13 of the POCSO Act using children for creating pornographic contents is considered as criminal offence and punishable with imprisonment which may even extend to life depending upon the nature of the act (S.14 of the POCSO Act). In such a case, filming child sexual abuse can itself be an offence and as such the principal accused (i.e., who is booked for such offence) may not be considered as an abettor within any meaning of Chapter V of the IPC (abetment) or S.16 of the POCSO Act, but he may be tried only for the offence thus committed.[8]

---

[7] From the personal experience of the author.
[8] Jeetoo Chawdhury, 1865, 4 WR (CR) 23.

Attempt to Commit Sexual Abuse on Children

While abetment to commit sexual abuse on children attracts specific punishment under the POCSO Act, attempt to commit offences also attracts punishment under S.18 of the POCSO Act. Unlike S.16, which defines the term 'abetment' in the light of sexual abuse of children for the purpose of POCSO Act, S.18 does not define the term 'attempt to commit a crime'. It prescribes punishment for attempt to commit a crime by stating,

> Whoever attempts to commit any offence punishable under this Act or to cause such an offence to be committed, and in such attempt, does any act towards the commission of the offence, shall be punished with imprisonment of any description provided for the offence for a term, which may extend to one-half of the imprisonment for life or, as the case may be, one-half of the longest term of imprisonment provided for that offence, or with such fine as is provided for the offence, or with both.

This again is an adaptation of the provision meant for attempt under S.511 of the IPC, which states:

> Whoever attempts to commit an offence punishable by this Code with imprisonment for life or imprisonment, or to cause such an offence to be committed, and in such attempt does any act towards the commission of the offence, shall, where no express provision is made by this Code for the punishment of such attempt, be punished with imprisonment of any description provided for the offence, for a term which may extend to one-half of the imprisonment for life or, as the case may be, one-half of the longest term of imprisonment provided for that offence, or with such fine as is provided for the offence, or with both.

Hence the issue of attempt to commit an offence under the POCSO Act can be analysed from the perspective of the IPC with special reference to POCSO Act.

As has been stated in S.18 of the POCSO Act as well as in S.511 of the IPC, penal liability to any act falling within the meaning of

S.18 of the POCSO Act may be attracted only when the concerned accused (i) attempts to do such offence, (ii) attempts to cause such an offence to be committed and (iii) in the course of such attempt, does any act, which may be some other sort of offence that he was not actually attempting to do or the offence that he was actually attempting to do. It may be pertinent to note that POCSO Act being a special Act focusing only on sexual abuse of children, special attention has been given to minute actions which may cause sexual abuse of children; for example, the provision for penetrative sexual assault including aggravated penetrative sexual assaults include slightest insertion of penis or any body parts or even any other object into the private parts of the child or mouth as an offence even if the accused may have actually attempted deep penetrative sexual assault but was prevented or apprehended while preparing for deep penetration. Further, penal liability is also attracted when, in the course of penetrative sexual assault, the accused may have actually sexually assaulted the child but could not perform actual penetrative sexual assault. However, in some notable cases, police as well as the courts have used S.18 in addition to the provisions meant for penetrative or non-penetrative sexual assault or sexual harassment.[9] But this further attracts the attention to detailed explanations of the meanings of the terms and nature of the offences that POCSO Act penalizes. The law is inclusive of the minute details because of the special place of children in the society and the need to protect them from all sorts of sexual abuses as had been laid down by the Optional Protocol to the CRC on the sale of children, child prostitution and child pornography.[10] The necessity to bring a separate provision penalizing attempt to commit an offence in this regard therefore needs special explanation. As Hidayatullah

[9] For example, see State v. Mohan, Sessions Case No. 144/13, decided on 2 February 2015, Unique ID Case No. 02404R0252922013. Available at: http://indiankanoon.org/doc/4799603/ (accessed on 12 February 2016).

[10] 'Optional Protocol to the Convention on the Rights of the Child on the Sale of Children, Child Prostitution and Child Pornography'. Adopted and opened for signature, ratification and accession by General Assembly resolution A/RES/54/263 of 25 May 2000 entered into force on 18 January 2002. Available at: http://www.ohchr.org/EN/ProfessionalInterest/Pages/OPSCCRC.aspx (accessed on 24 January 2018).

and Manohar[11] mentioned, every crime has some essential elements, which are (a) intention, (b) preparation and (c) attempt to commit the crime. The aim of the offender gets fulfilled only when these essential elements finally result in the committing of the offence, whether the one he wished to actually commit, or any other offence that had resulted in due to course while committing the actual offence. But mere intention to commit an offence cannot be penalized, nor can it be termed as 'attempt' unless it is being executed by some sort of preparation. Further, preparation of any act which may constitute crime may not attract penal liability unless 'he has passed beyond the stage of preparation'.[12] Hence, if any person harbours intention to commit sexual harassment within the meaning of S.11(iv), he may not be penalized for attempt to commit the offence under S.18 of the POCSO Act unless he has made preparation to execute the intention and that actually proceeds towards fulfilling the act as designed or prepared by him. The term 'attempt' is therefore understood as 'the direct movement towards the commission after the preparations are made'.[13]

It becomes interesting to note that even though Chapters II and III of the POCSO Act cover activities which may constitute child sexual abuse in detail under the purview of the term 'offences' understood in the perspective of POCSO Act, S.18 of the POCSO Act prescribes separate punishment for attempt to commit any offence under the POCSO Act. Noticeably, the JJ Act, 2015 does not have any provision addressing attempt to commit any offence or punishment thereof. In general, for attracting penal provisions regarding criminal attempt under S.511, IPC, the act of attempt may be examined through five tests, namely, the 'proximity rule', whereby the attempt may result in similar consequences but not the actual consequence or the offence which the offender was aiming for,[14] and which may attract penal provision for committing the offence which was actually committed

---

[11] M. Hidayatullah and V. R. Manohar, eds., *Ratanlal & Dhirajlal's The Indian Penal Code* (Nagpur: Wadhwa & Company, 1994), 606.

[12] Regina v. Padala Venkatasamy, 1881, I.L.R. 3 Mad. 4, 5.

[13] Queen v. Peterson, 1876, ILR 1 All 316; also see Hidayatullah and Manohar, *Ratanlal & Dhirajlal's The Indian Penal Code*, 608.

[14] See Sudhir Kumar Mukherjee v. State of West Bengal, 1974, 3 SCC 357.

and attempting to commit the designed offence; the doctrine of Locus Poenitentiae test, which may mean withdrawing oneself from committing the offence even though he had intention and preparation and not committing any offence in reality, and whereby the concerned may not be liable to penalties under S.511, IPC;[15] 'impossibility test', when the attempt to commit an offence results in an incomplete offence due to impossibility in finishing the act of committing offence, and he may be liable to punishment for attempt to commit the crime, provided it is shown that the means adopted to commit the crime could have actually resulted in committing the crime if the impossible situation would not have arrived;[16] 'equivocality test', where the act already committed is not a complete offence as per the intention and preparation of the offender, but unequivocally refers to the act which he was aiming for;[17] and the 'social danger test', whereby the offence thus attempted for may pose social danger and such danger can be inferred from the circumstances which were used to prepare for the offence and the probable consequences.[18] Child sexual abuse being a social crime, which has every potentiality to ruin a child from within, any attempt to commit any sort of child sexual abuse must be necessarily seen in the light of social danger test if not in the light of any other tests mentioned earlier. Any act of child sexual abuse, even the most trivial form of it, may set extremely dangerous example for others, especially the youth and adolescent children, especially in a country like India where inquisitiveness to know about sexual changes in the human body is hushed up by the society, thereby negatively motivating young persons to satisfy their adolescent sexual desires by learning from wrong sources, including the media and digital communication technology, and experimenting by way of sexual abuse on other children. Hence, this author feels that the police and the courts must use S.18 of the POCSO Act more within the meaning of social danger theory for any attempt to commit any form of sexual abuse of children.

---

[15] See Malkiat Singh v. State of Punjab, 1969, 1 SCC 157.
[16] Queen Empress v. Mangesh Jivaji, 1887, ILR 11 Bom 376.
[17] Narayanswami Pillai v. Emperor, AIR, 1932 Mad 507.
[18] R. v. Brown, 1889, 24 Q.B.D. 357.

Part III

Procedural Practices for Reporting, Investigation, Prosecution and Trials

CHAPTER 7

Reporting of Crimes, Preliminary Investigation and Witness/Victim Protection

Introduction

Sexual offences (especially, offences other than aggravated ones where the child develops immediate signs of torture such as bleeding, senselessness and so on) against children often go unnoticed because of four main reasons: (i) fear in the minds of the child victims anticipating heavy scolding and even physical hitting, slapping, thrashing and so on by the parents on hearing about the incident, (ii) fear in the minds of the child victims anticipating more sexual as well as physical assault by the offender him/herself, especially in cases where the child victims are threatened by the offenders to not to disclose anything to anyone including parents or caregivers, (iii) parent's or caregiver's fear of being tabooed due to reporting of the sexual victimization of the girl child and (iv) lackadaisical attitude and unawareness among police officials regarding sexual crimes done to children. Even the sexual offences of aggravated forms may also remain unreported in many cases due to the aforementioned reasons. What can be inferred from the earlier is, fear of graver harm and mental trauma on the victims as well as their families and lackadaisical attitude of the police may prevent victims or their family members from reporting child sexual abuse cases to the criminal justice machinery. It is an unfortunate fact that in this age of information technology, when the victims or responsible citizens can reach the police or the courts either by a phone call or web platform for crime reporting, the same is not taken well due to various reasons including the aforementioned facts. In India, reporting of crimes, whether cognizable[1] or non-cognizable,[2] by anyone including the victims or the witnesses has been recognized as a duty as well as a right under S.39 of the CrPC (which speaks about the duty of the public to give information of certain offences),[3] S.154 (for cognizable

[1] As per the First Schedule of the IPC, cognizable offences are those which are punishable with imprisonment for a term of more than three years. In such cases, police initiates action including investigation and arrest without the permission of the courts.

[2] As per the First Schedule of the IPC, non-cognizable offences are those which are punishable with imprisonment for a term which is less than three years. In such cases, police cannot initiate any action including investigation and subsequent arrest without the permission of the courts.

[3] S.39 of the CrPC speaks about the duty of individuals to report certain types of crimes and it states as follows:

1. Every person, aware of the Commission of, or of the intention of any other person to commit, any offence punishable under any of the following sections of the Indian Penal Code (45 of 1860), namely

i. sections 121 to 126, both inclusive, and section 130 (that is to say, offences against the state specified in Chapter VI of the said Code);

ii. sections 143, 144, 145, 147 and 148 (that is to say, offences against the public tranquility specified in Chapter VIII of the said Code);

iii. sections 161 to 165A, both inclusive (that is to say, offences relating to illegal gratification);

iv. sections 272 to 278, both inclusive (that is to say, offences relating to adulteration of food and drugs, etc.);

v. sections 302, 303 and 304 (that is to say, offences affecting life);

va. Section 364A (that is to say, offence relating to kidnapping for ransom, etc.);

offences)[4] and S.155 (for non-cognizable offences)[5] of the CrPC.

---

vi. section 382 (that is to say, offence of theft after preparation made for causing death, hurt or restraint in order to the committing of the theft);

vii. sections 392 to 399, both inclusive, and section 402 (that is to say, offences of robbery and dacoity);

viii. section 409 (that is to say, offence relating to criminal breach of trust by public servant, etc.);

ix. sections 431 to 439, both inclusive (that is to say, offence of mischief against property);

x. sections 449 and 450 (that is to say, offence of house-trespass);

xi. sections 456 to 460, both inclusive (that is to say, offences of lurking house-trespass); and

xii. sections 489A to 489E, both inclusive (that is to say, offences relating to currency notes and bank notes),

shall, in the absence of any reasonable excuse, the burden of proving which excuse shall lie upon the person so aware, forthwith give information to the nearest Magistrate or police officer of such Commission or intention;

For the purposes of this section, the term 'offence' includes any act committed at any place out of India which would constitute an offence if committed in India.

[4] S.154 of the CrPC (as amended vide S.13 of the Criminal Law Amendment Act, 2013) speaks about information about cognizable cases and states:

(1) Every information relating to the commission of a cognizable offence, if given orally to an officer in charge of a police station, shall be reduced to writing by him or under his direction, and be read over to the informant; and every such information, whether given in writing or reduced to writing as aforesaid, shall be signed by the person giving it, and the substance thereof shall be entered in a book to be kept by such officer in such form as the State Government may prescribe in this behalf.

(2) A copy of the information as recorded under sub-section (1) shall be given forthwith, free of cost, to the informant.

(3) Any person, aggrieved by a refusal on the part of an officer in charge of a police station to record the information referred to in sub-section (1) may send the substance of such information, in writing and by post, to the Superintendent of Police concerned who, if satisfied that such information discloses the commission of a cognizable offence, shall either investigate the case himself or direct an investigation to be made by any police officer Subordinate to him, in the manner provided by this Code, and such officer shall have all the powers of an officer in charge of the police station in relation to that offence.

Provided that if the information is given by the woman against whom an offence under section 326A, section 326B, section 354, section 354A, section 354B,

With the coming into force of the POCSO Act, reporting of sexual offences against children has become mandatory for every individual who may have knowledge of the same. Considering the fact that reporting of child sexual abuses may bring secondary traumatization especially due to revealing of the name and personal information of the victims, this Act has also provided provisions to safeguard the identity of the victims irrespective of their gender. Even though this Act has not specifically mentioned about any separate investigation procedure

---

section 354C, section 354D, section 376, section 376A, section 376B, section 376C, section 376D, section 376E or section 509 of the Indian Penal Code is alleged to have been committed or attempted, then such information shall be recorded, by a woman police officer or any woman officer:

Provided further that

(a) In the event that the person against whom an offence under section 354, section 354A, section 354B, section 354C, section 354D, section 376, section 376A, section 376B, section 376C, section 376D, section 376E or section 509 of the Indian Penal Code is alleged to have been committed or attempted, is temporarily or permanently mentally or physically disabled, then such information shall be recorded by a police officer, at the residence of the person seeking to report such offence or at a convenient place of such person's choice, in the presence of an interpreter or a special educator, as the case may be;

(b) the recording of such information shall be videographed;

(c) the police officer shall get the statement of the person recorded by a Judicial Magistrate under clause (a) of sub-section (5A) of section 164 as soon as possible.

[5] S.155 of the CrPC speaks about information as to non-cognizable cases and investigation of such cases and states:

(1) When information is given to an officer in charge of a police station of the commission within the limits of such station of a non-cognizable offence, he shall enter or cause to be entered the substance of the information in a book to be kept by such officer in such form as the State Government may prescribe in this behalf, and refer the informant to the Magistrate.

(2) No police officer shall investigate a non-cognizable case without the order of a Magistrate having power to try such case or commit the case for trial.

(3) Any police officer receiving such order may exercise the same powers in respect of the investigation (except the power to arrest without warrant) as an officer in charge of a police station may exercise in a cognizable case.

(4) Where a case relates to two or more offences of which at least one is cognizable, the case shall be deemed to be a cognizable case, notwithstanding that the other offences are non-cognizable.

other than that which has been mentioned in the CrPC and the JJ Act, 2015 and the JJ Act Rules, the POCSO Act and the POCSO Rules provide several guidelines in this regard. This chapter therefore addresses questions as to who can complaint. To whom the complaint should be made? What is the role played by Child Welfare Committee (CWC) when such cases are reported? Could a victim report crimes to the Childline and what role does it have in such cases? How can the victim's/witnesses' identity be protected? What is the procedure for preliminary investigation in child sexual abuse cases and whether the same is different from traditional investigation procedure as has been stated in the CrPC?

Reporting of Crime

Who Can Report?

S.19 of the POCSO Act speaks about reporting crimes. Subsection (1) of this Section states that notwithstanding anything contained in the CrPC, 1973, any person (including the chid), who has apprehension that an offence under this Act is likely to be committed, or has knowledge that such an offence has been committed, he shall provide such information to (i) the special juvenile police unit or (ii) the local police. As this provision explains, the following individuals are eligible to report the crime:

(a) Any adult or a child who has apprehension that an offence is likely to be committed;

(b) (d) Any adult or a child who has witnessed the occurrence of the offence; or

(c) A child who has been a victim of any offence as has been categorized under this Act.

These are the primary categories of complainants as per this Act and such persons must lodge their complaints to either the special juvenile police unit (SJPU) or the local police station. However, S.19(1) of this Act specifically does not mention about any other complainants including Childline. It needs to be understood that due to fear of social taboo many families as well as many children do not prefer to report cases to the police. Childline 1098 was created as an alternative solution to solve this issue. Childline Networking System created by Childline India Foundation (CIF) is a network which works through volunteers who connect with people including children through a toll free number: 1098.[6] As the missions of Childline suggests, it can be used as a platform to connect the victim to the proper machinery for reporting child abuses including child sexual abuses. The child victim, a child witness or a child apprehending danger, or any other adult who have knowledge of sexual abuse of any child may therefore contact Childline through telephone and seek help for further action, which may include rescue of the child as well as reporting the matter to the police including SJPU and to the CWC. However, in such cases, the child or the adult who may have contacted the Childline remains the main complainant and Childline cannot be treated as the main complainant. Similarly, in case any Childline volunteer comes across any case of child sexual abuse, he/she must be considered as an independent adult complainant as has been mentioned in Article 19(1). S.20(1) of the Act further extends the scope of S.19(1) for digital sexual abuse of children including creation, production and distribution of child pornography and obscene materials by making it mandatory to report such offences by certain special categories of persons, including any person engaged in any media, hotel, lodge, club, hospital, studio or photographic facility, by whatever name called, irrespective of the numbers of persons employed therein. S.20 therefore states:

> Any personnel of the media or hotel or lodge or hospital or club or studio or photographic facilities, by whatever name called, irrespective of the numbers of persons employed therein, shall, on coming across any material or object which is sexually exploitative of the child including pornographic, sexually-related or making obscene representation of a child or children through the use of any medium, shall provide such information to the Special Juvenile Police Unit, or to the local police, as the case may be.

---

[6] For more details about Childline, see http://www.childlineindia.org.in/cif.htm (accessed on 28 November 2015).

In this regard, the case of Yadava Manikanta, who was arrested by the CB-CID for creating paedophilic pages in Facebook,[7] must be mentioned again. This case was reported by a child right activist who was not a victim himself, but who came to know about such pages on Facebook. As it may be seen, S.20 and also S.19(1) of the POCSO Act encourage such sorts of reporting which may be made for the welfare of the children even though the complainant may not be directly involved in the victimization, but has specific knowledge about the offence being committed.

To Whom the Report Should be Made

Both S.19(1) and S.20 state that the report must be made to the Special Juvenile Police Unit or the local police. POCSO Act does not define the term 'Special Juvenile Police Unit'. The term has the same meaning as has been defined and explained under S.2(w) of the JJ Act, 2000. According to S.2(w) of the JJ Act, 2015.

> Special Juvenile Police Unit means a unit of the police force of a district or a city or, as the case may be, any other police unit like railway police, dealing with children and designated as such for handling of children under S.107 of the JJ Act.

S.63 of the JJ Act, 2015 further explains the SJPU in the following words:

> 1. In every police station, at least one officer, not below the rank of assistant sub-inspector, with aptitude, appropriate training and orientation may be designated as the child welfare police officer to exclusively deal with children either as victims or perpetrators, in co-ordination with the police, voluntary and non-governmental organisations.

> 2. To co-ordinate all functions of police related to children, the State Government shall constitute Special Juvenile Police Units in each district and city, headed by a police officer not below the rank

---

[7] For details of the case, see Chapter 5.

of a Deputy Superintendent of Police or above and consisting of all police officers designated under sub-section (1) and two social workers having experience of working in the field of child welfare, of whom one shall be a woman.

3. All police officers of the Special Juvenile Police Units shall be provided special training, especially at induction as child welfare police officer, to enable them to perform their functions more effectively.

4. Special Juvenile Police Unit also includes Railway police dealing with children.

As it may be understood from the wordings of S.107 of the JJ Act, 2015, the cases related to crime against children as well as crimes involving children as juvenile offenders should be reported to SJPU. When we speak about crimes, especially sexual crimes against children, it becomes necessary to explain the role of SJPU in dealing with such sorts of crimes. The police force is seen as the primary custodian of law and justice. The duties of the police as enshrined in the Indian Police Act emphasize upon the role of the police as protective as well as preventive, that is, it protects the individuals and the society from any apprehended harm. It also protects the victims of offences from further victimization by adopting proper legal mechanism to provide justice. The role of the police is also preventive by nature because it also ensures prevention of committing of any offence by strict vigilance and maintaining the law and order of the society. In general, the police are the primary reporting agency in the criminal justice mechanism whereby a victim can report a crime already committed or may also report about apprehended offences for seeking help to prevent the actual commission of the offence. However, when the victim is a child, the same may need special help from the police due to various factors including the age-related immaturity, physical and emotional traumatization and so on. For this, the police need to be given special training especially for handling children as victims and as juvenile offenders. This understanding was first reached in the United Nations Standard Minimum Rules for the Administration of Justice, 1985 (also known as Beijing Rules, 1985). Article 12 of the Rules articulates about special police force for such purposes under the title 'Specialization Within Police' and states:

> In order to best fulfil their functions, police officers who frequently or exclusively deal with juveniles or who are primarily engaged in the prevention of juvenile crimes shall be specially instructed and trained. In large cities, special police units should be established for that purpose.[8]

S.107 of the JJ Act, 2015 was enacted on the philosophy of Article 12 of Beijing Rule and it extended the scope of the provision to every district and city in India. According to S.107 of the JJ Act, 2015, every police office in every district, should have SJPU consisting of a police officer of the level of inspector, specially trained to handle cases of children, and who should be assisted by two social workers who are aware of child rights related issues, among whom, one should be woman. Such inspector should be also known as child welfare officer or juvenile police officer. Such unit may function under direct supervision of a deputy superintendent of police. At the police station level, two officers in the rank of subinspector or assistant subinspector may be trained specially to play the role of juvenile police officers and they must be assisted by two or more social workers.

As S.19(1) of the POCSO Act states, when a victim needs to report sexual offence relating to children, the victim must be directed to such juvenile police unit or juvenile police officer without any delay. In case there is no SJPU in the police station or the district police office, the victim can still report the crime to the station incharge or to the concerned police officer available at the district police office, who in turn, must follow the guidelines as has been stated in the CrPC, the JJ Act and also the POCSO Act in regard to dealing with child victims of sexual offences. In this regard, mention must also be made about the guidelines issued by the Hon'ble Delhi High Court in the case of *Court on Its Own Motion v. State and Anr.* in W.P.

---

[8] Available at: https://www.ncjrs.gov/pdffiles1/Digitization/145271NCJRS.pdf (accessed on 30 November 2015).

(Crl.) No. 930/2007.[9] In this case, the Hon'ble Delhi High Court had emphasized on the role of a lady officer not below the rank of subinspector for carrying out the investigation for sexual offence-related cases. POCSO Act is gender neutral and it recognizes sexual offences done to male, female as well as children who are not gender specific. Hence, it should be noted that even if the police stations or district police officers may have SJPUs consisting of required numbers of police officers and social workers, the unit must have women police officers as juvenile police officers especially when the case relates to sexual offences against children, more so girl children. It must also be noted that as has been held in the case of Childline India Foundation v. Allan John Waters (2011),[10] any concerned stakeholder can approach Childline for reporting the case. With the coming into force of the POCSO Act, the role of the Childline has been further clarified in this regard. Hence, when an offence is reported to Childline, it cannot act as SJPU, but the concerned Childline officer who receives the information must immediately inform the SJPU of the local police station or the district police officer before taking any action for the welfare of the child.

The Procedure for Receiving the Reports

For Adults: S.19(2), (3) and (4) read with Rule 4 of the POCSO Rules specifically mention about the procedures for receiving reports from the adults and child informants as well as victims. Subsection (2) of S.19 deals with the general procedure for receiving the reports by the police or the SJPU from adults. This provision states that every report given under Subsection (1) shall be (a) ascribed as entry number and recorded in writing, (b) be read over to the informant and (c) shall be entered in a book to be kept by the police unit. This provision is created on the basis of S.154 (Information in Cognizable Cases) and S.155 (Information as to Non-cognizable Cases and Investigation of Such Cases) of the CrPC. It must be noted that neither the POCSO Act nor the POCSO Act Rules specify about cognizable or non-bailable

---

[9] Court on Its Own Motion v. State and Anr., W.P. (Crl.) No. 930/2007.
[10] Childline India Foundation v. Allan John Waters, 2011, 6 SCC 261.

offences. Hence, reliance must be made upon Part II of the First Schedule (Classification of Offences Against Other Laws) of the CrPC, where it has been mentioned that whenever the punishment for offences has been restricted to less than three years, such offences must be considered as non-cognizable and bailable, whereas when the punishments for offences are indicated to begin from three years or the punishment is for more than three years, such offences must be considered as cognizable and non-bailable. As such, offences described and punished under Chapters II (Sexual Offences Against Children) and III (Using Child for Pornographic Purposes and Punishments Thereof) are all cognizable and bailable offences. Other than these provisions, except S.17 (Punishment for Abetment), other offences as described in Chapters IV (Abetment and Attempt to Commit an Offence), V (Procedure for Reporting of Cases) and the like can be non-cognizable and bailable. As such, when an informant reports any offence as described under Chapters II, III and S.17 of the POCSO Act, such report must be ascribed as an FIR within the meaning of S.154 of the CrPC by the police officer or the juvenile police officer of SJPU who receives the report (Rule 4(2)(a) of the POCSO Rules).[11] In case the reports are made for offences under other provisions including Chapters IV (except S.17), V and so on, procedures prescribed in S.155, CrPC for receiving general diary for non-cognizable cases must be followed by the police or the juvenile police officer of SJPU.

For Children: Subsections (3) and (4) of S.19, read with Rule 4 of the POCSO Rules, deal with reports made by a child informant or a victim. Subsection (3) states that where the report under Subsection (1) is given by a child, the same shall be recorded under Subsection (2) in a simple language so that the child understands contents being

---

[11] Rule 4(2)(a) of the POCSO Rules states:

Where an SJPU or the local police, as the case may be, receives information in accordance with the provisions contained under sub-section (1) of section 19 of the Act in respect of an offence that has been committed or attempted or is likely to be committed, the authority concerned shall, where applicable,—(a) proceed to record and register a First Information Report as per the provisions of section 154 of the Code of Criminal Procedure, 1973, and furnish a copy thereof free of cost to the person making such report, as per sub-section (2) of section 154 of the Code;

recorded. Subsection (4) states that in case contents are recorded in the language not understood by the child, or wherever it is deemed necessary, a translator or an interpreter, having such experience and on payment of such fees, as may be prescribed, shall be provided to the child if he fails to understand the same. As can be seen from these provisions, POCSO Act does not mention about how a designated juvenile police officer should dress which would make him/her appear different from regular police officers and more child friendly. When a child informant or a victim approaches the police, POCSO Act ensures that the communication must be child friendly so that the child in question does not feel traumatized by seeing a police officer in his/her regular uniform. It is for this reason that Subsection (1) in S.19 mentioned about SJPU for dealing with child informants or victims, which shall be specially trained to communicate with children according to their needs. Child victims are often left so traumatized that they may not be able to narrate the whole incident coherently and as per the legal requirements when it comes to mentioning specific terms including those such as 'genitals', 'crime', 'rape' and the like. For this, the law must aim to create a child-friendly environment right from the reporting stage. S.19(3) of the POCSO Act serves the purpose by providing instructions for recording the report of the child in a simple language and it has also been emphasized in the Model Guidelines under S.39 of the POCSO Act, 2012 for the use of professional and experts, prepared by Ministry of Women and Child Development in 2014.[12] It is also pertinent to note that children may also suffer sexual abuse due to child trafficking whereby children may be dislocated from their place of birth, habitat and general place of residence. In such cases, children may need assistance for reporting the offences or even interacting with the police for informing about such sexual abuses especially when they do not speak the local language where they have been trafficked. There may also be instances where children run away from their homes and may need to contact the police for care and protection. To provide proper justice to such children, S.19(4) provides that translators, interpreters and special educators must be

[12] See http://mohfw.nic.in/sites/default/files/953522324.pdf (accessed on 18 September 2016) for the full copy of the guidelines.

engaged in such cases. This provision is further supported by Rule 3 of the POCSO Rules, 2012, which speaks about interpreters, translators and special educators.[13] While using the services of such assistants, the police must also note about any personal choice expressed by the

[13] Rule 3 of the POCSO Rules states as follows:

Interpreters, translators and Special educators—(1) In each district, the DCPU shall maintain a register with names, addresses and other contact details of interpreters, translators and special educators for the purposes of the Act, and this register shall be made available to the Special Juvenile Police Unit (hereafter referred to as 'SJPU'), local police, magistrate or Special Court, as and when required.

(2) The qualifications and experience of the interpreters, translators, Special educators, and experts, engaged for the purposes of sub-section (4) of section 19, sub-sections (3) and (4) of section 26 and section 38 of the Act, shall be as indicated in these rules.

(3) Where an interpreter, translator, or Special educator is engaged, otherwise than from the list maintained by the DCPU under sub-rule (1), the requirements prescribed under sub-rules (4) and (5) of this rule may be relaxed on evidence of relevant experience or formal education or training or demonstrated proof of fluency in the relevant languages by the interpreter, translator, or special educator, subject to the satisfaction of the DCPU, Special Court or other authority concerned.

(4) Interpreters and translators engaged under sub-rule (1) should have functional familiarity with language spoken by the child as well as the official language of the state, either by virtue of such language being his mother tongue or medium of instruction at school at least up to primary school level, or by the interpreter or translator having acquired knowledge of such language through his vocation, profession, or residence in the area where that language is spoken.

(5) Sign language interpreters, Special educators and experts entered in the register under sub-rule (1) should have relevant qualifications in sign language or special education, or in the case of an expert, in the relevant discipline, from a recognized University or an institution recognized by the Rehabilitation Council of India.

(6) Payment for the services of an interpreter, translator, Special educator or expert whose name is enrolled in the register maintained under sub-rule (1) or otherwise, shall be made by the State Government from the Fund maintained under section 61 of the Juvenile Justice Act, 2000, or from other funds placed at the disposal of the DCPU, at the rates determined by them, and on receipt of the requisition in such format as the State Government may prescribe in this behalf.

(7) Any preference expressed by the child at any stage after information is received under sub-section (1) of section 19 of the Act, as to the gender of the interpreter, translator, Special educator, or expert, may be taken into

child informant or the victim regarding the person, gender of the interpreter/translator/special educator and the like (Rule 3(7) of the POCSO Rules) and such interpreter/translator/special educator must respect the privacy and dignity of the child victim whom they are asked to assist by not taking any unethical step which may infringe the privacy of the victims and disturb the confidentiality of the matter (Rule 3(10) of the POCSO Rules).

It must be noted that First Information Report (FIR) is not substantive evidence.[14] It is a fact report of occurrences when the offence took place.[15] But when the FIR is lodged with the police by the complainant or the victim him/herself, the officer receiving the FIR must read the statements provided by the complainant/victim and after entering it into writing, should also take the signature or the thumb impression of the complainant/victim as per the requirements of S.154, CrPC. It may be noted that even if the child complainant reaches out to Childline through toll-free phone number to complaint about sexual abuse, the Childline volunteer must immediately take note of the complaint and inform the police by way of S.19 of the POCSO Act read with S.154, CrPC. After receiving the report about

consideration, and where necessary, more than one such person may be engaged in order to facilitate communication with the child.

(8) The interpreter, translator, Special educator, expert, or person familiar with the manner of communication of the child engaged to provide services for the purposes of the Act shall be unbiased and impartial and shall disclose any real or perceived conflict of interest. He shall render a complete and accurate interpretation or translation without any additions or omissions, in accordance with section 282 of the Code of Criminal Procedure, 1973.

(9) In proceedings under section 38, the Special Court shall ascertain whether the child speaks the language of the court adequately, and that the engagement of any interpreter, translator, Special educator, expert or other person familiar with the manner of communication of the child, who has been engaged to facilitate communication with the child, does not involve any conflict of interest.

(10) Any interpreter, translator, Special educator or expert appointed under the provisions of the Act or its rules shall be bound by the rules of confidentiality, as described under section 127 read with section 126 of the Indian Evidence Act, 1872.

[14] State of Bombay v. Rusi Mistry, AIR 1960 SC 391.
[15] Sahadevan Rajan v. State of Kerala, 1992, Cr. LJ 2049 Ker.

occurrence of the offence, the police officer in charge, must provide the complainant with the free copy of the FIR lodged by the complainant/victim along with several necessary information including his name and designation, address and telephone number of the police station as well as his mobile number, and the name and designation of the police officer who supervises the officer who received the report or the FIR (Rule 4(1) and (2) of the POCSO Rules). However, as was held in the case of Shyam Deogharia,[16] all the requirements for filing FIR as has been mentioned under S.154(1) of the CrPC, including reducing it to writing, entering it in a proper format, affixing the signature or the thumb impression of the complainant, etc., are not mandatory and in cases especially where the complainant is a child, or the case involves child sexual abuse, such FIR may be considered by the courts as valid documents. But it has been noted that many police offices and police websites pressurise for following all the requirements so that any discrepancy in the FIR should not go against the prosecution case and make the case weak.[17] POCSO Act being a special law with specific punishments for child sexual abuse has every potential to be misused by perpetrators who may intend to lodge false complaints for harassing innocent people. For preventing such misuse, S.22 of the POCSO Act prescribes punishment for false complaints for adults when the said adult files a false complaint against another adult person with an intention to humiliate, extort or insult with penalties for imprisonment for a term of six months or both (S.22(1) of the POCSO Act). But considering the maturity level of the children, S.22(2) of the POCSO Act excuses children from such punishment in case it is found out to be a false complaint preferred by the child. However, where false complaint is made against another child by any adult, S.22(3) of the POCSO Act prescribes punishment with imprisonment for a term for one year or with fine or both.

---

[16] (1953)33 Pat. 122.

[17] For example, see guidelines relating to FIR published by Police Training School, Puducherry, where it has been mentioned that signature of the complainant/informant must be taken to ensure the valid source of the information. Available at: http://police.pondicherry.gov.in/police%20training/Hand%20Book%20on%20FIR%20by%20PTS%20on%2020.02.10.pdf (accessed on 28 January 2018).

Care and Protection of Child Victims and Preliminary Investigation

Role of Police/SJPU Post the Reporting Period

POCSO Act being a special law created mainly for the welfare of the children who are sexually abused and offended, it directs the police and other stakeholders including the CWC to get into action for rescuing and rehabilitation of the victim child immediately after receiving the report and before starting a formal investigation. S.19(5) and (6) of the POCSO Act therefore direct the SJPU to act swiftly after being intimated of the offence and after being satisfied that the child in question needs immediate care. The 2013 Model Guidelines by the Ministry of Women & Child Development specifically mention the guidelines to handle the preliminary inquiry stage by the police as well as by the CWC. As the Guidelines suggests, the police while enquiring with the child victim should not take up any mechanism that may further traumatize the child. Simple language should be used to encourage the child to narrate the whole incidence and direct questions, such as whether anyone touched the child victim's private parts and so on should be avoided even by the police officers. S.19(5) of the POCSO Act states that where SJPU or the local police is satisfied that the child against whom an offence has been committed is in need of care and protection, then, it shall, after recording the reasons in writing, make immediate arrangement to give him such care and protection (including admitting the child to the shelter home or to admitting him/her to nearest hospital) within 24 hours of the report as may be prescribed. S.27(1) of the POCSO Act further states that such medical examination can be done and the child should be shifted to nearest hospital or shelter home even before filing of the FIR by the SJPU especially when it is found that the child's condition is grave.[18] S.19(6) of the POCSO mentions about the procedural requirement for initiating the legal procedure for safeguarding the victim's rights by stating that

---

[18] CCL–NLSIU, 'Overview of the Procedures Under POCSO Act', 2013. Available at: https://www.nls.ac.in/ccl/jjdocuments/simplified.docx (accessed on 28 January 2018).

the Special Juvenile Police Unit, or local police, shall without unnecessary delay, but within a period of 24 hours, report the matter to the Child Welfare Committee and the special court or where no special court has been designated, to the court of session, including need of the child for care and protection and steps taken in this regard.

A clear reading of S.19(6) would show that contrary to S.157, CrPC (Procedure for Investigation Preliminary Inquiry),[19] police is not required to send the report to the special court immediately but within 24 hours, because the main object of S.19(6) is child welfare oriented, that is, to inform the special court about the steps taken and the requirements that are needed to be fulfilled for the welfare of the victim. Whereas the aim of S.157, CrPC is to protect the rights of the accused.[20] The role of SJPU does not end with sending the copy

---

[19] S.157, Cr PC: Procedure for investigation preliminary inquiry

(1) If, from information received or otherwise, an officer in charge of a police station has reason to suspect the commission of an offence which he is empowered under section 156 to investigate, he shall forthwith send a report of the same to a Magistrate empowered to take cognizance of such offence upon a police report and shall proceed in person, or shall depute one of his subordinate officers not being below such rank as the State Government may, by general or special order, prescribe in this behalf, to proceed, to the spot, to investigate the facts and circumstances of the case, and, if necessary, to take measures for the discovery and arrest of the offender; Provided that—

(a) When information as to the commission of any such offence is given against any person by name and the case is not of a serious nature, the officer in charge of a police station need not proceed in person or depute a subordinate officer to make an investigation on the spot;

(b) If it appears to the officer in charge of a police station that there is no sufficient ground for entering on an investigation, he shall not investigate the case.

(2) In each of the cases mentioned in clauses (a) and (b) of the proviso to subsection (1), the officer in charge of the police station shall state in his report his reasons for not fully complying with the requirements of that sub-section, and, in the case mentioned in clause (b) of the said proviso, the officer shall also forthwith notify to the informant, if any, in such manner as may be prescribed by the State Government, the fact that he will not investigate the case or cause it to be investigated.

[20] State v. Dasrath Sharma, SC No. 09/14, ID No.: 02401R0052622014, Delhi District Court, Additional Session Judge—01, Central (Delhi). Available

of the FIR to the special court, reporting the matter to the CWC and shifting the child for emergency medical care and shelter home only. The role is of continuous assistance and it includes informing the child and his/her guardian about additional information other than those specified under Rule 4(1) and (2) of the POCSO Rules. These are as follows:

- Availability of support services including counselling. If required, they must also assist in connecting the child and his or her family to persons providing support services.
- Child's right to legal aid and legal representation.
- Developments, including the arrest of the accused, applications filed and court proceedings.
- Availability of public and private emergency and crisis services.
- Procedural steps involved in a criminal prosecution.
- Availability of victims' compensation benefits.
- Status of the investigation of the crime, to the extent it is appropriate to inform the victim and to the extent that it will not interfere with the investigation.
- Filing of charges against a suspected offender.
- Schedule of court proceedings that the child is either required to attend or is entitled to attend.
- Bail, release or detention status of an offender or suspected offender.
- Rendering of a verdict after trial.
- Sentence imposed on an offender.

Medical Examination of the Victim

S.27 of the POCSO Act speaks about medical examination of the victim of sexual offence. In its four Subsections, S.27 establishes the following five rules:

---

at: http://indiankanoon.org/doc/166732240/ (accessed on 22 November 2015).

(1) Medical examination must be conducted on the child who has been victimized by any offence, including non-penetrative sexual assault (S.27(1)).

(2) Medical examination can be conducted even before the registration of the complaint or the FIR by the SJPU or the local police. Any concerned police officer who has been informed of the offence must take the child for medical examination in accordance with S.164A of the CrPC (S.27(1)).

(3) If the victim is a girl child, then the medical examination should be conducted by a female medical practitioner (S.27(2)).

(4) Medical examination shall be conducted in the presence of the parents or in the event of the parents remaining absent, in the presence of any guardian or caretaker whom the child trusts (S.27(3)).

(5) In case the parents or guardians are not present during the medical examination, it should be conducted in the presence of a woman nominated by the head of the medical institution (S.27(4)).

In this connection, mention must be made of 'Guidelines and Protocols: Medico-legal Care for Survivor/Victims of Sexual Violence', which was issued by Ministry of Health & Family Welfare, Government of India in March 2014.[21] This document of guidelines and protocols was the first of its kind in India and its primary objectives are to help the survivor/victims of sexual violence to get immediate medical assistance, to provide psychological counselling for coping with the trauma suffered due to sexual violence, to provide assistance for pregnancy detection, prevention of HIV, safe abortion (for unwanted pregnancy) and for gathering proper forensic evidences without harming the victim/survivor either physically or emotionally. Similar to the aims and objectives of the Model Guidelines under S.39 of the POCSO Act, 2012 for the use of professional and experts, prepared by Ministry of Women & Child Development in 2013,[22]

---

[21] See http://mohfw.nic.in/sites/default/files/953522324.pdf (accessed on 18 September 2016) for the full copy of the guidelines.

[22] See the full text of the model guidelines, 2013. Available at: http://wcd.nic.in/sites/default/files/POCSO-ModelGuidelines.pdf (accessed on 18 September 2016).

the 'Guidelines and Protocols' also aims for providing guidance for available legal aid to the victim/survivor. However, the 2014 guidelines was made specifically for child victims and it covered the issues for professional experts including experts in the fields of law, psychology, medicine, child care and social services. The 2014 guidelines was made for victims of all age groups and specifically for directing medico-legal professionals for assisting the victims. The speciality of the 2014 guidelines and protocols lies in the specific definitions of terms including 'victim', 'survivor', 'sexual orientation', 'gender identity', 'transgender' and so on.[23] These terms are specifically defined to bring all human beings irrespective of their gender and sexual orientation under the purview of this guidelines and also to set up mechanism which may heal the victim/survivor not only from the physical perspective but also from the psychological one. Among the guidelines mentioned in this document, medical examination of the child victims finds a special mention. Some of the important points as per this guidelines and protocols that the police as well as the health worker/doctor assisting the victim need to remember are as follows:

(i) Establishing a uniform method of medical examination in an order that should help to develop a proper chain of custody.

(ii) To start medical examination only after the victim/survivor or his/her guardian consents for the same. Often parents or guardians of minor children may not agree for medical examination. In such cases, the examiner should not pressurize for medical examination but should clarify as why and how it is done, and how the examination can be beneficial for the child. Even after such counselling, if the parents or guardians do not agree, the concerned person must record the no-consent statement and provide it to the police.

(iii) To offer best possible psychological counselling so that the victim may feel at ease to verbally narrate the incidences.

(iv) Not to show irritation, shock, disbelief, humiliation and the like to the victim irrespective of his/her gender, sexual orientation,

---

[23] See Annexure 7 for the detailed guidelines and protocols.

caste, creed, region, sexual habits and so on while conducting the examination.

(v) To conduct examination with the sole aim to gather forensic evidences. During this, the internal wound or the external wound either in the vagina or on the penis or in any other body part which may have been affected due to sexual abuse should not be aggravated.

(vi) Not to record past injuries as part of the present sexual abuse as this jeopardizes the forensic chain of custody.

(vii) In case the child is not comfortable with the accompanying adult, who may be the abuser himself/herself, the concerned person must conduct the medical examination in the presence of a female assistant from the hospital and in a screened place whereby the examination can be conducted in private.

(viii) Medical examination must be conducted under the supervision of a registered medical practitioner.

(ix) The victim/survivor and his/her family members must be told about the available facilities for further treatment including abortion and healing of internal as well as external injuries.

(x) While conducting the medical examination, the accompanying police officer should not be allowed to be present inside the room where examination is conducted.

(xi) The victim/survivor and his/her family must be made aware of victim compensation schemes and encouraged to apply for such schemes.

(xii) While conducting the medical examination, the health worker/doctor as well as the police officer must assure the victim/survivor that the latter is assured of confidentiality.

Both the 2013 and 2014 guidelines and protocols insist upon right to privacy and right against any forms of discrimination of children along with other essential child rights. Both these guidelines also emphasize upon the fact that medical examination of children should be done with utmost care and if the child or his/her parents resist the examination, it should be avoided and the concerned medical practitioner must record it in writing to provide it to the police. Once this stage of receiving initial report and preliminary investigation is over (including medical examination or excluding the same where in case the victim/survivor does not allow the medical examination), the police must within 24 hours report the matter to the CWC and also the special court.

Role of Child Welfare Committee for Inquiry and Care and Protection of Children

The JJ Act, 2000 (later amended in 2015) created the CWC for taking care of the cases related to children in need of care and protection.[24]

---

[24] S.2(14) of the JJ Act, 2015 defines 'child in need of care and protection' as a child

(i) who is found without any home or settled place of abode and without any ostensible means of subsistence; or

(ii) who is found working in contravention of labour laws for the time being in force or is found begging, or living on the street; or

(iii) who resides with a person (whether a guardian of the child or not) and such person—

(a) has injured, exploited, abused or neglected the child or has violated any other law for the time being in force meant for the protection of child; or

(b) has threatened to kill, injure, exploit or abuse the child and there is a reasonable likelihood of the threat being carried out; or

(c) has killed, abused, neglected or exploited some other child or children and there is a reasonable likelihood of the child in question being killed, abused, exploited or neglected by that person; or

(iv) who is mentally ill or mentally or physically challenged or suffering from terminal or incurable disease, having no one to support or look after or having parents or guardians unfit to take care, if found so by the Board or the Committee; or

(v) who has a parent or guardian and such parent or guardian is found to be unfit or incapacitated, by the Committee or the Board, to care for and protect the safety and well-being of the child; or

(vi) who does not have parents and no one is willing to take care of, or whose parents have abandoned or surrendered him; or

(vii) who is missing or run away child, or whose parents cannot be found after making reasonable inquiry in such manner as may be prescribed; or

(viii) who has been or is being or is likely to be abused, tortured or exploited for the purpose of sexual abuse or illegal acts; or

CWC plays a special role under the POCSO Act as the definition of child in need of care protection specifically embraces children who are sexually abused or are likely to be abused. S.19(6) of the POCSO Act says, the SJPU or local police shall, without unnecessary delay but within a period of 24 hours, report the matter to the CWC and the special court, or where no special court has been designated to the court of the session, including need of the child for care and protection and steps taken in this regard. POCSO Act or the POCSO Rules do not describe the powers of the committee in regard to cases which may be covered under the POCSO Act. The CWC's general powers are stated under S.29 of the JJ Act, 2015. In Subsection (1) of S.29, it is stated that 'the Committee shall have the authority to dispose of cases for the care, protection, treatment, development and rehabilitation of the children as well as to provide for their basic needs and protection of human rights'. Subsection (2) further states:

> Where a Committee has been constituted for any area, such Committee shall, notwithstanding anything contained in any other law for the time being in force but save as otherwise expressly provided in this Act, have the power to deal exclusively with all proceedings under this Act relating to children in need of care and protection.

It may be understood from the earlier discussion that the CWC is empowered to look after the rights of the children in regard to (i) care, (ii) protection, (iii) treatment, (iv) development, (v) rehabilitation of the children and (vi) to provide for their basic needs and protection of their human rights. It cannot go over board to pronounce any judgement in regard to any accused even if the accused is a juvenile, as it

---

(ix) who is found vulnerable and is likely to be inducted into drug abuse or trafficking; or

(x) who is being or is likely to be abused for unconscionable gains; or

(xi) who is victim of or affected by any armed conflict, civil unrest or natural calamity; or

(xii) who is at imminent risk of marriage before attaining the age of marriage and whose parents, family members, guardian and any other persons are likely to be responsible for solemnization of such marriage.

can be done by the JJB. This can further be elaborated with the help
of S.30 of the JJ Act, which speaks about CWC's power in regard
to inquiry for the violation of child rights. S.30(1) of the JJ Act lays
down the two-folded powers of the CWC in regard to inquiry; this
includes (a) to hold inquiry upon receipt of report from any person or
individual as has been mentioned in S.31 of the JJ Act in the prescribed
manner and (b) on its own or on the report from any person or agency
as mentioned in Subsection (1) of S.31, the CWC may pass an order
to send the child to a children's home for speedy inquiry by a social
worker or child welfare officer. S.36(2) of the JJ Act further states
that such inquiry under this Section shall be completed within four
months of the receipt of the order or within such shorter period as may
be fixed by the CWC, provided that the time for the submission of
the inquiry report may be extended by such period as the CWC may,
having regard to the circumstances and for the reasons recorded in
writing, determine. S.36(3) of the JJ Act limits the scope of the CWC's
power to pronounce its judgement by stating that after the completion of the inquiry if the CWC is of the opinion that the said child
has no family or ostensible support, it may allow the child to remain
in the children's home or shelter home until suitable rehabilitation is
found for him or until he attains the age of 18 years. Hence, S.19(6)
of the POCSO Act, and Rule 4 (Ss.3–12) read with Chapters V and
VI of the JJ Act, 2015 lay down the powers and duties of the CWC
which is limited to ensuring the care and protection of the child as
a victim. According to these provisions, the CWC can counsel the
child for reducing the trauma, can gather more information from the
victim which may corroborate the victim's testimony, can maintain
a register for reported cases of sexual offences against children, can
rehabilitate the victim in case he/she needs safer shelter, can reunite
the victim with parents/guardians in case he/she was sexually abused
as a trafficked child or in case he/she was subjected to sexual offence
when he/she was under an institutional care such as student hostel,
shelter home, orphanage home, school and so on and can appoint a
'support person' for assisting the child for the judicial process as well
as for availing victim compensation. The CWC can also lodge complaint on behalf of the victim with the police, can hold an inquiry upon
receipt of information from any individual or the victim him/herself

to provide the information to the police, can initiate action-oriented planning involving other stakeholders including concerned government departments, the District Child Protection Unit (DCPU), chief education officers, the district legal service authorities and the police and can forward petition for compensation under victim compensation scheme to the district legal services authority unless the victim him/herself or the special court had already initiated move towards claiming victim compensation for the victim. However, unlike the police or the SJPU, the CWC does not have the power to register any case against any individual who may be accused for sexual offences.[25]

As the 2013 Model Guidelines states, the CWC should adopt child-friendly methods to conduct preliminary inquiry with the child. It is noticed that in many cases inquiry conducted by the CWC or professional experts appointed by the CWC to help the latter in inquiry may reveal more information regarding the victimization. Noting this, the 2013 model guidelines has emphasized upon conducting the inquiry with the child in a child-friendly atmosphere where the child victim may have better opportunity to tell the exact incidences without being distracted by any object, persons, phone calls and the like. It has further been noted by the courts in many cases that children may be used as tools by the parents against the accused to take revenge of old enmity by tutoring them to say about supposed sexual offences by the accused.[26] In some cases, they may also be tutored by the police.[27] This not only violates basic norms of child rights but also may expose the children to the extreme negative or dark sides of criminal justice mechanism. This may be avoided if the CWC conducts the preliminary investigation in the manner laid down in the 2013 guidelines with the help of expert professionals if needed and provides the said investigation report to the court to avoid further unnecessary exposure of the child to such negative issues and to curb the time of the courts in disposing off the matters. CWC should also ascertain during such counselling and inquiry sessions as to whether the child needs to be

---

[25] Dr Letha J. v. State of Kerala, 2015 (1) KHC 234.
[26] See Chapter 9, note 16.
[27] Ibid.

rescued from the present accommodation where he/she is staying and be shifted to any other home, or whether he/she may continue staying in his/her present accommodation within three days of being intimated by the police and production of the child to them (Rule 4(2) and (3) of the POCSO Act).

In short, CWC can be described as the gateway for rehabilitation, reunion and care and protection of the victim.

Victim/Witness Protection at the Reporting Stage Under POCSO Act

It is essential to note that the law as well as legal instruments ensures complete privacy to the victim of sexual offences. In a country like India where sexual offences against children, especially girls, may bring fear of social exclusion for the whole family, all stakeholders engaged in protection of child rights must provide information regarding laws which guarantee victim/witness's identity protection to the victims and their families. Article 8(1)(e) and (f) of the Optional Protocol to CRC stated:

> State Parties shall adopt appropriate measures to protect the rights and interests of child victims of the practices prohibited under the present Protocol at all states of the criminal justice process, in particular by:
>
> (e) Protecting, as appropriate, the privacy and identity of child victims and taking measures in accordance with national law to avoid the inappropriate dissemination of information that could lead to the identification of child victims;
>
> (f) Providing, in appropriate cases, for the safety of child victims, as well as that of their families and witnesses on their behalf, from intimidation and retaliation;

Basing on these factors, the POCSO Act and the Rules ensure protection of identity of the child victims right from the reporting stage. S.23 of the POCSO Act speaks in this regard; it is both protective as well as punitive in nature. S.23(1) protects the identity of the child victim by preventing any person from making any report or making any comment about any child who may come under the purview of this Act, in the form of media, studio or photographic facilities without having complete and authentic information and in any way which may lower his/her reputation or infringe his/her privacy. S.23(2) further states that unless the special court permits for the interest of the child, no one shall disclose the photo, name, family identity, name of the school and information about the victim's neighbourhood in the form of any media. This particular provision therefore prohibits any media, including any social media and digital communication technology, publicity of any sexual victimization involving minors. Ss.3 and 4 pronounce punishment for publisher or owner of the media and the like and any individual who contravenes the provision with punishment of imprisonment which should not be less than six months but may extend to one year, pecuniary punishment or both. Rule 4 of the POCSO Act further ensures protection of privacy of the victim including that of his/her family by prohibiting any support person engaged by CWC and also medical professionals who may be engaged for medical examination of the victim from disseminating any information about the child or about his/her identity.

The 2013 Model Guidelines has further emphasized these facts from various aspects, including from the socio-legal-medical caregiver aspects. Taking right to privacy as a primary right for the children, it has emphasized upon several mechanisms to deal with these cases; these include appointing trained child counsellors for preliminary investigation by the CWC at places where the child may feel comfortable, providing protection and ensuring confidentiality to the victim and his/her family by the police, stressing upon maintaining ethical principles by the counsellors, the police, the CWC members, medical professionals, the lawyers and so on for securing privacy of the victim, emphasizing upon no discrimination of the child victim in the educational institution or at any other organization where the child may join for training for any vocational course and the like. But it is sad to note that in spite of model guidelines, the punitive laws preventing breaching of privacy of child victims and constant campaigning of the POCSO Act by some child rights activists and

NGOs working for child rights, the reporting rate is still very low in India. It is because many families and the victims themselves may still feel that reporting any type of sexual offence may invite unnecessary media highlight. Hence, it has been seen that while the rate of reports regarding penetrative sexual offences may be higher, reporting for non-penetrative sexual assaults including cybercrimes (such as using children for creation of pornographic contents or showing children porn contents) is extremely low. Unless the civil society, the police, the district legal services authority and the NGOs join hands in vigorous campaigning about POCSO Act, the model policy guidelines and the privacy protection guidelines stated in these laws as well as governmental efforts to bring genuine offenders under the scanner of law may never be fruitful.

CHAPTER 8

Juvenile Offenders of Sexual Offences

Introduction

One of the unique features of POCSO Act is the gender-based and gender-neutral categorization of the offenders and victims for specific offences. For example, with regard to offences of penetrative sexual assault and aggravated penetrative sexual assault under Ss.3 and 5 in Chapter II of the POCSO Act, the gender of the harasser has been categorized as male and that of the victims as both male and female children as well as those with undetermined gender. Similarly, the other types of offences also have gender-neutral categorization for offenders and victims. But simultaneously it may be noted that the scope of the POCSO Act expands to offenders of all age groups irrespective of their gender as there is no particular limitation of the age of the offender under this Act. However, the POCSO Act specifically does not mention anything about reporting of the crimes committed by juveniles or any particular category of trial and punishment for juvenile offenders committing sexual offences against fellow children. The JJ Act, 2015 fulfils this lacuna by introducing specific provisions for trial of juvenile offenders who may have committed any crimes including sexual offences. Prior to December 2015, the trials of juvenile offenders (who are above 16 years of age but below 18 years of age) were conducted by the JJB even if the juvenile would have committed sexual offences including rape. With the presidential assent on the JJ Act, 2015,[1] the amended JJ Act has become functional to extend its scope to cover such juveniles and provides methods to treat them separately as adults in specific cases. This particular feature of the juvenile justice administration was introduced after the heinous rape and subsequent death of Jyoti Singh, who is popularly known as 'Nirbhaya', who was raped by six persons including a juvenile on the night of 13 December 2012 in a moving bus at Delhi. This case, popularly known as Nirbhaya case, created a historic public outrage due to the manner in which the rape was conducted. The victim was gang raped, beaten and assaulted by the convicts including the juvenile offender. The convicts had inserted a rod and their hands inside the victim's vagina as well as rectum causing severe injury to her internal organs. As the judgement in the case of State Through Reference v Ram Singh & Others (2013)[2] reads, 'the perineal injury was severe' and there was a 'complete tear involving lower 2/3rd of posterior vaginal wall, recto vaginal septum, anus, anal canal, anterior rectal wall extending upwards into adjoining large intestine. This injury could have been caused by thrusting of blunt rod like object forcibly through vagina and/or anus'. Also, as per their opinion, 'During the struggle and withdrawal of rod like structure from abdomen, intestines prolapsed/herniated which led to irreparable damage, loss and severe injuries to large and small intestine'. However, in this particular judgement, the juvenile was not awarded any punishment by the High Court as he was being tried at the JJB, which later released him and shifted him into the care of an NGO for rehabilitation.[3] Against this order of release by the JJB, the Delhi Commission for Women filed an appeal to the Supreme Court through Swati Maliwal Jaihind, Chairperson Delhi

---

[1] PTI, 'Juvenile Justice Act: President Nod to Trial of Juveniles as Adults for Serious Crimes', *The New Indian Express,* 4 January 2016. Available at: http://www.newindianexpress.com/nation/Juvenile-Justice-Act-President-Nod-to-Trial-of-Juveniles-as-Adults-for-Serious-Crimes/2016/01/04/article3211424.ece (accessed on 28 January 2018).

[2] See Chapter 3, note 13.

[3] Krishnadas Rajagopal, 'Apex Court Dismisses Plea Against Release of Juvenile', *The Hindu*, 21 December 2015. Available at: http://www.thehindu.com/news/national/sc-dismisses-plea-against-juvenile-in-nirbhaya-case/article8013697.ece (accessed on 30 January 2018).

Commission for Women v. Raju Through Juvenile Justice Board & Ors.[4] The latter dismissed the plea against the release order on the ground of lack of proper sanction by the existing JJ Act, 2000 which did not prescribe any separate trial, like it did for adults, for juvenile offenders who are under the age of 18 years.[5] One of the contentions of the Supreme Court in this dismissal was that unless the government and the Parliament amend the existing JJ Act, 2000 to change the mode of trial of the juveniles accused and convicted of heinous crimes, the court cannot go beyond the lines of the law to satisfy the demands of the petitioners.

Basing on these technical loopholes, the government proposed for the amendment of the JJ Act, 2000 and the JJ Act, 2015[6] became functional on and from 1 January 2016 after the then Hon'ble President of India Pranab Mukherjee assented to the amendment of this Act. This chapter deals with specific provisions from the JJ Act, 2015 related to the juveniles in conflict with law with special highlight on juveniles accused of committing of heinous crimes including sexual offences (including those as has been categorized under Chapter II of the POCSO Act) and murder. This chapter is divided into three parts including the introduction. The second part will discuss about juveniles in conflict with law as has been stated in the JJ Act, 2015 with special reference to those convicted for various offences as has been categorized by the JJ Act, 2015, including the 'heinous crimes'. The third part will discuss about the JJB and its functions with special reference to juveniles convicted for heinous crimes.

Juvenile Offenders

The Overlapping Concept of Child in Conflict with Law and Child in Need of Care and Protection

The JJ Act, 2015 or any of its predecessors did not define the term 'juvenile offender', even though the term 'juvenile' is defined under

[4] Swati Maliwal Jaihind, Chairperson Delhi Commission For Women v. Raju Through Juvenile Justice Board & Ors, 2016 (1) Recent Apex Judgements 18.
[5] Ibid.
[6] JJ Act, 2015, Act no. 2 of 2015.

S.2(35) of the JJ Act, 2015 which states that 'Juvenile means a child below the age of 18 years'. The concept of juvenile offender is clarified under S.2(13) of the JJ Act, 2015 which uses the term 'child in conflict with law'.[7] According to this provision child in conflict with law 'means a child who is alleged or found to have committed an offence and who has not completed eighteen years of age on the date of commission of such offence'. The JJ Act, 2015 does not define the term 'offence', hence it may be assumed that the term has the same meaning as has been explained by the IPC.[8] The JJ Act, 2015 neither categorizes offences depending upon the nature of the same, as has been categorized by the POCSO Act.[9] However, a plain reading of the JJ Act, 2015 and of S.2(13) of the JJ Act, 2015 may show that juvenile offenders or children in conflict with laws may be broadly categorized under two heads: (a) children who may have done offences themselves and (b) children who may have been made to do offences by adults taking advantage of their situations. In the latter case, the JJ Act, 2015 has included such children who fall in the borderline of offender and victims by broadening the definition of child in need of care and protection in S.2(14) and including the child who is found working in contravention of labour laws for the time being in force or is found begging, or living on the street (S.2(14)(ii)); or who has been or is being or is likely to be abused, tortured or exploited for the purpose of sexual abuse or illegal acts (S.2(14)(viii)); or who is found vulnerable and is likely to be inducted into drug abuse or trafficking (S.2(14)(ix)); or who is being or is likely to be abused for unconscionable gains (S.2(14)(x)); or who is victim of or affected by any armed conflict, civil unrest or natural calamity (S.2(14)(xi)); or who is at

---

[7] The definition thus provided by S.2(13) of the JJ Act, 2015 has been carried over from the previous versions of the JJ Act, including JJ Act, 2000.

[8] S.40 of the IPC defines the term 'offence' by stating,

Except in the chapters and sections mentioned in clauses 2 and 3 of this section, the word 'offence' denotes a thing made punishable by this Code. In Chapter IV, [Chapter VA] and in the following section, namely, sections [64, 65, 67, 71], 109, 110, 112, 114, 115, 116, 117, [118, 119, 120] 187, 194, 195, 203, 211, 213, 214, 221, 222, 223, 224, 225, 327, 328, 329, 330, 331, 347, 348, 388, 389 and 445, the word 'offence' denotes a thing punishable under this code, or under any special or local law as hereinafter defined.

[9] See Part II of this book for the categorization of the offences.

imminent risk of marriage before attaining the age of marriage and whose parents, family members, guardian and any other persons are likely to be responsible for solemnization of such marriage (S.2(14) (xii)). The JJ Act, 2015 further understands this vulnerable position of children in conflict with law in S.8(3)(g) which speaks about the powers, functions and responsibilities of the JJB and states:

> The function and the responsibilities of the Board should include... transferring to the Committee, matters concerning the child alleged to be in conflict with law, stated to be in need of care and protection at any stage, thereby recognising that a child in conflict with law can also be a child in need of care simultaneously and there is a need for the Committee and the Board to be both involved.

Categorization of Offences (Including and Related to Sexual Offences) for Juvenile Offenders

Even though the JJ Act, 2015 does not categorize offences like the POCSO Act does, it mentions three distinct types of offences depending upon the terms of punishment as has been fixed by the IPC or any other law existing in India. These are as follows:

(i) Petty offences: S.2(45) of the JJ Act, 2015 states that 'petty offences' includes offences for which the maximum punishment under the Indian Penal Code or any other law for the time being in force is imprisonment up to three years.

(ii) Serious offences: S.2(54) of the JJ Act, 2015 states that 'serious offences' includes offences for which the punishment under the Indian Penal Code or any other law for the time being in force, is imprisonment between three to seven years.

(iii) Heinous offences: S.2(33) of the JJ Act, 2015 states that 'heinous offences' includes offences for which the minimum punishment under the Indian Penal Code or any other law for the time being in force is imprisonment for seven years or more.

It may be pertinent to note that as per the NCRB statistics, juveniles committing sexual offences are alarmingly growing. As such, the 2014 statistics may show that while 1 boy below the age of 12 years was apprehended for gang rape, 22 boys below the age of 12 years were apprehended for other sorts of rape (other than custodial gang rape, etc.). This statistics further showed that a total of 632 boys and 1 girl above the age of 12 but below the age of 16 were apprehended for rape. Further, 9 boys under the age of 12 and 136 boys above the age of 12 and under the age of 16 were apprehended for sexual harassment. Also, 20 boys above the age of 12 and under the age of 16 were apprehended for assault of women with intent to disrobe.[10] Even though Chapter 6 of the report shows about offences against children, including sexual offences, there are no specific statistics available on juvenile offenders committing sexual offences against children. As the Nirbhaya gang-rape case showed, when a juvenile is accused of committing an offence, the prosecution, the victim/s and the courts may often have to face critical questions regarding the manner in which the juvenile may be treated, that is, whether he may need only counselling and restorative legal treatment or stricter punishment like adults. This becomes a critical question especially when the juvenile commits sexual offences. It is for this very reason that when a juvenile is accused of committing sexual offences against minors, the offence must be seen both from the perspectives of POCSO Act and the JJ Act, 2015. Hence, keeping the categorization of the offences under the JJ Act, 2015 in mind, the offences under the POCSO Act and related laws including the IPC can be grouped for the purpose of dealing with children in conflict with law as shown in Table 8.1.

It may be pertinent to note that this categorization of the offences basing on the seriousness of the offences has also been introduced in many other jurisdictions such as that of South Africa, whereby S.6 of the Child Justice Act, 75 of 2008 also provides three sorts of crime categorization for the effective administration of juvenile justice.[11]

---

[10] See Table 10.4 of the NCRB report. Available at: http://ncrb.nic.in/ (accessed on 10 January 2016).

[11] For more detail, see Child Justice Act, 75 of 2008 of South Africa. Available at: http://www.justice.gov.za/legislation/acts/2008-075_childjustice.pdf (accessed on 28 January 2018).

Table 8.1 Categorization of the Offences as Per the Gravity of the Offence

Petty Offences (as per S.2(45) of the JJ Act, 2015)	Serious Offences (as per S.2(54) of the JJ Act, 2015)	Heinous Offences (as per S.2(33) of the JJ Act, 2015)
S.11 (sexual harassment) read with S. 12 (punishment for sexual harassment) of the POCSO Act	S.7 (sexual assault) read with S.8 (punishment for sexual assault) of the POCSO Act	S.3 (penetrative sexual assault) read with S.4 (punishment for penetrative sexual assault) of the POCSO Act
S.15 (punishment for storage of pornographic materials involving children) of the POCSO Act	S.9 (aggravated sexual assault) and S.10 (punishment for aggravated sexual assault) of the POCSO Act	S.5 (aggravated sexual assault) read with S.6 (punishment for aggravated sexual assault) of the POCSO Act
	S.13 (use of child for pornographic purposes) read with S.14(1 and 4) (punishment for the same) of the POCSO Act	S.13 (use of child for pornographic purposes) read with S.14(2, 3 and 5) (punishment for using child for pornographic purposes) of the POCSO Act
S.117 (abetment of commission of offence), S.120 (criminal conspiracy to commit an offence) read with S.120(b) (punishment for the same), S.292 (sale, etc., of obscene objects), S.293 (sale, etc., of obscene objects, etc., to young persons), S.306 of IPC, S.354C (voyeurism), S.354D (stalking), S.509 (word, gesture, etc., to harm the modesty of women) of IPC	S.32B (voluntarily throwing or attempt to throw acid), S.361 (kidnapping from lawful guardian), read with S.363 (punishment for the same), S.365 (kidnapping or abducting for secret wrongful confinement), S.366 (kidnapping, abducting, inducing or compelling woman to marry, etc.), S.366A (procuring of minor girl), S.503 (criminal intimidation) read with S.506 (punishment for the same)	S.299 (culpable homicide) read with S.304 (punishment for the same), S.300 (murder) read with S.302 (punishment for the same), S.306 (abetment to suicide of child or insane person), S.306 (abetment to suicide), S.307 (attempt to murder), S.308 (attempt to culpable homicide), S.326A (voluntarily causing grievous hurt by acid, etc.), S.377 (unnatural offences)

Source: Author.

Rights of the Juvenile Offenders

It needs to be understood that even if a juvenile is apprehended for committing any offences, including those as has been shown in Table 8.1, the treatment of the offender has to be different than those committed by the adult offenders. One of the main differences in the treatment of juvenile offenders thus lies in the penalties that can be awarded. S.12 of the JJ Act, 2015 states in this regard:

(1) When any person, who is apparently a child and is alleged to have committed a bailable or non-bailable offence, is apprehended or detained by the police or appears or brought before a Board, such person shall, notwithstanding anything contained in the Code of Criminal Procedure, 1973 or in any other law for the time being in force, be released on bail with or without surety or placed under the supervision of a probation officer or under the care of any fit person. Provided that such person shall not be so released if there appears reasonable grounds for believing that the release is likely to bring that person into association with any known criminal or expose the said person to moral, physical or psychological danger or the person's release would defeat the ends of justice, and the Board shall record the reasons for denying the bail and circumstances that led to such a decision.

(2) When such person having been apprehended is not released on bail under subsection (1) by the officer-in-charge of the police station, such officer shall cause the person to be kept only in an observation home in such manner as may be prescribed until the person can be brought before a Board.

(3) When such person is not released on bail under subsection (1) by the Board, it shall make an order sending him to an observation home or a place of safety, as the case may be, for such period during the pendency of the inquiry regarding the person, as may be specified in the order.

(4) When a child in conflict with law is unable to fulfil the conditions of bail order within seven days of the bail order, such child shall be produced before the Board for modification of the conditions of bail.

These distinguishing rights including other fundamental rights of the juvenile offenders are presented by the JJ Act, 2015 in the form of 16 general principles which are to be followed for the purpose of the administration of the JJ Act. S.3 of the JJ Act provides these general principles, which are as follows:

(i) Principle of presumption of innocence: Any child shall be presumed to be an innocent of any mala fide or criminal intent up to the age of eighteen years.

(ii) Principle of dignity and worth: All human beings shall be treated with equal dignity and rights.

(iii) Principle of participation: Every child shall have a right to be heard and to participate in all processes and decisions affecting his interest and the child's views shall be taken into consideration with due regard to the age and maturity of the child.

(iv) Principle of best interest: All decisions regarding the child shall be based on the primary consideration that they are in the best interest of the child and to help the child to develop full potential.

(v) Principle of family responsibility: The primary responsibility of care, nurture and protection of the child shall be that of the biological family or adoptive or foster parents, as the case may be.

(vi) Principle of safety: All measures shall be taken to ensure that the child is safe and is not subjected to any harm, abuse or maltreatment while in contact with the care and protection system, and thereafter.

(vii) Positive measures: All resources are to be mobilised including those of family and community, for promoting the well-being, facilitating development of identity and providing an inclusive and enabling environment, to reduce vulnerabilities of children and the need for intervention under this Act.

(viii) Principle of non-stigmatising semantics: Adversarial or accusatory words are not to be used in the processes pertaining to a child.

(ix) Principle of non-waiver of rights: No waiver of any of the right of the child is permissible or valid, whether sought by the child or person acting on behalf of the child, or a Board or a Committee and any non-exercise of a fundamental right shall not amount to waiver.

(x) Principle of equality and non-discrimination: There shall be no discrimination against a child on any grounds including sex, caste, ethnicity, place of birth, disability and equality of access, opportunity and treatment shall be provided to every child.

(xi) Principle of right to privacy and confidentiality: Every child shall have a right to protection of his privacy and confidentiality, by all means and throughout the judicial process.

(xii) Principle of institutionalisation as a measure of last resort: A child shall be placed in institutional care as a step of last resort after making a reasonable inquiry.

(xiii) Principle of repatriation and restoration: Every child in the juvenile justice system shall have the right to be re-united with his family at the earliest and to be restored to the same socio-economic and cultural status that he was in, before coming under the purview of this Act, unless such restoration and repatriation is not in his best interest.

(xiv) Principle of fresh start: All past records of any child under the juvenile justice system should be erased except in special circumstances.

(xv) Principle of diversion: Measures for dealing with children in conflict with law without resorting to judicial proceedings shall be promoted unless it is in the best interest of the child or the society as a whole.

(xvi) Principles of natural justice: Basic procedural standards of fairness shall be adhered to, including the right to a fair hearing, rule against bias and the right to review, by all persons or bodies, acting in a judicial capacity under this Act.

These principles are based on the three particular Articles of the UN CRC as adopted by the General Assembly on 1989. These are as follows:

(1) Article 37, which states:

States Parties shall ensure that:

(a) No child shall be subjected to torture or other cruel, inhuman or degrading treatment or punishment. Neither capital punishment nor life imprisonment without possibility of release shall be imposed for offences committed by persons below eighteen years of age;

(b) No child shall be deprived of his or her liberty unlawfully or arbitrarily. The arrest, detention or imprisonment of a child shall be in conformity with the law and shall be used only as a measure of last resort and for the shortest appropriate period of time;

(c) Every child deprived of liberty shall be treated with humanity and respect for the inherent dignity of the human person, and in a manner which takes into account the needs of persons of his or her age. In particular, every child deprived of liberty shall be separated from adults unless it is considered in the child's best interest not to do so and shall have the right to maintain contact with his or her family through correspondence and visits, save in exceptional circumstances;

(d) Every child deprived of his or her liberty shall have the right to prompt access to legal and other appropriate assistance, as well as the right to challenge the legality of the deprivation of his or her liberty before a court or other competent, independent and impartial authority, and to a prompt decision on any such action.

(2) Article 39, which states:

States Parties shall take all appropriate measures to promote physical and psychological recovery and social reintegration of a child victim of any form of neglect, exploitation, or abuse; torture or any other form of cruel, inhuman or degrading treatment or punishment; or armed conflicts. Such recovery and reintegration shall take place in an environment which fosters the health, self-respect and dignity of the child.

(3) Article 40, which states:

1. States Parties recognize the right of every child alleged as, accused of, or recognized as having infringed the penal law to be treated in a manner consistent with the promotion of the child's sense of dignity and worth, which reinforces the child's respect for the human rights and fundamental freedoms of others and which takes into account the child's age and the desirability of promoting the child's reintegration and the child's assuming a constructive role in society.

2. To this end, and having regard to the relevant provisions of international instruments, States Parties shall, in particular, ensure that: (a) No child shall be alleged as, be accused of, or recognized as having infringed the penal law by reason of acts or omissions that were not prohibited by national or international law at the time they were committed; (b) Every child alleged as or accused of having infringed the penal law has at least the following guarantees: (i) To be presumed innocent until proven guilty according to law; (ii) To be informed promptly and directly of the charges against him or her, and, if appropriate, through his or her parents or legal guardians, and to have legal or other appropriate assistance in the preparation and presentation of his or her defence; (iii) To have the matter determined without delay by a competent, independent and impartial authority or judicial body in a fair hearing according to law, in the presence of legal or other appropriate assistance and, unless it is considered not to be in the best interest of the child, in particular, taking into account his or her age or situation, his or her parents or legal guardians; (iv) Not to be compelled to give testimony or to confess guilt; to examine or have examined adverse witnesses and to obtain the participation and examination of witnesses on his or her behalf under conditions of equality; (v) If considered to have infringed the penal law, to have this decision and any measures imposed in consequence thereof reviewed by a higher competent, independent and impartial authority or judicial body according to law; (vi) To have the free assistance of an interpreter if the child cannot understand or speak the language used; (vii) To have his or her privacy fully respected at all stages of the proceedings.

3. States Parties shall seek to promote the establishment of laws, procedures, authorities and institutions specifically applicable to children alleged as, accused of, or recognized as having infringed the penal law, and, in particular: (a) The establishment of a minimum age below which children shall be presumed not to have the capacity to infringe the penal law; (b) Whenever appropriate and desirable, measures for dealing with such children without resorting to judicial proceedings, providing that human rights and legal safeguards are fully respected.

4. A variety of dispositions, such as care, guidance and supervision orders; counselling; probation; foster care; education and vocational training programmes and other alternatives to institutional care shall be available to ensure that children are dealt with in a manner

appropriate to their well-being and proportionate both to their circumstances and the offence.

(4) Article 41, which states, 'Nothing in the present Convention shall affect any provisions which are more conducive to the realization of the rights of the child and which may be contained in: (a) The law of a State party; or (b) International law in force for that State'.

Possible Socio-psychological Reasons for Juvenile Offenders Committing Sexual Offences Against Minors

While the Nirbhaya case posed a serious question regarding the treatment of juvenile offenders of sexual offences from the age group of 16–18 specifically, it also motivated many researchers and lawmakers to think afresh about causes of juvenile behaviours relating to sexual offences. The issue of juveniles committing sexual offences against children may attract further research interest. Due to strict secrecy maintained by many government organizations including the observation homes, special homes, the JJB and the Special Courts dealing with sexual offences against children, not many analytical views are available regarding the reasons behind such offensive sexual behaviours of juvenile offenders in India. However, in the United States, a few studies have been conducted to know the reasons of such sexual deviances targeting children by children. The common factors that have been noted by most of the researchers and this author are as follows:

(a) Sexual offences by children against children may be less aggressive than that committed by adult offenders, because in many cases juvenile sex offenders may have done this on an experimental basis.[12]

(b) The typology of sexual offences committed against children may vary from showing porn clippings to fondling fellow children over

---

[12] David Finkelhor, Richard Ormrod, and Mark Chaffin, 'Juveniles Who Commit Sex Offenses Against Minors', *Juvenile Justice Bulletin*, 2009. Available at: https://www.ncjrs.gov/pdffiles1/ojjdp/227763.pd (accessed on 18 September 2016).

the clothes, to touching and grabbing fellow children in a sexual way, date rape or even gang rape.[13]

(c) Early adolescence curiosity about sex may lead to committing sexual offences on younger children or older children.[14] Further, repression of sexual queries mainly due to fear of orthodox elders in the family or in the schools may also motivate children to learn from personal experiments.

(d) Role play by children with fellow children (e.g., acting like Romeo–Juliet or even sexual scenes as shown in the cinema, other media, etc.) may also push them to commit sexual offences including sexual touching, kissing and vaginal or anal sex. Studies have shown that in such occasions, children often exhibit sexual advances such as touching body parts in a sexual manner and anal or vaginal sex with other fellow children without thinking about the consequences.[15]

(e) Often juveniles committing sexual offence, including date rape, fondling and anal or vaginal sex, misinterpret the silence or shocked nature of their 'partners' as consent to carry on with the sexual activities.[16]

(f) Juveniles may also commit aggressive sexual offences including cyber sexual offences as a measure to take revenge for emotional break-up with partners.[17]

(g) Aggressive sexual abuse by juveniles may also be committed as part of ragging.[18]

---

[13] Ibid.

[14] Human Rights Watch, *Raised on the Registry: The Irreparable Harm of Placing Children on Sex Offender Registries in the US*, 2013, 28. Available at: https://www. hrw.org/sites/default/files/reports/us0513_ForUpload_1.pdf (accessed on 28 January 2018).

[15] Ibid., 29.

[16] See Chapter 1, note 16.

[17] See Chapter 5, note 12.

[18] See 'The Menace of Ragging in Educational Institutions and Measures to Curb It', Report of the Committee Constituted by the Hon'ble Supreme Court of India in SLP No. 24295 of 2006. Available at: http://dos.iitd.ac.in/anti-ragging/ menace.pdf (accessed on 28 January 2018).

Apart from these various socio-psychological factors, this author feels that there may be some other factors as well which motivate juveniles to commit sexual offences on fellow children; these may include sudden exposure to sexual activities of elders in the family and wish to 'enjoy' the same by the juvenile him/herself.[19] It may be pertinent to note further that pampered childhood and extremely lenient elders in the family due to the gender of the juvenile (especially for boys) may also push the juvenile to commit sexual offences to other children, especially when the juvenile feels confident that he would not be held responsible for such activities.[20] It is for these aforementioned factors that the juvenile offenders committing sexual offences against children may need special legal treatment. The next chapter deals with the procedure and forum in this regard.

[19] This information was gathered by the author from the information shared by staff of District Child Protection Unit and CWC in Tirunelveli.
[20] Ibid.

CHAPTER 9

Prosecution and Trial

Introduction

Sexual offences against children (whether done by adults or minors) need a separate legal understanding when it comes to prosecution and trials. It needs to be understood that many cases of sexual offences against children go unreported in India because either the parents of the victims fear for social taboo for their entire family as well as for the victim/s, or the criminal justice machinery may not be equipped enough to deal with the cases. Victims of sexual offences, especially children, may feel extremely traumatized to provide testimony again and again in front of different persons. Similarly, it may not be advisable to prosecute cases of such nature in courts which are handling cases where both the parties are adults. As referred to and discussed in Chapters 7 and 8, children can be tutored both by the parents/caregivers or the police to provide false testimony only to take revenge upon the defendants/accused. There needs to be a strong infrastructure including judges, lawyers, child psychologists and individual experts who may have sufficient understanding of child psychology, the nature of the cases, therapeutic effects of the law and the proceedings on the victims as well as the accused. To cater to this purpose, the POCSO Act, 2012 introduced Special Courts which are empowered to deal with cases within the scope of the POCSO Act, 2012 exclusively. However, it must be noted that while the Special Courts under

POCSO Act are empowered to deal with all sorts of sexual offences against children, there are exceptions when the offenders are minors. In such cases, the role of JJB and the children's courts must also be considered. This chapter therefore deals with these issues including some specific questions such as whether JJB and children's court may step into the role of Special Courts in such circumstances and how the prosecution should proceed in all cases of sexual offences against children.

Pre-trial Management

All criminal cases go through several stages before reaching the final stage where judgement is delivered by the courts. These stages necessarily follow procedures established by the CrPC, 1973. There is no exception of this rule for cases of sexual offences targeting children. However, the stages may vary in such cases considering the nature of the offences and the victims and sometimes the offenders who may be minors. Generally, the pre-trial procedure may follow the following stages as shown in Figure 9.1.

This pre-trial management of cases by the police can be divided into three groups: (i) pre-trial management of cases for child in need of care and protection, (ii) pre-trial management of cases for child in conflict with law and (iii) pre-trial management of cases for adults. It is discussed in detail in the following:

(i) **Pre-trial management of cases for child in need of care and protection:** When we say child in need of care and protection within the perspective of the POCSO Act, it necessarily means child victims of sexual abuse of any sort as has been shown in Chapters II and III of the POCSO Act. It must be noted that children victimized due to immoral trafficking and abused by way of prostitution and sexual abuse thereby, due to sexual abuse by way of ragging, child marriage or victimized by any sort of sexual abuse within the meaning of Chapters II and III of the POCSO Act by any individual must be brought under the broad scope of the POCSO Act. In all these cases, pre-trial management of the case by the police must follow the steps as have been mentioned

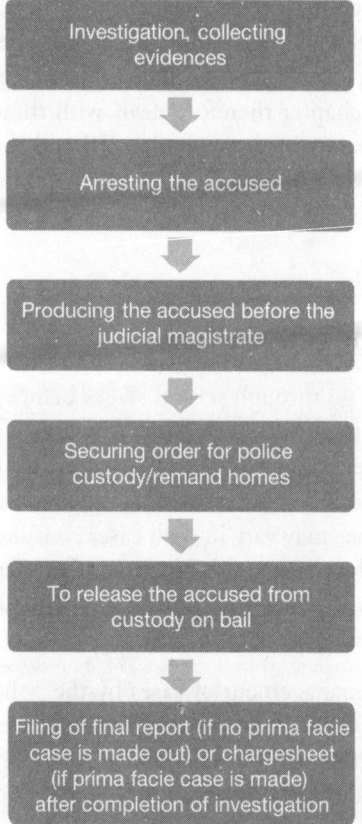

Figure 9.1 *Pre-trial Procedure for Offences Against Children*
Source: Author.

in Chapter 7 of this book, whereby the police after finishing preliminary investigation must inform the CWC and both the CWC and the police should follow the procedure as stated in Chapter 7 of this book.

(ii) **Pre-trial management of cases for child in conflict with law:** Such children in conflict with law may mean children who have committed sexual abuse on children. It must be noted that the POCSO Act expands its scope to include perpetrators of all ages and gender and as such child offenders must go through pre-trial and trial process as has been mentioned in the CrPC, read with JJ Act, 2015 and the JJ Act Rules, 2000. After receiving the information of the offence, the typical procedures which follows thereafter are:

(a) Preliminary investigation, which includes recording the information of the informant as per S.154, CrPC,[1] rescuing

---

[1] S.154, CrPC (Information in Cognizable Cases) states:

(1) Every information relating to the commission of a cognizable offence, if given orally to an officer in charge of a police station, shall be reduced to writing by him or under his direction, and be read over to the informant; and every such information, whether given in writing or reduced to writing as aforesaid, shall be signed by the person giving it, and the substance thereof shall be entered in a book to be kept by such officer in such form as the State Government may prescribe in this behalf.

(2) A copy of the information as recorded under sub-section (1) shall be given forthwith, free of cost, to the informant.

(3) Any person, aggrieved by a refusal on the part of an officer in charge of a police station to record the information referred to in sub-section (1) may send the substance of such information, in writing and by post, to the Superintendent of Police concerned who, if satisfied that such information discloses the commission of a cognizable offence, shall either investigate the case himself or direct an investigation to be made by any police officer Subordinate to him, in the manner provided by this Code, and such officer shall have all the powers of an officer in charge of the police station in relation to that offence.

Provided that if the information is given by the woman against whom an offence under section 326A, section 326B, section 354, section 354A, section 354B, section 354C, section 354D, section 376, section 376A, section 376B, section 376C, section 376D, section 376E or section 509 of the Indian Penal Code is alleged to have been committed or attempted, then such information shall be recorded, by a woman police officer or any woman officer:

Provided further that

(a) in the event that the person against whom an offence under section 354, section 354A, section 354B, section 354C, section 354D, section 376, section 376A, section 376B, section 376C, section 376D, section 376E or section 509 of the Indian Penal Code is alleged to have been committed or attempted, is temporarily or permanently mentally or physically disabled, then such information shall be recorded by a police officer, at the residence of the person seeking to report such offence or at a convenient place of such person's choice, in the presence of an interpreter or a special educator, as the case may be;

the child victim and shifting him/her to safer custody and apprehending the accused juvenile;

(b) As per S.11(1) of the JJ Rules, 2007, as soon as the juvenile is apprehended, the police officer apprehending the juvenile must inform three persons immediately—the designated juvenile officer or the child welfare officer either in the same police station or in the nearest police station to take care of the case (S.11(a), JJ Rules, 2007); the parents of the juvenile with special information about the apprehension, the address of the JJB where the juvenile would be produced and the date and time when the parents of the juvenile need to be present before the Board (S.11(b) of the JJ Rules, 2007) and the probation officer to enable him to obtain information regarding the juvenile's socio-economic background and other related information which may assist the JJB in the trial of the case (S.11(1)(c), JJ Rules, 2007).

(c) No police officer may detain the juvenile in the police lockup immediately after the arrest. But the juvenile must be shifted to observation home pending the inquiry and before producing the juvenile before the JJB. It may be necessary to note here that S.10(1) of the JJ Act, 2015 states:

> As soon as a child, alleged to be in conflict with law, is apprehended by the police, such child shall be placed under the charge of the special juvenile police unit or the designated child welfare police officer, who shall produce the child before the Board without any loss of time but within a period of twenty-four hours of apprehending the child excluding the time necessary for the journey, from the place where such child was apprehended. Provided that in no case, a child alleged to be in conflict with law shall be placed in a police lockup or lodged in a jail.

If the juvenile is apprehended for any offence of serious or heinous crime as has been shown in the table in Chapter 8 of

---

(b) the recording of such information shall be videographed;

(c) the police officer shall get the statement of the person recorded by a Judicial Magistrate under clause (a) of sub-section (5A) of section 164 as soon as possible.

this book or for any petty offence which has been made along with any serious or heinous crime as shown in Figure 9.1, the juvenile so apprehended may be detained in the observation home prior to production before the JJB, for preparation of the social background report and considering the need of the juvenile's care, protection and counselling, as has been mentioned under S.12 of the JJ Rules, 2007, which states:

> The State Government shall recognize only such voluntary organizations that are in a position to provide the services of probation, counselling, case work, a safe place and also associate with the police or the juvenile or the child welfare officer from the Special Juvenile Police Unit, and have the capacity, facilities and expertise to do so as protection agencies that may assist the police or the juvenile or the child welfare officer from the police at the time of apprehension, in preparation of the report containing social background of the juvenile and circumstances of apprehension and the alleged offence, in taking charge of the juvenile until production before the Board, and in actual production of the juvenile before the Board within twenty-four hours.

(d) The JJ Rules, 2007 in S.11(11) states:

> In dealing with cases of juveniles in conflict with law the police or the juvenile welfare officer or the child welfare officer from the nearest police station, shall not be required to register an FIR or file a chargesheet, except where the offence alleged to have been committed by the juvenile is of a serious nature such as rape, murder or when such offence is alleged to have been committed jointly with adults; instead, in matters involving simple offences, the police or the juvenile or the child welfare officer from the nearest police station shall record information regarding the offence alleged to have been committed by the juvenile in the general daily diary followed by a report containing social background of the juvenile, circumstances of apprehension and the alleged offence, and forward it to the Board before the first hearing.

Keeping in mind this provision, it must also be remembered that POCSO Act being a special law, the principle of *Generelaia Specialibus Non Derogant* (special law prevails over general law) must be considered. As such, the police may proceed to prepare charge sheet when the offences are of serious and heinous nature and petty offences clubbed up with heinous or serious offences or done under the instruction of or with the adults.

(e) Producing the juvenile before the JJB within 24 hours of the arrest either by the SJPU officer or the child welfare officer or in case the same is not available, by the officer who has apprehended him (S.11(2), JJ Rules, 2007). In case there is a delay for producing within 24 hours, then producing the child within shortest possible time before the Board in case it is sitting on that day or before any individual member of the Board as per S.10 of the JJ Rules, 2007 read with S.7(2) of the JJ Act, 2015, in case the Board is not sitting on that particular day.

(iii) **Pre-trial management of cases for adults:** As soon as the police is informed about the offence within the scope of the POCSO Act, after registering the FIR as per S.154, CrPC, and rescuing the child victim where the victim needs such rescuing, the police must proceed with the following steps:

(a) Arrest the accused as per the regular provisions of CrPC, especially under S.41 of the CrPC which speaks about the power of the police to arrest without warrant.[2] However, it must be

---

[2] S.41 of the CrPC states:

(1) Any police officer may without an order from a Magistrate and without a warrant, arrest any person:

(a) who has been concerned in any cognizable offence, or against whom a reasonable complaint has been made, or credible information has been received, or a reasonable suspicion exists, of his having been so concerned; or

(b) who has in his possession without lawful excuse, the burden of proving which excuse shall lie on such person, any implement of house-breaking; or

(c) who has been proclaimed as an offender either under this Code or by order of the State Government; or

noted that in the absence of any police officer in charge of a police station or any other officer who is in charge of the investigation of the offence, a subordinate officer may arrest the accused on a written order of the former as per S.55 of the CrPC.[3] In cases falling under the scope of POCSO Act, this is

---

(d) in whose possession anything is found which may reasonably be suspected to be stolen property and who may reasonably be suspected of having committed an offence with reference to such thing; or

(e) who obstructs a police officer while in the execution of his duty, or who has escaped, or attempts to escape, from lawful custody; or

(f) who is reasonable suspected of being a deserter from any of the Armed Forces of the Union; or

(g) who has been concerned in, or against whom a reasonable complaint has been made, or credible information has been received, or a reasonable suspicion exists, of his having been concerned in, any act committed at any place out of India which, if committed in India, would have been punishable as an offence, and for which he is, under any law relating to extradition, or otherwise, liable to be apprehended or detained in custody in India; or

(h) who, being a released convict, commits a breach of any rule made under subsection (5) of section 356; or

(i) for whose arrest any requisition, whether written or oral, has been received from another police officer, provided that the requisition specifies the person to be arrested and the offence or other cause for which the arrest is to be made and it appears there from that the person might lawfully be arrested without a warrant by the officer who issued the requisition.

(2) Any officer in charge of a police station may, in like manner, arrest or cause to be arrested any person, belonging to one or more of the categories of person specified in section 109 or section 110.

[3] S.55, CrPC (Procedure when police officer deputes subordinate to arrest without warrant):

(1) When any officer in charge of a police station or any police officer making an investigation under Chapter XII requires any officer subordinate to him to arrest without a warrant (otherwise than in his presence) any person who may lawfully be arrested without a warrant, he shall deliver to the officer required to make the arrest an order in writing, specifying the person to be arrested and the offence or other cause for which the arrest is to be made and the officer so required shall, before making the arrest, notify to the person to be arrested the substance of the order and, if so required by such person, shall show him the order.

extremely necessary to apprehend the accused who may try to conceal the evidences or may try to escape the clutches of law in case it is found that the station in charge or investigating officer is absent to execute the arrest. However, while making the arrest, the concerned officer must follow the principles set in S.46 of the CrPC (arrest how made) and should not cause death or grievous hurt to the person so apprehended.[4]

(b) The arrested person must be informed about the grounds of arrest and his rights as an arrested person, including that of seeking bail under S.50 (person arrested to be informed of grounds of arrest and of right to bail) and S.50A (obligation of person making arrest to inform nominated person about the arrest, etc.) of CrPC. The arrested person must also be searched (S.51, CrPC) and if it is a case of aggravated sexual offence/s, the weapon must be seized then and there (S.52, CrPC). Further, when the accused is charged with offences like rape or attempt to rape or any other types of sexual assault within the meaning of POCSO Act, he/she must be medically examined to gather evidences relating to the offence (S.53A, CrPC). However, it needs to be remembered that when the

---

(2) Nothing in sub-section (1) shall affect the power of a police officer to arrest a person under section 41.

[4] S.46, CrPC Procedure when police officer deputes subordinate to arrest without warrant. Arrest how made:

(1) In making an arrest the police officer or other person making the same shall actually touch or confine the body of the person to be arrested, unless there be a submission to the custody by word or action.

(2) If such person forcibly resists the endeavour to arrest him, or attempts to evade the arrest, such police officer or other person may use all means necessary to effect the arrest.

(3) Nothing in this section gives a right to cause the death of a person who is not accused of an offence punishable with death or with imprisonment for life.

(4) Save in exceptional circumstances, no woman shall be arrested after sunset and before sunrise, and where such exceptional circumstances exist, the woman police officer shall, by making a written report, obtain the prior permission of the Judicial Magistrate of the first class within whose local jurisdiction the offence is committed or the arrest is to be made.

accused is a woman, the arrest must be made by a woman officer, must be made before sunset and must be made to be examined by a lady doctor (S.46(4) of the CrPC).

(c) The arrested person must be produced before the concerned police officer in charge of the station or the magistrate within 24 hours (S.56, CrPC). The arrestee may never be put up in the lock-up for a long time beyond 24 hours if he is produced before the officer in charge of the police station.[5] He must be produced before the magistrate within the shortest possible time (S.76, CrPC). In case there is a delay in producing the arrested person within 24 hours, the officer who apprehended the accused must submit in writing the causes for delay.

(d) In case the person is apprehended from the spot of the occurrence of the offence, the police must seize all the evidence necessary for proving the charge as per S.102 of the CrPC.[6] However, when the case relates to cybercrime, the officer apprehending arrest must take care to not to destroy any evidence stored digitally.[7] Once the evidence including the

---

[5] Khatri & Ors v. State of Bihar & Ors, 1981, 1 SCC 627.

[6] S.102, CrPC states:

(1) Any police officer may seize any property which may be alleged or suspected to have been stolen, or which may be found under circumstances, which create suspicion of the Commission of any offence.

(2) Such police officer, if subordinate to the officer in charge of a police station, shall forthwith report the seizure to that officer.

(3) Every police officer acting under sub-section (1) shall forthwith report the seizure to the Magistrate having jurisdiction and where the property seized is such that it cannot be, conveniently transported to the Court or where there is difficulty in securing proper accommodation for the custody of such property, or where the continued retention of the property in police custody may not be considered necessary for the purpose of investigational, he may give custody thereof to any person on his executing a bond undertaking to produce the property before the Court as and when required and to give effect to the further orders of the Court as and when required and to give effect to the further orders of the Court as to disposal of the same.

[7] For a guideline in investigating cyber offences, stakeholders may see Chapter 18 ('Investigating Cyber Crimes') of the CBI manuals regarding investigation of

electronic devices such as the computer, mobile phone, any parts of the electronic device/s are collected, the same must be given to the cyber forensic experts to exclude necessary information in case the officer so apprehending does not have mechanism to store the electronic devices and the data in his own police station for safe production to the court.[8]

(e) Once the police officer registers the FIR, he must apprehend the offender even if he is not present within the jurisdiction of his own station. In such case, he can pursue the offender in any place in India under S.48 of CrPC (pursuit of offenders in other jurisdiction) and may take necessary legal step to bring the offender back to the jurisdiction.

(f) No accused person shall be restrained for an unnecessary long time. The arrested person may be released on bail in case of bailable offences by the police officer who apprehended him or by a magistrate. S.59 of the CrPC thus states:

> No person who has been arrested by a police officer shall be discharged except on his own bond, or on bail, or under the special order of a Magistrate. The police officer in charge of a police station, who had arrested the accused, can release him on bail as per S.436 of CrPC.

S.436, CrPC further states in Clause (i):

> When any person other than a person accused of a non-bailable offence is arrested or detained without warrant by an officer in charge of a police station, or appears or is brought before a Court, and is prepared at any time while in the custody of such officer or at any stage of the proceeding before such Court to give bail, such person shall be released on bail:

> Provided that such officer or Court, if he or it thinks fit, may, instead of taking bail from such person, discharge him on his executing a bond without sureties for his appearance as hereinafter provided:

---

crimes. For more, see http://cbi.nic.in/aboutus/manuals/Chapter_18.pdf (accessed on 20 March 2017).

[8] Ibid.

Provided further that nothing in this section shall be deemed to affect the provisions of sub-section (3) of section 116 or section 446A.[9]

Prosecution and Trial

Prosecution and trial of cases of sexual offences against children may be categorized into two groups for the purpose of this chapter: (i) cases where offenders are juveniles and (ii) cases where offenders are adults. The issues are broadly discussed as follows:

(i) **Prosecution and trial of cases where offenders are juveniles:** Once the juvenile is apprehended by the designated police officer, he must be produced before the nearest JJB within 24 hours of apprehension. While the POCSO Act under Chapter VII, S.28 has created special courts to try the cases of sexual offences of children exclusively, S.34(1) of the POCSO Act shifts the responsibility of trying the cases of juveniles to the JJBs. Hence in such cases, JJBs constituted under S.4 of the JJ Act, 2015, steps in the shoes of special courts as designated by the POCSO Act. However, as S.8(2) of the POCO Act states, 'the powers conferred on the Board by or under this Act may also be exercised by the High Court and the Children's Court, when the proceedings come before them under section 19 or in appeal, revision or otherwise'.

When the juvenile is produced before the Board, the latter must hold inquiry under S.14 of the JJ Act, 2015 regarding the (i) gravity of the nature of the case to understand whether it is a heinous crime, serious crime or a petty crime, (ii) the mental maturity of the juvenile in case he/she is above 16 but under the

---

[9] S.436(ii), however, states:

Notwithstanding anything contained in sub-section (1), where a person has failed to comply with the conditions of the bail-bond as regards the time and place of attendance, the Court may refuse to release him on bail, when on a subsequent occasion in the same case he appears before the Court or is brought in custody and any such refusal shall be without prejudice to the powers of the Court to call upon any person bound by such bond to pay the penalty thereof under section 446.

age of 18 (S.15 of the JJ Act, 2015) and (iii) the ascertaining of the age of the juvenile in case he appears to be above 18 (S.94(2) of the JJ Act, 2015, (presumption and determination of age)). Even if the person apprehended has crossed the age of 18, but produced before the JJB or the special court for offences committed by him when he was a juvenile, the prosecution and trial must be carried on as if he was still less than 18 years of age. However, after the initial inquiry, if the Board is satisfied that the juvenile has not committed heinous offence or is eligible to be released on bail, the first priority of the Board should be to release such juvenile on bail with or without surety (S.18 of the JJ Act, 2015). In cases where procedure for bail needs to be delayed due to various reasons, including further inquiry and production of social inquiry reports, the Board must send the juvenile to the remand home, namely the observation home (S.39(2) of the JJ Act, 2015) and make sure that the juvenile is treated with care and protection based on the principles stated in S.3 of the JJ Act, 2015. But it must be noted that the bail for the juvenile in certain cases of heinous or serious nature may not be given on the date of the production of the juvenile before the Board itself. The Madras High Court (Madurai bench) in the case of Ajith Kumar & Others v. State represented by Inspector of Police & Others, 2016[10] considered the application under S.12 of the JJ Act, 2015[11] and opined as follows:

---

[10] Crl. O.P.(MD) Nos. 1785, 1941, 2073, 2047 and 2224 of 2016.
[11] S.12 of the JJ Act, 2015 states:

(1) When any person, who is apparently a child and is alleged to have committed a bailable or non-bailable offence, is apprehended or detained by the police or appears or brought before a Board, such person shall, notwithstanding anything contained in the Code of Criminal Procedure, 1973 or any law for the time being in force, be released on bail with or without surety or placed under the supervision of a probation officer or under the care of any fit person: Provided that such person shall not be so released if there appears reasonable grounds for believing that the release is likely to bring that person into association with any known criminal or expose the said person to moral, physical or psychological danger or the person's release would defeat the ends of justice, and the Board shall record the reasons for denying the bail and circumstances that led to such a decision.

From the above, it is clear that a juvenile in conflict with law is statutorily entitled to bail, even though he is involved in a non-bailable offence. The Juvenile Justice Boards in Tamil Nadu do not mechanically refuse bail in all the cases. In serious offences like attempt to murder, murder, etc., there is every possibility of the victim party retaliating and that may expose the juvenile to 'moral, physical or psychological danger'.... Whether in a given case, the juvenile in conflict with law will be exposed to 'moral, physical or psychological danger' is a fact that can be assessed only by the Juvenile Justice Board, where members are trained to gauge the situation. Therefore, this Court should not give a blanket order in all the cases to the Juvenile Justice Board to release the juvenile in conflict with law on bail on the very same day of his production. Such direction will go contrary to the mandates of Section 12(1) of the Old Act as well as New Act. No direction under Section 482 of the Code can be given contrary to the express statutory provisions under a Special Act.

This author feels that the Madras High Court had taken a very matured decision in this regard because the nature of the crime committed by the accused showed that he had passed derogatory comments about women of another community, which may have led to communal violence. Also, the court did not want to infringe into the jurisdiction of the JJB.

However, the proceedings of trial and prosecution of the JJB post releasing the juvenile on bail, must proceed according to Chapter VIII of the POCSO Act (Proceedings and Powers

---

(2) When such person having been apprehended is not released on bail under sub-section (1) by the officer-in-charge of the police station, such officer shall cause the person to be kept only in an observation home in such manner as may be prescribed until the person can be brought before a Board.

(3) When such person is not released on bail under sub-section (1) by the Board, it shall make an order sending him to an observation home or a place of safety, as the case may be, for such period during the pendency of the inquiry regarding the person, as may be specified in the order.

(4) When a child in conflict with law is unable to fulfil the conditions of bail order within seven days of the bail order, such child shall be produced before the Board for modification of the conditions of bail.

of Special Courts and Recording of Evidence), which is commonly discussed under the next heading. But keeping in view the presence of juveniles as offenders, the Board must also follow procedures of fast and speedy inquiry as has been stated under S.14 of the JJ Act, 2015 (Inquiry by Board Regarding Child in Conflict with Law). Further, the JJ Act, 2015 provides special attention to juveniles above 16 years of age, who may have committed heinous or serious crimes. According to S.15 of the JJ Act, 2015, the Board shall conduct a preliminary assessment for knowing his mental and physical capacity towards committing the crime and understanding the consequences thereof. It needs to be remembered that such inquiry should not be confused as trial.[12] Once the board is satisfied that the juvenile can be tried by the Board, the trial must be conducted as any other trial in summons cases (S.15(2) of the JJ Act, 2015). In such cases and in all other cases where juvenile offenders are involved, the Board may either release him on probation, or may order for therapeutic counselling for him, or may order to put him in special home in special cases. But if the juvenile is proved to be mentally matured enough to understand the consequences of the offence, he must be tried by the children's court as per S.19 of the JJ Act, 2015. In such case, if the children's court is of opinion that the juvenile needs to be tried as adult, then he must be sent to a place of care and safety for three years[13] and on reaching the age of 21, he must

---

[12] See Explanation of S.15 of JJ Act, 2015.

[13] S.18(1)(g) of the JJ Act, 2015 states:

(1) Where a Board is satisfied on inquiry that a child irrespective of age has committed a petty offence, or a serious offence, or a child below the age of sixteen years has committed a heinous offence, then, notwithstanding anything contrary contained in any other law for the time being in force, and based on the nature of offence, specific need for supervision or intervention, circumstances as brought out in the social investigation report and past conduct of the child, the Board may, if it so thinks fit...direct the child to be sent to a special home, for such period, not exceeding three years, as it thinks fit, for providing reformative services including education, skill development, counselling, behaviour modification therapy, and psychiatric support during the period of stay in the special home: Provided that if the conduct and behaviour of the child has been such

be shifted to regular jail (Ss.19(3) and 20 of the JJ Act, 2015). However, throughout the prosecution and trial. the juvenile must be given opportunity to be heard, to avail legal aid and under no circumstances the victim child should be brought in direct contact with the juvenile in any stage of the trial even if it is necessary for identification.

(ii) **Prosecution and trial where offenders are adults:** Unlike prosecution and trial of cases for juvenile offenders, when the offenders are adults, the prosecution and trial need to proceed in designated Special Courts meant to try cases within the meaning of POCSO Act. In this connection, a detailed discussion on the Special Courts within the meaning of Chapters VII and VIII of the POCSO Act is given here:

Special Court: The POCSO Act was created with a special aim to create a specific set of court system for a speedy disposal of sexual offences against children. S.28 of the POCSO Act provides for setting up a Special Court in each district, which would be a court of session by nature.[14] Proviso to this section further states:

> Provided that if a Court of Session is notified as a children's court under the Commissions for Protection of Child Rights Act, 2005 (4 of 2006), or a Special Court designated for similar purposes under any other law for the time being in force, then, such Court shall be deemed to be a Special Court under this section.

Further, S.28(2 and 3) also speaks about the scope of the courts by stating that the Special Court shall not only be eligible to try the offences under the POCSO Act but also other offences with which the offender may have been charged with in the same trial. It further says that in case the offender is charged with offences relating to cybercrime targeting children, the Special Court shall also have the jurisdiction to try offences under S.67B of the IT

---

that, it would not be in the child's interest, or in the interest of other children housed in a special home, the Board may send such child to the place of safety.

[14] Also see Unknown v. Dhananjoy Singh @ Motu & Anr., C.R.R. No. 2562 of 2014, in the High Court at Calcutta, on 8 April 2015.

Act in so far as it relates to obscene, sexually explicit publication, production, distribution of contents depicting children in any act, conduct or manner or facilitating child abuse online. For conducting the prosecution and trial, Special Courts shall follow CrPC in general with special focus to the POCSO Act. The POCSO Act further states that each Special Court shall have a special public prosecutor within the meaning of CrPC, who should be a lawyer of not less than 7 years of experience.[15]

The prosecution in Special Courts specially meant for cases under the POCSO Act must follow the regular prosecution and trial procedure as mentioned in the CrPC. But considering the punishments, it should be understood that the Special Courts have to follow the procedures of trials in warrant cases. While speaking about the powers of the Special Court, the Act has further stated that the Special Court has the power to assume that a person has in reality committed or abetted or attempted to commit the offence if an accused is prosecuted for committing, abetting or attempting to commit any offence under the POCSO Act unless it is proved contrarily (S.29). However, this does not mean that the so prosecuted would not have the right to defend. In such cases, the accused would have all the rights generally available to any accused in criminal cases as has been conferred under the Constitution and the CrPC. Further, the Special Court has the power to presume the existence of culpable mental state on the part of the accused, which includes intention, motive, knowledge of a fact and the reason to believe in or reason to believe a fact (S.30 of the POCSO Act). The provision further states that even if the court shall presume the existence of the culpable mental state, the accused may have the defence to disprove the existence of culpable mental state. In this regard mention must be made of the recent amendments made in the JJ Act, 2015. As has been stated in the aforementioned paragraph, in case the accused is a juvenile above the age of 16 years and he/she is charged with heinous offence, the JJ Board has the primary power to assess the

---

[15] P. Shanmugavel Raj v. State, Criminal Revision Case (MD) No. 743 of 2013 and M.P. (MD) Nos. 1 and 2 of 2013.

mental status of the accused and provide its opinion on the issue as whether the said accused possess enough mental maturity. The Special Court can exercise its powers to presume existence of culpable intentions if the JJB opines that the juvenile possess such mental status. Further, S.30(2) also says that a fact is said to be 'proved' when the Special Court believes it to exist beyond reasonable doubt and not merely on proof of the existence on preponderance of probability. Further, the Special Courts may take cognizance of offence without the accused being committed to trial upon receiving a complaint of facts which constitute such offence or upon receiving a police report (S.33(1) of the POCSO Act). The prosecutorial procedures regarding cross examination, chief examination and the like by the special prosecutor or the counsel appearing for the child must be conducted through the Special Court itself and no direct question can be put to the victim child. The court should also ensure that the environment of the court should be child friendly. The child should be given frequent breaks within the trial, especially the questioning session, and no aggressive question should be asked to the child. Further, the child should be allowed to be accompanied by adults and should also be allowed to be represented by lawyer. He/she should be allowed to use the services of interpreter as well. The child in no case should be made to see the accused, but mechanism should be used so that the accused can hear the statement of the child and communicate with his/her lawyer. Also, for this purpose, the court can also arrange for single mirror video conferencing system or may use curtain to protect the identity of the child and his/her identity should be protected unless there is a specific reason for publishing the identity (S.36 of the POCSO Act). The Special Court must also ensure that the course of examining the child must be completed within the maximum period of one month since the date the court takes cognizance of the case and any delay in such case must be recorded by the court. The trials must be conducted in camera and only if the court is of opinion that the child victim should be examined in any place other than the court, it may issue for a commission for this purpose and proceed with examination in the said place (S.38 of the POCSO

Act). The Special Court must also ensure that the full trial must be completed within one year (S.35(2) of the POCSO Act). In case the child is put up for safer custody in any special care home through the CWC, the latter should ensure that the child can avail all sorts of help and support person to attend the court, know about the proceedings and again get back to safe custody. The support person[16] and the SJPU must also periodically inform the child about the pre- and post-trial developments of the case and should also inform the child and his/her parents or caregivers about the final order and compensation if any (S.12 of the POCSO Rules, 2012) that may be prescribed to the child by the Special Court (S.33(8) of the POCSO Act).[17] However, such order for compensation must be executed through the District Legal Services Authority.

---

[16] S.2(f) of the POCSO Rules, 2007 defines 'support person' as a person assigned by a CWC, in accordance with Subrule (8) of Rule 4, to render assistance to the child through the process of investigation and trial, or any other person assisting the child in the pre-trial or trial process in respect of an offence under the Act.

[17] For example, see Sc No: 135/13 State v. Kapil Tyagi, FIR No. 43/13, ID No. 02405R0-120342013, where the court granted compensation for ₹50,000 to the victim to provide restorative and compensatory justice. The court also ordered that the learned Secretary, Delhi State Legal Services Authority (DSLSA), North District, New Delhi shall ensure that the said amount is given to the parents of the victim within one month on receipt of this order and shall further ensure that the said amount is disbursed in such a manner that the same be used for welfare and rehabilitation of the victim.

Part IV

Sentencing and Rehabilitation

CHAPTER 10

Sentencing, Rehabilitation and Social Reintegration of Children

Introduction

One of the main objectives of the POCSO Act had been to recognize every minute sexual offences done to the children and penalize the same to achieve the aims laid down by UN CRC, 1989 and the Optional Protocol to the CRC on the Sale of Children, Child Prostitution and Child Pornography. Laws can be retributive,[1]

---

[1] Retributive justice theory considers that the best response for crime is proportionate punishment. It is more offender oriented whereby it aims to teach the offender about his mistakes by way of punishments. For more details, see Neil Vidmar, 'Retributive Justice: Its Social Context', in *The Justice Motive in Everyday Life*, eds. M. Ross and D. T. Miller (Cambridge University Press, 2001). Available at: https://ssrn.com/abstract=293782 or http://dx.doi.org/10.2139/ssrn.293782 (accessed on 15 June 2016).

restorative[2] or therapeutic.[3] When law is used as a tool to prevent social evils like sexual abuse of children, it must be framed to meet the needs of the victim. The first responsibility of the law should be to prevent the abuser to be in contact with the victim again may be during his/her lifetime to safeguard the child physically and emotionally. Further, the law should also aim to establish strict precedence to prevent such abuse by sentences which would be retributive but at the same time beneficial for the victim. Also, since sexual abuse on female children may result in pregnancy and unwanted motherhood, the aim of the law should be to provide welfare measures to tackle these problems. But at the same time when the offenders are young offenders, law cannot use the same penology to restrict certain basic fundamental rights for such children forever. In such cases the aim of the law should be more correctional in nature and bring the child offender to an understanding as to why and how such acts may be deterrent not only for the victim but also for the offender himself. In this chapter, these issues are discussed broadly.

Penology for Sexual Abuse of Children

Prior to the introduction of POCSO Act, punishment for sexual abuses against children were awarded mainly on the basis of selected

---

[2] Restorative justice theory considers that the crime done to individuals or groups, etc. necessarily brings obligations and liabilities of the offender to correct the harm through restorative mediation process. It is more victim oriented compared to retributive justice theory. For more details, see H. Zeher, *The Little Book of Restorative Justice* (Vermont: Good Books, 2002).

[3] Therapeutic jurisprudence sees how the positive use of laws may heal the wrong. As Wexler and Winick explained, therapeutic Jurisprudence is 'an interdisciplinary approach to legal scholarship that has a law reform agenda, therapeutic jurisprudence seeks to assess the therapeutic and counter-therapeutic consequences of the law and how it is applied as well as to increase the former and diminish the latter. It is an approach to the law that uses the tools of the behavioural sciences to assess the law's therapeutic effects and, when consistent with other important legal values, to reshape law and legal processes in ways that can improve the psychological functioning and emotional wellbeing of the individuals affected.' See David B. Wexler and Bruce J. Winick, 'Therapeutic Jurisprudence', in *Principles of Addiction Medicine* (4th ed.). Available at: http://ssrn.com/abstract=1101507

provisions of Indian Penal Code, which included rape (S.375 read with S.376), procuration of minor girls (S.366A), unnatural offences (S.377) and also through provisions such as ITPA, 1986 which was created to tackle trafficking of children for prostitution, etc. Other sorts of non-penetrative sexual abuse had been dealt with through traditional IPC provisions, which were not age specific.[4] The highest penalty prescribed under these provisions was capital punishment for rape and also when it resulted in the death of the victim (S.376A, IPC).[5] With the introduction of the POCSO Act, attempt was made to bring all sorts of sexual abuses against children under one legal provision and provide uniform punishment to all offences and offenders irrespective of gender for any kinds of sexual abuse targeting children of any gender. Punishment under the POCSO Act can be grouped under three heads according to the nature of the crimes: (i) punishment for heinous crimes, (ii) punishment for serious crimes and (iii) punishment for petty crimes.[6] As such, these punishments differ according to the period of jail terms, the pecuniary amount that the accused may have to pay and the rigorousness of the jail term. But it may further be noted that the POCSO Act is not restrictive to enlarging the gravity of punishment. For example, S.42 of the POCSO Act states:

> Where an act or omission constitute an offence punishable under this Act and also under any other law for the time being in force, then notwithstanding anything contained in any law for the time being in force, the offender found guilty of such offence, shall be liable to punishment only under such law or this Act, as provides for punishment which is greater in degree.

Keeping this in mind, it may be seen that the POCSO Act prescribes punishment for not less than seven years of imprisonment which may extend to life imprisonment under S.4 for penetrative sexual assault. This provision also provides for paying of the fine, even though the amount of the fine is not mentioned under this section or in any section in POCSO Act. Further, S.6 of the POCSO Act also pronounces

---

[4] These have been discussed in previous chapters of this book.

[5] See Chapter 3, note 13.

[6] For the category of such crimes, see Table 8.1 in Chapter 8.

punishment to the maximum level of life imprisonment and also fine in case of aggravated sexual offence, which may or may not result in death or grievous harm to the child. In such case, if the offender is also charged with provision for murder under S.302 or S.376 of the IPC for rape which prescribes punishment for death due to the gravity of nature of the crime, the special court should accept the punishments pronounced under the latter rather than the former. Similarly, if an accused is charged with provisions from IT Act, 2000 (amended in 2008), especially S.67B (punishment for publishing or transmitting materials depicting children in sexually explicit acts and the like) and also under any of the provisions under S.14 of the POCSO Act (punishment for using children for pornographic purposes), then in that case the court must consider the amount of fine (₹10 lakhs) as well as heavier punishment, whichever may be beneficial for the restoration of justice. The punishments for the offences within the meaning of POCSO Act, as prescribed under the POCSO Act, is provided in Table 10.1 in comparison with other punishments for offences of sexual abuse targeting women in general and also children. Table 10.1 may be used to understand which provision may be pulled in by the courts to provide heavier punishments to the accused.

It must also be remembered that right to bail is an inherent right for all accused persons, especially for cases which are made as bailable.[7] As has been stated earlier in the book, no provision in POCSO Act clarifies which offences are bailable and which are non-bailable. For this, one needs to look into the First Schedule of the CrPC depending upon the time limit of the punishments. However, bail in cases of bailable offences must be given only after scrutinizing the whole case properly. However, in no case, the courts can take any decision which may add more insult to the injury of the child victim. In this connection mention must be made of the judgement of Madras High Court where the court ordered the rapist to mediate the crime of rape of a minor to compensate for the social taboo that she had to bear for the rape.[8] Such sorts of decisions may not only violate the rights of

---

[7] Rasiklal v. Kishore, 2009, 4 SCC 446.

[8] V. Mohan v. State Represented by Inspector, All Women Police Station, Vridhachalam, Cuddalore District, M.P. No. 2 of 2014 in Crl. A no. 402 of

Table 10.1 Punishments for Several Offences Under the POCSO Act, IT Act and IPC

Penetrative sexual offence	Minimum 7 years to maximum life term of imprisonment and fine under S.4 of the POCSO Act. Rigorous imprisonment for minimum 10 years to maximum life imprisonment and fine under S.6 of the POCSO Act	Minimum 7 years and maximum life imprisonment and fine (S.376(1), IPC) Minimum rigorous imprisonment for 10 years to maximum life imprisonment and fine (S.376(2), IPC) Minimum 20 years or life imprisonment or capital punishment under S.376A, IPC Minimum 2 years to maximum 7 years and fine under S.376B, IPC Minimum rigorous imprisonment for 5 years to maximum 10 years and fine under S.376C, IPC Minimum 20 years and maximum life imprisonment and fine under S.376D, IPC Life imprisonment or with death under S.376E, IPC	–
Non-penetrative sexual assault	Minimum 3 years and maximum 5 years with fine under S.8 of the POCSO Act Minimum 5 years and maximum 7 years under S.10 of the POCSO Act	Minimum 2 years and fine under S.354, IPC Minimum 3 years and maximum 7 years and fine under S.354B, IPC	Maximum life imprisonment, minimum 10 years of imprisonment with fine under S.377, IPC

(Continued)

Table 10.1 (Continued)

Stalking	Maximum 3 years and fine under S.11 of the POCSO Act	Maximum 3 years of imprisonment and fine under S.354D, IPC for the first conviction and maximum 5 years for the second conviction	–
Sexual harassment	Ditto	Maximum 3 years with rigorous imprisonment or fine or both under S.354A(I, II, III), IPC	–
Voyeurism	No specific mention[a]	Minimum 3 years and maximum 5 years and fine under S.354C, IPC	–
Using children for pornographic purposes	Minimum 5 years to life imprisonment in certain cases under S.14 of the POCSO Act	–	Maximum 5 years of imprisonment with fine of ₹10 lakhs in the first conviction and maximum 7 years of imprisonment with ₹10 lakhs fine under S.67B of the IT Act, 2000 (amended in 2008)
Showing pornographic images	Maximum 3 years of imprisonment and fine under S.12 of the POCSO Act	Maximum 3 years with rigorous imprisonment or fine or both under S.354(iii), IPC	
Storing child porn images for commercial purposes	Maximum 3 years of imprisonment or fine or both under S.15 of the POCSO Act		

Source: Author.

[a] For details about how such cases may be dealt with for offences against children, see Chapter 5 of this book.

the child for a fair principles of law, it may also turn extremely traumatizing for the child as well. The court must also show leniency for the welfare of the victim. Consider the recent decision of the Gujarat High Court allowing a rape victim to terminate 24-weeks pregnancy.[9] Such decisions may not only allow the victims to heal physically but may also help the victim to come out of the trauma.

The sentencing and bail policy may be different for the offenders who are minors.[10] In such cases, the provisions of JJ Act, 2015 and the JJ Act rules must be followed. Further, the sentencing must also include therapeutic sentences as has been mentioned in the JJ Act.[11] These may include community services such as cleaning public places, counselling and correctional teachings which may help to deviate the minds from such mental status. In this regard, it must be mentioned that juvenile offenders must be encouraged to continue their schooling and vocational courses in order to allow them to mix with general children, though with strict monitoring. As the Madurai bench of the Madras High Court emphasized in the case mentioned previously, children must be taught to respect women as well as fellow human beings first. The correctional administration in the juvenile observation homes must be framed keeping this in mind. Further, neither the POCSO Act nor the JJ Act nor the IT Act speaks anything about handling juvenile offenders of cybercrimes targeting women and children. This author feels that such children must also be treated in a manner similar to that of other juvenile offenders who may have been sentenced for other sorts of sexual harassment. IT Act, 2000 (amended in 2008) prescribes for heavy pecuniary fines for digital crimes and it is expected that the parents pay the fine, which actually encourages

---

2014. Also see, 'Madras HC Passes Order Permitting Person Convicted of Rape of a Minor to Settle the Matter Through Mediation', *Live Law*, 24 June 2015. Available at: http://www.livelaw.in/madras-hc-passes-order-permitting-person-convicted-of-rape-of-a-minor-to-settle-the-matter-through-mediation/ (accessed on 20 October 2016).

[9] See, for instance, Anju Cletus, 'Gujarat HC Allows Rape Victim to Terminate 24-week Pregnancy', *Live Law*, 23 February 2016. Available at: http://www.livelaw.in/gujarat-hc-allows-rape-victim-to-terminate-24-week-pregnancy/

[10] Refer to Chapter 9 for a detailed discussion on this.

[11] Ibid.

the children to commit more such crimes thinking that the parents would be supportive every time such offences are committed. This attitude must be changed.

Rehabilitation and Social Reintegration of Victim Children

Special courts under POCSO Act must ensure rehabilitation and social reintegration as a part of sentencing while disposing off the cases. The POCSO Act Rules and the JJ Act and the Rules emphasize upon this issue in various segments of the provisions.[12] This restorative approach of the laws is needed for two main reasons: (a) for the physical and mental well-being of the victim and (b) for meeting the financial needs of the victim. Any sexual assault may have deep impact on the child both physically and emotionally. As has been categorized by the POCSO Act, sexual offences may be divided into two groups: those which are inflicted by strangers and those which are inflicted by people on whom the child trusts. In the former, there is every possibility that the child may not only suffer from physical and emotional trauma, the family may be ostracized fearing taboo. In the second case, the victim may have to live in constant fear and pressure from the abuser, who also plays the role of caregiver. It is for this reason that the law prescribes retributive as well as therapeutic sentences for the abuser and the victim. The sentence should be retributive because the sentence shall punish the abuser and make him/her to pay for his mistakes which could be used for victim compensation; the sentence should also be therapeutic because the immediate rescue and shifting of the victim from the custody of the abuser may provide better healing for the victim. The law further ensures that no information about the victim should be published outside.

This further enhances the confidence of the victim to fight the crime without any victim blaming. But the situation may in reality be very different with the advancement of digital communication technology where many people may feel circulating rape videos or the

---

[12] See earlier chapters of this book.

images of the incidence may actually engage people positively. This author feels that this is absolutely a wrong idea and this must also be brought under the purview of privacy provisions under the POCSO Act. It may be pertinent to note that in India, like the United States or the United Kingdom, 'no contact orders', are still not popular for crimes of stalking or sexual abuse.[13] The courts must consider this while sentencing. Further, while the victims are rescued and sent to shelters or homes, possibilities must also be explored for foster care in case the assaulter lives in the family itself and the child needs homely atmosphere to come out of the trauma. S.2(29) of the JJ Act, 2015 defines foster care as placement of a child, by the committee for the purpose of alternate care in the domestic environment of a family, other than the child's biological family, that has been selected, qualified, approved and supervised for providing such care. The CWC can take such decisions for the welfare of children. Such families are chosen by the District Child Protection Unit after careful perusal of the social enquiry records of the family (S.44 of the JJ Act, 2015).

This author feels that only when sentencing and social reintegration scenario is used in a more focused way, the victims may be encouraged and motivated to report the crimes more which, in return, may help stop the growth rate of the crimes.

[13] D. Halder, 'Cyber Stalking Victimisation of Women: Evaluating the Effectiveness of Current Laws in India from Restorative Justice and Therapeutic in Jurisprudential Perspectives', *Temida* 13, no. 3–4 (2015), str. 103–130.

Epilogue

CHAPTER 11

Conclusion

This book discusses about child sexual abuse and the new developments in socio-legal understanding regarding this in India. The concept of child sexual abuse cannot be restricted to any specific form or
within specific gender (e.g., 'males are always perpetrators and females
are always victims'). The discussions on child sexual abuse laws may
however be divided into three periods, namely, (i) pre-POCSO Act,
(ii) POCSO Act and (iii) post-Independent Thought v. Union of
India judgement, which pronounced sexual intercourse with child
bride as rape. In the period earlier to POCSO Act, the understanding
regarding the gender of the victims and the perpetrators was extremely
narrow. The POCSO Act brought in a new understanding whereby
the Parliament recognized the rights of any child (irrespective of gender
and gender orientation) against sexual exploitation. The POCSO Act
also broadened the concept of the gender of offender irrespective
of age. Simultaneously, JJ (Amendment) Act, 2015 broadened the
understanding regarding dealing with matured teens who may have
committed heinous crimes along with other developments in the arena
of management of juvenile delinquency. POCSO Act also categorized
sexual offences targeting children depending upon the nature of the
same. the new developments also ensured that the child sexual abuse
cases would be looked after by a completely revised set of institution
consisting of the judicial officers, lawyers, and people including social

activists, health workers, child psychologists and from school teaching fraternity, who may effectively communicate with victim children as well as juvenile perpetrators. These developments have tremendously affected the reporting of crimes to designated authorities. As such, the new laws have simplified the reporting mechanism whereby the child may him/herself contact the helpline, the police or the CWC directly to report about sexual exploitation. The Act also ensures that not only the child but also the parents, any other relative or well-wishers who may wish to lodge a report of sexual exploitation of the child may be properly verified and may avail right to privacy to not only to protect the child, but also to protect him/herself from any sort of vengeance from the perpetrator. But in spite of such developments, several recent incidences may show that the new laws may have failed to prevent the escalation of crime statistics targeting children.[1] What is the cause for such steep escalation of the numbers of the offences then?

It is obvious that new or amended laws cannot be 100 per cent successful in changing the social outlook and create fear in the minds of people regarding the consequences of offences that may be committed by them. In the Independent Thought case (criminalizing child marital rape), Justice Madan B. Lokur had very rightly observed that in spite of prevailing laws criminalizing child marriages, India still has thousands of young child brides. They are subjected to sexual victimization almost on a daily basis which not only hampers their physical health but also hampers their mental health. This is sexual victimization of girl children within the family system. But there are also umpteen numbers of examples of sexual victimization of girls and boys within the family as well as within institutions including schools, hostels and also in public places. Schools and NGOs along with the government have taken certain child-friendly measures to sensitize children to understand what is sexual touch and how to report it with the help of the caregivers, parents or through digital technology. But

---

[1] This is evident from the latest statistics regarding child sexual abuse provided in the pp. 4–5 in 'Crime in India 2016 Statistics'. Available at: http://ncrb.nic.in/StatPublications/CII/CII2016/Press%20release-Crime%20in%20India%202016.pdf (accessed on 7 December 2017).

as Wexler[2] pointed out, sex offenders in majority of cases may not their admit their guilt. According to him:

> Sex offenders usually are extremely unwilling to admit guilt, even when the state's evidence is impressive, and therefore, they often seek to plead 'no contest', or nolo contendere. A nolo plea permits the sex offender to accept the consequences of a conviction without going to trial and without admitting guilt.[3]

Noticeably, in India, plea bargaining has been introduced in 2006 vide introducing S.265A-L, CrPC and the law specifically excludes plea bargaining for the cases targeting women and children below 14 years of age and for offence where punishment includes jail term for a period below 7 years. POCSO Act prescribes punishment for more than seven years in sexual assaults. However, the punishment prescribed for offences of sexual harassment including using the child for pornographic purposes, etc., have been categorized as offences with lesser punishments. While in the earlier cases plea bargaining is automatically not applicable, in later cases, the accused can use plea bargaining if the victim is above 14 years of age. But in all cases, the onus lies on the criminal justice machinery to win confidence of the child victims and their parents so that they can cooperate with the criminal justice machinery and they are refrained from becoming perpetrators themselves. This book there suggests to include therapeutic jurisprudential approach in dealing with child sexual abuse cases. Therapeutic jurisprudence suggests that agents of law including lawyers, judges and in certain cases the police may act as therapeutic agents to heal the pain of the crime by effectively understanding the nature of the crime, efficiently carrying on investigation and prosecution and above all, through proper dialogue and communication with the victim and the offender.[4] This book has shown that both POCSO Act and

---

[2] See David Wexler, 'Therapeutic Jurisprudence and the Criminal Courts', *William & Mary Law Review* 35, no. 1(1993): 285. Available at: http://scholarship.law.wm.edu/cgi/viewcontent.cgi?article=1781&context=wmlr (accessed on 12 November 2017).

[3] Ibid.

[4] Ibid.

the JJ Act, 2015 and its rules to a certain extent carry the therapeutic jurisprudential approach.

However, this book also suggests that criminal justice machinery especially the courts, the child welfare committees and the JJB officials should also take therapeutic jurisprudential approach while dealing with child sexual abuse. This author has observed that in many occasions CWC members suggest children including older children to turn more devotional to shun the mentality of 'eloping' with 'boyfriends' or to refrain from watching sexually explicit online contents that may be conveyed to them or shown to them by their peers or groomers, or to refrain from juvenile delinquency including sexually harassing peers, classmates, female teachers, older girls and so on. Further, both CWC and JJB members may pass several insulting or teasing remarks to the victims blaming their roles in the victimization process and also to the juvenile offenders. Also, in several cities CWC, JJB and special courts may not even have proper infrastructure to speak with the child victims or juvenile offenders *in camera*. Child victims and their parents may feel withdrawn specifically for this very reason. This makes the whole system anti-therapeutic. It is therefore suggested that more training and education of the stakeholders including the CWC members, JJB members, judges and lawyers and police personnel should be held under proper expert guidance. Further, the infrastructure must also be developed to make the whole system child friendly. The child victims should be sensitized more about reporting mechanisms. In this regard, the government, the courts and the stakeholders may also consider applying innovative methods to communicate with the child victims to know the exact facts; for example, this author suggested the use of creative dance movements that can be shown to young children to communicate with them. Such dance movements may indicate which body parts were touched or violated or who did it[5] and may be shown by the trained volunteers who may be considered as special educators or

---

[5] D. Halder and S. Gupta, 'Multifaceted Dance Forms as Therapy for Child Victims of Sexual Abuse: A Therapeutic Jurisprudential Approach'. Paper presented at the 6th International and 10th Biennial Conference of the Indian Society of Victimology, 23–25 February 2017, at Nirma University, Ahmedabad, organized by the Institute of Law, Nirma University, Ahmedabad.

interpreters within the meaning of S.38 of the POCSO Act.[6] Similarly, consideration may also be made of the use of dolls to not only to pacify young victims, but also to help them express which body parts were violated and whether any of the body parts of the harassers was/were inserted into the vagina of the victim.[7] It is hoped that if the courts, lawyers, police and other stakeholders including the government consider the suggestions made earlier; the aims, objectives and optional protocols of CRC as well as those of the POCSO Act and the JJ Act, 2015 may be reached. It is to be noted that the recent Criminal Law Amendment ordinance 2018 has considerably amended laws prescribing punishment for rape, especially of minors. As per this ordinance, S.376AB has been introduced to IPC to enhance punishment for rape of minors of upto 16 years of age to rigorous life imprisonment for 20 years which is extendable to life or death penalty under certain circumstances. Under this provision, convicted person is also liable for fine to meet the medical and rehabilitation expenses of the victim. The ordinance also mentions that in case of rape and gang rape of children below 12 years, the convicted may also be awarded death sentence. While amending POCSO Act, this ordinance has stated that for all such offences, the offence which is higher between POCSO Act and IPC should apply. While the author feels that inclusion of fine in the sentence for the welfare of the victim could make the law therapeutic in nature, it must be noted that proper awareness and implementation of the law is extremely necessary to make it a welfare law.

[6] S.38 of the POCSO Act speaks about assistance of an interpreter or expert while recording evidence of child and states:

(1) Wherever necessary, the Court may take the assistance of a translator or interpreter having such qualifications, experience and on payment of such fees as may be prescribed, while recording the evidence of the child. (2) If a child has a mental or physical disability, the Special Court may take the assistance of a special educator or any person familiar with the manner of communication of the child or an expert in that field, having such qualifications, experience and on payment of such fees as may be prescribed to record the evidence of the child.

[7] For example, see PTI, '5-year-old Explains Sexual Assault on Her Through Barbie Doll', *The Indian Express*, 16 June 2017. Available at: http://www.newindianexpress.com/nation/2017/jun/16/5-year-old-explains-sexual-assault-on-her-through-barbie-doll-1617469.html (accessed on 12 September 2017).

Index

About the Author

Debarati Halder is Professor and Head at the Centre for Research on Law and Policy in United World School of Law, Gandhinagar, Gujarat. She is honorary managing director of the Centre for Cyber Victim Counselling (CCVC), India. She is the founder secretary of South Asian Society of Criminology and Victimology. She received her LLB from the University of Calcutta and her Master's Degree in International and Constitutional Law from the University of Madras and PhD degree from the National Law School of India University (NLSIU), Bengaluru.

Dr Halder has published three books, two authored books and an edited book, and many articles in international peer-reviewed journals including the *British Journal of Criminology*, *Journal of Law and Religion*, *Annals in Criminology*, *Victims and Offenders* and *Temida*. She served as resource person for many government and non-government organizations. She has been on the Panel Advocate to Child Welfare Committee, Juvenile Justice Board and Juvenile Home at Tirunelveli, Tamil Nadu. She has been invited as an expert resource person and consultant for UNICEF's project on state of children: *Digital World of Children and Cyber Security Handbook*. Dr Halder has served as vice-president for kids and teens division and internet safety advocate for Working to Halt Online Abuse (WHOA) from 2008 to 2015.

Other titles in this series:

Law of Business Contracts in India, Sairam Bhat (ed.)

Water and the Laws in India, Ramaswamy R. Iyer (ed.)

Protection of Himalayan Biodiversity: International Environmental Law and a Regional Legal Framework, Ananda Mohan Bhattarai

Social Justice and Labour Jurisprudence, Sharath Babu and Rashmi Shetty

Social Legislation of the East India Company: Public Justice versus Public Instruction, Nancy Gardner Cassels

Natural Resources Conservation Law, Sairam Bhat

Business and Human Rights, Manoj Kumar Sinha (ed.)

Crime and Justice in India, N. Prabha Unnithan (ed.)

In Custody: Law, Impunity and Prisoner Abuse in South Asia, Nitya Ramakrishnan

Law and Economics (Volume I: Theory and Volume II: Practice), Subhashis Gangopadhyay and V. Santhakumar (eds)

Separated and Divorced Women in India: Economic Rights and Entitlements, Kirti Singh

Women and Law: Critical Feminist Perspectives, Kalpana Kannabiran (ed.)

The Protection of Geographical Indications in India: A New Perspective on the French and European Experience, Delphine Marie-Vivien

Sports Law in India: Policy, Regulation and Commercialisation, Lovely Dasgupta and Shameek Sen (eds)

About the Author

Debarati Halder is Professor and Head at the Centre for Research on Law and Policy in United World School of Law, Gandhinagar, Gujarat. She is honorary managing director of the Centre for Cyber Victim Counselling (CCVC), India. She is the founder secretary of South Asian Society of Criminology and Victimology. She received her LLB from the University of Calcutta and her Master's Degree in International and Constitutional Law from the University of Madras and PhD degree from the National Law School of India University (NLSIU), Bengaluru.

Dr Halder has published three books, two authored books and an edited book, and many articles in international peer-reviewed journals including the *British Journal of Criminology, Journal of Law and Religion, Annals in Criminology, Victims and Offenders* and *Temida*. She served as resource person for many government and non-government organizations. She has been on the Panel Advocate to Child Welfare Committee, Juvenile Justice Board and Juvenile Home at Tirunelveli, Tamil Nadu. She has been invited as an expert resource person and consultant for UNICEF's project on state of children: *Digital World of Children and Cyber Security Handbook*. Dr Halder has served as vice-president for kids and teens division and internet safety advocate for Working to Halt Online Abuse (WHOA) from 2008 to 2015.

Other titles in this series:

SAGE was founded in 1965 by Sara Miller McCune to support the dissemination of usable knowledge by publishing innovative and high-quality research and teaching content. Today, we publish over 900 journals, including those of more than 400 learned societies, more than 800 new books per year, and a growing range of library products including archives, data, case studies, reports, and video. SAGE remains majority-owned by our founder, and after Sara's lifetime will become owned by a charitable trust that secures our continued independence.

Los Angeles | London | New Delhi | Singapore | Washington DC | Melbourne

WOMEN IN
SCIENCE AND
TECHNOLOGY

Thank you for choosing a SAGE product!
If you have any comment, observation or feedback,
I would like to personally hear from you.

Please write to me at **contactceo@sagepub.in**

Vivek Mehra, Managing Director and CEO, SAGE India.

WOMEN IN SCIENCE AND TECHNOLOGY

CONFRONTING INEQUALITIES

NAMRATA GUPTA

Los Angeles | London | New Delhi
Singapore | Washington DC | Melbourne

First published in 2020 by

SAGE Publications India Pvt Ltd
B1/I-1 Mohan Cooperative Industrial Area
Mathura Road, New Delhi 110 044, India
www.sagepub.in

SAGE Publications Inc
2455 Teller Road
Thousand Oaks, California 91320, USA

SAGE Publications Ltd
1 Oliver's Yard, 55 City Road
London EC1Y 1SP, United Kingdom

SAGE Publications Asia-Pacific Pte Ltd
18 Cross Street #10-10/11/12
China Square Central
Singapore 048423

Published by Vivek Mehra for SAGE Publications India Pvt Ltd. Typeset in 10.5/13 pt Berkeley by Zaza Eunice, Hosur, Tamil Nadu, India.

Library of Congress Cataloging-in-Publication Data Available

ISBN: 978-93-5328-748-1 (HB)

SAGE Team: Abhijit Baroi, Sandhya Gola, Madhurima Thapa and Rajinder Kaur

CONTENTS

DETAILED CONTENTS

FOREWORD

A grand natural experiment is about to take place as India plans to double its university student population and advance a significant number of its academic institutions to the front ranks of global metrics. Will this scale-up replicate and preserve the gender inequities in India's science, technology and innovation systems—relentlessly and precisely documented by Dr Namrata Gupta, the country's leading gender S&T analyst—or will it break with embedded unequal traditional practices, in science and society, and use an expansion moment to foreground women as equals, utilizing the talents of all genders, castes and regions?

Dr Gupta's ovular study goes beyond documenting a 'patrifocal' gender system (one that prevented her making an international conference visit, as an individual, not too many years ago) to lay out pathways of reform in institutions and culture to bring along recalcitrant individuals and break historic patterns of inequity. It will take leadership of committed individuals and enlightened institutions to create a 'virtual Gandhi' for gender equality, with India and South Africa showing the way as they did for non-violent regime change. In solidarity for 'gender satyagraha', I am delighted to invite you to be inspired by the perspicacious volume you are about to encounter.

Professor Henry Etzkowitz is the Founder and President of the International Triple Helix Institute. He is the co-author of *The Triple Helix* and *Athena Unbound: The Advancement of Women in Science and Technology*.

ACKNOWLEDGEMENTS

This book is a product of an academic journey that began with my M.Phil on the social history of higher education from the University of Delhi, followed by doctorate on women faculty in science and engineering institutes in 2002 from IIT Kanpur. Thereafter, projects funded by the Indian Council of Social Science Research (with affiliation to IIT Kanpur) helped me to carry out research studies on the issues facing women in S&T. I am thankful to my M.Phil dissertation supervisor Professor Aparna Basu for teaching me the ropes. I am particularly thankful to my doctoral thesis supervisor Professor A. K. Sharma for his constant appreciation and support for all my endeavours. I am immensely thankful to all the participants, particularly the scientists who spared their valuable time for my questions in my various research projects.

I am grateful to Professor Henry Etzkowitz for providing the Foreword for this book. Collaboration with him and his team on women in STEM at various times in my academic journey hitherto has been a great experience apart from being productive.

I would also like to thank SAGE Publications, New Delhi, particularly the commissioning editor Abhijit Baroi, production editor Sandhya Gola, and the editorial and design team for their painstaking editing, great cover and support throughout.

My parents' efforts and blessings, and sister Renu's loving support have laid the very foundation of this road to my academic journey.

I am thankful to my husband, Vinay, for believing in me and for his constant encouragement and motivation, and my daughters, Neha and Manya, for being understanding and patient with me during the writing of this book. They have been a constant source of inspiration to me.

Introduction
Context and Theoretical Overview

FOCUS AND PURPOSE

This work examines the position of women in S&T at various levels of education and in various professions. Women in S&T generally constitute an urban educated middle class in India aspiring for white-collar jobs. The book analyses how trends related to women's position in S&T education and professions reflect a gendered social normative structure typically upheld by this class and how gendered sociocultural norms are reproduced in behaviours and interactions in families/schools/institutes/organizations impacting women's position in S&T. The book combines feminist perspectives, perspectives of gender and organization, and of gender and science in understanding gender inequalities.

While the book deals with women in S&T in different professions, it particularly emphasizes the position of women scientists (i.e., those doing research in science, technology, engineering and mathematics [STEM]) in labs and academia because of the significance of intellectual capital in a knowledge-based economy. For the first time, a section on 'gender parity' (p. 9) was included in STI Policy 2013, which recognized the importance of women in science, technology and innovation activities. Encouraging women in science and using the full potential of the women scientists is essential for a place in the global knowledge community and for global competitiveness.

In the following sections, the relationship between S&T and economic development is discussed followed by an introduction to the gender gap in education and professions in general. It then discusses the perspectives on gender inequalities in S&T professions including biological versus sociological explanations for gender gap in S&T, organizations as sites and institution of science as masculine. The Introduction further discusses the caste and class background of those in S&T professions and concludes by outlining the Indian studies on the subject, the book's approach and the chapterization.

WOMEN, S&T AND DEVELOPMENT

Science and technology (S&T) has been recognized as central to the national growth and development in India (Department of Science & Technology 2013). Scientific and technological knowledge, its access and development for societal ends and economic performance is apprehended as increasingly significant. India's share in research publications has increased by about 68 per cent between 2009 and 2013 as per Scopus database, and the growth rate of scientific publications (as per the same database) at 13.4 per cent has been much above the average growth rate of 4.4 per cent in the world; its share of publications is 4.4 per cent in 2013 and it ranked 6th, ahead of France, Spain and Italy. Yet its research lacks global attention as its share of citations is around 3 per cent (Ministry of Science & Technology 2017). The proportion of scientific personnel is small compared to population at 218 per million in 2015, ranking below Chile, Kenya and many other countries (Ministry of Science & Technology 2017; Noorden 2015). The proportion of GDP spent on R&D remains quite small. India's gross expenditure on R&D (GERD) is only 0.69 per cent of the GDP as against that of the developed countries with 2 per cent of GDP on an average (and even China at 2.05%).[1] This investment is critical for growth of S&T infrastructure as well as manpower. Cultivating indigenous S&T capability requires use of human resources to their full potential. According to UNESCO (2007):

> Maintenance of an indigenous S&T workforce allows countries to be more than consumers of technological exports of other nations, and allows

citizens to actively improve their own situations and economic well-being. A country that does not recognize this and consequently does not invest in national S&T capacity, will find itself falling further and further behind.

Thus, growth of S&T workforce is critical to any nation which cannot afford to ignore women's (or half of its population's) participation.

Growth in participation of women in economy is abysmal at present. Ranked 108th in gender gap index by the World Economic Forum in 2018, its rank in economic opportunity and participation is among the lowest at 142 among 149 nations (WEF 2018). McKinsey Global Institute predicts 18 per cent addition to India's GDP by 2025 from improving gender equality (Woetzel et al. 2018). Harnessing potential of women is likely to pave way for a more effective way of recruiting, training and retaining labour which will benefit both men and women (Alvesson and Billing 2009) and make good business sense (Rapoport et al. 2002).

Gender equality in S&T is also an issue of human equity. The term 'gender equality' is sometimes used interchangeably with 'gender equity'. However, they differ in meanings:

> Gender Equity is the process of being fair to men and women. To ensure fairness, measures must often be put in place to compensate for the historical and social disadvantages that prevent women and men from operating on a level playing field. Equity is a means. Equality is the result.[2]

Gender equality is not about equal numbers, it implies equal rights, opportunities and responsibilities which should not depend upon whether one is a man or a woman. Gender inequality in S&T careers is a product of complex of social, cultural, structural and institutional issues that marginalize women.

WOMEN IN EDUCATION AND PROFESSIONS: GENDER GAP

Women's participation in higher education has improved considerably. There is a near-gender parity in senior secondary education enrolment levels as per the Ministry of Human Resource Development (MHRD) report (Ministry of Human Resource Development 2016). In terms of performance, girls in class XII tend to outperform boys, as, for instance, in 2010 with 81.5 per cent of girls that appeared actually passed the exams compared to 73.2 per cent boys (Ministry of Human Resource Development 2016: Table 11B; p. 9). Of the total number of students enrolled in 2017–2018, in the Undergraduate (UG) Arts courses and Social Sciences, about 52 per cent are women; 48.6 per cent in Science and 28.6 per cent in Engineering and Technology (Ministry of Human Resource Development 2018: Table 12). As per this All India Survey on Higher Education 2017–18 (AISHE) report, in the Medical Science stream in UG, share of women's enrolment to the total exceeds men. AISHE survey shows that women's participation increased sharply since 2010–2011 in all Masters courses. Women constitute 45 per cent doctoral students in science and 30 per cent in engineering.

As the aforementioned figures indicate, women's participation in science education is not lagging behind men in UG courses, except in engineering. The figures though lower for engineering are high compared to many of the developed countries. Proportion of women in engineering at bachelor's level in the USA is about 20 per cent (NSF 2017: 7). However, the proportion of women in elite educational institutes of S&T is very low. It was about 8–9 per cent in the IITs and the number was declining until the government introduced supernumerary seats for women at the IITs from 2018. Science is favoured over engineering for girls and engineering is encouraged for patrifocal reasons. In all areas of S&T, women encounter issues with regard to doctoral education such as going abroad for doctorate or post-doctorate, a system of education which is hierarchical and masculine with stereotypes infiltrating even the elite institutes.

Compared to their participation in education, the educated women's participation in labour force is considerably low; also, their participation is declining. This is despite considerable economic growth since the 1990s. Between 1990 and 2013, GDP growth averaged 6.4 per cent (Fletcher, Pandey and Moore 2015) and is 6.2 per cent in 2017, while the world average is 2.5 per cent in 2016

(World Bank 2017a); the share of services in GDP increased from 34.6 to 48.9 per cent between 1990 and 2017 (World Bank 2017b).

The low participation rate of women is a striking feature of the Indian labour force. With only 27 per cent female labour force participation (FLFP; as percentage of female population ages 15+), India's FLFP rate is among the lowest in the world. The global average is 52 per cent and in South Asia it is 29 per cent (Choudhary et al. 2018). In contrast, male labour force participation (MLFP; as percentage of male population ages 15+) in India is on an average at 78.8 per cent, which is higher than the world average of 75.2 per cent (World Bank 2018). Long-term trends suggest that FLFP rates in India have declined from 34.1 per cent in 1999–2000 to 27.2 per cent in 2011–2012 (World Bank 2018); that the recent drop in FLFP is primarily accounted for by the rural female labour force (Andres et al. 2017).

The relationship between FLFP and literacy levels is even more striking in India. The FLFP rate is highest among illiterates and college graduates in both rural and urban areas (Andres et al. 2017). This creates a U-shaped relationship between level of education and FLFP (while being linear for men). FLFP for urban educated 'college and above' is estimated to be about 35–36 per cent in 2011–2012 (Andres et al. 2017: 16; Figure 3) and has fallen by about 6.5 percentage points in the urban areas since 2004–2005 (17; Table 9). The decline is verified by other studies, for instance, with respect to the age cohort 30 and above, the percentage of women with graduate degrees and above and out of the labour force has increased from 62.7 per cent to 65.2 per cent between 2013–2014 and 2015–2016 (Ghai 2018: 20).

Reports point to a low proportion of educated women in professions which is still lower in high positions. According to Woetzel et al. (2018), while proportion of women among tertiary educated graduates is 43 per cent, proportion of women among entry level professionals is 25 per cent but falls to 4 per cent in senior management. Their proportion as board members has risen to 11 per cent due to legal mandate of one woman on board of all listed companies. A UN report (Nair 2012) found that while India has a high representation of women in administrative and managerial positions, it has a low representation of women in decision-making positions. The proportion of women as Fellows of national science academies constitutes not more than 10 per cent (Indian Academy of Sciences, National Academy of Sciences, and Indian National Science Academy, 2016)

The participation of doctorate women in S&T professions reflects similar trends and the figures are much lower than those stated earlier. There is a high participation of women in S&T doctoral education (30%–45% as mentioned earlier) but they constitute only 14 per cent of (full-time equivalents) researchers (NSTMIS 2017). Gender gap in scientific research is worldwide. However, it is particularly wide in India, and proportion of women researchers is lower than the average for South and West Asia. The world average for the share of women in research is 28.8 per cent; it is 32.3 per cent for the USA and Western Europe, and 18.5 per cent for South and West Asia (UNESCO 2018).

These statistics are the visible manifestations of gender inequality among educated women including those in S&T in India. The invisible role of gender in creating barriers for women in S&T and thereby perpetuating inequalities has been the subject of research worldwide as discussed further.

BARRIERS FOR WOMEN IN S&T

In explanations of how and why gender inequalities occur, studies on women in S&T highlight the role of sociocultural norms, the organizations as sites for construction of gender and institution of S&E as masculine in creating barriers for women in S&T. 'Gender' is not merely a sociocultural system of roles based on sex which are transmitted through socialization. It is an institutionalized system of social practices for constituting social relations of inequality between men and women (Risman 1998). Cultural beliefs about gender are produced and reproduced in interactions, behaviours and practices at homes, organizations and all relational contexts. However, there are persistent beliefs about innate differences suggesting the arguments of male biological superiority for dominance of men in S&T. These arguments and the role of culture are dealt with in the following section.

BIOLOGY VERSUS CULTURE

Feminists question the traditional belief that women are unfit/ less suited to do science/math than men. Technically, while 'sex' refers to the biological/physical distinction of being male/female, 'gender' is patterned, socially produced distinctions between male and female, feminine and masculine (Acker 1992). The biological/ physical distinctions have been related to few women in higher positions or as high achievers in mathematics and sciences. For instance, differences in which side of brain men and women utilize have been found to be associated with mathematical skills in the literature on spatial ability and neo-spatial abilities analysed by researchers (e.g., Halpern et al. 2007; Xie and Shauman 2003). Neo-social Darwinists believe that biological 'difference' is a product of evolution, in which women seem either to have been left behind (in the development of quantitative and spatial abilities) or to lack innate qualities and dispositions suited to science and mathematics (Cronin 2005). However, experience alters brain structures and functioning, so causal statements about brain differences and success in math and science are circular (Halpern et al. 2007). Biological differences also have a sociological explanation and depend on the situational contexts in which women live (Bem 1993). A wide range of sociocultural forces including family, neighbourhood, peer and school influences; training and experience; and cultural practices contribute to sex differences in mathematics and science achievement and ability (Halpern et al. 2007). Even if men have higher aptitude than women in mathematics, it would not explain why more women on an average have higher aptitude than careers that require mathematics (Etzkowitz and Gupta 2006). The decision to choose S&T career option is influenced by the wider context of society and is influenced by stereotypes (Powell, Dainty and Bagilhole 2012). Gender beliefs can bias individuals' expectations for their own competence in the situation independently of their underlying abilities. In analysing why so few women compared to men choose to pursue highly rewarded S&T careers, Correll (2001) showed that girls attributed less math ability to themselves than did boys with the same math test scores and grades.

In India, biological arguments do not explain a very high percentage of women, about 45 per cent of total, enrolled in doctorate in mathematics (Ministry of Human Resource Development 2018) and only 10–15 per cent women as scientists or researchers in STEM. Also, various scholars working on women in S&T in India disagree that in India there is a linking of biological or psychological traits to women's participation in mathematical sciences in society. These researchers point out that women's innate ability to perform in mathematics is not doubted in India (Mukhopadhyay 1994; Subrahmanyan 1998; Venkatesh 2015). Nevertheless, there are evidences to the contrary. Biological arguments, such as women are more hardworking and men have higher cognitive skills, are common which result in women being discouraged by their professors from applying for higher studies or a woman faculty applicant being questioned stringently at interview committees or pushed towards experimental areas of study (Subramanian 2007). However, gender biases operate in women's subject/career choices irrespective of the belief in innate mathematical/cognitive abilities. Thus, for instance, it is the gendered expectations of parents for success and a gendered discourse in families that create male privilege in S&T fields even before embarking on a career (as discussed in Chapter 1). Further, in India, the biological difference maps on significantly to the functional differences (Sur 2009) implying that since women are biologically different, their functions should differ. The relationship between biological differences and gendered expectations continue to be intrinsic to the Indian society and impact women scientists and other women professionals through biases at the workplace and in institutions of science.

In general, the education and careers of women in India have been influenced by patriarchal culture referred to as 'patrifocality' by Mukhopadhyay and Seymour (1994). 'Patrifocality' refers to the kinship and family structures and ideology that give precedence to men over women and overall imply subordination of the individual to family. Unlike the system implied in patriarchy, it is not a monolithic system in which males predominate in all settings and social contexts. Rather, 'patrifocality' is the complex linkage between the hierarchical family structure and male dominance and emphasizes lineage purity through control of marriage and female sexuality. Traditionally, control of females, particularly female sexuality, has been linked to caste status; purity of caste is contingent upon purity of women (Chakravarti 2004). In effect, the upper castes are more conservative in following the patrifocal ideology (Mukhopadhyay and Seymour 1994). Educational and marital decisions are family decisions; age and educational hypergamy (groom as more educated, higher in age than bride), universality of marriage, women's centrality in domestic sphere with a dichotomy of 'public–private' sphere continue to exist although more so among the upper castes and middle classes. Culturally, patriarchal systems associate women with the domestic roles. According to UN data, women do three times more unpaid care and domestic work than men.[3] Entrenched patriarchal systems like that of India have a more rigid association of women with domestic roles or the 'private' sphere. In India, a time use survey shows that women spend six times more number of hours a day than men on unpaid work such as household chores, shopping, etc.[4] Women's employment has been found to be significantly related to gender such as women opting out due to marriage (Fletcher et al. 2017). There is a strong relation between women's empowerment and employment with southern and north-eastern states faring better in terms of women's employment and empowerment in general than the northern states (Jain 2018). Cultural norms that marginalize women to mother and homemaker roles create a higher imbalance in men–women ratios in science in the developing world than in the developed ones (Campion and Shrum 2004). Patriarchal sociocultural norms construct and reproduce gender in institutional and organizational settings. These norms along with the unique context of S&T create disadvantages for women.

GENDER AND S&T: PROFESSIONAL CULTURE

Cultural beliefs about gender or gender schemas and stereotypes are stronger in the male-dominated professions such as science and engineering (Valian 1999). The stereotypical image of a scientist is male (Schiebinger 1999). In most countries, the growth of women's representation in education or influx of more women in pipeline has not fulfilled the expectation of a similar proportion in S&T professions and very few reach leadership positions (UNESCO 2015). Women are under-represented at scientific workplaces and in careers in most countries of the world (Rathgeber 2009). Gender stratification exists in employment, rank, salary and productivity, and also varies by discipline indicating horizontal segregation (Fox 1999; Long and Fox 1995).

A vast literature on women in S&T has analysed the discrepancies in opportunities and status of women scientists in academia. Although Merton ([1942]1973) did not mention gender as a source of lack of 'universalism' in science, various studies since then have pointed out gender as accounting for 'particularism' in appointment and evaluation of women scientists (Long and Fox 1995). Barriers to women range from lack of mentorship, problems of travel and odd hours (Hogan et al. 2010; Mason and Ekman 2007) to bias in evaluation of research and competence (Foschi 2000; Steinpreis, Anders and Ritzke 1999; Wenneras and Wold 1997); women's research is likely to be cited less than men's (Larivière et al. 2013); they are less likely to be selected for prominent awards reflecting 'Matilda effect' (Lincoln et al. 2012). The authors found that the ghettoization of women's accomplishments into a category of 'women-only' awards implicitly support the cultural belief that women's scientific efforts are not as important as those of men thus marginalizing women's research. Evidence shows a 'triple burden' on women scientists in different parts of the world, indicating the negative impact of masculine culture in science, normative cultural values and organizational structures (Gupta et al. 2005).

The reasons for such discriminatory practices in research careers are to be found in the professional culture of science. Professionally, contacts and networks constitute social capital; however, women face exclusion from professional networks (Etzkowitz et al. 2000) and confront problems of collaboration (Fox 2001). 'Male model' of full-time devotion to science disadvantage women. There are sexist beliefs about competence in selection and evaluation of applications for hiring (Moss-Racusin et al. 2012). Particularism is enhanced for women immigrants in Western countries as a stereotypical scientist is not only a male but also a White male. Such women are exposed to discriminatory practices and are constructed as less competent than the norm (Harding 1986; Husu 2001; Mählck and Thaver 2010; Subramanian 2009).

Proportions of women in engineering professions tend to be lower than those in education in most countries. In the UK, for instance, women constituted 15.8 per cent engineering and technology graduates in 2005–2006 and more than half across all subjects and in 2006 women formed only 5.4 per cent of engineering professionals aged 16–65 (Powell et al. 2009). Masculinity of the engineering domain is primarily an issue of women being excluded from the engineering culture. Technical culture 'expresses and consolidates relations among men' thereby excluding women (Wajacman 1991: 137). Women engineers are simultaneously highly visible as women yet invisible as engineers (Faulkner 2009).

Women in S&T professions deny that gender matters; this is because of a strong link between achievement and meritocracy (Britton 2017; Rhoton 2011). Also, drawing attention to their gender often marks them as outsiders in a male-dominated realm (Rhoton 2011). Powell and Sang (2015) found that often women themselves feel that men are more suited to the 'masculine professions' because they have masculine capital, that is, stereotypically masculine skills and capacities, which enable men to be better engineers, architects, etc. This is 'symbolic violence' or an internalization of sexism, but women do not perceive it as such, because their situation seems to be the natural order of things. Symbolic violence is not physical, but may take the form of people being denied resources, treated as inferior or being limited in terms of realistic aspirations.

ORGANIZATIONS: DOING GENDER

Similar to any profession, S&T careers are practised in organizations and hence gender stereotypes that operate in other professions also operate for women in S&T. While there is overt discrimination, as, for instance, wage gap (Peterson and Morgan 1995), invisible barriers operate in organizations which are sites of 'doing gender'. Gender is a process that is constantly being enacted in everyday situations (Linstead and Pullen 2006); this process, referred to as 'doing gender' (West and Zimmerman 1987) involves a complex of perceptual, interactional and micro-political activities casting particular pursuits as expressions of masculine and feminine natures. Cultural beliefs play a significant role in doing gender. For instance, women are seen as more communal and men as more agentic and instrumental (Eagly, Wood and Diekman 2000). Women are viewed as less competent in general but 'nicer' and better at communal tasks even though these tasks themselves are less valued (Conway, Pizzamiglio and Mount 1996; Fiske et al. 2002). A manager's role is typically perceived to be a masculine one (Heilman 2012). Organizing processes such as gender in recruitment, differential gender-based evaluations and informal interactions (such as exclusion from meetings and informal groups or being ignored at meetings) reproduce inequalities (Acker 2006).

Gender exists as a background frame in interactions (Ridgeway and Correll 2004) and becomes salient in masculine professions. Engineering and physical sciences are strongly gender-typed in the USA. Thus, in IT firms, the background gender frame creates a stronger bias against women's competence than in biotech settings (Ridgeway 2009). When the domain is culturally defined as masculine, such as engineering, the beliefs about the male competence are buttressed by the presumptions of their specific gender skills (Ridgeway and Correll 2004). When the domain is 'feminine' such as caretaking, the evaluations are weakly influenced by the gender skills; the general presumption of men's greater competence is counterbalanced and sometimes overvalued compared to the assumptions about women's special, gender-typed skills. Thus, while women experience glass ceiling or invisible barriers to their rise to higher positions in male-dominated professions such as science, men experience glass escalator in predominantly female occupations.

Gender inequality is experienced as 'tokenism' (Kanter 1977) in organizations particularly in the male-dominated professions, such as S&T. As per the theory, a low numerical representation of women have several negative consequences for them such as overwhelming pressure to perform due to a heightened visibility, exaggeration of differences by the majority leading to isolation due to boundary heightening and tendency to stereotype the minority (role encapsulation). However, a mere increase in numbers in a department or the system does not suggest enhanced status. The 'paradox of critical mass'

(Etzkowitz et al. 2000) is that when number of women increase in a department, they get divided into subgroups; for instance, bifurcation along generational fault lines. An increased presence of women in science in Hungary and Poland was due to a number of negative factors such as significant decreases in salaries, status and resources, and the shift of male scientists to the better remunerated and prestigious posts in the private sector in the country or abroad (UNESCO 1999).

Women in S&T experience what Hall and Sandler (1982) referred to as 'chilly climate' in organizations. MIT (1999) on status of women faculty in science observed that many tenured faculty found themselves marginalized and excluded from significant roles in their departments and this was accompanied by differences in salary, space, awards, resources and response to outside offers between men and women faculty with women receiving less despite professional accomplishments equal to those of their male colleagues. Some researchers have found that women complete UG engineering programmes less because of the chilly climate marked by hostile classroom and campus experiences (Hartman and Hartman 2008; Seymour and Hewitt 1997; Vogt, Hocevar and Hagedorn 2007).

Type of organizations has been found to be significant in the creation of equity climate for the women scientists. For instance, Smith-Doerr (2004) found that women scientists working in small, for-profit companies are eight times more likely than their university counterparts to head a research lab. This is because of the organizational flexibility, absence of large hierarchical bureaucracies and a lack of old boys' networks in such companies. Recent researches have shown that hierarchy and bureaucratic structure by themselves might not be detrimental to gender equity (Roth and Sonnert 2011). According to Ridgeway (2009), less hierarchical structures help to mitigate the negative effects of femininity for women scientists.

As elsewhere, in India also, there is overt as well as covert discrimination in organizations employing educated professionals. For graduates and above, the wage gap is high at 24 per cent in urban areas (Ghai 2018: 17). From the limited research that documents the professional women's experiences at the workplace in India, it is evident that women perceive it as a biased environment. For example, in a study of Indian firms (Nath 2000), although performance management and reward structures were considered gender-free, women managers still reported that extra hard work was required from them to prove their worth. Gupta (2017) highlights the prevalence of gender stereotypes in Indian private sector R&D and according to Basu (2008) lack of interaction due to gender segregation accounts for the persistence of most of the stereotypes regarding women. In one study (Kundu 2003), men employees rated women employees as being less qualified, less competent and less productive than women rated themselves. Women believed that they had less chance of receiving working facilities, promotions and salary increases than men. Patel and Parmentier (2005) found that the hiring of women engineers in India, including those in the IT sector, often reflects gendered assumptions: that a woman's primary responsibility is towards her family, or that the woman will leave the job once she gets married.

WOMEN IN S&T: CASTE AND CLASS BACKGROUND

Women in S&T are usually urban upper castes and middle class as shown, for instance, in studies on women scientists (Gupta 2016, 2017). NIAS–IAS report (Kurup et al. 2010) states that about 80 per cent of women in research belong to the General castes and those women in science not doing research also belong to upper castes (79%); about 66 per cent of women in research live in cities. Women working in IT are middle class (Radhakrishnan 2009) and usually from better economic backgrounds than men and are more qualified (NASSCOM 2018). Most students qualifying the entrance exam of the elite IITs are from middle classes (Indian Institute of Technology Kanpur 2018).

Historically, women in S&T have been mostly from the upper castes. Traditionally, knowledge has been the preserve of the Brahmins. As a single-minded pursuit of knowledge, oblivious to personal needs and desires, a scientist is like an ascetic, the latter being deeply revered in Indian tradition (Sur 2009). An ascetic is a male and a Brahman male is the repository of all knowledge traditionally. The new elite that arose in the British period (the bhadralok) was the first to take up modern Western ideas and Western science. This elite was drawn from the Hindu upper castes (Raj 1991). The social and cultural capital enjoyed by the upper castes enabled them to continue their hegemony over science and scientific enterprise in the post-independence period. The advantage of upper castes in terms of social position and education enabled women from these families to enter science. Research continues to be dominated by upper caste men and women particularly in the realm of pure sciences (Chadha and Achuthan 2017).

While being upper caste in composition, women in S&T are usually from middle classes. Researchers of the Indian middle class have pointed out the ideological significance of this class in conceptualizing the Indian nation (Deshpande 2003; Fernandes 2000; Radhakrishnan 2009). The educated middle class grew in the colonial period. Modern nationalist culture was projected as binary of 'outer/inner', 'material/spiritual', 'world/home' and India/East was seen as superior to the West in 'spiritual' and purity of the middle-class woman along with a gendered notion of middle-class domesticity was central to this project. The binary was also a way of resolving preference for Western science while being loyal to Indian nationalism. Acutely conscious of the Western superiority in modern science, Indians faced racism as they were denied access to all higher scientific and technical positions (Basu 1991) and had limited access to research in S&T. According to Partha Chatterjee (1989), nationalists sought to reconcile the desire to pursue Western science and their opposition to colonialism. Through the division of the cultural sphere into material and spiritual, S&T were seen as part of the 'material', and 'spiritual' referred to the Indian sociocultural sphere where women became the chief definers of the 'spiritual' sphere. Logically, therefore, the category of 'women' could not fit in this ideological positioning of science/'material' as easily as men could.

Nevertheless, influenced by the nationalist movement of the colonial times and the encouragement of women's education by social reformers, women scientists took up the Gandhian way of life (simple ascetic life, wearing khadi; Sur 2009); however, they rejected the Gandhian view that since women are biologically different, their functions should differ and that education should aid their primary functions of homemaker. Adoption of simple life by women scientists at the time transformed scientific calling into asceticism and helped to create acceptance in public spaces (Sur 2009).

In the immediate post-independence period, the Nehruvian idea of Indianness was defined in secular and socialist terms (Radhakrishnan 2011) which stood in tense contradiction to Hindu rightist ideals. In the Nehruvian India, the old 'middle class' was made up of government workers. Liberalization and globalization since the 1990s has led to the emergence of the 'new middle classes' (Fuller and Narasimhan 2007); this coupled with the growing Hindu nationalist forces has revitalized the ideas of role of Hindu piety, moralism with central role of family. The new middle class does not differ from the old in terms of their composition but in how they perceive their position in nation, characterized by often conservative cultural or nationalist values coupled with a conscientious integration into the global political economy (Radhakrishnan 2009). The globalization forces and growth of education has brought a greater acceptance of women in public spaces (Thapan 2007) but a pursuit of a highly successful career remains circumscribed (Radhakrishnan 2011). The post-colonial notion of Indian culture is gendered as it gives primacy to family and a central role to women in the family.

Studies of urban women professionals show that there is a simultaneous existence of individualization and collectivism in their lives. Belliappa (2013) found that professional women in urban India continue to define individual subjectivity in collective terms (individual self as part of family). They uphold family as a 'core value' of global Indian identity and this helps enact 'respectable femininity' at the workplace and in their personal lives (Radhakrishnan 2009). The post-colonial societies do not reflect simply a process of growing individualization. It is complicated by the re-appropriation of tradition. For instance, women's relationship with in-laws is a re-versioning of joint families as they assist in women's work outside home reflecting 'relational reflexivity' or ability to construct self in relationship to others (Belliappa 2013).

The position of women scientists in academia/research varies from women in newer S&T professions such as IT in some ways. IT is a new field unencumbered by conservative gender and internal hierarchies and set patterns of work at the workplace. As multinational companies and Indian firms vie for the best talent in IT, the industry has been at the forefront of the global best practices. In contrast, the Indian infrastructure of science is mainly in the government sector and developed in the post-independence period under state patronage and hence is bureaucratized in most of its organizations. The diversion of state attention to its labs and later the IITs has taken the focus away from the universities many of which lack sufficient funds. However, women scientists are drawn from a similar socio-economic background as women in other S&T professions and thus share the composition and values of the new middle class with primacy to family and women's central role in it. The idealization of traditional roles of women creates a tenuous position within the scientific community. Specific schemes for women such as childcare leave and separate awards for women scientists, although well intended, appears to marginalize them. The most essential task in gender equality therefore is the integration and respect for women scientists within their scientific community.

There is a lack of understanding of the gendered perceptions of men of the similar socio-economic background and in the similar professional and educational domains, of how the identification of national culture with family and positioning of women as the pivot of the family affects day-to-day workplace interactions and construct masculinity in public spaces. Masculinity, or the values, experiences and meanings that are interpreted as masculine and are ascribed mostly to men in a particular cultural context (Alvesson and Billing 2009: 72), is constructed through social process of interactions and practices. This book attempts to show, among other things, how construction of masculinity in educational institutes and at the workplace disadvantage women in S&T.

INDIAN STUDIES ON WOMEN IN S&T

There is a lack of research on women in S&T. Sociologists of science focus on the scientific community in India, research productivity and role of S&T in unleashing social change in India (e.g., Pattnaik 2013) but they lack focus on gender and science. The studies of post-colonial science focus on the spatial location as being advantageous and disadvantageous for Indian scientists (Abraham 2006) on the development of science in India in its various phases from colonial period to bureaucratic control of science in the Nehruvian phase (Krishna 2001). History and philosophy of science is silent about the question of women in science as, for instance, among those conceptualizing post-colonial science as an assault on Indian indigenous forms of learning (Shiva 1989) or those viewing it as a modern enterprise that would lift India from its social and economic problems (Sheshadri 1994, as cited in Sur 2009).

Studies on Indian women in science started emerging since the 1970s after the formation of the Indian Women Scientists' Association in 1975 which conducted a small exploratory study on the members of its association (Subrahmanyan 1998). Thereafter, a survey of women scientists at Bhabha Atomic Research Centre (Begum and Balaraman 1975) found that due to socialization in a patriarchal culture and a lack of childcare facilities, women have to work harder than men (for a summary, see Subrahmanyan 1998: 35). Problems related to the interactional environment and the role of perceptions was first pointed out by Gurnani and Sheth (1984). Chakravarthy (1986) reported very few women scientists holding senior posts in central research institutions. She also emphasized the role of prejudices, lack of infrastructural support and dual burden for women scientists.

More detailed studies on women in S&T have emerged since the 1990s. Based on a large-scale survey of science degree holders, a first of its kind, Krishnaraj (1991) demonstrated how patriarchy operates at both levels: the place of work and family. Jaiswal (1993) studied the professional status of women scientists and engineers vis-a-vis men scientists and engineers in organizations. He found that women were at a lower level of the professional hierarchy, and there was latent discrimination against women, both at the organizational level and in relationships. Kumar (2001) found that career paths for women are flatter than for men, and that a disparity in academic rank exists even when differential productivity is taken into account. A pioneering study on women in science and engineering education has been by Mukhopadhyay and Seymour (1994) who showed that patrifocal family structure and ideology were important in women's underrepresentation in science and engineering education.

Ethnographic studies such as that of Subrahmanyan's (1998) study of women academic scientists at an Indian university deal with the problems encountered by them due to gender. Based on the study of the elite academic institutes—the IITs—disadvantages for women academics and doctoral students in the informal milieu have been pointed out Gupta (Gupta and Shrama 2002; Gupta 2007). Study of Council of Scientific and Industrial Research (CSIR) labs (Gupta 2016) and private pharmaceutical labs (Gupta 2017) highlight the role of hierarchy and patriarchy in creating barriers for women. Study of women scientists at Kerala has contributed to the study of networking and collaboration (Palackal, Anderson and Miller 2007).

A few studies in the recent times have compared scientific productivity of women and men scientists in various fields (Gupta, Kumar and Aggarwal 1999; Hasan et al. 2012; Upadhye et al. 2014). However, there are lack of studies on the relationship between research productivity and various social variables, such as marriage, children and age.

There is a considerable growth of the narratives by the women scientists themselves in the recent years which provide valuable insights into their position. For instance, a feminist study of science in recent times drew upon the narratives of women practitioners of science collating them into a section (namely, 'Review of Women's Studies') of a journal (EPW 2017). The articles in this section focus on low representation of women in science and gender-based discrimination against them. It finds the common themes of diminishing sense of self-worth, lack of belonging and pervasiveness of upper caste male culture among these narratives of women scientists. Another category of collection of narratives is that compiled by the women scientists themselves, such as Lilavati's Daughters (Godbole and Ramaswamy 2008).

Surveys conducted by government departments have been significant in understanding the position of women scientists. First such survey (INSA 2004) pointed out women's lack of representation in S&T education, careers, leadership positions and awards. A survey jointly conducted by women scientists and social scientists (Kurup et al. 2010) studied barriers for women doctorates in science who were working and not working. It found that organizational factors were important in creating such barriers.

This book attempts to weave together the available evidence from various sources to understand the invisible barriers in the lives of women in S&T from education to careers.

THE BOOK'S APPROACH AND CHAPTERS

In exploring the contours of women's journey from education to careers, the book adopts the approach that while there are biological differences between men and women, it is gender or the socially constructed norms, roles and behaviours that support difference and reproduce inequality. Gender is a performance of this cultural male–female difference system which informs not only micro-interactions but also institutions and structures. Women in S&T are disadvantaged by patriarchal norms, masculinity of the professional culture and an organizational milieu elsewhere also. However, national cultural beliefs about gender, internal systems of science/its institutions and developing country status create national similarities and dissimilarities in the manner in which the gender process operates and therefore require nation-specific solutions. This work aims to highlight the invisible gender inequalities in the domain of Indian S&T and to create a discourse in organizations on gender issues so as to enable full utilization of the potential of women workforce in S&T. The chapterization is as follows:

Chapter 1 focuses on the historical and social context of women's education; on the relationship between education of women and construction of gender in the Indian society, particularly, among the urban middle classes and on education in the pre-college period.

Chapter 2 is divided into two parts. Part I of the chapter gives an overview of the higher education system, choice of courses, institutes and the relationship between gender and decisions made at this level. The sociocultural norms and those related to masculinity/femininity tend to be reproduced and reconstructed not only through such choices/decisions but also through interactions involving the youth. This is dealt with in Part II.

Chapter 3 analyses position of women in some of the key professions related to S&T such as information technology, medicine and S&T entrepreneurship. It specially focuses on inequalities of representation in scientific research in labs and academia, the issues related to productivity and evaluation.

Chapter 4 focuses on gender in science organizations such as academia and labs. It shows how, on one hand, certain structural and normative factors favour men and, on the other hand, certain sociocultural norms devalue women in public spaces which help to maintain and reproduce masculinity at the workplace.

Chapter 5 analyses the existing discourse, initiatives and policies encouraging women in S&T from higher education onwards; it highlights the limitations of the existing discourse, the need for a change of perspective and chief areas of concern in moving towards gender equality. It discusses programmes elsewhere that encourage women in research/academia, importance of men's participation in bringing change, suggests policy changes and directions for future research.

NOTES

1. GERD: Higher education sector versus government sector: In India, 50 per cent of GERD is accounted for by the government. GERD is mainly driven by the government sector comprising of central government 45.1 per cent, state governments 7.4 per cent, higher education 3.9 per cent and public sector industries 5.5 per cent with private sector industries contributing 38.1 per cent during 2014–2015. An 80 per cent of central government funds go to 8 major central agencies, DRDO accounted for the maximum share of 37.8 per cent of R&D expenditure followed by Department of Space (DoS), Department of Atomic Energy (DAE), Indian Council of Agricultural Research (ICAR), CSIR, Department of Science and Technology (DST), Department

of Biotechnology (DBT) and Indian Council of Medical Research (ICMR) (Ministry of Science & Technology 2017). These agencies fall under different ministries, for example, DRDO under defence ministry, DST, DBT under Ministry of Science and Technology; or may report directly to PM as in the case of Department of Space. Higher education sector comprises central and state universities, deemed and private universities and institutes of national importance such as the IITs. This sector is under the MHRD.

2. Available at portal.unesco.org/en/files/11483/10649049699Definitions.doc/ Definitions.doc (accessed on 2 August 2019).
3. Available at http://www.unwomen.org/en/digital-library/multimedia/2017/7/ infographic-spotlight-on-sdg-5 (accessed on 2 August 2019).
4. Available at http://www.oecd.org/gender/balancing-paid-work-unpaid-work-and-leisure.htm (accessed on 2 August 2019).

REFERENCES

Abraham, Itty. 2006, 21–27 January. 'The Contradictory Spaces of Postcolonial Techno-Science'. *Economic & Political Weekly* 41 (3): 210–217.

Acker, Joan. 1992. 'Gendering Organizational Theory'. In *Gendering Organizational Theory*, edited by A. J. Mills and P. Tancred, 248–260. Thousand Oaks, CA: SAGE Publications.

———. 2006. 'Inequality Regimes: Gender, Class and Race in Organizations', *Gender & Society* 20 (4): 441–464.

Alvesson, M., and Y. Billing. 2009. *Understanding Gender and Organizations*. New Delhi: SAGE Publications.

Andres, Luis A., Basab Dasgupta, George Joseph, Vinoj Abraham, and Maria Correia. 2017. 'Precarious Drop. Reassessing Patterns of Female Labor Force Participation in India'. Policy Research Working Paper No. 8024. World Bank Group. Available at http://documents.worldbank.org/curated/en/559511491319990632/pdf/WPS8024.pdf (accessed on 2 August 2019).

Bem, S. L. 1993. *The Lenses of Gender: Transforming the Debate on Sexual Inequality*. New Haven, CT: Yale University Press.

Basu, Aparna. 1991. 'The Indian Response to Scientific and Technical Education in Colonial Era 1820–1920'. In *Science and Empire: Essays in Indian Context, 1700–1947*, 126–138. New Delhi: Anamika Prakashan.

Basu, S. 2008. *Gender Stereotypes in Corporate India: A Glimpse*. New Delhi: Response Books.

Begum, Roshan J., and K. Balaraman. 1975. 'Contemporary Social Problems of Women Engineers and Scientists in India'. Paper presented at the Fourth International Conference of Women Scientists and Engineers, Poland.

Belliappa, J. 2013. *Gender, Class and Reflexive Modernity in India*. Basingstoke: Palgrave Macmillan.

Britton, D. M. 2017. 'Beyond the Chilly Climate: The Salience of Gender in Women's Academic Careers'. *Gender and Society* 31 (1): 5–27.

Campion, P., and W. Shrum. 2004. 'Gender and Science in Development: Women Scientists in Ghana, Kenya and India'. *Science, Technology and Human Values* 29 (4): 459–485.

Chadha, Gita, and Asha Achuthan. 2017, 29 April. 'Feminist Science Studies. Intersectional Narratives of Persons in Gender-Marginal Locations in Science'. *Economic & Political Weekly* 52 (17): 33–36.

Chatterjee, Partha. 1989. 'Colonialism, Nationalism, and Colonialized Women: The Contest in India'. *American Ethnologist* 16 (4): 622–633.

Choudhary, Afra R., Ana C. Areias, Saori Imaizumi, Shinsaku Nomura, and Futoshi Yamauchi. 2018. 'Reflections of Employers' Gender Preferences in Job Ads in India'. An Analysis of Online Job Portal Data. Policy Research Working Paper No. 8379. World Bank Group. Available at http://documents.worldbank.org/curated/en/548581522089881652/pdf/WPS8379.pdf (accessed on 2 August 2019).

Conway, M., M. T. Pizzamiglio, and L. Mount. 1996. 'Status, Communality and Agency: Implications for the Stereotypes of Gender and Other Groups'. *Journal of Personality and Social Psychology* 71: 25–38.

Correll, S. J. 2001. 'Gender and the Career Choice Process: The Role of Biased Self-Assessments'. *American Journal of Sociology* 106 (6): 1691–1730.

Cronin, H. 2005, March. 'The Vital Statistics: Evolution, Not Sexism, Puts Us at a Disadvantage in the Sciences'. *The Guardian Weekly*, 18–24.

Department of Science & Technology. 2013. *Science, Technology and Innovation Policy 2013*. Available at http://www.dst.gov.in/st-system-india/science-and-technology-policy-2013 (accessed on 2 August 2019).

Deshpande, Satish. 2003. *Contemporary India: A Sociological View*. New Delhi: Viking Penguin.

Eagly, A. H., W. Wood, and A. B. Diekman. 2000. 'Social Role Theory of Sex Differences and Similarities: A Current Appraisal'. In *The Developmental Social Psychology of Gender*, edited by T. Eckes and H. M. Trautner, 123–174. Mahwah, NJ: Erlbaum.

EPW. 2017. *Economic & Political Weekly* 52 (17): 52–60.

Etzkowitz, H., and N. Gupta. 2006. 'Women in Science: A Fair Shake?' *Minerva* 44 (2): 185–199.

Etzkowitz, H., C. Kemelgor, and B. Uzzi. 2000. *Athena Unbound: The Advancement of Women in Science and Technology*. Cambridge, MA: Cambridge University Press.

Faulkner, Wendy. 2009. Doing Gender in Engineering Workplace Cultures. II. Gender In/Authenticity and the In/Visibility Paradox. *Engineering Studies* 1 (3): 169–189.doi:10.1080/19378620903225059

Fernandes, Leela. 2000. 'Restructuring the New Middle Class in Liberalizing India'. *Comparative Studies of South Asia, Africa and the Middle East* 20 (1–2): 88–111.

Fiske, S. T., A. J. C. Cuddy, P. Glick, and J. Xu. 2002. A Model of (Often Mixed) Stereotype Content: Competence and Warmth Respectively Follow from Perceived Status and Competition. *Journal of Personality and Social Psychology* 82 (6): 878–902.

Fletcher, Erin K., Rohini Pande, and Charity Troyer Moore. 2015. Women and Work in India: Descriptive Evidence and a Review of Potential Policies. Working Paper No. 339. Center for International Development at Harvard University. Available at https://www.hks.harvard.edu/sites/default/files/centers/cid/files/publications/faculty-working-papers/women_work_india_cidwp339.pdf (accessed on 2 August 2019).

Foschi, M. 2000. Double Standards for Competence: Theory and Research. *Annual Review of Sociology* 26: 21–42.doi: 10.1146/annurev.soc.26.1.21. Available at http://www.annualreviews.org/doi/abs/10.1146/annurev.soc.26.1.21 (accessed on 2 August 2019).

Fox, M. F. 1999. 'Gender, Hierarchy, and Science'. In *Handbook of the Sociology of Gender*, edited by J. S. Chafetz, 441–457. New York, NY: Kluwer Academic/Plenum Publishers.

———. 2001. Women, Science, and Academia: Graduate Education and Careers. *Gender & Society* 15 (5): 654–666.

Fuller, C., and H. Narasimhan. 2007. Information Technology Professionals and the New-Rich Middle Class in Chennai (Madras). *Modern Asian Studies* 41 (1): 121–150.doi:10.1017/S0026749X05002325

Ghai, S. 2018. 'The Anomaly of Women's Work and Education in India'. Working Paper No. 368. ICRIER. Available at http://icrier.org/pdf/Working_Paper_368.pdf (accessed on 2 August 2019).

Godbole, R., and R. Ramaswamy, eds. 2008. *Lilavati's Daughters: The Women Scientists of India*. Bangalore: Indian Academy of Sciences.

Gupta, B. M., Suresh Kumar, and B. S. Aggarwal. 1999. 'A Comparison of Productivity of Male and Female Scientists of CSIR'. *Scientometrics* 45 (2): 269–289. Available at http://link.springer.com/article/10.1007%2FBF02458437?LI=true#page-20 (accessed on 2 August 2019).

Gupta, Namrata. 2007. 'Indian Women in Doctoral Education in Science and Engineering: A Study of Informal Milieu at the Reputed Indian Institutes of Technology'. *Science Technology and Human Values* 32 (5): 507–533.

———. 2016. 'Perceptions of the Work Environment: The Issue of Gender in Indian Scientific Research Institutes'. *Indian Journal of Gender Studies* 23 (3): 437–466.doi: 10.1177/0971521516656079

———. 2017. 'Gender Inequality in the Work Environment: A Study of Private Research Organizations in India'. *Equality, Diversity and Inclusion: An International Journal*.doi:10.1108/EDI-04-2016-0029.

Gupta, N., and A. K. Sharma. 2002. 'Women Academic Scientists in India'. *Social Studies of Science* 32 (5–6): 901–915.

Gupta, Namrata, Carol Kemelgor, Stefan Fuchsand, and Henry Etzkowitz. 2005. Triple Burden on Women in Science: A Cross-Cultural Analysis. *Current Science* 89 (8): 1382–1386.

Gurnani, S., and M. Sheth. 1984. 'Women Scientists in India: Their Position and Role'. *Interdisciplinary Science Reviews* 9 (3): 259–270. Available at https://www.tandfonline.com/doi/abs/10.1179/isr.1984.9.3.259 (accessed on 2 August 2019).

Hall, Roberta M., and Bernice R. Sandler. 1982. The Classroom Climate: A Chilly One for Women? Washington, DC: Project on the Status and Education of Women. Available at http://eric.ed.gov/PDFS/ED215628.pdf (accessed on 22 March 2019).

Halpern, D. F., C. P. Benbow, D. Geary, R. Gur, J. S. Hyde and M. A. Gernsbacher. 2007. 'The Science of Sex Differences in Science and Mathematics'. *Psychological Science in the Public Interest* 8: 1–51.

Harding, S. 1986. *The Science Question in Feminism*. Milton Keynes: Open University Press.

Hartman, H., and M. Hartman. 2008. 'How Undergraduate Engineering Students Perceive Women's (and Men's) Problems in Science, Math and Engineering'. *Sex Roles* 58 (3–4): 251.doi:10.1007/s11199-007-9327-9

Hasan, S. A., Mahender Kumar Sharma, Sushila Khilnani, and R. Luthra. 2012. 'Research Productivity of Female Research Scholars and Their Migration Pattern in Pursuit of Higher Education and Research'. *Current Science* 103 (6): 611.

Heilman, M. E. 2012. 'Gender Stereotypes and Workplace Bias'. *Research in Organizational Behavior* 32: 113–135. Available at https://doi.org/10.1016/j.riob.2012.11.003 (accessed on 2 August 2019).

Hogan, Alice, K. Zippel, L. M. Frehill and L. Kramer. 2010. 'Report of the International Workshop on International Research Collaboration'. Arlington, VA: National Science Foundation.

Husu, L. 2001. 'Sexism, Support and Survival in Academia: Academic Women and Hidden Discrimination in Finland'. Dissertation, Department of Social Psychology, University of Helsinki, Finland.

Indian Institute of Technology Kanpur. 2018, August. Joint Implementation Committee Report, Vol. I. Kanpur: IIT Kanpur. Available at https://drive.google.com/file/d/12x1uG0BeGqO2r9OJi43Ag5YVAjF2alIi/view (accessed on 2 August 2019).

INSA. 2004. *Science Career for Indian Women: An Examination of Indian Women's Access to and Retention in Scientific Careers*. New Delhi: Indian National Science Academy. Available at https://www.ias.ac.in/public/Resources/Initiatives/Women_in_Science/report.pdf (accessed on 2 August 2019).

Jain, D. 2018, 8 March. *What Prevents Women from Working in India?* Available at https://www.livemint.com/Politics/jedAN6zwNy0V0eXmc2vMGM/What-prevents-women-from-working-in-India.html (accessed on 2 August 2019).

Jaiswal, R. P. 1993. *Professional Status of Women: A Comparative Study of Women in Science and Technology*. Jaipur: Rawat Publications.

Kanter, R. M. 1977. *Men and Women of the Corporation*. New York, NY: Basic Books.

Krishna, V. V. 2001. 'Reflections on the Changing Status of Academic Science in India'. *International Social Science Journal* 53 (163): 231–246.

Krishnaraj, Maithreyi. 1991. *Women and Science: Selected Essays*. Bombay: Himalaya Publishing House.

Kumar, Neelam. 2001. 'Gender Stratification in Science: An Empirical Study in the Indian Setting'. *Indian Journal of Gender Studies* 8 (1): 51–67.

Kundu, Subhash C. 2003. 'Workforce Diversity Status: A Study of Employees' Reactions'. *Industrial Management & Data Systems* 103 (4): 215–226.

Kurup, Anitha, R. Maithreyi, B. Kantharaju, and Rohini Godbole. 2010. Trained Scientific Women Power: How Much Are We Losing and Why? IAS–NIAS Research Report. Available at http://eprints.nias.res.in/142/1/IAS-NIAS-Report.pdf (accessed on 2 August 2019).

Larivière, V., C. Ni, Y. Gingras, B. Cronin, and C. R. Sugimoto. 2013. 'Global Gender Disparities in Science'. *Nature* 504 (7479): 211–213.

Lincoln, A. E., S. Pincus, J. B. Koster, and P. S. Leboy. 2012. 'The Matilda Effect in Science: Awards and Prizes in the US, 1990s and 2000s'. *Social Studies of Science* 42 (2): 307–320. Available at https://journals.sagepub.com/doi/10.1177/0306312711435830 (accessed on 2 August 2019).

Linstead, S., and A. Pullen. 2006 'Gender as Multiplicity: Desire, Difference and Dispersion'. *Human Relations* 59 (9): 1287–1310.

Long, Scott J., and Mary F. Fox. 1995. 'Scientific Careers: Universalism and Particularism'. *Annual Review of Sociology* 21: 45–71.

Mählck, Paula, and Beverly Thaver. 2010. 'Dialogue on Gender and Race Equality: Conversations between Sweden and South Africa'. Equality, Diversity and Inclusion: *An International Journal* 29 (1): 23–27.

Mason, Mary Ann, and E. M. Ekman. 2007. *Mothers on the Fast Track: How a Generation Can Balance Family and Careers*. New York, NY: Oxford University Press.

Merton, R. K. [1942]1973. 'The Normative Structure of Science'. In *The Sociology of Science*, edited by R. K. Merton, 267–278. Chicago, IL: University of Chicago Press.

Ministry of Human Resource Development. 2016. *Educational Statistics at a Glance*. New Delhi: Department of School Education & Literacy, Ministry of Human Resource Development, Government of India. Available at http://mhrd.gov.in/sites/upload_files/mhrd/files/statistics/ESG2016_0.pdf (accessed on 2 August 2019).

———. 2018. *All India Survey on Higher Education 2017–18*. New Delhi: Department of Higher Education, Ministry of Human Resource Development, Government of India. Available at http://aishe.nic.in/aishe/viewDocument.action?documentId=245 (accessed on 2 August 2019).

Ministry of Science & Technology. 2017. *Research & Development Statistics at a Glance 2017–18*. New Delhi: Department of Science & Technology, Ministry of Science & Technology, Government of India. Available at http://www. nstmis-dst.org/statistics-Glance-2017-18-2.pdf (accessed on 2 August 2019).

MIT. 1999. 'A Study on the Status of Women Faculty in Science at MIT'. *The MIT Faculty Newsletter* 11 (4). Available at http://web.mit.edu/fnl/women/women. html (accessed on 2 August 2019).

Moss-Racusin, C. A., J. F. Dovidio, V. L. Brescoll, M. J. Graham, and J. Handelsman. 2012. 'Science Faculty's Subtle Gender Biases Favor Male Students'. Proceedings of the National Academy of Sciences of United States of America 109 (41): 16474–16479. Available at https://www.pnas.org/content/109/41/16474 (accessed on 2 August 2019).

Mukhopadhyay, C. C. 1994. 'Family Structure and Indian Women's Participation in Science and Engineering'. In *Women, Education and Family Structure in India*, edited by C. C. Mukhopadhyay and S. Seymour, 103–134. Boulder, CO: Westview Press.

Mukhopadhyay, C. C., and S. Seymour. 1994. 'Introduction and Theoretical Overview'. In *Women, Education and Family Structure in India*, edited by C. C. Mukhopadhyay and S. Seymour, 1–33. Boulder, CO: Westview Press.

Nair, Sudha. 2012. National Assessments on Gender Equality in the Knowledge Society. Country Results: India. WISAT. The Elsevier Foundation. Available at http://wisat.org/wp-content/uploads/National_Scorecard_India_Reduced. pdf (accessed on 2 August 2019).

NASSCOM. 2018. Women and IT Scorecard—India. The Open University, UK. Available at http://gsm-it.com/userassets/Publications/GSM-IT_SCORECARD-INDIA_2018_Final.pdf (accessed on 2 August 2019).

Nath, G. 2000. 'Gently Shattering the Glass Ceiling: Experiences of Indian Women Managers'. *Women in Management Review* 15 (1): 44–52.

Noorden, R. V. 2015, 13 May. 'India by the Numbers. Highs and Lows in the Country's Research Landscape'. *Nature*. Available at https://www.nature.com/news/india-by-the-numbers-1.17519 (accessed on 2 August 2019).

NSF. 2017. Women, Minorities, and Persons with Disabilities in Science and Engineering. National Center for Science and Engineering Statistics Directorate for Social, Behavioral and Economic Sciences. *National Science Foundation*. Available at https://www.nsf.gov/statistics/2017/nsf17310/static/downloads/nsf17310-digest.pdf (accessed on 2 August 2019).

NSTMIS. 2017. S&T Indicators 2017–18. *Tables*. Available at http://www.nstmis-dst.org/SnT-Indicators2017-18.aspx (accessed on 2 August 2019).

Palackal, A., M. Anderson, and B. Paige Miller. 2007. 'Internet Equaliser? Gender Stratification and Normative Circumvention in Science'. *Indian Journal of Gender Studies* 14 (2): 231–257.

Patel, R., and M. J. C. Parmentier. 2005. 'The Persistence of Traditional Gender Roles in the Information Technology Sector: A Study of Female Engineers in India'. *Information Technologies and International Development* 2 (3): 29–46.

Pattnaik, B. K, ed. 2013. *Readings in Indian Sociology, Vol. 6*. Sociology of Science and Technology in India. New Delhi: SAGE Publications.

Peterson, T., and L. A. Morgan. 1995. 'Separate and Unequal: Occupation-Establishment Sex Segregation and Gender Wage Gap'. *American Journal of Sociology* 101: 329–365.doi: 10.1086/230727

Powell, A., and K. J. C. Sang. 2015. 'Everyday Experiences of Sexism in Male-Dominated Professions: A Bourdieusian Perspective'. *Sociology* 49 (5): 919–936.

Powell, Abigail, Andrew Dainty, and Barbara Bagilhole. 2012. 'Gender Stereotypes Among Women Engineering and Technology Students in the UK: Lessons from Career Choice Narratives'. *European Journal of Engineering Education* 541–556. Available at https://doi.org/10.1080/03043797.2012.724052 (accessed on 2 August 2019).

———. 2009. 'How Women Engineers Do and Undo Gender: Consequences for Gender Equality'. *Gender, Work and Organization* 16 (4): 411–428. Available at https://onlinelibrary.wiley.com/doi/full/10.1111/j.1468-0432.2008.00406.x (accessed on 2 August 2019).

Radhakrishnan, Smitha. 2009. 'Professional Women, Good Families: Respectable Femininity and the Cultural Politics of a "New" India'. *Qualitative Sociology* 32 (2): 195–212.

———. 2011. *Appropriately Indian: Gender and Culture in a New Transnational Class*. New Delhi: Orient Blackswan.

Raj, Kapil. 1991. 'Knowledge, Power and Modern Science: The Brahamins Strike Back'. In *Science and Empire: Essays in Indian Context, 1700–1947*, edited by A. Rahman, 115–125. Delhi: Anamika Prakashan.

Rapoport, R., L. Bailyn, J. Fletcher, and B. Pruitt. 2002. *Beyond Work–Family Balance: Advancing Gender Equity and Workplace Performance*. San Francisco, CA: Jossey-Bass.

Rathgeber, Eva M. 2009. 'Women and Girls in Science and Technology: Increasing Opportunities in Education, Research and Employment, UN'. Available at http://www.un.org/womenwatch/daw/egm/impact_bdpfa/EP4%20-%20 Rathgeber_final.pdf (accessed on 2 August 2019).

Rhoton, Laura A. 2011. 'Distancing as a Gendered Barrier: Understanding Women Scientists' Gender Practices'. *Gender & Society* 25 (6): 696–716.

Ridgeway, C. L. 2009. 'Framed Before We Know It: How Gender Shapes Social Relations'. *Gender & Society* 23 (2): 145–160.

Ridgeway, C. L., and S. J. Correll. 2004. 'Unpacking the Gender System: A Theoretical Perspective on Gender Beliefs and Social Relations'. *Gender & Society* 18 (4): 510–531.

Risman, B. 1998. Gender Vertigo: American Families in Transition. New Haven, CT: Yale University Press.

Roth, W. D., and G. Sonnert. 2011. 'The Costs and Benefits of "Red Tape": Antibureaucratic Structure and Gender Inequity in a Science Research Organization'. *Social Studies of Science* 41 (3): 385–409.

Schiebinger, Londa. 1999. *Has Feminism Changed Science?* Cambridge, MA, and London: Harvard University Press.

Seymour, E., and Nancy M. Hewitt. 1997. *Talking About Leaving: Why Undergraduates Leave the Sciences.* Boulder, CO: Westview Press.

Shiva, V. 1989. *Staying Alive. Women, Ecology and Development.* London: Zed Press.

Smith-Doerr, Laurel. 2004. *Women's Work: Gender Equality vs. Hierarchy in the Life Sciences.* Boulder, CO: Lynne Rienner.

Steinpreis, Rhea A., Katie A. Anders, and Dawn Ritzke. 1999. 'The Impact of Gender on the Review of the Curricula Vitae of Job Applicants and Tenure Candidates: A National Empirical Study'. *Sex Roles* 41 (7): 509–528.

Subrahmanyan, L. 1998. *Women Scientists in the Third World: The Indian Experience.* New Delhi: SAGE Publications.

Subramainam, Banu. 2009. 'Snow Brown and the Seven Detergents. A Metanarrative on Science and the Scientific Method'. In *Women, Science, and Technology: A Reader in Feminist Science Studies 2nd ed.*, edited by Mary Wyer, Mary Barbercheck, Donna Cookmeyer, Hatice Ozturk and Marta Wayne, 40–45. New York, NY: Routledge.

Subramanian, Jayasree. 2007. 'Perceiving and Producing Merit: Gender and Doing Science in India'. *Indian Journal of Gender Studies* 14 (2): 259–284.

Sur, Abha. 2009. 'Dispersed Radiance. Women Scientists, in C. V. Raman's Laboratory'. In *Women and Science in India*, edited by Neelam Kumar, 98–136. New Delhi: Oxford University Press.

Thapan, Meenakshi. 2007. 'Adolescence, Embodiment and Gender Identity: Elite Women in a Changing Society'. In *Urban Women in Contemporary India: A Reader*, edited by Rehana Ghadially, 31–45. New Delhi: SAGE Publications.

UNESCO. 1999. Women in Science—Quality and Equality for Sustainable Human Development. World Conference on Science, Budapest, 5–7 November 1998. Available at http://www.unesco.org/science/wcs/meetings/eur_bled_e_98.htm (accessed on 2 August 2019).

———. 2007. 'Gender Indicators in Science, Engineering and Technology: An Information Toolkit'. Available at http://unesdoc.unesco.org/images/0015/001504/150434e.pdf (accessed on 2 August 2019).

———. 2015. *UNESCO Science Report: Towards 2030.* Available at https://unesdoc.unesco.org/ark:/48223/pf0000235406_eng (accessed on 2 August 2019).

———. 2018. *Women in Science.* Fact Sheet No. 51. UNESCO Institute for Statistics. Available at http://uis.unesco.org/sites/default/files/documents/fs51-women-in-science-2018-en.pdf (accessed on 2 August 2019).

Upadhye, Rekha P., Priya Vijay Girap, Shalini Tewari, Tara Ashok, K. Bhanumurthy, and Ratan Kumar Sinha. 2014. 'Journal Publication Productivity of Women Scientists at Bhabha Atomic Research Centre, India'. *International Journal of Nuclear Knowledge Management* 6 (3). Available at https://doi.org/10.1504/IJNKM.2014.058939 (accessed on 2 August 2019).

Valian, V. 1999. *Why So Slow? The Advancement of Women*. Cambridge, MA, and London: MIT Press.

Venkatesh, Sujatha. 2015. 'Forms of Social Asymmetry and Cultural Bias: Of Gender and Science in India and the World'. *Transcience* 6 (1): 1–19.

Vogt, C., D. Hocevar, and L. Hagedorn. 2007. 'A Social Cognitive Construct Validation: Determining Women's and Men's Success in Engineering Programs'. *Journal of Higher Education* 78 (2): 337–364.

Wajacman, J. 1991. *Feminism Confronts Technology*. University Park, PA: The Pennsylvania State University Press.

WEF. 2018. The Global Gender Gap Report 2018. Available at http://www3. weforum.org/docs/WEF_GGGR_2018.pdf (accessed on 2 August 2019).

Wenneras, C., and A. Wold. 1997. 'Nepotism and Sexism in Peer-Review'. *Nature* 387: 341–343.

West, C., and D. Zimmerman. 1987. 'Doing Gender'. *Gender and Society* 1 (2): 125–151.

Woetzel, Jonathan, Anu Madgavkar, Kevin Sneader, Oliver Tonby, Diaan-Yi Lin, John Lydon, Sha Sha, Mekala Krishnan, Kweilin Ellingrud, and Michael Gubieski. 2018. The Power of Parity: Advancing Women's Equality in Asia Pacific. MGI Report. Available at https://www.mckinsey.com/featured-insights/gender-equality/the-power-of-parity-advancing-womens-equality-in-asia-pacific (accessed on 2 August 2019).

World Bank. 2017a. GDP Growth (Annual %). Available at https://data.worldbank. org/indicator/NY.GDP.MKTP.KD.ZG?end=2017&start=1990&year_low_ desc=false) (accessed on 2 August 2019).

———. 2017b. Services, Value Added (% of GDP). Available at https://data. worldbank.org/indicator/NV.SRV.TOTL.ZS?end=2017&start=1990 (accessed on 2 August 2019).

———. 2018. Labor Force Participation Rate, Male (% of Male Population Ages 15+) (Modeled ILO Estimate). Available at https://data.worldbank.org/indica-tor/SL.TLF.CACT.MA.ZS (accessed on 2 August 2019).

Xie, Y., and K. A. Shauman. 2003. *Women in Science: Career Processes and Outcomes*. Cambridge, MA: Harvard University Press.

Indian Culture, Gender and S&T Education

Through a son he conquers the worlds, through a son's son he obtains immortality, but through his son's grandson he gains the world of the sun.

—Manusmriti (X: 137)[1]

In childhood a female must be subject to her father, in youth to her husband, when her lord is dead to her sons; a woman must never be independent.

—Manusmriti (V: 148)[2]

This chapter provides a historical and sociocultural context of women's education with focus on their participation in S&T education. A history of women's education reflects changes in the position of women and thereby gender relations in the society. The Introduction discussed that 'gender' is socially constructed and that the normative roles attributed to men and women reproduce gender in different social, institutional and historical contexts. This chapter shows how the contemporary Indian sociocultural context of women's education in S&T is marked by both continuity and change in the gender relations in the country. It also analyses construction of gender in the Indian society, particularly among the urban middle classes, and its impact on education in the pre-college period.

HISTORICAL CONTEXT OF WOMEN'S EDUCATION

In India, the Vedic period (until about 500 BC) is identified with a period of limited surplus economy coinciding with a lack of deep-seated class inequalities and the caste system in its nascent phase (Desai and Krishnaraj 2004). This early caste system was actually the *varna* system in which the Brahmins, Kshatriyas, Vaishyas and Shudras are hierarchically arranged with Brahmins at the highest position and the Shudras at the bottom. A lack of stratification in this period is also reflected in a limited nature of gender hierarchy. For instance, birth of a daughter was not a source of anxiety; women had access to education which led to the emergence of women scholars such as Lilavati who was a mathematician; Gargi who held philosophical discussions and of women composers of Vedic hymns (Basham 1967: 179; Basu 1999: 135).

Rigidity of the caste hierarchy in the post-Vedic period is intrinsically related to a decline in the position of women (Desai and Krishnaraj 2004). Gender inequalities acquired normative structure through Manusmriti or the Law Code written around 200 AD (Thapar 1966: 121) which codified laws of social structure given by Manu, the ancient lawgiver. The Code established Brahamanical supremacy and declared the oldest male member of the kin as the patriarchal head; women and the Untouchables (positioned outside the varna system but within the Hindu fold) were declared unfit for learning; women were to be subservient to men, that is, father–husband–son, at different stages of her life (Desai and Krishnaraj 2004). Thus, the decline in women's education went hand in hand with the crystallization of a patriarchal system that glorified the birth of son, elevated husband to the status of god to be worshipped with a host of accompanying rituals that subordinated women. Women's access to education declined steeply with some exceptions in the Kshatriya and Brahmin families; by the time the British conducted indigenous education surveys in the 1820s and 1830s, there were no girls in traditional village schools or in the schools of higher learning (Basu 1999).

Christian missionaries in the colonial period (1800 AD onwards till 1947) were the first to open schools for girls followed by the liberal official and non-official English men and women. Wood's Despatch of 1854 was the first official expression of interest in girls' education. Soon, Indian social reformers and women from upper caste/class, with some notable exceptions such as Jotiba Phule (born into agricultural caste), also took up the cause of girls' education (Basu 1999). The general view including those of the Indian social reformers was that education of women would aid in their becoming better wives and mothers (Chanana 2001). There were animated debates even among the Indian social reformers about objectives of educating women. Very few (mostly radicals) argued for women's education from gender equity point of view, that is, education that would shake the unjust and hierarchical society. For a majority, women were the custodians of traditional Indian values and their education would help in fulfilling those traditional roles better (Mazumdar 2012: xviii). Separate schools for girls were common in the areas dominated by 'purdah' (Chanana 2001). Many intellectuals of the time favoured single-sex schools, for instance, Siqueira (1939: 146) says: 'Experience rather seems to show that boys become girlish and girls boyish when they are educated in mixed schools'. Education for women was seen as an ideal method to tide over the complexities of transition from tradition to modernity; to provide an educated wife for men of ambition (Forbes 2008: 69).

Most intellectuals of the time saw gender role differentiation as the basis of curriculum differences, particularly at secondary education level, justifying women's exclusion from mathematics and science and of men from fine arts (Chanana 2001). It was argued that since women were not expected to take up jobs after education, they should be taught subjects relevant for their domestic roles such as botany, sociology and psychology; while subjects like physics, chemistry and mathematics (PCM) should have a subordinate role (e.g., Chiplunkar 1930: 232–241; Siqueira 1939: 142). For instance, according to Chiplunkar, secondary education should include knowledge of elementary sciences such as botany, zoology, physics, chemistry 'as applied to household needs and requirements' (p. 236). Ideal science was home science and this was part of the curriculum of the girls' high schools by the 1920s. All India Women's Conference (AIWC), founded in 1927, perceived women's education as important for women's equality and women were to be educated to be not only better wives but also to be lawyers, doctors, etc. However, this education was to be within the dominant reformist and nationalist framework of the times. Their efforts led to the establishment of Lady Irwin College for women in 1932 in Delhi with a certificate course in home science (Basu 2005: 195). A few women such as Menon and Choksi were radicals who believed that education should lead to intellectual development and that physics and mathematics should form part of the curriculum for women (Chanana 2001: 112). Choksi (1929), for example, wrote on alteration of curriculum debate: 'Its (education) purpose should finally be to produce accurate, far-reaching and critical thought' (p. 68).

Gendered notions about education were held by both colonial officials as well as the Indian intelligentsia. This is best expressed in the medical education for women. Medical education for Indian women arose as part of the colonial discourse of 'white man's burden' and control over *zenana* or women's quarters (Burton 2009; Forbes 2009). Much hesitation marked awarding medical degrees in the 1870–1880s to Indian women due to gendered notions on women's intellectual capabilities and their aptitude for science among medical men at the helm of affairs, both Indian and European (Forbes 2009: 6). Kadambini Basu was the first woman to graduate from Medical College, Bengal (later called the Calcutta Medical College) in 1886. Apart from the degree programme (MB), there was the Lady Certificate Programme requiring passing of university entrance examination. Given the social prejudices related to treatment of Indian women by male doctors, it was deemed imperative that women be treated by women medical practitioners. However, there were not enough women doctors from India or England to staff the hospitals and dispensaries under the Dufferin Fund set up for this purpose in the 1880s (Forbes 2009: 5). The Hospital Assistant Course was introduced for this purpose; entry to it required a simple entrance exam with no formal education in science; it was a three-year course which involved little science. Indian intelligentsia did not object to it as women were seen to be different from men, in charge of home and hearth, who needed education suitable to their nature; further, since women's problems were mostly related to childbirth and reproduction, their problems could be dealt with privately by women through this course (Forbes 2009). Thus, the programme designed to bring 'Western medicine' to Indian women reflected prejudices related to women's scientific education.

Engineering education developed as part of the colonial requirement for personnel for civil and construction works. The Roorkee

College for Civil Engineering came up in 1848 and was unique in concept in England also (INSA 2001). With the establishment of universities of Calcutta, Madras and Bombay in 1857, faculties of art, science, law, medicine and engineering came in to being. The three engineering colleges at Calcutta (Shibpur), Pune and Madras (Guindy) were affiliated to the universities in their respective presidencies (INSA 2001). By 1907, 45 affiliated colleges were established in three presidency regions where 91 lecturers, most of them of Indian origin, conducted science and engineering courses at the undergraduate (UG) and postgraduate levels (Krishna 1997). Between the 1910s and the 1920s, about 2,134 degrees were awarded to the Indian students in all the sciences (Mahalanobis 1971, cited in Krishna 1991).

Women in engineering were unheard of at least till the 1940s. There is no research yet on the history of women in engineering education in India. The earliest evidence of women in engineering emerges from Guindy (Madras). Leela George and A. Lalitha were the first to graduate, entering the College of Engineering at Guindy in 1940 and passing out in 1943 (Mohan 2017). Women engineers emerged from those engineering colleges that had been established initially, such as, Guindy and Shibpur (Bengal).

Due to sex segregation and prejudices against female education, it remained mostly an urban phenomenon (Chanana 2001) and all levels of education were heavily male-dominated. There were only 10 per cent girls of school-going age that were enrolled in schools in British India (Basu 1999). In 1946–1947, there were 36 girls for 100 men in primary schools, 14 in high schools; the numbers tapered off in university education with only 7 women for 100 men in colleges of professional education and 12 in colleges of general education and universities (Chanana 2001: 97). More specifically, by 1950–1951, the proportion of women to total enrolment in university education was 16.1 per cent in arts, 7.1 per cent in science, 0.16 per cent in technology (19 women enrolled out of total of 12, 094) and 16.3 per cent in medicine (Chanana 1993: 129). Thus, arts and medicine had emerged as fields with maximum participation of women in the period following independence.

After independence (1947), all areas of study were thrown open for both women and men. However, secondary education boards of different states continued exclusion of girls from science and mathematics and of boys from fine arts even in the 1950s. Finally, in 1961, Committee on Differentiation of Curricula for boys and girls proposed a common curriculum (Mazumdar 2012).

POST-INDEPENDENCE EDUCATION: GROWTH AND INEQUALITIES

There has been a tremendous expansion of education at all levels since independence, both in terms of infrastructure and enrolments. In 1950–1951, there were 74 secondary (up to class IX–X) and senior secondary schools, that is, up to class XI–XII (Ministry of Human Resource Development 2016: 17; Table 19). In 2015–2016, there were about 2.5 lakh such schools (Ministry of Human Resource Development 2018b: 3; Table 6). In 2015–2016, overall there were 1,522,346 schools, 799 universities of all types (central, state, public and private, deemed, institutes of national importance and those under State Legislature Acts, and open universities); 39,071 colleges and 11,923 stand-alone Institutions (Ministry of Human Resource Development 2018b: 3). Since liberalization and privatization in the 1990s, a considerable increase in infrastructure of higher education lies in the private sector. At present, there are 78 per cent of the colleges in the private sector, aided and unaided, accounting for 67.3 per cent of the enrolment (Ministry of Human Resource Development 2018a: iii).

The government recognizes that 'Education is the single most important factor to ensure gender equality and empowerment' (Ministry of Human Resource Development 2016: A2). In 1951, the literacy rate was 7.93 per cent for women and 24.95 per cent for men (Chanana 2001). In 2011, literacy rate (a 'literate' is a person of 7+ age group who can read and write in any language with understanding) for women was 64.6 per cent for women and 80.9 per cent for men in 2011 (Ministry of Human Resource Development 2016: 2). Although these figures reflect considerable growth in literacy, they also indicate gender disparity in literacy levels. Further, there are social inequalities related to access to education as urban students outperform rural students by a large margin in learning outcomes in subjects of English, mathematics, science and social science (Ministry of Human Resource Development 2016: A3). The average annual dropout rate is very high in secondary school (class IX–X) at about 18 per cent for both boys and girls overall, but much higher at 27 per cent for the ST and 19 per cent for the SC in 2013–2014; this dropout is lower at senior secondary level at about 1.5 per cent overall, 1.81 per cent for the SC and 2.94 per cent for ST (Ministry of Human Resource Development 2016: 8; Table 10). A high dropout rate at the secondary school level suggests inability of certain sections to educate children in secondary school and beyond particularly among the SC/ST. Interestingly, the same table shows that the dropout rate for the SC/ST boys is higher compared to the girls of the SC/ST in secondary and senior secondary school.

SENIOR SECONDARY EDUCATION: CRITICAL YEARS AND SCIENCE-RELATED DECISIONS

There is near parity in gross enrolment ratio (GER)[3] of boys and girls at secondary and senior secondary level in the country (Ministry of Human Resource Development 2017). As per the Unified District Information System for Education (UDISE) 2015–2016, the GER of boys and girls at secondary level is 79.16 per cent and 80.97 per cent, respectively, and GER of boys and girls at senior secondary level is 55.95 per cent and 56.41 per cent, respectively. However, parents prefer private schools for boys 'which reflects a broader sort of inequality' (Ministry of Human Resource Development 2018b: ii). In terms of performance, girls in class XII tend to outperform boys, as, for instance, in 2010 with 81.5 per cent of girls that appear actually passing the exams compared to 73.2 per cent boys (Ministry of Human Resource Development 2016: 9; Table 11B).

Senior secondary education or classes XI and XII in school (for 16–18 years old) constitute critical years for the career of a student. This stage occurs just prior to higher education in India or the college education. The student in these two years (class XI–XII) studies a stream of learning which roughly decides his/her subject options for college and thereby career options for the future. There are primarily three streams in most schools at senior secondary level: (a) arts/social sciences, (b) science (PCM; or PCB, i.e., physics, chemistry, biology) and (c) commerce. Here, our focus is on the science streams. Study of PCM is required for appearing in the engineering entrance exams while PCB stream is essential for medical sciences. Those in the PCM stream usually opt for engineering/pure science courses in undergraduation (UG) level and those in PCB opt for medical courses or biology-related courses at the UG level. The science stream offers future subject options greater than any other stream at the UG level. Thus, those in the science stream can shift to arts or commerce in UG but the vice versa is not possible; those in the commerce stream can move to arts but not to sciences. Further, it is possible to give medical entrance even while opting for PCM in case a student opts for biology as an elective.[4] Science is considered as the best option and humanities is the last option, while commerce is gradually becoming popular (Gautam 2015). Science stream, particularly PCM, is most popular. According to a report (NCEE 2005):

> The most prestigious stream (which also has the highest cut-off in terms of marks required in the grade 10 exams) is the science stream, the second is commerce, and the third is humanities (arts). Students in the sciences stream almost always study mathematics, physics, and chemistry. (9)

Students of all streams sit for the exams conducted by the national or state boards in class XII. Those wanting to pursue professional education, such as medical or engineering, additionally sit for their entrance examinations.

The enrolment figures of boys and girls in various streams at the senior secondary level are not available. Nevertheless, figures for enrolment in higher education (graduation onwards) indicate that the enrolment proportion of women is higher than men in medical sciences and humanities. Of the total number of students enrolled in UG in medical sciences, women are 61.1 per cent; the similar statistic for sciences is 48.6 per cent and 28.6 per cent for engineering and technology (Ministry of Human Resource Development 2018a: Table 12). This indicates that the proportion of girls opting for PCM in the senior secondary school might be less than those opting for PCB. Although some students from PCM substream might have shifted to arts/commerce in graduation, the same is true for PCB also.

Family plays an important role in educational decisions (Mukhopadhyay and Seymour 1994) such as what stream to opt for, and father's role in such decisions is particularly significant (Gautam 2015). The decisions are often based on gendered considerations. This is due to the nature of Indian patriarchy with the middle classes, upper castes being the chief carriers of patriarchal values in Indian society (Mukhopadhyay and Seymour 1994) as discussed further.

Indian Patriarchy and Relation with Education

Indian society, as noted in the previous sections, has been historically patriarchal. This patriarchal system is family oriented, referred to as 'patrifocality' by Mukhopadhyay and Seymour (1994). For instance, it requires subordination of the individual goals and interests to the welfare of the family. Thus, marital decisions and later educational decisions for the children became family decisions. Features of patrifocality include patrilineal inheritance and patrilocal descent and residence that reinforce the centrality of males (e.g., a daughter shifts her residence and allegiance to her husband's family after marriage); gender-differentiated family roles (women's nurturing role and domestic roles versus men's economic roles); an ideology of appropriate female behaviour emphasizing chastity, obedience, domesticity and adaptability. Concern with 'purity' (of lineage) through protection of women's sexuality traditionally led to restrictions on male–female interaction which reinforced women's domestic roles, confining them to 'private' sphere as opposed to the 'public' (or economic) sphere. This ideology also constricted women's education in professional fields and professional employment (Dube 2001; Mukhopadhyay and Seymour 1994). These restrictions have applied more to the middle classes and upper castes than others (Mukhopadhyay and Seymour 1994; Subrahmanyan 1998). While there are regional variations in constructions of gender with the North being the patriarchal heartland, and the South and the Eastern regions being more diluted in the potency of patriarchy (Datta 2005), there is a broad similarity of patriarchal norms (Mukhopadhyay and Seymour 1994).

The patriarchal system and the accompanying construction of gendered identities in the colonial period received further ideological thrust as part of the nationalist discourse to define the 'Indian' identity as opposed to the Western. According to Chatterjee (1993), while the supremacy of the White man in the outer/material world was obvious, a reconstituted national identity idealized Indian home and woman's centrality in it as part of the inner/spiritual domain.

Patriarchy has undergone considerable changes since the colonial period. Social practices such as Sati, child marriage and purdah are almost non-existent, and daughters have an equal right to property. Although the 'joint family' continues to be an 'ideal type', the traditional joint family (the most common form of which is the parents, their earning sons and the latter's spouses and children residing together) has declined (Nimkoff 2005). Further, marital decisions are increasing with the consent of the son/daughter in question, although not necessarily based on the bride and groom's familiarity with each other (Desai and Andrist 2010).

An ideal woman was a homemaker until a few decades ago. Now an ideal woman is a woman more visible in public spaces (Thapan 2007). With growth in education, urbanization and opportunity for employment, 'women are much freer now to come out of their homes' (Singh 2009: 14). However, construction of an ideal woman as primarily devoted to family continues and even received a fresh lease of life with the rise of Hindutva forces in the 1990s (Radhakrishnan 2011). This is particularly relevant in case of middle-class families which form the focus of our narrative.

The Indian middle class has been typically perceived to be an educated section of urban society who are seeking white-collar jobs or are employed in those (Sridharan 2004). The educated urban sections, such as the students and professionals in science and engineering, constitute the 'middle class'. For instance, most of the students at the prestigious colleges such as the Indian Institutes of Technology (IITs) are from the middle classes as indicated by their father's professions.

Fathers of about 44 per cent students admitted are in government/ private service, about 13 per cent in doctor/engineering/law/teaching and research/architecture/pharmacy professions; about 8 per cent in agriculture, 15 per cent in business, 3.5 per cent self-employed and rest as 'others'/unknown (IIT Kanpur 2018 [Chapter 14]: 3). Although those from income (father's) group of 8 lakhs and above formed only 12 per cent of those registered for Joint Entrance Examination (JEE) Advanced, they constituted about 23 per cent of those who got admission (Chapter 14: 2). About 77.3 per cent of those admitted belonged to cities, and only 12.5 per cent from towns and 10.2 per cent from the villages (Chapter 14: 1).

Although small numerically (about 153 million; Shukla 2010), the Indian middle class has played a conspicuous role ideologically (Deshpande 2003; Fernandes 2006). While multiple identities within this broad 'middle class' exist and are being added, there is a certain 'middleclassness' that defines the attitudes and values of this section due to common patterns of formal education, consumption and lifestyle aspirations (Donner 2012). For instance, education and careers are extremely important for the middle class as a source of mobility and jobs are much sought after in the engineering and management fields (Kumar 2011). Another significant aspect of middleclassness is the expression of Indianness through focus on family (Donner 2012; Radhakrishnan 2011). Sancho (2015) argues that Indian parents aggressively support their children through their education and build up marketable skills while at the same time appearing to be detached and 'only spending money'.

Studies (Gupta 2012, 2015; Varma 2011) show considerable family support for the women that opt for the science stream in class XI and for science/engineering later during higher education. Women's education in science and more remarkably in the engineering field (offshoot of the PCM stream) has witnessed a growth in participation over the years reflecting critical changes in the patriarchal system. The proportion of women enrolled in engineering and technology courses at UG level was 0.2 per cent in 1950–1951, which rose to 3.8 per cent in 1980–1981, 16 per cent in 1995 and to 28.6 per cent in 2017–2018 (Gupta 2012; Ministry of Human Resource Development

2018a: Table 12). The question thus arises: what has changed in the Indian society due to which there is an enhancement of women's S&T education? Is there any continuity in the patriarchal structure? Although there is a growth of women in engineering, what limits their proportion to one-third while that in medicine is more than half? Do the subject choices reproduce the Indian sociocultural context? These questions are dealt with in the following sections.

SUBJECT DECISIONS FOR GIRLS IN SENIOR SECONDARY SCHOOL

Considerations of parents in making educational decisions are often gendered (Gupta 2012). For instance, in case of daughters, the subject to be chosen is related not only to the family decision of whether the daughter should have a career-oriented education but also to the marital obligations of the parents. Thus, in accordance with the rules of hypergamy, parents must find a groom who is more educated and older than their daughter. In many castes and religions, parents of a professionally educated woman would find it difficult to search for a groom who was more educated than their daughter and one who would also allow her to pursue a career. Mukhopadhyay (1994) found parents unwilling to expend resources on their daughters' academic career due to the assumption that, after marriage, benefits of their education would accrue to their husband and his family. However, in recent years, a professional degree eases marital negotiations for the woman's parents apart from empowering the daughters (Gupta 2015). A daughter's professional education brings prestige to the young woman and her family and assures her a respectable job.

Change is particularly visible since the late 1990s due to liberalization and globalization. Engineering degree requiring PCM at school has become an attractive option for girls due to its association with computer-related branches. The latter are considered 'appropriate' for girls (Varma 2010) and access to engineering education has become enhanced due to privatization of education and mushrooming of engineering colleges (Gupta 2012). Further, since liberalization, there is an availability of jobs in this field (Gupta 2015). PCM stream is also desirable for those wishing to take up science courses later. However, the stream requires a study of mathematics which is considered to be a masculine domain in the West. Growth of women in engineering has ignited debates among scholars whether women's mathematical abilities have ever been doubted in India.

Western studies indicate that women experience 'math anxiety' because mathematics is perceived to be inappropriate for girls; as a result, they must somewhat deny their femininity in order to achieve in mathematics (Fennema and Sherman 1977). American girls' performance in mathematics and science is still impacted by traditional gender beliefs that regard women as 'incompetent' or biologically unsuited for mathematics; it is also affected by gender socialization which is reflected in family attitudes and early negative classroom experiences (Etzkowitz, Kemelgor and Uzzi 2000). The profession of a 'scientist' is ascribed as a 'man's job' and boys and girls identify a typical scientist as male.

Contrary to the Western experience, the beliefs about women's incompetency in mathematical or mechanical activities or notions of differences in intrinsic intellectual ability do not appear in the Indian sociocultural context (Mukhopadhyay 2009). In India, women are believed to have the same potential as men but are constrained by the social contextual factors (p. 163). Varma (2011), in context of computer education of girls in India, also found that mathematics does not appear as a male domain and that gender does not play any role in acquiring mathematical and problem-solving skills. A study on women in a low reputed state engineering college for women (Gupta 2012) found that fathers of 96 per cent of respondents and mothers of 93 per cent respondents believed that women were no less capable than men in science and math; also, parents actively support mathematics and science education for their daughters by hiring tutors for them. At present, proportion of women in postgraduation (PG) in mathematics exceeds that of men at about 60 per cent and in PhD, it is about 45 per cent (Ministry of Human Resource Development 2018a).

Another study that corroborates that mathematical ability of girls is not doubted is that of Das and Singhal (2017). It found gender gap in mathematics at primary school level in rural areas but not in the urban areas. Further, the rural gender gap in mathematics scores was a product of the societal factors such as parents discussing science and related issues more with sons than daughters, involvement of girls with household chores, boys' involvement in outdoor activities and lack of nutrition among girls. The study does not report any intrinsic or biological differences being perceived in the society.

However, there are evidences to the contrary also and certain studies indicate persistence of doubts over women's ability to do mathematics. For instance, according to Gautam (2015), the participants in their senior secondary school found that boys and teachers questioned mathematical ability of girls. This was supplemented by gendered classroom experiences as boys got greater attention in 'masculine' subjects of mathematics and physics than girls did; stereotypes that girls are good in rote learning and boys in conceptual understanding tend to persist. In another study, while women researchers clearly reject stereotypes about a woman's ability to pursue science and engineering, men researchers do not reject these stereotypes with the same vehemence as women (Gupta 2007). Nevertheless, despite stereotypes, there is a growing cluster of women in undergraduate sciences and mathematics the reasons for which are equally gendered (as discussed in Chapter 2). Within sciences, there is greater enrolment in biological sciences (as seen in UG level figures indicated earlier). Interest in biological sciences among women is a function of sociocultural experiences. For instance, a study (Gafoor 2017) shows that despite their similar achievement levels, boys at senior secondary level had higher interest in physics, and girls had higher interest in biology and chemistry. These interest levels, according to the author, relate more to their out-of-school experiences rather than innate abilities.

The interests of a son/daughter appear secondary to the primary role of gendered considerations in the family's subject choice decisions. These decisions are gendered for boys also. According to Gautam (2015: 37), in urban middle-class families, 'even if brothers were not considered "good students," they still "had to take science." Male siblings were not given the option of pursuing arts and commerce'.

Further, in such families, the decision to take science was made keeping in mind mainly two professions: medicine for girls and engineering for boys. Although women's participation in engineering has increased, this is mainly owing to the computer-related fields of engineering. Engineering is still male-dominated with only 28 per cent women in graduation. This is because education for boys is intrinsically related to a construction of masculinity and male privilege.

Construction of Masculinity, Socialization and Relation with Education

Study of masculinity deepens our understanding of the underlying drivers of gender inequality; it helps to focus on men and highlights that patriarchy also puts dictates on men (Edström, Das and Dolan 2014). While patriarchy refers to a system of social organization that is organized around the idea of male superiority over females, it is the social processes, interactions, behaviours, actual division of tasks that constructs masculinity and femininity (Srivastava 2006). The focus of the earlier studies on gender was primarily on women and the construction of their identity. However, recent years have witnessed a growing understanding that gender relations cannot be understood without making men and masculinities visible. Masculinity can be defined as values, experiences and meanings that are culturally interpreted as masculine and are ascribed to men more than women in a particular cultural context (Alvesson and Billing 2009: 72).

A dominant form of masculinity reflecting Indian patriarchal norms is constructed in the urban, middle-class students particularly through early socialization at home and school. Socialization is a process through which individuals learn ways of a given society or a group so that they can function within it (Elkin and Handel 1989). Family is the first exposure of a child to understand the norms of the society. The process also involves gender socialization, that is, learning society's rules and regulations dichotomized as either masculine or feminine and behaving in ways socially accepted as a male or female; it is in family that boys realize their privileged status and its relation to power (Adams and Coltrane 2005).

Male privilege and dominance is reproduced in Indian families through differential socialization of sons and daughters and these differences are rooted in the Indian society's son preference (Srivastava 1997). Traditional Hindu society exhibits son preference as son is required for cultural rites, girls are to be married (with dowry) and in the process lost to parents and, therefore, a liability, son carries forward the family name, belongs to the family, takes care of the aged parents and is therefore an asset. Srivastava (1997) found that urban mothers (65%), urban grandmothers (72%), rural mothers (74%), rural grandmothers (96%) overwhelmingly preferred a son to a daughter. According to Chowdhury (2008), while restrictions, pressures and regulations for girls are enormous, for boys, there is little restriction and opposition at all for their behaviour, actions and thoughts, and are overprotected and over cared for. Girls tend to conform to rules of the game and enforce the rules as well, whereas boys use flexible rules and change them to suit their convenience.

Schools appear as institutionalized mechanisms for construction of masculinity. Analysis of school curriculum has shown that traditional meanings of masculine and feminine continue to persist despite the government pronouncements on providing women empowering education (Bhog 2002). For instance, men are valourized for their achievements and their personal life is rarely mentioned in the school texts of classes III, V and VIII; on the other hand, in the description of valiant women, the achievements of Rani of Jhansi and Marie Curie are 'normalized' through their participation in cooking, washing, cleaning and praying (p. 1641). Science education itself is value-laden. Drawing from the feminist critique of gender and science, Raveendran and Chunawala (2015) analysed science curriculum documents and the NCERT class XII biology textbook; they found that the curriculum/ chapters reflect the masculine, positivist discourse of science and supported technologies that pose risk to the woman's body.

Construction of masculinity is closely associated with educational attainments of boys. Due to the patriarchal emphasis on the male as an asset, a greater societal focus and parental expectations regarding science and math achievement of boys than of girls exists. The discourse on whether math capability of girls is doubted or not is perhaps of less relevance in India and it is more important to understand how the society views the achievements of men and women. Thus, Mukhopadhyay remarks that even among the well-off, education-oriented families, educational achievement, especially in the scientific fields, is viewed differently for girls than boys (1994: 108–109). Men's academic achievement is celebrated more than that of women as it will bring long-term economic and social benefits to the family while the girl's achievement has little long-term value for the natal family. Further, even if there is parental support, women moving ahead of men in mathematics and science might not be looked on favourably among the male peers and teachers. For instance, a respondent in Gupta and Sharma's (2003) study on women academic scientists reported:

> In the final year of school, I topped among all the schools in the city. The boys' schools did not like it and I received a lot of junk mail. I faced a lot of harassment and only the support of my parents helped me through this crisis. (p. 287)

Masculinity is also associated with technology in many parts of the world. As Mellström (2004) says, there is a materially and symbolically powerful relationship between men and technology, both historically and in contemporary societies (p. 369). This relationship affects use of electronic and mechanical toys and gadgets from the childhood which negatively impacts women's careers in STEM (science, technology, engineering and mathematics). Western studies show that culture of engineering involves preoccupation with tinkering (McIlwee and Robinson 1992). Most women engineers have not grown up tinkering and do not share the same obsession; for a woman to be closely involved in technology is to reject meaningful social and emotional relationships (Faulkner 2001).

In the Indian context, boys tend to have greater access to electronic gadgets. For instance, in a study at Trivandrum (a capital city), among the 283 students of class VIII–XII with mobile phones, 64 per cent were boys (Varghese, Nivedhitha and Krishnatray 2013). There are 'engineering for kids' centres in metropolitan cities for 4–15-year olds which brings STEM to kids in a fun and challenging ways. As one centre reported (Bhyana 2017), the activities include building simple models like that of a car and introduction to basic concepts such as distance, speed and direction in a fun manner; attaching motors and sensors to the animal models made of Lego and then programming them through simple steps on computer. At another centre, they also explained how everyday machines like fans work and how cars move to get them thinking about technology. However, girls make up less than 20 per cent of the class at most of these centres. As per this report, robotics professionals say that parents and schools need to get rid of the mindset that only boys are inclined towards robotics. Thus, masculinity is related to tinkering in India as elsewhere. This notion of masculinity and its relationship with the concept of male as an asset construct engineering as a masculine field in India. The entry in the two sought-after professions of engineering and medical requires extensive preparation which has led to coaching centres. The trends in coaching reflect family choices that vary for sons and daughters. This gendered nature of coaching and medical/engineering decision is discussed in the following section.

'Coaching' for Entry in Medical and Engineering: Gendered Decisions

Since 1991, there has been a mushrooming of private coaching centres. Education is the fulcrum of middle-class aspirations, and coaching centres for the final school year symbolize the mobility aspirations of this class (Sancho 2015). This is because this year's examinations constitute the bedrock of future higher education and jobs. As discussed earlier, examinations for entry in institutes of higher education in engineering and medicine are in addition to the class XII exams. However, these entrance exams require coaching at the senior secondary school level because they need training and skills of a higher level than those required for the class XII board examinations. Coaching is not essential, but it enhances the chances of securing admission. For instance, IIT Kanpur (2018) shows that out of 60,420 of those who registered for the JEE Advanced exam[5] and took coaching, about 10.5 per cent (6,326/60,420) finally got admission into an IIT; while out of 97,253 students who registered and did self-study, only 5.32 per cent (5,183) finally got admission (Chapter 14: 1).

Studies show a lack of female students at the coaching centres for engineering entrance examinations. For instance, Singh and Pathak (2010) found that more women than men were not being given professional coaching for such examinations. Further, almost all the students who did well in JEE had taken coaching, but the percentage of women in coaching centres in major cities of India did not exceed 24 per cent. Gupta's (2012) study corroborates this, as out of about 58 per cent of respondents at a lower level women's engineering college (69/118) who appeared for JEE (equivalent to JEE Advanced at the time of this study), only 30 per cent (21/69) had taken coaching. Out of 10.4 lakh students appearing for JEE Mains in 2018, more than 60 per cent (6.46 lakh) were boys (*The Times of India* 2018). Fewer women appear for JEE Advanced held for admission to prestigious science and engineering institutes. In 2018, percentage of girls that registered for JEE Advanced was 20.4 per cent of total (33,811/165,656); they constituted 20 per cent of those who (31,021/155,158) appeared and 13.06 per cent (4,179/31,988) of those who qualified (IIT Kanpur 2018 [Chapter 4]: 1). This low percentage of girls that qualify suggests lack of coaching since girls are well represented in the merit lists of class XII Central Board of Secondary Education (CBSE) boards and are often toppers in the PCM stream (Rao et al. 2016; Singh and Pathak 2010). It also suggests a lack of expectations from girls, and such families that do not impart coaching usually prefer to send their daughters to a nearby engineering college (Gupta 2012).

The situation for medical entrance is different for women. The selection of students in most of the medical colleges is based on the score obtained in the objective type exams such as NEET-UG or National Eligibility cum Entrance Test for admission into UG medical courses at government and private medical colleges.[6] It is a 3-hour exam and contains multiple choice questions on subjects of PCB. It is conducted by the CBSE. Coaching starts usually from class XI and is believed to be desirable for getting a good rank; it is regarded as tough and enjoys prestige similar to the JEE. There is a lack of studies on gender issues related to medical coaching. However, unlike the JEE exams, girls' participation in medical entrance exams appears to exceed that of boys. For instance, in 2018, about 13.3 lakh students registered for the NEET-UG examination held for 66,000 seats in medical and dental courses across the country, of whom about 7.5 lakh (about 56.4%) were girls and 5.8 lakh were boys (CBSE 2018). Proportion of girls for coaching for medical does not lag behind boys. According to a head of a coaching institute at Hyderabad:

> For medical coaching, we see six girls to three boys. In engineering, it is the reverse. Engineering has a lot of mathematics in the curriculum. The general notion is that girls are more suited for studying biology. (*Deccan Chronicle* 2017)

Girls are half or more of the total students for medical coaching at Kota (Rao et al. 2016). Hence, expenditure on girls or sending them far from home for coaching or for degree later are not the obstacles for women's entry in medical. This leads to the questioning of the hypothesis that parents are unwilling to spend money on the coaching of girls, as found in case of women's entry in engineering (e.g., Mukhopadhyay 1994). The monetary investment for girls' education depends on subject choice decision. Engineering continues to be viewed less favourably than medicine for girls as seen in the statistics for women that appear in such entrance exams (as given earlier). The preference for medical career for girls is due to various gendered factors. According to Chakrabarty (2010):

> Parents usually prefer the professional career of a doctor (compared to engineering) for their daughters, as it offers flexible working hours, independent work through private practice, social prestige and good earning. (p. 420)

As apparent from the national entrance exam figures, proportion of boys vis-à-vis girls who appear is lesser for medical entrance than for JEE Mains. The question then arises why is engineering preferred for men and not medicine? A successful medical career requires greater period of study including 5.5 years of UG, 3 years of PG and maybe 2 years of super specialization; while a Bachelor of Medicine and Bachelor of Surgery (MBBS) can practice medicine but the degree has little market value; On the other hand, 4 years of UG in engineering can fetch a job with decent salary which is further enhanced by a PG degree in management (Bansal 2005). Clearing JEE or a good rank in

NEET are equally difficult, but entry in IITs guarantees a good career while a medical graduate would still have to slog out for several more years. A doctor needs to establish reputation, but, once established, can make a higher amount of money than an engineer. A successful doctor lacks time for vacation and family. Also, it is easier to go abroad for higher studies after Bachelor of Technology (B.Tech) than after MBBS.

In short, it implies that a successful career is easier to achieve through engineering than medicine. Yet career in medical is preferred for girls. A study of medical college students shows that girls received more encouragement from their families to pursue medicine than boys (Agrawal et al. 2015). This appears to be contradictory as women receive encouragement for medicine from their families even though it is difficult to achieve a successful career in medicine. However, preference for medicine for women is due to historical and sociocultural reasons. Historically, medicine has been considered prestigious for women since the colonial period and being related to biology it appears to be suited to women's aptitude. Further, encouraging daughters for medicine is also probably because of various other gendered factors: highly successful careers are not desired for women and therefore the concerns that might plague regarding a son becoming a doctor (a successful one) are not overwhelming in case of daughters. Studies suggest higher parental expectations from boys for academic and career achievements (Basu et al. 2017; Larsen 2011). Women are expected to use their education to be independent financially, while men are expected to be 'successful' in careers (Gupta 2007). As Kapadia (2017: 153) puts it, girls in middle-class urban families are raised to be achievement-oriented and their aspirations encouraged, but they are persuaded to exercise restraint so that their aspirations do not result in compromise of their gendered roles in family and home. The ideas of educating and empowering women versus placing traditional limitations on those coexist (Radhakrishnan 2011). In effect, it implies that a woman might become a doctor as it enables financial independence and status, but the practice or the choice of specialization should allow her to meet the gendered obligations, for instance, private practice at home and flexible work hours, as suggested by Chakrabarty (2010), would help in balancing home and work.

The coaching at senior secondary level has become a menace, a 'shadow education' (Orberg 2017). Coaching represents a failure of the institutions to select the best students for professional courses. Kota in Rajasthan is the largest coaching market in the country. Kota coaching industry has about 110,000 strong student population with yearly turnover including fees and living costs around 200 million Euros (Orberg 2017). They have a large number of successful qualifiers in JEE and NEET. It also has the highest suicide rates among the students with about 57 students committing suicide in five years (Poonam 2016). Student suicides have also been reported from other coaching centres such as those at Andhra Pradesh and Telangana (Dailybite 2017). The premium attached to being doctors and engineers and lack of other respectable jobs fuel parental pressure. Gruelling study schedule, large student population in the coaching class and difficulty in coping with the preparation, lack of friends and cultural differences with peers might lead to isolation and depression.

The stress in the two years of higher secondary school affects both boys and girls. In a study on academic stress among students of class XI–XII (Deb, Strodl and Sun 2015), about 63 per cent students reported stress due to academic pressure with no significant differences across gender. About 66 per cent students reported pressure due to parental expectations for better academic performance. Although there is a higher parental pressure on boys than girls, the difference is not significant (Deb et al. 2015: Table 2). Perhaps both sexes experience academic pressure due to gendered expectations of parents, for boys to obtain a lucrative career and for girls to obtain high status jobs to meet patrifocal concerns of parents (e.g., Gupta 2012). The subject preferences for women such as preference of medical over engineering, of science over humanities are governed by the concerns of women's profession being balanced by domestic roles.

CONCLUSIONS

From the ancient times when women were denied the right to education, India has come a long way. A major fillip to education for women occurred after independence with growth in infrastructure and access.

However, professional education in general and for women specifically grew after opening of the higher education to private sector and growth of jobs after liberalization after the 1990s. The growth in women's education has been marked by continuity and change in the patrifocal ideology which both encourages and places limits on women's educational choices and growth.

A gendered discourse in families has an impact on the subject choices and the overall planning of families for education/careers of their children. Studies show that urban middle-class families are involved extensively in the strategic planning of their child's academic and professional future (Chopra 2005; Gautam 2015). This extensive involvement, in terms of financial and emotional, becomes even more evident in the preparation (or coaching) for the entrance exams of engineering and medical UG programmes.

Educational decisions in S&T are related to male privilege and hierarchical relations between men and women. Son preference is accompanied by parental attention on sons for professional education; boys experience pressures of parental expectations of being successful in education and later in careers as they are supposed to be the breadwinners and take care of ageing parents. However, the process also constructs hierarchical gender relations, imparting power to men and producing male privilege which is internalized through socialization experiences. It also constructs women as secondary to men in the discourse on successful careers. The parental focus on sons for science and engineering education and careers marks the beginning of the marginalization of women in the 'public' sphere. The masculine dominance and the patriarchal structure is reproduced and reconstructed in higher education in science and engineering as discussed in the next chapter.

NOTES

1. Manusmriti or the Manav Dharam Shastra are the laws given by the ancient sage Manu on topics such as duties, rights, laws, conduct, virtues and others. It was one of the first Sanskrit texts translated during the British rule of India in 1794 by Sir William Jones and used to formulate the Hindu law by the

colonial government. It has been translated several times. Here, the text refers to the following: Buhler, George, translator. *The Laws of Manu*. Available at http://www.sacred-texts.com/hin/manu.htm (accessed on 5 August 2019).

2. Ibid.

3. GER = Number of students enrolled in a given level of education, regardless of age, expressed as a percentage of the official school-age population corresponding to the same level of education. Available at http://uis.unesco.org/node/334661 (accessed on 5 August 2019).

4. In class XI–XII, a student has five subjects. One language is compulsory; the three subjects in PCM stream/PCB are fixed and one elective can be taken. A student from PCM stream can opt for biology as an elective.

5. Students must take the JEE Mains exam to get admission into the university for the UG engineering programme. Only top 200,000 scorers in JEE Mains, which includes students from all categories (GE, OBC [NCL], SC, ST and PD as per reservation policy with different merit lists prepared for each category) are eligible to appear in JEE Advanced. The JEE Advanced is a common admission test for students seeking admission to UG programmes of all IITs and ISM Dhanbad. The JEE Advanced has two objective type papers. Each paper consists of PCM. Duration of each paper is 3 hours. JEE Mains consists of one objective type paper with questions on PCM.

6. NEET-UG: The NEET-UG is an entrance examination in India for students who wish to study graduate medical course (MBBS) and dental course (Bachelor of Dental Surgery [BDS]) in government or private medical colleges and dental colleges. NEET-UG (UG) for MBBS and BDS courses is currently conducted by the CBSE. NEET-UG replaced the All India Pre Medical Test (AIPMT) and all individual MBBS exams conducted by states or colleges themselves in 2013.

REFERENCES

Adams, Michele, and S. Coltrane. 2005. 'Boys and Men in Families: The Domestic Production of Gender, Power, and Privilege'. In *Handbook of Studies on Men & Masculinities*, Vol. 14, edited by Michael S. Kimmel, Jeff Hearn and R. W. Connell, 230–248. Thousand Oaks, CA: SAGE Publications.

Agrawal, Meena J., Madhura Y. Bedekar, and Deepa S. Nair. 2015. 'Gender Differences in Motivational Factors Towards Medical Career Choice'. *IOSR Journal of Research & Method in Education (IOSR-JRME)* 5 (4): 53–56.

Alvesson, M., and Y. Billing. 2009. *Understanding Gender and Organizations*. New Delhi: SAGE Publications.

Bansal, Rashmi. 2005, 7 February. *Doctor or Engineer? Which Has More Money and Demand?* Available at http://www.rediff.com/getahead/2005/feb/07rashmi.htm/ (accessed on 2 August 2019).

Basham, A. L. 1967. *The Wonder That Was India*. New Delhi: Rupa and Co.

Basu, Aparna. 1999. 'Women's Education in India: Achievements and Challenges'. In *From Independence Towards Freedom: Indian Women Since 1947*, edited by Bharati Ray and Aparna Basu, 135–157. New Delhi: Oxford University Press.

———. 2005. 'A Century and A Half's Journey: Women's Education in India, 1850s to 2000'. In *Women of India: Colonial and Post-Colonial Periods*, edited by Bharti Ray, 183–207. New Delhi: PHISPC, Centre for Studies in Civilizations.

Basu, S., X. Zuo, C. Lou, R. Acharya, and R. Lundgren. 2017. 'Learning to Be Gendered: Gender Socialization in Early Adolescence among Urban Poor in Delhi, India, and Shanghai, China'. *Journal of Adolescent Health* 61 (4S): S24–S29. Available at https://www.ncbi.nlm.nih.gov/pubmed/28915988 (accessed on 2 August 2019).

Bhayana, Neha. 2017. When Parents Started to Enroll Their Kids in Robotics Classes! *The Economic Times*. Available at https://economictimes.indiatimes.com/articleshow/56848071.cms?utm_source=contentofinterest&utm_medium=text&utm_campaign=cppst (accessed on 2 August 2019).

Bhog, Dipta. 2002. 'Gender and Curriculum'. *Economic & Political Weekly* 37 (17): 1638–1642.

Burton, A. 2009. 'Contesting the Zenana: The Mission to Make Lady Doctors for India, 1874–1885'. In *Women and Science in India: A Reader*, edited by Neelam Kumar, 21–54. New Delhi: Oxford University Press.

CBSE. 2018. *Statistics of NEET(UG) 2018*. Available at https://cbseneet.nic.in/cbseneet/ShowPdf.aspx?Type=E0184ADEDF913B076626646D3F52C3B49C39AD6D&ID=25293F2761D658CC70C19515861842D712751BDC (accessed on 2 August 2019).

Chakrabarty, B. 2010. 'Some Additional Aspects of Gender Asymmetry'. *Current Science* 99 (4): 420.

Chanana, Karuna. 1993. 'Accessing Higher Education: The Dilemma of Schooling Women, Minorities, Scheduled Castes and Scheduled Tribes in Contemporary India'. In *Higher Education Reform in India*, edited by Philip G. Altbach and Suma Chitnis, 115–154. New Delhi: SAGE Publications.

———. 2001. *Interrogating Women's Education: Bounded Visions, Expanding Horizons*. Jaipur: Rawat Publications.

Chatterjee, Partha. 1993. *The Nation and Its Fragments: Colonial and Postcolonial Histories*. Princeton, NJ: Princeton University Press.

Chiplunkar, G. M. 1930. *The Scientific Basis of Women's Education*. Pune: S. B. Hudlikar. Available at https://archive.org/details/in.ernet.dli.2015.83360 (accessed on 2 August 2019).

Choksi, M. 1929. 'Some Impressions of Women's Colleges'. In *Women in Modern India*, edited by E. V. Gedge and M. Choksi, 63–77. Bombay: D. B. Taraporevala Sons. Available at https://archive.org/stream/in.ernet.dli.2015.200558/2015.200558.Women-In#page/n79/mode/2up/search/63 (accessed on 2 August 2019).

Chopra, R. 2005. 'Sisters and Brothers: Schooling, Family and Migration'. In *Educational Regimes in Contemporary India*, edited by R. Chopra, P. Jeffery and H. Reifeld, 299–315. New Delhi: SAGE Publications.

Chowdhury, A. 2008. 'The Cultural Construct of Troubles with Boys in India'. *Journal of Human Ecology* 24 (4): 297–303.

Dailybite. 2017, 23 October. 'Student Suicides are our Collective Shame. Education Mustn't be a Battle unto Death'. *DailyO*. Available at https://www.dailyo.in/variety/students-suicide-coaching-institutes-exam-pressure/story/1/20204.html (accessed on 2 August 2019).

Das, Upasak, and Karan Singhal. 2017, 23–25 November. 'Gender Differences in Mathematics Performance: Evidence from Rural India'. Paper prepared for the IARIW-ICIER Conference New Delhi, India. Available at http://www.iariw.org/India/singhal.pdf (accessed on 2 August 2019).

Datta, Anandita. 2005. 'MacDonaldization of Gender in Urban India'. *Gender, Technology and Development* 9 (1): 125–135. doi: 10.1177/097185240500900107

Deb, Sibnath, E. Strodl, and Jiandong Sun. 2015. 'Academic Stress, Parental Pressure, Anxiety and Mental Health among Indian High School Students'. *International Journal of Psychology and Behavioral Sciences* 5 (1): 26–34. doi:10.5923/j.ijpbs.20150501.04

Deccan Chronicle. 2017, 3 July. *Fewer Girls at Coaching Centre Too*. Available at https://www.deccanchronicle.com/nation/current-affairs/030717/fewer-girls-at-coaching-centres-too.html (accessed on 2 August 2019).

Desai, N., and M. Krishnaraj. 2004. 'An Overview of the Status of Women in India'. In *Class, Caste and Gender*, edited by Manoranjan Mohanty, 296–319. New Delhi: SAGE Publications.

Desai, S., and L. Andrist. 2010. 'Gender Scripts and Age at Marriage in India'. *Demography* 47 (3): 667–687. Available at http://www.ncbi.nlm.nih.gov/pmc/articles/PMC3000052/ (accessed on 2 August 2019).

Deshpande, Satish. 2003. *Contemporary India: A Sociological View*. Bangalore: Penguin Books.

Donner, H. 2012. *Being Middle-Class in India: A Way of Life*. Abingdon: Routledge.

Dube, Leela. 2001. *Anthropological Explorations in Gender: Intersecting Fields*. New Delhi: SAGE Publications.

Edström, Jerker, Abhijit Das, and Chris Dolan. 2014. 'Introduction: Undressing Patriarchy and Masculinities to Re-Politicise Gender'. *IDS Bulletin* 45 (1): 1–10.

Elkin, F., and G. Handel. 1989. *The Child and Society: The Process of Socialization*, 5th ed. New York, NY: McGraw-Hill.

Etzkowitz, H., C. Kemelgor, and B. Uzzi. 2000. *Athena Unbound: The Advancement of Women in Science and Technology*. Cambridge: Cambridge University Press.

Faulkner, Wendy. 2001. 'The Power and the Pleasure? A Research Agenda for "Making Gender Stick" to Engineers'. *Science, Technology, & Human Values* 25 (1): 87–119.

Fennema, E., and J. Sherman. 1977. Sex-related Differences in Mathematics Achievement, Spatial Visualization and Affective Factors, *American Educational Research Journal* 14 (1): 51–71.

Fernandes, L. 2006. *India's New Middle Class: Democratic Politics in an Era of Economic Reform*. Minneapolis, MN: University of Minnesota Press.

Forbes, Geraldine. 2008. 'Education for Women'. In *Women and Social Reform in Modern India: A Reader*, edited by Sumit Sarkar and Tanika Sarkar, 83–112. New Delhi: Permanent Black.

———. 2009. 'No Science for Lady Doctors in Nineteenth Century Bengal'. In *Women and Science in India: A Reader*, edited by Neelam Kumar, 3–20. New Delhi: Oxford University Press.

Gafoor, K. Abdul. 2017, 23–24 February. 'Influence of Out-of-School Experiences and Learning Styles on Interest in Biology, Chemistry and Physics among Higher Secondary Boys and Girls in Kerala'. Paper presented at the National Conference on Quality Education in Present Educational Scenario, Umiam, Meghalaya, India. Available at https://eric.ed.gov/?id=ED581524 (accessed on 2 August 2019).

Gautam, Meenakshi. 2015. 'Gender, Subject Choice and Higher Education in India: Exploring "Choices" and "Constraints" of Women Students'. *Contemporary Education Dialogue* 12 (1): 31–58.

Gupta, Namrata. 2007. 'Indian Women in Doctoral Education in Science and Engineering: A Study of Informal Milieu at the Reputed Indian Institutes of Technology'. *Science Technology and Human Values* 32 (5): 507–533.

———. 2012. 'Women Undergraduates in Engineering Education in India: A Study of Growing Women's Participation'. *Gender, Technology and Development* 16 (2): 153–176.

———. 2015. 'Rethinking the Relationship between Gender and Technology: A Study of the Indian Example'. *Work Employment & Society* 29 (4): 661–672.

Gupta, Namrata and Arun K. Sharma. 2003. 'Patrifocal Concerns in the Lives of Women in Academic Science: Continuity of Tradition and Emerging Challenges'. *Indian Journal of Gender Studies* 10 (2): 279–305.

IIT Kanpur. 2018. Report of the Joint Implementation Committee. Volume I. Available at https://drive.google.com/file/d/12x1uG0BeGqO2r9OJi43Ag5YV AjF2alli/view (accessed on 2 August 2019).

INSA. 2001. *Pursuit and Promotion of Science*. Available at http://www.iisc.ernet. in/insa/ch6.pdf (accessed on 2 August 2019).

Kapadia, Shagufta. 2017. *Adolescence in Urban India: Cultural Construction in a Society in Transition*. New Delhi: Springer.

Krishna, V.V. 1991. The Emergence of the Indian Scientific Community. *Sociological Bulletin* 40 (1/2): 89–107.

———. 1997. 'A Portrait of the Scientific Community in India: Historical Growth and Contemporary Problems'. In *Scientific Community in the Developing World*, edited by J. Gaillard, V. V. Krishna and Roland Waast, 237–280. New Delhi: SAGE Publications.

Kumar, N. 2011. 'The Middle-Class Child: Ruminations on Failure'. In *Elite and Everyman: The Cultural Politics of the Indian Middle Classes*, edited by A. Baviskar and R. Ray, 220–245. New Delhi: Routledge.

Larsen, M. 2011. *Vulnerable Daughters in India: Culture, Development and Changing Contexts*. New Delhi: Routledge.

Mazumdar, V. 2012. *Education, Equality and Development: Persistent Paradoxes in Indian Women's History*. New Delhi: Pearson.

McIlwee, Judith S., and J. Gregg Robinson. 1992. *Women in Engineering: Gender, Power, and Work Place Culture*. Albany, NY: SUNY Press.

Mellström, Ulf. 2004. 'Machines and Masculine Subjectivity Technology as an Integral Part of Men's Life Experiences'. *Men and Masculinities* 6 (4): 368–382. doi:10.1177/1097184X03260960

Ministry of Human Resource Development. 2016. *Educational Statistics at a Glance*. New Delhi: Department of School Education & Literacy, Ministry of Human Resource Development, Government of India. Available at http://mhrd.gov.in/sites/upload_files/mhrd/files/statistics/ESG2016_0.pdf (accessed on 2 August 2019).

———. 2017. *Gross Enrolment Ratio of Boys and Girls*. Press Information Bureau. Available at http://mhrd.gov.in/sites/upload_files/mhrd/files/gross.pdf (accessed on 2 August 2019).

———. 2018a. *All India Survey on Higher Education 2017–18*. New Delhi: Department of Higher Education, Ministry of Human Resource Development, Government of India. Available at http://aishe.nic.in/aishe/viewDocument.action?documentId=245 (accessed on 2 August 2019).

———. 2018b. *Educational Statistics at a Glance*. New Delhi. Available at https://mhrd.gov.in/sites/upload_files/mhrd/files/statistics-new/ESAG-2018.pdf (accessed on 2 August 2019).

Mohan, S. 2017. *The Resilient Builder: Leelamma (George) Koshie, Kerala's First Woman Engineer*. Available at https://www.linkedin.com/pulse/resilient-builder-leelamma-george-koshie-keralas-shantha-mohan-ph-d-/ (accessed on 2 August 2019).

Mukhopadhyay, Carol C. 1994. 'Family Structure and Women's Participation in Science and Engineering'. In *Women, Education and Family Structure in India*, edited by Carol C. Mukhopadhyay and S. Seymour, 103–132. Boulder, CO: Westview Press.

———. 2009. 'How Exportable are Western Theories of Gendered Science? A Cautionary Word'. In *Women and Science in India: A Reader*, edited by Neelam Kumar, 137–177. Oxford: Oxford University Press.

Mukhopadhyay, Carol C., and S. Seymour. 1994. 'Introduction'. In *Women, Education and Family Structure in India*, edited by Carol C. Mukhopadhyay and S. Seymour, 1–36. Boulder, CO: Westview Press.

NCEE. 2005. *India Education Profile*. Available at http://www.ncee.org/wp-content/uploads/2013/10/India-Education-Report.pdf (accessed on 2 August 2019).

Nimkoff, M. F. 2005. 'The Family in India: Some Problems Concerning Research on the Changing Family in India'. In *The Family in India: Structure and Practice*, edited by T. Patel, 71–80. New Delhi: SAGE Publications.

Orberg, J. W. 2017. 'Uncomfortable Encounters Between Elite and "Shadow Education" in India—Indian Institutes of Technology and the Joint Entrance Examination Coaching Industry'. *Higher Education* 76 (1): 129–144. Available at https://doi.org/10.1007/s10734-017-0202-5 (accessed on 2 August 2019).

Poonam, S. 2016, 1 June. 'Why 57 Young Students Have Taken Their Lives in Kota'. *Huffpost*. Available at https://www.huffingtonpost.in/2016/06/01/life-and-death-in-kota_n_10232456.html (accessed on 2 August 2019).

Radhakrishnan, S. 2011. *Appropriately Indian: Gender and Culture in a New Transnational Class*. New Delhi: Orient Blackswan.

Rao, Yogita, Shreya Roy Choudhary, and Shoeb Khan. 2016, 24 June. Are Girls Good at Maths? Toppers Are in Medicine. *TOI*. Available at https://www.pressreader.com/india/the-times-of-india-new-delhi-edition/20160624/281960312051138 (accessed on 2 August 2019).

Raveendran, A., and S. Chunawala. 2015. 'Reproducing Values: A Feminist Critique of a Higher Secondary Biology Textbook Chapter on Reproductive Health'. *Indian Journal of Gender Studies* 22 (2): 194–218. Available at https://doi.org/10.1177/0971521515578244 (accessed on 2 August 2019).

Sancho, David. 2015. *Youth, Class and Education in Urban India: The Year that Can Break or Make You*. Milton Park: Taylor & Francis.

Shukla, R. 2010. *How India Earns, Spends and Saves—Unmasking the Real India*. New Delhi: SAGE Publications and NCAER-CMCR.

Singh, J. P. 2009. *Problems of India's Changing Family and State Intervention*. Available at http://undesadspd.org/LinkClick.aspx?fileticket=UWi5XFLDzB4 (accessed on 2 August 2019).

Singh, Vijay A., and Praveen Pathak. 2010. 'Gender Asymmetry in Selection Tests at the Pre-College Level'. *Current Science* 98 (11): 1432–1433.

Siqueira, T. N. 1939. *The Education of India: History and Problems*. Madras: Oxford University Press. Available at https://archive.org/details/in.ernet.dli.2015.507462 (accessed on 2 August 2019).

Sridharan, E. 2004 'The Growth and Sectoral Composition of India's Middle Class: Its Impact on the Politics of Economic Liberalization'. *India Review* 3 (4): 405–428.

Srivastava, A. K. 1997. 'The Changing Place of Child in Indian Families: A Cross-Generational Study'. *Trends in Social Science Research* 4 (1): 191–200.

Srivastava, Sanjay. 2006. 'The Voice of the Nation and the Five-Year Plan Hero: Speculations on Gender, Space, and Popular Culture'. In *Fingerprinting Popular Culture: The Mythic and the Iconic in Indian Cinema*, edited by Vinay Lal and Ashis Nandy, 122–155. New Delhi: Oxford University Press.

Subrahmanyan, Lalitha. 1998. *Women Scientists in the Third World: The Indian Experience*. New Delhi: SAGE Publications.

Thapan, Meenakshi. 2007. 'Adolescence, Embodiment and Gender Identity: Elite Women in a Changing Society'. In *Urban Women in Contemporary India: A Reader*, edited by Rehana Ghadially, 31–45. New Delhi: SAGE Publications.

Thapar, Romila. 1966. *A History of India 1*. London: Penguin Books.

The Times of India. 2018, 9 April. *IIT JEE Main 2018: 10.5 Lakh Students Appeared for the Examination*. Available at https://timesofindia.indiatimes.com/home/education/news/iit-jee-main-2018-10-5-lakh-students-appeared-for-the-examination/articleshow/63677318.cms (accessed on 2 August 2019).

Varghese, Titto, D. Nivedhitha, and Pradeep Krishnatray. 2013. 'Teenagers' Usage of Social Networking Media in a South Indian State'. *International Journal of Scientific & Engineering Research* 4 (12): 622–636.

Varma, R. 2010. 'Computing Self-Efficiency among Women in India'. *Journal of Women and Minorities in Science and Engineering* 16 (3): 257–274.

———. 2011. 'Indian Women and Mathematics for Computer Science'. *IEEE Technology and Society Magazine* 30 (1): 39–46.

Higher Education in S&T

Gendered Domains and Institutes

This chapter is divided into two parts. Part I of the chapter gives an overview of the higher education system, choice of courses, institutes and the relationship between gender and decisions made after the final year of school (class XII). Entry in higher education, that is, education after clearing the final year of school is marked by the need to make choices which has considerable bearing on one's career. For the science students, these choices include which institute to opt for and which course to study within the broad science streams selected earlier. This section analyses how choices of students at this stage, and later placements or career decisions, particularly those related to higher studies and moving abroad, exhibit gendered sociocultural norms. Such decisions are a product of a social structure in which the family plays a major role. The sociocultural norms and those related to masculinity/femininity tend to be reproduced and reconstructed not only through such choices/decisions but also through interactions involving the youth. Part II of this chapter aims to delve deeper in social institutions to analyse how gender is constructed therein through such interactions. Homes, schools and professional colleges appear as sites of such construction impacting youth. A skewed gender ratio in professional S&T colleges are fertile arenas for reproduction and reconstruction of gendered social norms.

Part I
Gender in Higher Education in S&T: Macro-Trends

There is a horizontal segregation in higher education as women's proportion in certain branches defies the logic of merit, that is, higher rankers in entrance exams would opt for more sought-after branches. Certain fields in engineering from the UG level itself and in medicine at the master's level are perceived as masculine/feminine. Further, women's proportion at different stages of higher education in PCM-related fields does not exhibit a continuous slide or leakages. The PCM-related fields are STEM fields without life sciences and social sciences. Elite institutes tend to have a lower proportion of women particularly in these fields. An increase in proportion in masters tends to be a part of a discourse in families that is gendered. Placements in the professional colleges appear discriminatory. More men than women tend to migrate abroad for higher studies, particularly in S&T. However, gender constructs can be a burden on men as indicated by studies on the mobility of students abroad.

WOMEN'S PROPORTION IN VARIOUS COURSES IN S&T: MASCULINE/FEMININE BRANCHES

The enrolment proportions in UG courses indicate horizontal segregation or concentration in certain fields of education. Of the total number of students enrolled in the UG arts courses, 52.7 per cent are women; 50.1 per cent in social sciences, 48.6 per cent in science and 28.6 per cent in engineering and technology (Ministry of Human Resource Development 2018: Table 12). As per this report, in the medical science stream, share of women's enrolment to the total exceeds men at 61.1 per cent; similar is the case in education stream, with 64.6 per cent women; law is male-dominated with 33.1 per cent women in the stream.

Within science, no separate statistics are available for enrolments in PCM and biosciences at the UG level. The 'leaky pipeline' in science education, which describes the phenomenon of more women than men dropping out of the higher education as they move from graduation to PhD (Miller and Wai 2015) does not seem to apply to India. There is an increase in enrolment proportion of women from UG to PG and then drops again in doctoral studies for science and engineering, excepting medical sciences. This is true for 2010–2011 as well as 2017–2018. For instance, the proportion of women in 'all sciences' ('all sciences' excludes home science, veterinary science and social sciences) in 2017–2018 is about 48.6 per cent in UG, 61 per cent in PG and about 45 per cent in PhD (Table 2.1). In biosciences, while the proportion of women in total enrolment in PG is at about 70 per cent it is below half in PhD in 2017–2018 at 48.4 per cent, which is a considerable drop compared to about 57 per cent in PhD in 2016–2017 (Ministry of Human Resource Development 2017: Table 13); however, the overall proportion in PhD in science at 45.6

Table 2.1 *Percentage of Women to Total Enrolment in Science and Engineering at Various Levels*

		Percentage of Women		
	Faculties	UG	PG	PhD
2010–2011	Physics	–	46.45	29.54
	Chemistry	–	44.3	36.97
	Math	–	51.72	38.83
	Bioscience	–	61.48	53.1
	All sciences	46.51	52.01	39.84
	Engineering/technology	29.15	31.83	23.46
	Medical sciences (total)	53.5	42.68	36.50
2017–2018	Physics	–	57.8	35.8
	Chemistry	–	57.3	40.8
	Math	–	59.6	44.9
	Bioscience	–	69.9	48.4
	All sciences	48.6	61.2	45.6
	Engineering/technology	28.6	37.4	30.8
	Medical sciences (total)	61.1	57.1	43.3

Source: Ministry of Human Resource Development (2013): Table 12, 13; Ministry of Human Resource Development (2018): Table 12, 13.

per cent remains similar from the previous year's 44.7 per cent which suggest increases in some other science subjects. For instance, there is an increase in women PhD enrolments in chemistry, maths, botany, biotechnology and environmental sciences compared to 2016–2017, indicating a growing demand in these fields. Home science remains the women's field with women's proportion at 85 per cent at the UG level, 91.2 per cent in PG and 86 per cent in PhD (Ministry of Human Resource Development 2018: Table 13). The UG enrolment ratio of women in sciences has been almost static with an increase of only about 2 per cent from 2010–2011 to 2017–2018 (Table 2.1).

Proportion of women in UG arts at about 50 per cent is only slightly higher than the women in sciences at about 48 per cent at the UG level (Ministry of Human Resource Development 2018). Globalization and market forces since the 1990s have made pure sciences less lucrative; they are less attractive commercially and draw fewer job opportunities compared to the other branches of science and engineering (Chanana 2001; Krishna 2001). This has led to a rise in the proportion of women in the now 'low status' pure sciences and mathematics. This trend of 'feminization' of pure sciences is also due to the association of prestige to science compared to humanities degrees for women as those opting for science are perceived as bright students by society (Gautam 2015) and due to its role in improving the marriage prospects of women (Gupta 2007).

In contrast to science, engineering is male-dominated with women constituting about 28 per cent of enrolment in UG level, although the percentage is high compared to the Western countries. In the USA, the proportion of women in engineering has been increasing but remains around 20 per cent at bachelor's level (NSF 2017: 7). Liberalization in India in the early 1990s paved way for privatization of higher education and creation of jobs, particularly in the IT/computer sector which gave fillip to women's higher education in engineering among the urban middle classes. Most private colleges offer only computer-related courses, such as information technology (IT), electrical and electronics engineering (EEE), electronics and communication engineering (ECE) and computer science and engineering (CSE; Gupta 2012). A high percentage of women in engineering occurs mainly due to the 'choice' for computer-related branches as discussed later.

In engineering and technology, women's proportion in UG in 2010–2011 was 29.15 per cent which declined to 28.6 per cent in 2017–2018 (Ministry of Human Resource Development 2013, 2018). In the same period, the proportion of women has increased at the PG and the PhD level. Even at the UG level, there is an increase in actual numbers. There were 699,025 women enrolled in UG engineering and technology courses in 2010–2011 which increased to 1,149,631 in 2017–2018, which is a 64.5 per cent increase. Nevertheless, the decline in women's proportion is a change in trend over the years as the proportion of women enrolled in engineering and technology courses rose from 16 per cent in 1995 to 23 per cent in 2005–2006 (Chanana 2004). Between 1970 and 1995, the increase in absolute numbers in enrolment of women in engineering represented a compound annual growth rate (CAGR) of 14.4 per cent (Banerjee and Muley 2008; Chanana 2004). On the other hand, this CAGR from 2010–2011 to 2017–2018 is merely 0.07 per cent. In case of men, the increase in absolute numbers is 68.9 per cent (from 1,698,593 in 2010–2011 to 2,869,748 in 2017–2018). A decline in proportion of women in 2017–2018 appears to be part of a general decline with number of men declining (from 2,980,998 in 2016–2017) by about 1.1 lakh from 2016–2017 to 2017–2018, about 0.37 per cent decline in a year; compared to a much steeper decline for women in the one-year period (numbering 1,180,254 in 2016–2017) which is 2.59 per cent; this trend appears to have reversed as women's proportion rose marginally to 28.8 per cent, as per the 2018–2019 report of the Ministry, even though there is a decline in absolute numbers of both men and women, indicating a sharper decline in number of men since the previous year. Declining numbers in UG engineering is now a definite trend.

Within engineering, there are 17 substreams with highest UG enrolment in mechanical engineering (ME) followed by computer engineering (COE), ECE, civil (CE) and electrical engineering (EE) in the order of declining enrolment. However, the percentage share of women to total enrolment in ME is a mere 4.8 per cent; in COE 42.1 per cent; 44.4 per cent in ECE; 20.8 per cent in CE and 27.4 per cent in EE. Women enrolment in IT and computer applications at the UG level is 41.6 per cent (Ministry of Human Resource Development 2018: Table 12). Thus, overall, women's preferred branch in engineering is related to computers. This is in contrast to some of the Western countries; in the USA, the proportion of women earning degrees in computer sciences has been declining since 1995 and is below 20 per cent at present (NSF 2017: 6). According to a UNESCO report (2015: 93), computer science shows a steady decrease in female graduates since 2000 and this decline is particularly marked in high-income countries. Between 2000 and 2012, the share of women graduates in computer science slipped in Australia, New Zealand, South Korea and the USA.

In the West, the computers are associated with male attributes such as highly technical skills, requirement of long and anti-social hours of work on the machine, and those working on it are perceived as 'nerds' or geeks who are typically male (Ensmenger 2010; Wajcman 1991). According to Rasmussen and Håpnes (1991), the primary reason for the decline in the number of women entering computer science in Norway is the disliked 'nerd' image. In India, the preference of women for computer-related branches of engineering indicate that theories that associate computers with masculinity are not universally applicable. In many Asian countries, including India, computers are not viewed as masculine. In India, computers are viewed as woman-friendly and this is due to gendered assumptions. For instance, the jobs associated with computers are considered 'safe' for women, as they are office-based and require only mental and not physical strength (Varma 2010). The gender gap in ME (less than 5% in UG are women) reflects social prejudices against women in terms of women working with machines other than computers. This is also related to the masculine work culture at the machine-based industries and therefore lack of preference for the branch by the families for their daughters. Although ME is viewed as masculine in various countries, the proportion is higher in the developed countries. In the USA, the proportion of women among the UGs in ME is about 13 per cent but at the elite MIT, through the proactive approach of the department, it has reached 49.5 per cent (O'Leary 2017). In the UK, 9 per cent graduates were in ME in 2010–2011 (Peers 2016).

The gendering of engineering fields is further seen in the allocation of branches in the institutes where students take up branches according to their rank in the merit list.

BRANCH CHOICE/ALLOCATION IN UG ENGINEERING: IS THERE A CORRELATION WITH RANK?

There is no gender-segregated data on allocation of branches after JEE Advanced/JEE Mains. Hence, individual colleges and their departments have to be studied to understand the pattern of branch chosen. A study of the registration data at IIT Kanpur shows that the choice for branch (or department) of engineering represents a complex picture when analysed through gender lens (Table 2.2). The introduction of super-numerary seats since 2018 requires all branches to have at least 14 per cent women. The study of proportions in branches before 2018 gives an idea of how branch selection works for women without additional seats for them.

As can be seen from Table 2.2, women constituted 8.12 per cent of the total B.Tech students in IIT Kanpur in 2014–2015, second semester. A highest percentage (23.5%) of women is in bioscience and bioengineering. The lowest are in ME at 1.35 per cent. The seats for various departments in most colleges in India, including the IITs

Table 2.2 *Total Number of Men and Women Registered for BTech in 2014–2015 Second Semester at IIT Kanpur*

Branch (or Department)	Men	Women	Percentage of Women
Aerospace engg	155	8	4.9
Bio-sc & Bioengg	101	31	23.5
Chemical engg	246	42	14.58
Civil engg	348	24	6.45
CSE	338	27	7.4
Electrical engg	474	35	6.87
Mech. engg	364	5	1.35
Mat. Sc & engg	291	33	10.2
Engg. Sc-Mech.	1		
Total	2,318	205	8.12
Percentage of total	91.87	8.12	

Source: Registration Data of UG students in 2014–2015-II Semester.

are decided rank-wise. Thus, the highest ranking candidate usually opts for CSE. This is because of the availability of jobs, future career prospects and the salaries drawn.

Closing ranks for various branches give the rank of the student who was last to enter the branch. If the closing rank is high, it shows that the branch is popular. For instance, the closing ranks for various branches in 2016 at IIT Kanpur in Round 6 of counseling[1] indicate the following: CSE closes the earliest (rank 230), followed by electrical, mechanical, chemical (ChemE), aeronautical engineering (AE), CE, material science and engineering (MSE), biological sciences and bioengineering (BSBE). However, there appears to be horizontal segregation within engineering branches. Thus, while ME is third in popularity as seen in the closing ranks, proportion of women is the lowest in ME among all the branches as seen from Table 2.2. Similar is the case of AE also. A highest percentage of women are in BSBE which is also the lowest in popularity order.

As noted earlier, the national figure for the proportion of women in the top branch of CSE is above 40 per cent which implies that many non-IITs and private colleges have a high proportion of women in this branch; on the other hand, the percentage of women in ME at IIT Kanpur and the national figure for mechanical at less than 5 per cent are both paltry. Thus, there are factors other than ranking through merit which operate in case of selection of branches. While a high closing rank and a low proportion of high women rankers account for a low proportion of women in computer science in IITs, the high national figure is due to CSE and related branches being viewed as women-friendly, as discussed earlier; ME still carries the image of having to work with machines and therefore considered inappropriate for women which translate not only into less numbers in education at most engineering institutes but also lesser jobs for women in this field due to similar views of companies offering placements and therefore less attractive for women.

There is some evidence of a waning interest in engineering as noted earlier in the decline of figures enrolled for UG programme in engineering and technology; also, government (All India Council for

Technical Education) closed about 150 private engineering colleges in 2016–2017, about 95 in 2017–2018 and 30 for 2018–2019 (AICTE Web[2]) due to poor intake and poor performance. About 50,550 of those shortlisted for the JEE Advanced exam did not appear in 2016 (JEE-Advanced Report 2016).

On the other hand, there appears to be a rising interest in medical UG course. The proportion of students enrolled for MBBS programme has risen continuously in the last three years (from about 1.6 lakhs to 1.9 lakhs from 2013–2014 to 2015–2016 to 2.4 lakhs in 2017–2018) while it has come down for B.Tech/B.E. from about 43 lakhs to 42 lakhs to 39 lakhs (Ministry of Human Resource Development 2018: 40). Government plans to raise the number of seats in MBBS by about 85,000 in the next three years and establish 24 medical colleges (Sharma 2018). However, decline in interest in engineering has not resulted in a higher proportion of women (unlike the trend of 'feminization' in sciences). In fact, as shown earlier, the enrolment figures for UG engineering show a decline in the proportion of women. Interestingly, there is a rise in proportion of women in UG medical sciences (Table 2.1).

PCB students can opt for various sciences related to biological sciences apart from medicine, such as dentist, paramedical, veterinary science, marine biology, etc. However, on clearing the NEET-UG exam, one can opt for either MBBS or BDS. The top rankers usually prefer MBBS. For instance, in 2017, in the first round of counselling, the opening and closing ranks for MBBS (for all government colleges in unreserved category) were 1 and 5,799 respectively; and for BDS, they were 3,792 and 10,920, respectively (NEET 2018). Women constitute half the proportion in MBBS (121,628/241,601) but are about 72 per cent of the total (67,539/93,766) in dentistry (BDS; Ministry of Human Resource Development 2018: Table 11).

CHOICE OF INSTITUTES FOR ENGINEERING/ MEDICAL/SCIENCE

Counseling[3] decides the medical college one studies in and the top rankers opt for the prestigious government colleges. For example,

Table 2.3 *Proportion of Women in Medical Institutes in 2017–2018 (Some Examples)*

	UG (5 Years)	PG (3 Years)
AIIMS (autonomous)	24.5% (98/399)	39.8%% (333/837)
KGMC (public)	37.5% (465/1239)	49.9% (282/565)
CMC (private)	57.1% (229/401)	51.7% (206/398)

Source: NIRF (2019). Also, see https://www.nirfindia.org/2019/MedicalRanking.html (accessed on 6 August 2019).

closing rank in NEET 2017 for Maulana Azad Medical College (MAMC) was 49; at Lady Hardinge, 369; King George Medical College (KGMC) 725; at Vardhman Mahavir Medical College (VMMC) & Safdarjung Hospital, 82 (NEET 2018). Overall, women constitute a lower proportion in the UG and PG medical programme in the elite government institutes (Table 2.3) and higher in private institutes such as the prestigious Christian Medical College (CMC) at Vellore.

In some government colleges, the proportion of women can be high. For instance, in a government medical college in Pune (Maharashtra Institute of Medical Education and Research [MIMER]), the proportion of women is more than 50 per cent (Agrawal et al. 2015). There are elite women's medical colleges as well; for instance, Lady Hardinge Medical College is a prestigious women's college in Delhi with 200 seats. About 2.8 lakh students sat for the entrance exam of the MBBS programme of the elite All India Institute of Medical Sciences (AIIMS) for 700 seats in 2017. Of these, more than 50 per cent (1.5 lakh) were women and of those who qualified, about 47 per cent were women (HT 2017). The army medical colleges have a fixed seat ratio based on sex with a higher number of seats for men than women; for example, Armed Forces Medical College (AFMC), Pune, had 105 seats for men and 25 for women in 2017 (AFMC 2017).[4]

About 25 per cent and above proportion of women in even the most prestigious medical colleges appears as contrast to the proportion of women in the elite engineering institutes. A total of 847 female candidates, which constituted only 8 per cent of the total 10,576 seats, were offered admission across all IITs and ISM Dhanbad in 2016 (JEE-Advanced Report 2016: 11). This was a drop from the previous year (JEE-Advanced 2015), when total number of women offered provisional admission in IITs after JEE Advanced was 900 out of 9,974 (i.e., 9.02%). Even with supernumerary seats for women and rise in intake to 14 per cent in the IITs in UG, the proportion is presently lower than in the elite medical colleges.

Statistics available for JEE-Advanced 2015 show that among those who take admission, a higher proportion of women compared to men tend to opt for the elite 5 IITs (out of 23) at Delhi, Kanpur, Madras, Kharagpur and Bombay. Thus, of the 900 girls offered admission, 516 or 57.33 per cent went to the top 5 institutes, as compared to 47.12 per cent (4,275/9,074) men. Thus, it seems that choosing the top IITs is more important for women than for men, which implies that women might be giving a higher preference to the institute rather than the branch of engineering compared to men. A higher preference for the institute than the course of one's choice in the educational decisions of women is also suggested by Gautam (2015) who found that at the UG level, women's subject choice was compromised. However, participants in their study gave priority to the location of the institute (nearby college preferred), to the availability of an attached hostel and in some cases to single-sex institute. For girls that qualify for an IIT, being at the top institute irrespective of the location seems to be important. It guarantees job and status while the branch of study is perhaps given less weightage.

Those who clear JEE Mains are eligible to opt for engineering colleges other than the IITs, which could be public or private. The former include the National Institutes of Technology or NITs (30 in number) and 23 Indian Institutes of Information Technology (IIITs) which are next to the IITs in prestige. Some private engineering colleges, such as, Birla Institute of Technology and Science (BITS), Manipal and Vellore Institute of Technology (VIT) conduct their own entrance exams. Then there are state engineering colleges, and private ones affiliated to the state universities where admission is through state engineering exam; they have some quota for the state candidates with a fixed (usually smaller) percentage of seats for all India candidates (through JEE Mains score). Percentage of women is usually more in NITs than at the IITs; for example, it was 19 per cent (women in all four years of UG programme) in NIT Surathkal in 2017–2018 (615/3,215: NIRF 2019);

and about 14 per cent (508/3,566) in NIT Allahabad. Percentage of women in private engineering colleges is also higher than IITs but varies: for VIT, percentage of women out of total enrolled for all 4 years in all UG programmes was 16 per cent in 2017–2018; 18.9 per cent in Manipal Institute of Technology, 12.2 per cent in BITS Pilani and 19.3 per cent in Thapar (NIRF 2019). At some private engineering colleges, the percentage could be around 35 per cent (Mittal 2013). About 75 per cent of all engineering UGs are now taught in private engineering colleges (Banerjee and Muley 2008).

Private engineering/medical colleges have provided access to students who aspire for higher education in these fields but are unable to make it to the elite institutes, which are mostly government funded. The criteria for admission to most private professional institutes/colleges are less tough than criteria for admission to public institutes. While medical colleges for women had existed even during colonial period, several women's engineering colleges have also emerged since the 1990s. Cummins College of Engineering for Women at Pune, established in 1991, was the first such college in the country.[5] In 2012, the state of Uttar Pradesh (UP) had 15 women's engineering colleges approved by the All India Council for Technical Education (Gupta 2012). However, the quality of education is questionable in many private engineering and medical colleges. Only a small percentage of these colleges show up in the ranking of the top 50 engineering colleges. More than 90 per cent of the private engineering colleges are affiliated colleges that have little academic autonomy (Banerjee and Muley 2008). Similar is the case with private medical schools which are 53.8 per cent (205/381) of all the medical schools in 2013 (Solanki and Kashyap 2014). As these authors point out, the quality of education in most private institutes is suspect, their contribution towards any pedagogical innovation or excellence is negligible and are only concentrated in a few richer states.

Despite differences in the quality of education imparted in the private colleges as compared to the elite government-funded institutes, there are certain factors common to all the students who enter engineering or medical UG programme. For instance, studying PCM/PCB at class XI–XII level demands dedication of considerable time and energy from a student. It requires considerable support from the family. The daughter needs to be freed of all household responsibilities. Resources are required to provide for tuition or coaching without which competing in entrance exams of engineering/medical or even appearing for class XII examinations (which are conducted by national or state boards) is tough. Finally, UG engineering and medical education is quite expensive in private professional engineering and medical colleges. The education fees is quite low in prestigious government-funded medical colleges, for example, less than 4,000 p.a. in MAMC but much higher in the elite IITs.[6] On the other hand, fees in private medical colleges is exorbitant compared to the private engineering colleges (e.g., Manipal charges about 12–15 lakhs for B.Tech, 4-year course but the KMC at Manipal charges about 50 lakhs for MBBS, 5.5 years course).[7] This suggests that course fee or expenditure on professional education does not deter middle-class families to make a choice for their daughters to become doctors or engineers.

Further, for research available on engineering, students in many of the affiliated private women's colleges have not distinguished themselves academically yet as, Gupta (2012) found, their parents are keen on their engineering education. The parents took interest in their daughter's PCM education and did not wish them to take humanities in class XI–XII. The parents do not necessarily impart JEE coaching to their daughters but enrol them for tuitions; finally, they look for engineering institutes that are nearby, preferably single-sex. Perhaps, such conclusions will apply to medical education also as professional education provides status and job which meets the patrifocal aspirations of parents of arranging a 'suitable' match for their daughters; it fits with the needs of the groom side as an earning bride is increasingly considered an asset among the middle classes (Dalmia 2004). For young women, professional education brings independence and a chance to build a career (Gupta 2015).

INSTITUTES FOR SCIENCE AND MATHEMATICS

Most universities offer science and mathematics courses from UG (usually 3-year course) to PhD. The enrolments in universities are based on the class XII examination results. In the elite Delhi University, the cut-off percentages for honours courses in science and mathematics are usually above 90 per cent in the sought-after colleges.[8] Apart from this, Indian Institutes of Science Education and Research (IISERs; 7 IISERs at present) were established by the GOI from 2006 onwards for imparting high-quality science education.[9] IISERs offer 5-year BS–MS programme and PhD programme. The enrolments in BS–MS take place through three different channels, all tough routes: ranking in JEE Advanced, holders of Kishore Vaigyanik Protsahan Yojana (KVPY) scholarship, entrance exam of the IISERs.[10] The IITs also run science programme offering bachelor's (4-year programme, not available at all IITs), PG (2-year MSc and integrated MSc of 5 years) and PhD. They recruit students through nationwide exams, JEE Advanced in UG/integrated MSc degree and joint entrance exam (JAM in MSc) in PG. Indian Institute of Science (IISc) and National Institute of Science Education and Research (NISER) are also reputed national-level institutes with basic science courses. BS programme at IISc offers specialization in a science subject, but the knowledge imparted carries a strong flavour of engineering and an exposure to social science disciplines. The percentage of women in the science programmes of these elite institutes is usually low. Table 2.4 gives figures for IIT Kanpur.

A low proportion of women in Physics in BSc/MSc at IIT Kanpur (4.8%; Table 2.4) reflects lack of preference by women for this branch compared to chemistry and math. Closing ranks[1] indicate highest preference for math, followed by physics and chemistry. Thus, registration data show that while women high rankers opt for math, they do not prefer physics and probably opt for engineering at those ranks. This might be owing to higher job placements for math graduates (indicated

Table 2.4 *Percentage of Women in Bachelor of Science/MSc Integrated in 2014–2015 Second Semester at IIT Kanpur*

Branch	Women/Total	Percentage of Women
Chemistry	11/87	12.6
Physics	5/104	4.8
Math & Scien. Computing	28/214	13.1

Source: Registration Data of UG students in 2014–2015-II Semester.

by a high closing rank) compared to physics. Since PG figures for physics in nationwide statistics is above 50 per cent (Table 2.1), a low percentage at the IIT cannot be due to gender stereotypes related to physics elsewhere (Gonsalves, Danielsson and Pettersson 2016).

At IISc, out of the total 456 students in all 4 years of UG programme, only 71 (15.6%) were women in 2017–2018 and in 2-year PG out of 866 students, 155 (17.9%) were women in the same year (NIRF 2019). There is a lack of studies on women students in science at IISERs and their gender issues. As per the IISER Thiruvananthapuram's annual report (2016: 18), out of 144 students selected in the BS–MS programme, almost half (73) were women. However, such data are not available for all IISERs.

IS THERE AN ATTRITION OF WOMEN IN ENGINEERING?

An issue that leads to a comparison with the West is that of attrition of women from UG engineering. Unlike the Western universities, the educational system in India does not allow switching the allotted engineering branch or the programme. Hence, there is no possibility of attrition and there can only be a dropout. However, there are very few dropouts even in the tough IIT system. For instance, at IIT Kanpur, dropouts in the UG programme are insignificant at 0.004 per cent on an average per year (Registrar Office IIT Kanpur 2016). Of the 15 students that dropped out since 2011, there was not a single woman.[11]

Research in the West has found that for the women who persist in engineering, there is a positive relationship between 'tokenism' and academic performance and women tend to overachieve and have higher grade point averages (GPAs) than men UG students in engineering because only particularly confident and well-qualified women enter and persist in engineering fields and women compensate minority status by striving for particularly high achievement (Alexander and Thoits 1985; Sonnert and Fox 2012). In India, there are few studies on this aspect. A research study[12] on an IIT (IIT-X) and a private engineering college, referred to as PRC, found that the performance of women was better than men in both the institutes (ICSSR 2017).

Table 2.5 *Mean CPI (Out of 10) of Men and Women in BTech*

Institute	Gender	N	Mean	Std. deviation	Std. Error Mean	Sig. (p)
PRC	Women	228	7.76	1.26	0.084	0.00**
	Men	460	7.22	1.32	0.062	
IIT-X	Women	151	7.53	1.4	0.113	0.04*
	Men	515	7.27	1.4	0.061	

Note: **p < 0.01; *p < 0.05.
Source: ICSSR (2017).

Table 2.5 shows that the average cumulative performance index (CPI calculated out of 10) of women is higher than men in both the institutes and the difference in the means is significant. This affirms the findings elsewhere regarding the positive effect of tokenism. In India, the gendered social structure also leads to a greater academic focus of women and a higher involvement of men in the extra-curricular activities as discussed in Part II of this chapter.

PLACEMENTS

Most engineering colleges invite companies for an on-campus recruit-ment of students. For instance, at IIT Kanpur, from the statistics obtained from the Students' Placement Office (SPO) for 2015, about 200 companies visited the campus, 356 students of B.Tech registered for placements and 305 (85.75%) were placed.[13] CPI is an important criterion for placement and all those with CPI between 9 and 10 were successfully placed. Banerjee and Muley (2008) also found the percent-age placed to be about 85 per cent at IIT Bombay (p. 41). Placement percentage of students at some of the reputed private colleges is also above 80 per cent (Banerjee and Muley 2008; NIRF 2019). The salary package received by students of government institutes such as IITs and NITs is on an average higher than in private colleges. In 2017–2018, median salary of UG students placed at IIT Madras was about 13 lakhs per annum; at VIT/Manipal, median salary was about 5 lakhs (NIRF 2019).

There is a lack of gender-based data on placements either at college level or at macro level. According to Choudhury's (2014) study, male students are more likely than females to be employed in the job market; the lower participation of female graduates in the labour market is primarily due to their poorer access to government engineering institutions. Further, Choudhury (2014) found that within private institutes, women have a lesser chance of on-campus employment than men; discrimination is even more pronounced in earnings offered to women than in the employment prospects with male engineering graduates earning around 54 per cent more than females.

From the study conducted at an IIT and a private university, it appears that companies offer different job profiles to men and women (ICSSR 2017). Interviews with students showed that the companies are biased in favour of men in case of jobs involving technical work (engineering technology and production) and in favour of women where the job profile is non-technical such as consultancy, management and finance. Since the number of women is low and the companies must meet the diversity goals (particularly since Companies Act, 2013), women from the IITs get hired easily. As Shruti (CSE, fifth semester, IIT-X; names of the students interviewed have been changed) said, 'The recent trend is that companies take at least one girl (i.e., offer placement). Since the number of girls is less, it is easy for them to be selected'. Similarly, Shikha (CSE, dual degree, ninth semester, IIT-X) said, 'in order to maintain gender ratio, some companies hire more girls'. However, as Akshi (ChE, seventh semester, IIT-X) said, 'Girls are favoured by certain companies, Credit Swiss, Investment Banking, they might hire one girl for 10 boys but core companies don't favour girls'.

Does job type have an effect on earnings and what are its gender ramifications? Studies have found that most IIT graduates (Kamath 2011; Sohoni and Kathuria 2014) do not choose S&T-related jobs or the jobs related to their branch of study. Consultancy, management and finance (which are unrelated to the training received in bachelors) are preferred over S&T jobs. One of the important reasons for such preference is that the non-technical fields offer higher salaries than core engineering jobs (Choudhury 2014; Kamath 2011). Choudhury (2014) found that the job type did not have any significant impact on women's earnings while it was significant for men (high salary for non-technical compared to technical jobs).

It appears that women engineers might be clustering even more than men into non-technical or non-S&T jobs as technical jobs are considered a male domain. Companies ask gendered questions for technical jobs, particularly in traditionally masculine branches such as CE and ME (ICSSR 2017). For instance, Preety (CE, eighth semester, PRC) said that a big construction company asked her during the interview, 'have you handled heavy stuff; will you be able to talk to labourers; how will you handle the site; why did you take up Civil Engineering?' Labour market is not encouraging towards women in ME; while ME might also involve computer-managed designing, social prejudices work against girls (Nair 2012). Thus, job segregation begins even before the students complete their degree course in engineering. There is a strong link between the job prospects and subject choices of both women and men (Nair 2012) and this is witnessed in low numbers of women in branches such as ME.

IT industry has been a huge source of employment generation in the 1990s and early decade of the new millennium. There are reports of a slowdown thereafter and decline in the profits of the leading IT companies such as Infosys and TCS due to a changing business environment (Goswami 2017; NASSCOM 2017). The industry is transforming itself in the light of emergence of new technologies; the NASSCOM expects the IT-BPM industry to grow at about 8 per cent in 2017 (NASSCOM 2017), although the earlier growth used to be in double digits (Gupta 2015). Has this slowdown impacted placements of students in IT sector? Placement data from IIT Bombay show that between 2012–2013 and 2016–2017, the number of offers made by the IT sector dropped by 34 per cent.[14] However, its impact on placement of girls is not known and NASSCOM claims that hiring of women at entry level is equal to men. As NASSCOM's Diversity and Inclusion (D&I) website reports: 'The Indian IT-BPM industry has always been favourable for women, even more so now. Women represent 51 per cent of entry level hiring, and have a 50 per cent higher chance of getting job offers' (NASSCOM Web[15]). Yet women constitute about one-third of total workforce in IT and about 24 per cent of women employees are managers (NASSCOM web). This indicates a significant concentration of women at the junior positions in IT. Women drop off in big numbers after the first five years of employment, only 26 per cent hold engineering roles and very few reach leadership positions (Nagpal 2017).

POSTGRADUATION STUDIES:
SCIENCE, MEDICINE AND ENGINEERING

The feminization of science witnessed in the high enrolments of girls in 'all sciences' in UG continues at the PG level. At the PG level, between 2010–2011 and 2017–2018, there is an increase of about 8 to 11 per cent in the proportion of women in PCM and 'all sciences' and about 2–7 per cent at the PhD level (Table 2.1). The proportion of women in PG enrolment for PCM is above 55 per cent in 2016–2017 (Table 2.1); this proportion drops substantially at the PhD stage, but still remains above 35 per cent. Further, women continue to dominate biosciences at PG level, dropping just below half at PhD levels (Table 2.1). The figures for women's proportion in PG and PhD in PCM compares well with the Western countries. For instance, in the USA, proportion of women earning degrees in physics at all levels is about 20 per cent; in mathematics, it is about 40 per cent at bachelors and masters but 30 per cent at doctoral level (NSF 2017: 6).

The proportion of women in medical sciences has arisen between 2010–2011 and 2017–2018, as seen from Table 2.1, at all the levels from UG to PhD. Unlike some of the Western countries, the profession of medicine is not considered a male profession in India (Chanana 1988). However, the figures show the leaky pipeline in medicine. The proportion of women drops from UG to PG to doctoral studies (Table 2.1). PG studies in medicine involve choice of specialty. As Table 2.6 shows, there is a horizontal segregation here, similar to that witnessed for various branches in UG engineering.

Men are preponderant in numbers in branches such as general medicine, general surgery, orthopaedics, radiology and cardiology. As expected, women are high in proportion in gynaecology and nursing. They are also clustered in dentistry, physiotherapy and pathology at the PG level and in almost all fields men are more than women at the

Table 2.6 *Enrolment at PhD and PG Level (2017–2018)*

	PhD			PG		
	M	F	Total	M	F	Total
Paediatrics	90	43	133	1,369	1,147	2,516
Dentistry	200	171	371	5,253	8,932	14,185
Nursing	80	349	429	2,237	9,225	11,462
General medicine	95	61	156	5,720	3,225	8,945
General surgery	8	3	11	3,749	1,093	4,842
Physiotherapy	92	65	157	1,692	3,088	4,780
Gynaecology	3	11	14	451	2,170	2,621
Pathology	6	4	10	740	1,590	2,330
Orthopaedics	22	2	24	1,808	74	1,882
Radiology	27	6	33	949	577	1,526
Cardiology	169	29	198	113	12	125
Plastic surgery	41	8	49	20	3	23

Source: Ministry of Human Resource Development (2018; Table 13). Available at http://aishe.nic.in/aishe/viewDocument.action;jsessionid=DEA03818CE18AB28D219F1B7273AE7A9?documentId=245 (accessed on 6 August 2019).

doctoral level. Studies show that male-dominated disciplines such as surgery and orthopaedics are more lucrative (INSA 2004). The preference of women for branches such as dentistry is worldwide and stems from the opportunity they provide for autonomy and flexibility to manage work hours and thus balance home and family (Pallavi and Rajkumar 2011). Certain branches such as pathology are paraclinical branches in which women have dominated for several decades (Nagarajan 2016). However, figures also indicate that more men than women are entering paediatrics in PG and PhD, though the field has been traditionally preferred by women (Sood and Chadda 2010).

Defying the leaky pipeline again, there is an increase in proportion of women from B.Tech to M.Tech, from about 28 per cent to about 37 per cent in 2017–2018 (with similar figures in 2018–2019). A study (Thakkar et al. 2018) found that masters (M.Tech) in computer science was encouraged by the families as it was a matter of honour and a boost to the marital profile of the participants. Degrees were at times printed on the wedding invitations and helped negotiate dowry. Further, the master's degree offered women more freedom in a socially acceptable way to postpone marriage or work. The increase could also be perhaps because teaching might be preferred for women, which is also indicated by Parikh and Sukhatme (2004). These authors found that about one-third of women with B.Tech were employed in technical educational institutes. Since then, there have been changes in the AICTE norms; and as per 2010 AICTE regulations, M.Tech is essential to teach at entry level in technical institutions (AICTE 2012–2013: 121, pt 8.2).[16] The masculine demand and supply structure of the market enhances the possibility of a fewer men joining higher studies after B.Tech. Thus, more men tend to get jobs after B.Tech due to gender segregation in the job market (Gupta 2015); and men are expected to start earning as soon as they graduate and are under pressure to build successful careers (Mittal 2013). Further, Sohoni and Kathuria (2014) in their study of an IIT found that, except for the dual degree students placed abroad or in the IT sector, M.Tech students receive less salary on an average than the UG students. This might be another reason for a lesser proportion of men joining M.Tech after completing B.Tech, compared to women.

However, proportion of women drops from M.Tech to PhD (in 2017–2018 from about 37% to 31%: Table 2.1) suggesting that a proportion of men that do M.Tech and move to PhD is higher than women, who seem to drop out after M.Tech. Doctoral studies in engineering is viewed as a hurdle for women's marriage as there is a danger of becoming overeducated, overaged for being marriageable; for those women hoping to pursue PhD after marriage, issues related to geographic mobility and in-laws' support act as barriers (Thakkar et al. 2018). However, what is intriguing is that such constraints do not seem to apply to women doing PhD in biosciences or mathematics where the proportion of women is 48 per cent and 45 per cent, respectively. While a student completes masters in science in 5 years in most universities, M.Tech is usually completed after 6 years of college studies. Is the loss of one year sufficient to be overage for marriageability for those aspiring for PhD in engineering? One reason for a low proportion of women pursuing PhD in engineering is jobs being more easily available after masters in engineering than in science. But the same applies to men also. Perhaps, the real issue is, PhD in sciences is valued less than PhD in engineering and therefore women with doctorates in sciences will still not be over-educated and families can find 'more qualified' grooms. However, more research is required on this aspect.

WOMEN'S MIGRATION ABROAD FOR HIGHER EDUCATION

Other than job and higher education within India, another option for those who graduate is to move abroad for higher education. At present, the total number of mobile students abroad is 278,383 (UNESCO–UIS 2018). This is a phenomenal increase of about three and a half times since 2000 when the number was 62,342 (Hercog and van de Laar 2017). Among the students going abroad for higher studies from India, 40 per cent go to the USA (UNESCO–UIS 2018). Of those students who went to the USA in 2012, only 18 per cent opted for UG studies while 81 per cent sought PG (EY-FICCI 2014: 15). India accounts for the second largest outflow of students after China (Sondhi 2015). Expanding incomes, economic growth and rising tertiary enrolments are key reasons for Indian growth in mobile postgraduates (British Council 2014).

Globally, women and men are equally represented in the mobile student community (Sondhi 2015). The movement is also related to women's participation in tertiary education, which is 46 per cent in China, and women are 55 per cent of its mobile student flow; in India, the trend is reverse, with tertiary participation of women at 39 per cent but women comprising only 27 per cent of the international student mobility flow (Gallagher et al. 2009; Sondhi 2015; UIS 2010). There is a paucity of studies on the gender aspect of student migration. In a survey of students who had studied abroad, it was found that those enrolled in STEM programmes exhibit maximum male bias with 69 per cent males and 31 per cent females (Sondhi 2015).

The same study (Sondhi 2015) reported that most students had completed the first degree (UG) and were enrolled in the master's programme abroad; that studying in better universities, better job prospects and mitigating the fear of failure in a highly competitive Indian education system were common reasons for studying abroad. It also found that women who study abroad belong to a higher social class with highly educated parents working in high-income positions, while men belong to families from various socio-economic groups. Further, concerns of gender inequality of the Indian labour market, particularly in engineering and IT, motivated some women to opt for higher studies abroad; while parents sought to send their daughters abroad for a better future (with respect to work and marriage), parents of sons were reluctant due to concerns that their son might not return (making future of eldercare uncertain). According to the author, this suggests a noticeable change in the gender role expectations for girls, while men still have to grapple with traditional roles; and that daughter's emigration for education is aimed at negotiating better marital prospects and an unequal labour market. Hercog and van de Laar (2017) found that obligation towards family are put in the first place in the children's decisions to move abroad. Thus, given the fact that daughters traditionally have fewer obligations towards their parental families than sons, Sondhi's findings indicate how Indian patriarchy can create difficulties for sons (in this case, in their decision to move abroad).

Part II
Gender Construction among
the Educated Urban Youth

Part I of this chapter reveals a nationwide picture of the gender issues in higher education in S&T. However, this picture does not bring out the role of gender in the lives of young men and women while at home or pursuing education. This section delves deeper into the society to unravel as to how gender is constructed at homes and educational institutes during the youth period. Studies that focus on how daily doings construct gender make us aware of 'doing of gender' (West and Zimmerman 1987) and such awareness is important if we have to reduce or weaken rigid gender divisions and the consequences of such construction (Alvesson and Billing 2009: 68). Gender identity is constantly being reinvented and rearticulated in every setting and it is the 'codified aggregation of gendered interactions' (Connell, Hearn and Kimmel 2005: 7). Studies of masculinity point out that educational institutes offer site for 'constructing appropriate ways of being male' (Swain 2005: 213). For instance, having a girlfriend reinforces heterosexual masculinity (Renold 2000) and that girlfriend is a trophy or a status symbol (Swain 2005). Aggression may be a way of acting out or 'doing' masculinity; being 'male' is to be aggressive, noisy, showing less feelings and constructing girls as the 'other' (Messerschmidt 1993; Swain 2005).

GENDERED SOCIAL WORLDS

The construction of gender in family in India brings into existence separate domains for men and women, and also reinforces patrifocal ideology among the youth. For instance, in a study (Ram, Strohschein and Gaur 2014) of the male and female youth (aged 15–24 years), it was found that the youth inhabit different social worlds; that both male and female youth commonly faced gender-discriminatory practices within their households, with sons given preference in education, freedom to roam and to perform household tasks outside home. Data also showed greater freedom to males to spend money or buy clothes. Also, female youth expressed more gender-egalitarian attitudes than male youth.

Further, the youth grapple with their physicality, with their individuality versus parental control and the growing role of media in their lives. Men as male bodies and the physicality become highlighted for adolescents in schools. For instance, a study of boys, girls and teachers in Delhi secondary schools (Iyer 2014) found association between masculinity and violence with corporal punishment meted out to boys but not girls implying that boys are stronger and can take it; it found conflicting masculine identities: 'heroes' who were lovers and fighters, and 'good boys' who focused on studies and respected girls. While good boys distanced themselves from media portrayals of men as sexual predators, even 'heroes' found it difficult to define a positive masculine sexuality; the latter exemplified in the statement of a participant, 'anyone who is interested in sex is treated like a criminal' (6). Thus, Indian norms inhibiting interaction among opposite sex impedes construction of a self-assured masculinity.

The control exercised over the son in the patriarchal system is mainly through father who is both the provider and the ultimate authority. His authority is seldom challenged openly but there is resentment: a 'subtle trend of private defiance' (Bansal 2013: 242) as the young urban men (college-going, 20–29 years old) freed from physical proximity through hostel life try to indulge in irreverence; although not performing too well academically, it is considered a trade-off; peer group emerges as a source of guidance, support and information lowering their reliance on parents. In case of daughters, fathers are protectors and guardians of their chastity and girls strive to meet their expectations of a 'good girl' (248).

The young are impacted by globalization and infiltration of Western media through the Internet, television and magazines. The young middle-class urban girls experience dilemma in construction of their identity in post-colonial context as they express a desire to be independent but also emphasize their commitment to family (Thapan 2007). In India, as elsewhere, the 'self' or the identity of the teens is constructed through the social networking sites' profiles. The modes of sharing their emotions and building impressions among Indian teens are quite similar to their global counterparts (Diwakar 2016). However, the self-identity of teens in Indian middle-class families is characterized by morality typical of the class as girls feel conscious of the need to maintain chastity with respect to sexual relations (Diwakar 2016: 174). Thus, attributes of women as family oriented and sexually chaste continues to define femininity.

It is with this understanding as a backdrop that gender relations in educational institutes become visible which is discussed further. The socialization within family reproduces cultural constructions of gender and this is carried forward and reconstructed in the college-going youth. The operation of gender construction is discussed with reference to engineering institutes in India such as the IITs and private institutes.

CASE OF AN IIT

The IITs lack a critical mass of women. The term 'critical mass' indicates the attainment of a numerical level of a group that brings comfort or familiarity with the education environment and the lack of critical mass results in feelings of loneliness and isolation (Laden and Hagedorn 2000). A critical mass helps in the growth of a supportive peer culture. As mentioned earlier, the overall proportion of girls in the IITs has been about 8–9 per cent of the total since the beginning of this millennium. This percentage is lower than the national average (of 28%). Earlier, the percentage was rising at the IITs. For instance, at IIT Bombay, the percentage of women obtaining B.Tech degrees increased from 1.8 per cent in 1972 to 7.9 per cent in 2005 (Sukhatme and Parikh 2006); at IIT Kanpur, women constituted 6.5 per cent of total students registered for B.Tech in 2010 (Registration data: 2010–2011 first semester) which increased to 8.12 per cent in 2014 (Registration Data: 2014–2015 second semester).[17] However, the ratio declined in the recent years. The intake fell from 9 per cent in 2015 to 8 per cent in 2016 as mentioned earlier. The move to raise the proportion of women through supernumerary quota started from 2018. But this has not made a substantial difference in the overall ratio at present. For instance, at IIT Kanpur, the ratio of women in 2019 in UG programme for all years stands at about 9 per cent (275/3,285: IIT Kanpur website[18]). The proportion reflects in the structures, as, for instance, hostels; IIT Kanpur has 11 halls (or hostels) for men and only 2 are for women. There is no apparent discrimination in the formal or written rules.

There is a lack of research on informal relations using gender perspective at the UG level. On the basis of available primary and secondary sources such as the study (ICSSR 2017) conducted at an IIT and a private engineering college, some articles, books and news reports, the following sections exemplify how gender is reproduced and constructed in educational institutes that severely lack in a critical mass of women.

The informal relations between men and women during academic activities are marked by the Indian norm of separation between sexes and stereotyping. For instance, at IIT-X, within the lecture halls, women usually sit in the front rows and men would leave out a couple of rows (if numbers allowed) and then sit together. Since girls in most classes are miniscule in numbers, they have few girls from whom to seek help for academics. The lack of social capital forces many to rely on their own merit (human capital), thus working harder than boys (Mittal 2011).

Informal interaction between the opposite sexes reproduces gendered norms prevalent in society. Social norms inhibiting interaction of opposite sexes due to which dating is uncommon coupled with an intense study required in the last two years of school (before joining the engineering college) deprives students of knowledge about how to interact with the members of the opposite sex (who are not related). According to Ria (Female, EE, seventh semester): '(boys) ... are too desperate to have girlfriends. Having studied for JEE for two years, they have not had any interaction with girls. College time is visualized as a time for such interaction, influenced by movies and all....' Further, the social norms stress on female modesty but celebrate 'freedom' of behaviour in boys. This along with a skewed sex ratio creates an unfavourable environment for a mature interaction based on respect for women. According to Ria, 'it is easy to make initial friendships with boys but it is difficult to carry it forward because most of them want to move beyond friendship' (ICSSR 2017: 47). Women are unwilling to move to that stage. Break-up might result in harassment, such as the 'boyfriend' tarnishing the image of a woman on the social media (Nirvak 2014).

As mentioned earlier, families usually accord greater freedom of movement and behaviour to their sons than daughters. This differential pattern of socialization is reflected in the non-academic life of the students. Men are considerably more involved in non-academic activities compared to women. As elsewhere, sports constitute a major arena of construction of masculinity (Swain 2005). A women's football or cricket team is usually absent at the IITs. Women are less involved in outdoor sports and there is less culture of computer games among the women in the hostel. Women also lack participation in technical and cultural activities due to domination of men in those. This is partly because of the presence of a large number of men's hostels (or halls); also, the culture of competition among the halls during cultural festivals create hegemony of senior men who occupy dominant positions in student groups and are familiar with the nature of activities to be carried out. Pooja Goyal, an alumnus of IIT Delhi in the 1990s, remarks:

> The boys did not know how to interact with girls. There were ten hostels for boys on one side of the IIT Delhi campus, and there was one hostel for girls on the other end. And all the cultural activities took place on the boys' end. (Madhok 2015)

Another reason for a lack of participation in non-academic activities is that most of the meetings for various activities take place late in the night (e.g., activities related to robotics) which makes it difficult for women.

The senior men play a major role in construction and reproduction of peer group culture. The orientation period is an initiation into a behaviour that is considered a dominant form of masculinity. For instance, new male students are forced into using a language that is abusive and full of dirty expletives; they might be shown porn movies and videos in the hostels (ICSSR 2017; Nirvak 2014). As a woman student remarked, 'ragging often involves asking out a girl or just commenting something about her. They consider girls as a property to increase repo (sic) among friends' (Nirvak 2014: 1). Thus, peer group culture creates a dominant version of heterosexual masculinity by defining masculinity as aggression, objectification and negation of femininity.

Senior women seem to have internalized the hegemonic male culture. For example, student guides (senior women) advise the new students to initially maintain a low profile; to not wear Western dresses and to not to draw attention to themselves; they advise them how to talk and behave with men; 'that we should not smile when boys talk to us' (Nirvaak 2014). Girls are expected to behave according to cultural gendered expectations. For instance, 'We (girls) are being judged constantly. If she talks a lot, she is a "slut" and if she doesn't talk, she has an attitude….' (ICSSR 2017). Maligning and shaming girls on Facebook is common under disguised names which can easily be identified. Thus, hegemonic masculine culture is regressive.

Hegemonic masculinity embodied in the peer group culture is considered toxic by many male students also. However, it tends to subordinate other forms of masculinities. Thus, men's interaction with women is refined when they are alone with a woman compared to in a group. The women reported (ICSSR 2017), 'there are sectors of really nice people (boys); Boys behave differently when they interact with you individually and when they are in the group' (Seema, MSE, sixth semester: *names changed*). As a male student noted (Vijay, 5thsem, EE), 'it's a herd mentality'. Pressure on men to conform to group norms was noted by women. 'There is peer pressure on the boys. Lot of guys want to take a stand against all this' (Abha, sixth semester, ChE). Typically, peer groups are the main bearer of gender definitions rather than individual men (Connell 2000).

Leadership positions in student bodies further buttress the masculine peer group culture. At IIT-X, members in the Students' Senate, nominees of the Student Gymkhana, heads of organizing committees for student festivals are usually men. Further, 'all meetings (of student bodies) are usually held after midnight and this is not suitable to many of us; also boys (tend to) smoke, drink … don't want girls around, use loose language amongst themselves' (Seema, MSE, sixth semester). Gendered positions in student bodies impart power to men in the peer group and thereby contribute to a masculine hegemony. One manifestation of this hegemony is 'micro-aggressions'. There are instances of sexist humour through innocuous jokes (Mittal 2011) and objectification by the dominant group through skits and inter-hostel competitions directed at girls in general or even specifically targeting women through disguised names (Nirvaak 2014).

These aggressions are a function of power. In response to the question *why did the incidents of inappropriate humour targeting girls and other micro-aggressions took place*, responses included: 'Boys feel they are powerful' (Bharat, Male, ME, second semester); 'boys feel superior' (Vishnu, fifth semester, CE); 'boys want to show dominance'; this is mainly because of (the influence of) movies (Sanjiv, seventh semester,

EE). While flouting of gendered restrictions by women invites informal sanctions, the norms of decency flouted by men tend to be ignored by girls because of a lack of numbers and a lack of power.

The system professes gender neutrality. However, certain rules appear to create problems for women. For example, at IIT Kanpur, no time is specified for returning to one's hostel. Students of opposite sex cannot enter hostels between 12.00 a.m. and 6.00 a.m. At IIT Bombay, the time of no entry for opposite sex starts at 10 p.m. and is 8 p.m. at IIT Madras. The entry of men in women's hostels deprives women of privacy (Nirvaak 2014). At times, warden of a women's hostel has been a male which makes communication of problems for women difficult. This affirms the study of engineering institutes by Nair (2012), who found that gender-neutral principles of institutions reinforce gender inequality prevalent in society and policy decisions favouring women students are unwelcome.

The system is increasingly becoming more gender sensitive. This is due to the students' greater willingness to complain and chances of those grievances being redressed. For instance, in response to the complaints of women about defamation in a Hall day, at IIT Kanpur, six students were found guilty by the then Women's Cell (constituted in 2013) and the Academic Senate punished one with one year's suspension and the rest five with a semester drop. The Government of India has made an Internal Complaint Cell mandatory in all educational institutes.

Presence of women who cracked a tough exam itself is a challenge to the masculine image of engineering. Male students recognize that some women might be equally or more intelligent and perform better academically than them. While some women succumb to the masculine culture in subscribing to the dominant viewpoint, some others challenge it by raising their voice through complaints, as mentioned earlier. Sexism on the campus might disillusion some women as they believe that social attitudes will not change. For instance, a woman graduate from CSE from an IIT writing on her experience in an IIT anonymously on Quora (2015), 'good grades did not correlate with respect people had for ... girls while it did with guys and guys would never respect a girl irrespective of her grades'. According to Parul

Mittal, class of 1995 at IIT Delhi, 'It was a completely male-dominated institution. I felt like a complete outlier' (Madhok 2015).

However, most women are critical of the traditional norms that inhibit aspirations of women and they have high aspirations and confidence regarding their career advancement. Thus, in their refusal to be constrained at least in their private lives, these women are also laying the ground for rebellion.

THE PRIVATE INSTITUTES OF S&T

Although the percentage of women is higher in private colleges than at the IITs, they are still a minority group. Hence, problems related to tokenism manifest themselves here also. For instance, at PRC (ICSSR 2017), where women are about 20 per cent of the total, men formed their own informal groups through social media (e.g., WhatsApp) and women usually did not form a part of such informal groups of men. This created information deficit among women due to which they had to struggle more in working out projects, dealing with changes in class schedules, etc. According to Preety (CE, eighth semester), 'group decisions are taken without informing girls sometimes ... decisions regarding change of dates for a trip were made without even asking us'. Thus, an overwhelming majority of men manage to sideline women for important tasks. As Preety further comments, 'when we had a role-play in a communication course, girls were given only anchoring'.

Most hostels, whether in government or private institutes, have different timings for hostel entry of men and women due to 'security' reasons and women are recalled to their hostels in the evenings earlier compared to boys. However, many private colleges implement the rules more strictly for women than for men. Both the early recall of women and strict implementation has gendered implications. For instance, at a college (PRC) surveyed (ICSSR 2017), the deadline for return of women in the hostel is 8.30 or 8.00 p.m. (summer and winter timings, respectively) and for men it is 10.30 p.m. While this is discriminatory enough, the men's timings are not strictly adhered to. According to a male student, Pranveer (day scholar, CE, eighth semester), the few times his friends have stayed overnight at his place, they did not inform the authorities. This shows that the attendance register in men's hostels is not maintained strictly. On the other hand, women are fined even if they are late by 5 minutes. The timings translate into denial of access to resources and create several other problems for women. For instance, it affects access to library or any help that they might need for their male/female colleagues (in other hostels) after 8.30 p.m. at night. It hampers taking up leadership positions or acting as an organizer of events because such positions requires attending meetings and working after 8.30 p.m. Usually, one rises to the headship of societies through hard work and skills. However, headship for women is a problem due to the 8.30 pm rule. According to Pranshu (CSE, sixth semester), 'Usually these societies want one boy in high position because of girls' hostel time. Late night meetings would be difficult. One girl voted herself down from Vice-President to General Secretary in my society'. It also creates problems in collaborating for projects. According to Alok, ECE, sixth semester, 'even in project deadline it is difficult to collaborate because girls cannot stay beyond 8 p.m.'

The time restrictions by the system are done in the name of 'safety' and 'security' for girls, creating an impression of women as vulnerable and therefore rather than guaranteeing safety of women in the campus, such institutes resort to curbing their freedom through stricter controls on them vis-à-vis the men. They are also easier to control and intimidate than men due to socialization in patriarchal norms (value of obedience and docility in girls). Such controls give power to boys and create gender stratification in the college with girls as subordinate. There have been protests by women of such colleges against discriminatory rules without any concrete results and led to even adverse action against the complaining girls.[19]

At single-sex (women's) engineering colleges, tokenism is absent; however, there are gender-related issues. As one study reported (Gupta 2012), concern for women's security lead to a close, almost repressive supervision. There are several rules and regulations that restrict students' movement off campus. For day scholars, there are special college buses plying in the city; as one student said, 'if a day scholar wants to go back home after coming to college because she is unwell, the basic assumption is that she is pretending, and long-winded procedures have to be followed, so the whole purpose is lost' (Gupta 2012: 169). According to the director of the institute, parents expect and demand strict security arrangements from the authorities.

Thus, hegemony of men and men's practices in rational S&T educational institutes create an ideological arena for male dominance in public spaces in general. The recent decision of the government to raise the number of seats for girls to initially 14 per cent and by 2,026 to 20 per cent in each IIT is a step that might help in creating a less discriminatory environment for girls. However, even in the institutes with a higher ratio of women (as in PRC), gender issues exist. Without institutional and systemic emphasis on gender equality, it will remain difficult to tackle gender inequality in S&T education and careers later. Those who are students today are professionals tomorrow and the seeds of gender inequality sown early in society take roots in educational institutes and grow further in S&T careers as seen in the next chapters.

CONCLUSIONS

This chapter addresses the issue of horizontal segregation within S&T fields and construction of gender in S&T institutes. The two issues are related as it is the existing masculinity/femininity constructions that result in segregation of fields which in turn feed further into gender construction in S&T. Women's enrolment in computer science is encouraged as it is considered 'appropriate' for women, and ME is considered masculine. Sciences are preferred for women compared to humanities or engineering due to patrifocal reasons. Movement from bachelors to PG might be marked by a higher proportion of women due to significance of PG in the patrifocal scheme as in the case of M.Tech. Gendered constructions of fields appear malleable as enrolments of women in most S&T fields fall at the doctoral level. Thus, drop in the proportion of women from PG to doctorate in mathematics is about 15 per cent, in engineering and technology 7 per cent and medical sciences 14 per cent (Table 2.1). Thus, both branch and level of education appear as factors in creating gender divisions in S&T fields. Further, the career options and placements indicate gender discrimination. However, gender does not impact women alone. In case of men, their decision to go abroad for higher studies is hampered more by family considerations than in case of women.

Professional education in S&T, particularly engineering and medical, has received considerable encouragement with privatization providing access to such education to students who could not make it to elite institutes. Women's entry in such professional fields implies huge investments of time, money and energy which the families are willing to expend on their daughters. This is an encouraging sign, yet the socialization of sons and daughters remain marked by patrifocal attitudes and constructions of masculinity and femininity are carried forward even in the most elite institutes. The highly skewed gender ratio in the latter creates an aggressive version of masculinity; however, private institutes and all girls' institutes also reflect gender discrimination prevalent in the system.

Influenced by globalization and liberalization, the society is experiencing a change and continuity in its norms. While the growing presence of women in S&T fields and their career aspirations depict change, the traditional normative context is reproduced in the nature of choices for various S&T fields and in interactions which reflect masculine hegemony. Does the proportion of women in S&T professions reflect trends similar to those witnessed in education? What is the nature of relationship between gendered expectations and women's professional roles? Does this relationship manifest changes in the recent years? How is gender 'done' in organizations employing S&T personnel? These and other related questions are dealt with in the next chapters in the context of S&T professions.

NOTES

1. Available at https://josaa.nic.in/webinfocms/public/view.aspx?page=46 (accessed on 6 August 2019).

Closing ranks for various programmes at IIT Kanpur after Round 6 in 2016 for General Category:

Programme Name (4 Years, B.Tech)	Closing Rank
Aerospace engineering	2,988
Electrical engineering	798
Civil engineering	3,333
Computer science and engineering	230
Mechanical engineering	1,394
Chemical engineering	2,569
Materials science and engineering	4,148
Biological sciences and bioengineering	5,433
Physics	3,110
Math and scientific computing	976
Chemistry	6,084

2. https://www.facilities.aicte-india.org/dashboard/pages/angulardashboard. php#!/closedinstitute

3. Medical counselling: The Directorate General of Health Services (DGHS), on behalf of the Medical Counselling Committee (MCC), will conduct the NEET 2018 counselling for admissions to 15 per cent All India Quota (AIQ) seats in government medical and dental colleges across all states (except J&K), 100 per cent seats in deemed and central universities, seats reserved for wards of insured persons (IP quota) in Employees' State Insurance Corporation (ESIC) medical colleges and seats at the AFMC, Pune. NEET counselling 2018 for the remaining 85 per cent state quota seats (100% in case of J&K) in government medical and dental colleges and seats in other private and self-financing institutions in all states will be conducted by the respective state counselling authorities.

4. AFMC, Pune, prefers men doctors: The candidates selected in addition to being doctors will also be functioning as officers of the Indian Armed Forces, wherein, they have to be both physically and psychologically robust to be able to undergo the rigors of life in the Armed Forces... (AFMC 2017: 2).

5. Cummins College.

6. Fees at MAMC: See website of the college available at http://mamc.ac.in/oldsite/ugstud.htm#fees (accessed on 6 August 2019). Tuition fees at IIT is about Rupees 1.24 lakh for first semester in 2017–2018. See page 3 of the file at https://www.iitk.ac.in/dosa/data/Fee-structure-for-1st-sem-2017-18.pdf (accessed on 6 August 2019).

7. Fees for engineering at Manipal: https://manipal.edu/mit/programs/programlist/btech.html (accessed on 6 August 2019); the KMC at Manipal fees details

are available at: https://manipal.edu/kmc-manipal/programs/program-list/mbbs-graduation-in-medicine.html (accessed on 6 August 2019).

8. Cut-offs for Hindu College which is a reputed DU college are available on the college website at http://www.hinducollege.ac.in/download/2017/cutoffs/2.pdf (accessed on 6 August 2019).

9. IISERs have been declared by an Act of Parliament as institutions of national importance through National Institutes of Technology (Amendment) Bill, 2010, which was passed by Rajya Sabha in 2012 and are intended to be the leading institutes in the country in the field of basic sciences.

10. Admission process at IISERs are given at IISER's website at https://www.iiseradmission.in/?page_id=8 (accessed on 6 August 2019).

11. List of withdrawn students from Academic Section was communicated by IIT Kanpur on 30 March 2017 through e-mail.

12. Two engineering institutes were studied as part of the ICSSR project (vide F.No. 02/248/2014-2015/ICSSR/RPR) with findings reported in ICSSR (2017). The IIT studied was one of the oldest IITs and is referred to as IIT-X. Modelled on the MIT, the IITs were intended to be world-class institutes incorporating courses in humanities to develop technically trained persons with well-rounded personalities (Indiresan and Nigam 1993). There are 23 IITs at present.

PRC University was established in 1956 in the state of Punjab. Today, the University is considered among the leading privately managed engineering institutions of the country. National Assessment and Accreditation Council, an autonomous body funded by the UGC, has accredited the University with 'A Grade'. The institutes have been kept anonymous to honour the confidentiality promise made to them.

Semi-structured interviews at IIT-X and PRC were conducted by the author in 2015–2016 face-to-face with the students pursuing engineering courses for the B.Tech. In all, 40 interviews were conducted, including 21 women and 19 men, within the institute campuses. Snowball technique was used to gather sample. Each interview lasted for about 45 minutes to 75 minutes. The names of the participants have been changed to protect their identity.

13. Received information from SPO at IIT Kanpur through private communication via e-mail dated 5 May 2015.

14. Details of placements at IIT Bombay are available at http://placements.iitb.ac.in/ (accessed on 6 August 2019).

15. Diversity and Inclusion.http://www.nasscom.in/about-us/what-we-do/diversity-and-inclusion

16. Faculty Norms—Prescribed by AICTE for Various Programmes. Available at: http://www.satiengg.in/PDF/Faculty_Norms_AICTE.pdf (accessed on 2 August 2019).

17. This data was obtained from the office of the Dean of Academic Affairs (DOAA).

18. Office automation Division-statistics-gender-wise. http://www.iitk.ac.in/

19. Girls at some of the private colleges have protested against the authorities against discriminatory rules, particularly those related to hostel timings. This has evoked

disciplinary action also at some places. Available at https://www.change.org/p/vit-university-give-women-equal-rights-and-stop-suppressing-free-speech and http://www.tribuneindia.com/news/chandigarh/education/thapar-girls-protest-against-hostel-timings/384457.html (accessed on 6 August 2019).

REFERENCES

AFMC. 2017. *Information Brochure*. Available at http://www.afmc.nic.in/PDFfiles/AFMC%20MBBS%202017%20INFORMATION%20BROCHURE.pdf (accessed on 2 August 2019).

Agrawal, M. J, M. Y. Bedekar, and D. S. Nair. 2015. 'Gender Differences in Motivational Factors towards Medical Career Choice'. *IOSR Journal of Research & Method in Education* 5 (4): 53–56.

AICTE. 2012–2013. *Approval Process Handbook*. Available at http://www.old.aicte-india.org/downloads/approval_process_12_13_051011.pdf (accessed on 2 August 2019).

Alexander, Victoria D., and Peggy A. Thoits. 1985. 'Token Achievement: An Examination of Proportional Representation and Performance Outcomes'. *Social Forces* 64 (2): 332–340.

Alvesson, M., and Y. Billing. 2009. *Understanding Gender and Organizations*. New Delhi: SAGE Publications.

Banerjee, R., and V. P. Muley. 2008. *Engineering Education in India*. Sponsored by Observer Research Foundation; Department of Energy Systems Engineering, IIT Bombay Powai, Mumbai. Available at https://www.gedcouncil.org/sites/default/files/Engineering+Education+in+India+Dec1608-1.pdf (accessed on 20 February 2011).

Bansal, Parul. 2013. *Youth in Contemporary India. Images of Identity and Social Change*. New Delhi: Springer.

British Council. 2014. *Postgraduate Student Mobility Trends to 2024*. Education Intelligence. Available at https://www.britishcouncil.org/sites/default/files/postgraduate_mobility_trends_2024-october-14.pdf (accessed on 6 August 2019).

Chanana, Karuna, ed. 1988. *Socialisation, Education and Women: Explorations in Gender Identity*. New Delhi: Orient Longman.

———. 2001. *Interrogating Women's Education: Bounded Visions, Expanding Horizons*. Jaipur: Rawat Publications.

———. 2004, 1–3 December. 'Gender and Disciplinary Choices: Women in Higher Education in India'. Paper prepared for the UNESCO Colloquium on Research and Higher Education Policy. Knowledge, Access and Governance: Strategies for Change, Paris.

Choudhury, Pradeep K. 2014. What Explains the Gender Discrimination in Employment and Earnings of Engineering Graduates in India? Development Studies Association of Ireland, DSAI Working Paper No. 2014/003. Available

at https://www.dsaireland.org/sites/default/files/2018-02/choudhury_
wps2014003.pdf (accessed on 6 August 2019).

Connell, R. W. 2000. *The Men and the Boys*. Berkeley, CA: University of California Press.

Connell, R. W., J. Hearn, and M. S. Kimmel. 2005. 'Introduction'. In *Handbook of
Studies on Men & Masculinities*, edited by Michael S. Kimmel, Jeff Hearn and
R. W. Connell, 1–12. Thousand Oaks, CA: SAGE Publications.

Dalmia, S. 2004. 'A Hedonic Analysis of Marriage Transactions in India: Estimating
Determinants of Dowries and Demand for Groom Characteristics in Marriage'.
Research in Economics 58 (3): 235–255.

Diwakar, Vaishali. 2016. '"It's Complicated": The Construction of Indian Middle-
Class Teens in Social Media'. *Journal of Creative Communications* 11 (2):
161–182.

Ensmenger, Nathan. 2010. *The Computer Boys Take Over: Computers, Programmers,
and the Politics of Technical Expertise*. Cambridge, MA: MIT Press.

EY-FICCI. 2014. *Higher Education in India: Moving Towards Global Relevance
and Competitiveness*. FICCI Higher Education Summit 2014. Available
at http://www.ey.com/Publication/vwLUAssets/EY_-_Higher_educa-
tion_in_India/$FILE/EY-higher-education-in-india.pdf (accessed on 6
August 2019).

Gallagher, Michael, Abrar Hasan, Mary Canning, Howard Newby, Lichia Saner-
Yiu, and Ian Whitman. 2009. *OECD Reviews of Tertiary Education: China*.
OECD. Available at https://www.oecd.org/china/42286617.pdf (accessed on
2 August 2019).

Gautam, M. 2015. 'Gender, Subject Choice and Higher Education in
India. Exploring "Choices" and "Constraints" of Women Students'.
Contemporary Education Dialogue 12 (1): 31–58. Available at https://doi.
org/10.1177/0973184914556865 (accessed on 2 August 2019).

Gonsalves, A. J., A. Danielsson, and H. Pettersson. 2016. 'Masculinities and
Experimental Practices in Physics: The View from Three Case Studies'. *Physical
Review Physics Education Research* 12, 020120.

Goswami, Ranjit. 2017, 22 August. 'Is India's IT Sector Malfunctioning?'
Eastasiaforum.Economics, Politics and Public Policy in East Asia and the Pacific.
Available at http://www.eastasiaforum.org/2017/08/22/is-indias-it-sector-
malfunctioning/ (accessed on 2 August 2019).

Gupta, Namrata. 2007. 'Indian Women in Doctoral Education in Science and
Engineering: A Study of Informal Milieu at the Reputed Indian Institutes of
Technology'. *Science Technology and Human Values* 32 (5): 507–533.

———. 2012. 'Women Undergraduates in Engineering Education in India: A
Study of Growing Women's Participation'. *Gender, Technology and Development*
16 (2): 153–176.

———. 2015. 'Rethinking the Relationship between Gender and Technology: A
Study of the Indian Example'. *Work Employment & Society* 29 (4): 661–672.

Hercog, Metka, and Mindel van de Laar. 2017. 'Motivations and Constraints of Moving Abroad for Indian Students'. *Journal of International Migration & Integration* 18 (3): 749–770.doi:10.1007/s12134-016-0499-4

HT. 2017, 23 June. *AIIMS MBBS 2017 Results: Men Outperform Women, Only 4,905 Out of 2.8 Lakh Candidates Clear Exam.* Available at https://www.hindustantimes.com/education/aiims-mbbs-2017-results-men-outperform-women-only-4905-of-2-84-lakh-candidates-clear-exam/story-05fBvANVR-BLaMbHpqCy0dP.html (accessed on 6 August 2019).

ICSSR. 2017. *Women in Undergraduate Engineering in India: A Study of Gender in Academic Environment.* ICSSR report. Report submitted to ICSSR (vide F.No. 02/248/2014-15/ICSSR/RPR). New Delhi: ICSSR.

IISER Thiruvananthapuram. 2016. *Annual Report (2015–2016).* Available at http://www.iisertvm.ac.in/assets/uploads/downloads_buffer/2018_06_12_21_48_57/annual_report_15_16_english.pdf (accessed on 6 August 2019).

Indiresan, P. V., and N. C. Nigam. 1993. 'The Indian Institutes of Technology: Excellence in Peril'. In *Higher Education Reform in India: Experience and Perspectives,* edited by P. G. Altbach and S. Chitnis, 334–364. New Delhi: SAGE Publications.

INSA. 2004. *Science Career for Indian Women: An Examination of Indian Women's Access to and Retention in Scientific Careers.* Available at http://insaindia.org/science.htm (accessed on 2 August 2019).

Iyer, Padmini. 2014, 11 November. 'Negotiating Masculinities and Meaning to "Be a Man" at School in New Delhi, India'. Paper presented at the 2nd MenEngage Global Symposium, New Delhi. Available at http://sro.sussex.ac.uk/55744/1/Iyer_%282014%29_Negotiating_masculinities_and_learning_to_%27be_a_man%27_at_school_in_Delhi.pdf (accessed on 2 August 2019).

JEE (Advanced) 2015. Information at: https://drive.google.com/file/d/1-bVLg9CuWNXzXDhv950QIJ8IK3jCg-Jg/view

JEE (Advanced) 2016. *Joint Implementation Committee Report. Volume I.* Available at https://www.iitk.ac.in/new/data/jee-report/JEE-2016-Report.pdf (accessed on 6 August 2019).

Kamath, Anant. 2011. 'Does Technical Education in India Contribute to its Core-HRST? A Case Study of IIT Madras'. *Science and Public Policy* 38 (4): 293–305.doi:10.3152/030234211X12924093660156; Available at http://www.ingentaconnect.com/content/beech/spp (accessed on 2 August 2019).

Krishna, V. V. 2001. 'Reflections on the Changing Status of Academic Science in India'. *International Social Science Journal* 53 (168): 231–246.

Laden, B. V., and L. S. Hagedorn. 2000. 'Job Satisfaction among Faculty of Color in Academe: Individual Survivors or Institutional Transformers?' *New Directions for Institutional Research* 2000 (105): 57–66.

Madhok, Disha. 2015, 15 June. 'What Happened to the Women Who Graduated from IITs in the 90s?' *Quartz India.* Available at https://qz.com/424276/

what-happened-to-the-women-who-graduated-from-iits-in-the-90s/ (accessed on 2 August 2019).

Messerschmidt, J. W. 1993. *Masculinities and Crime: Critique and Reconceptualization of Theory*. Lanham, MD: Rowman & Littlefield.

Miller, D. I., and J. Wai. 2015. 'The Bachelor's to Ph.D. STEM Pipeline No Longer Leaks More Women than Men: A 30-Year Analysis'. *Frontiers in Psychology* 6. Available at https://doi.org/10.3389/fpsyg.2015.00037 (accessed on 2 August 2019).

Ministry of Human Resource Development. 2013. *All India Survey on Higher Education 2010–2011*. New Delhi: Department of Higher Education, Government of India. Available at http://mhrd.gov.in/sites/upload_files/mhrd/files/statistics/AISHE201011.pdf (accessed on 3 August 2019).

———. 2017. *All India Survey on Higher Education 2016–17*. New Delhi: Department of Higher Education, Government of India. Available at http://aishe.nic.in/aishe/viewDocument.action;jsessionid=429CC9A01D7DBD3DAF701BFAB10B86C1?documentId=239 (accessed on 3 August 2019).

———. 2018. *All India Survey on Higher Education 2017–2018*. New Delhi: Department of Higher Education, Government of India. Available at http://aishe.nic.in/aishe/viewDocument.action?documentId=245 (accessed on 3 August 2019).

———. 2019. *All India Survey on Higher Education 2017–2018*. New Delhi: Department of Higher Education, Government of India. Available at http://aishe.nic.in/aishe/viewDocument.action?documentId=262

Mittal, Parul A. 2011. *Heart Breaks and Dreams: Girls @ IIT*. New Delhi: Srishti Publishers and Distributors.

Mittal, Richa. 2013. 'Gender Disparity in Engineering Colleges: Is the Difference in the Preferred Learning Style the Reason?' *Institute for Learning Styles Journal* 1 (Spring): 11–34. Available at https://pdfs.semanticscholar.org/acb5/33b11568e9098c8f92263a4bd1f7c3aae70a.pdf (accessed on 2 August 2019).

Nagarajan. 2016, 11 January. 'More Women Study Medicine, But Few Practise'. *Times of India*. Available at https://timesofindia.indiatimes.com/india/More-women-study-medicine-but-few-practise/articleshow/50525799.cms (accessed on 2 August 2019).

Nagpal, Mohita. 2017, 8 September. Women in Tech: There are 3 Times More Male Engineers to Females. NASSCOM. Available at https://community.nasscom.in/community/discuss/dni/blog/2017/09/08/women-in-tech-there-are-3-times-more-male-engineers-to-females (accessed on 6 August 2019).

Nair, Sreelekha. 2012. 'Women in Indian Engineering: A Preliminary Analysis of Data from the Graduate Level Engineering Education Field in Kerala and Rajasthan'. Occasional Paper No. 58, CWDS, New Delhi. Available at http://www.cwds.ac.in/wp-content/uploads/2016/09/Women-in-IndianEngineering58.pdf (accessed on 2 August 2019).

NASSCOM. 2017. *IT-BPM Industry in India 2017: Strategic Review*. Available at http://www.nasscom.in/knowledge-center/publications/it-bpm-industry-india-2017-strategic-review (accessed on 6 August 2019).

NEET. 2018. *NEET 2018: Counselling, Result, Cut Off, Answer Key*. Available at http://mbbsneet.in/neet-government-colleges-cutoff/ (accessed on 6 August 2019).

NIRF. 2019. *India Rankings 2019 and ARIIA 2019*. Available at https://www.nirfindia.org/2019/Ranking2019.html (accessed on 6 August 2019).

Nirvaak. 2014. 'Aao Saare Pahan len Aaiena' (Come let us all wear mirrors). Cultural Council. IIT Kanpur. Available at https://issuu.com/nirvaakiitk/docs/nirvaak (accessed on 6 August 2019).

NSF. 2017. *Women, Minorities, and Persons with Disabilities in Science and Engineering*. National Center for Science and Engineering Statistics, Directorate for Social, Behavioral and Economic Sciences. National Science Foundation. Available at https://www.nsf.gov/statistics/2017/nsf17310/static/downloads/nsf17310-digest.pdf (accessed on 6 August 2019).

O'Leary, Mary Beth. 2017, 31 July. 'Closing the Gender Gap in Mechanical Engineering'. *MIT News*. Available at http://news.mit.edu/2017/closing-the-gender-gap-in-mit-mechanical-engineering-0731 (accessed on 2 August 2019).

Pallavi, S. K., and G. C. Rajkumar. 2011. 'Professional Practice among Woman Dentist'. *Journal of International Society of Preventive and Community Dentistry* 1 (1): 14–19.doi:10.4103/2231-0762.86376

Parikh, P. P., and S. P. Sukhatme. 2004. 'Women Engineers in India'. *Economic & Political Weekly* 39 (2):193–201.

Peers, Sarah. 2016. *Statistics on Women in Engineering*. Women's Engineering Society. Available at https://www.wes.org.uk/sites/default/files/Women%20in%20Engineering%20Statistics%20March2016.pdf (accessed on 6 August 2019).

Quora. 2015, 12 December. *Are Girls Treated Well in all IITs?* Available at: https://www.quora.com/Are-girls-treated-well-in-all-IITs (accessed on 6 August 2019).

Ram, Usha, Lisa Strohschein, and Kirti Gaur. 2014. 'Gender Socialization: Differences between Male and Female Youth in India and Associations with Mental Health'. *International Journal of Population Research*: 11. Available at https://doi.org/10.1155/2014/37145 (accessed on 6 August 2019).

Rasmussen, B., and T. Håpnes. 1991. 'Excluding Women from the Technologies of the Future: A Case Study of the Culture of Computer Science'. *Futures* 23 (10): 1107–1119.

Registrar Office, IIT Kanpur. 2016, 16 November. *Information Regarding Provisionally Admitted Question for the Lok Sabha*. Kanpur: IIT Kanpur.

Renold, E. 2000. '"Coming Out": Gender, (Hetero)Sexuality and the Primary School'. *Gender and Education* 12 (3): 309–326.

Sharma, Priyanka. 2018, 11 February. 'Increased MBBS Seats Bring Cheer to Medical Aspirants'. *India Today*. Available at https://www.indiatoday.in/mail-today/story/increased-mbbs-seats-bring-cheer-to-medical-aspirants-1166968-2018-02-11 (accessed on 2 August 2019).

Sohoni, Milind, and Vinish Kathuria. 2014, 12 December. 'The Elite University: Are We Too Selective?' In *Fundmatics*, edited by IIT Bombay Alumni Association, 2–22. Available at https://www.cse.iitb.ac.in/~sohoni/sel.pdf (accessed on 2 August 2019).

Solanki, Anjali, and Surender Kashyap. 2014. 'Medical Education in India: Current Challenges and the Way Forward'. *Medical Teacher* 36 (12): 1–5. Available at https://www.researchgate.net/publication/265392776_Medical_education_in_India_Current_challenges_and_the_way_forward (accessed on 2 August 2019).

Sondhi, Gunjan. 2015. 'Indian International Students: A Gender Perspective'. In *India Migration Report 2015: Gender and Migration*, edited by S. I. Rajan, 104–119. New Delhi: Routledge. Available at https://www.researchgate.net/publication/283018927_Indian_international_students_A_gender_perspective (accessed on 2 August 2019).

Sonnert, G., and M. F. Fox. 2012. 'Women, Men, and Academic Performance in Science and Engineering: The Gender Difference in Undergraduate Grade Point Averages'. *The Journal of Higher Education* 83 (January/February): 73–101.

Sood, Mamta and R. K. Chadda. 2010. 'Women in Medicine'. *Indian Journal of Gender Studies* 17 (2): 277–285.

Sukhatme, S. P., and P. P. Parikh. 2006. 'A Silent Revolution: Assessing Output of Women Graduates & Post-Graduates from IIT, Bombay'. Available at http://www.ircc.iitb.ac.in/~webadm/update/Issue1_2006 (accessed on 6 August 2019).

Swain, Jon. 2005. 'Masculinities in Education'. In *Handbook of Studies on Men & Masculinities*, edited by Michael S. Kimmel, Jeff Hearn and R. W. Connell, 213–229. Thousand Oaks, CA: SAGE. Available at http://dx.doi.org/10.4135/9781452233833.n13 (accessed on 2 August 2019).

Thakkar, D., N. Sambasivan, P. Yardi, P. Sudarshan, and K. Toyama. 2018. 'The Unexpected Entry and Exodus of Indian Women in CS and HCI, CHI 2018'. Paper No. 352. Proceedings of the 2018 CHI Conference on Human Factors in Computing Systems.

Thapan, Meenakshi. 2007. 'Adolescence, Embodiment and Gender Identity: Elite Women in a Changing Society'. In *Urban Women in Contemporary India: A Reader*, edited by Rehana Ghadially, 31–45. New Delhi: SAGE Publications.

UIS. 2010. *Global Education Digest*. Montreal: UNESCO Institute for Statistics.

UNESCO. 2015. 'Is the Gender Gap Narrowing in Science and Engineering?' In *UNESCO Science Report. Towards 2010*. Available at https://en.unesco.org/sites/default/files/usr15_is_the_gender_gap_narrowing_in_science_and_engineering.pdf (accessed on 6 August 2019).

UNESCO–UIS. 2018. *Global Flow of Tertiary-Level Students*. Available at http://uis.unesco.org/en/uis-student-flow (accessed on 6 August 2019).

Varma, R. 2010. 'Computing Self-Efficiency among Women in India'. *Journal of Women and Minorities in Science and Engineering* 16 (3): 257–274.

Wajcman, Judy. 1991. *Feminism Confronts Technology*. University Park, PA: Pennsylvania State University Press.

West, C., and D. Zimmerman. 1987. 'Doing Gender'. *Gender and Society* 1 (2): 125–151.

Women in S&T Professions

3

This chapter analyses the position of women in some of the key professions related to S&T such as scientific research, IT, medicine and S&T entrepreneurship. The first part deals with women's careers in non-academic/non-research careers in S&T; the second part analyses the position of women in S&T academia/research. The next chapter specifically delves into the organizational context of scientific research in academia and labs.

Part I
Non-academic Careers in S&T
VISIBLE DISCRIMINATION IN S&T PROFESSIONS

Although the Indian constitution guarantees equality to women in pay and work opportunities, there remain discrepancies. Gender pay gap occurs mostly in the private sector since salaries in the government jobs do not vary on the basis of sex. Gender pay gap has been found to be about 23–25 per cent among urban workers with graduation and above (Ghai 2018; MoSPI 2018).[1] This gender pay gap in India is more than China and less than USA and UK (Korn Ferry 2018). It declines when we compare men and women at the same level and the same company to 0.4 per cent in India (global average at 1.5%; Korn Ferry 2018). The gap in India, as elsewhere (e.g., the UK where gender pay gap increases with age and experience),[2] is mainly due to a lesser number of women in the best-paying parts of the labour market, including senior roles and functions such as engineering and technical disciplines. Thus, the pay gap seems to rise as women rise to higher positions. According to Monster Salary Index survey,[3] the pay gap widens as one gains experience and women tend to be underpaid as much as 30 per cent in supervisory positions.

Gender pay gap is higher in most of the S&T sectors than in others. As per one survey (Hewitt 2016), it is the highest in the manufacturing and technology sectors, closely followed by financial institutions and pharmaceuticals, while it is lowest in the fast-moving consumer goods/fast-moving consumer durables (FMCG/FMCD) sector. The pay gap is inversely proportional to the percentage of women in the workforce (Hewitt 2016). Thus, disadvantages to women due to a skewed ratio includes wage gap apart from those found by Kanter (1977) in informal relations. Since these findings apply to all professionals in the corporate sector, they might be applied to S&T professionals employed in the sector as well.

There is vertical segregation with women concentrated at lower levels of employment in S&T professions. The following sections discuss this aspect and other issues in the S&T professions such as IT and medicine, and also women's role in entrepreneurship.

WOMEN IN IT: THE GROWTH AND CHALLENGES

Women's participation in IT is higher both in comparison to other sectors in the country, and in comparison to representation in the sector in other countries. The increase in numbers of women in engineering education and the mushrooming of several private engineering colleges since the 1990s catered to a growth in demand for engineers in the IT industry. IT–BPM is the largest private sector employer—delivering 3.7 million jobs; this industry is contributing about 7.9 per cent of GDP at present—compared to 1.2 per cent in 1999–2000 (IT & ITES 2005–2006, 2018). There has been some slowdown in terms of hiring—the industry added 230,000 jobs in 2011–2012 (Gupta 2015) and 105,000 in 2017–2018 (IT & ITES 2018). However, private equity/venture capital in IT services has grown at the CAGR of 27.25 per cent in financial year 2017–2018 (IT & ITES 2018). Further, while the economy grew in terms of GDP from 6.4 per cent in 2013 to 6.9 per cent in 2017, the revenues from IT–BPO (now IT–BPM)[4] industry have grown much faster at CAGR of 9.5 per cent between 2013 and 2018 according to the World Bank statistics.[5]

Women constituted 21 per cent of the total IT workforce in 2001 (NASSCOM 2001), increasing to about 30 per cent in 2012 (NASSCOM 2013, cited in Gupta 2015); 28% according to Sudha 2012). At present, for FY 2017–2018, the IT and ITES sector employs 34 per cent women according to Ministry of Electronics & Information Technology.[6] This is higher than the 20.5 per cent average level of female participation in the formal economy in 2011, for which statistics are available (OGD 2012–2015) and higher than either in public or private sector separately. The women's participation in the organized public sector is lower at 18.07 per cent than in the organized private sector at 24.3 per cent (OGD 2012–2015). Women's participation in IT workforce is second highest among all non-agricultural sectors in the country after e-commerce (67.7%) and retail (52%; NASSCOM 2018; Raghuram et al. 2017).

This participation in IT is also higher in comparison to the participation in the sector in other countries. For instance, in 2014, women held about one-fourth of all computing occupations in the USA, although they make up more than half of the US workforce (Women's Bureau 2015). The percentage of computing occupations held by women has been declining in the USA since 1991, when it reached a high of 36 per cent (Ashcraft, McLain and Eger 2016).

The growth of women in the IT sector is aided by the fact that computers enjoy a woman-friendly image and fit into the overall gendered sociocultural context. As mentioned earlier, specialization in computers is suitable for women (Parikh and Sukhatme 2004); the jobs associated with computers are considered 'safe' for women (Varma 2010) and offer a career in software which commands the highest social approval (Bagchi 1999). A woman being skilled in computers is not regarded as abnormal, which is also reflected through cinema. According to Pal (2010: 7), in the South Indian films, 'we see a burst of female software engineers on screen' including films with a reversal of roles, with the female lead being an accomplished technologist and the male lead as professionally subservient.

The sociocultural context of the fillip in women's participation is supported by organizational context of the IT professions. The IT sector offers white-collar jobs with comparatively high salary, easy international mobility, gender-neutral policy based on knowledge-centric skills' possession, flexible work routine and physically less demanding work process in comfortable indoor work environment (Kumar 2001; Shanker 2008; Upadhya 2006). Some other factors that have led to this trend include transportation, parental leave, anti-harassment, health care and an emphasis on recognizing and supporting women's needs (especially mothers; Raghuram et al. 2017). In 2012, only 22 per cent of the companies had more than 20 per cent women at senior level; by 2015, the number of such firms had increased to 33 per cent (Raghuram et al. 2017). The number of companies achieving 30 per cent at the C-Suite level has been increasing at 2 per cent a year from 2012 (NASSCOM 2018).

Around 2006, the Indian infotech industry then faced with talent shortage launched initiatives to attract more women into the workforce. IT industry, a relatively new industry (about 30 years old at present), was unencumbered by a traditional masculine culture. It has been the first to recognize the significance of diversity and inclusion (D&I) of which gender has been a major component. It is seen as business imperative, particularly since they operate in a highly competitive environment and talent acquisition and its retention is important; diversity is seen as key to innovation (Buddhapriya 2013). Wipro Technologies launched its Women of Wipro (WoW) initiative, as part of the Wipro Diversity Council, in 2008. The objectives of WoW are to reduce the attrition of women employees, facilitate increased numbers of women managers at a senior level and develop Wipro as an equal opportunity employer with world-class practices to nurture women employees. Infosys has several programmes for gender diversity. It won the first NASSCOM-India Today Award for Gender Inclusivity in 2007 and American society for training and development award in 2009 (Buddhapriya 2013). Meenu Bhambhani, head of corporate social responsibility with Mphasis, now a Hewlett-Packard unit (Duttagupta 2010), says:

> The Indian IT industry is definitely ahead on the issue of respecting diversity and goes much beyond lip-service or tokenism. Diversity policies focus

not only on granting certain entitlements but also on creating support systems that lead to a level-playing field.

Diversity has been recognized as a good business proposition as well. NASSCOM points out that corporations with at least 10 per cent women on company boards have 2.5–5 per cent higher returns on equity, firms where women are at least 30 per cent of C-Suite have 15 per cent higher profitability than others (Raghuram et al. 2017).

However, the IT sector exhibits a mixed picture in terms of a gendered environment. The gender diversity initiatives of the firms helped to enhance the representation of women in the workforce. By 2011, HCL, Wipro and Infosys had about one-fourth to one-third women workforce, but few in leadership positions. At Infosys, for instance, only 4.8 per cent were at senior management level (Buddhapriya 2013).

At present, although representation of women in the IT workforce is roughly commensurate with percentage representation enrolled in bachelors in engineering (about 28%), it is less than those enrolled in bachelors in computer-related branches (COE, IT, ECE, computer applications) where women's representation is about 40 per cent (as in Chapter 2). This suggests attrition and/or change of sector of employment. As per one source, percentage of women engineers unemployed is as high as 40 per cent.[7] Although there is unemployment among men engineers also, experts believe that more women than men engineers are unemployed (Parikh and Sukhatme 2004).

Further, there is gender pay gap at all levels, lowest for 3–5 years' experience level and highest for 6–10 years of experience, as reported by Monster Salary Index (Monster India 2016: 17–26). Also, there is vertical and horizontal segregation. An analysis indicates that over 51 per cent of entry-level recruits are women; over 25 per cent of women are in managerial positions but <1 per cent are in the top level/C-Suite (Raghuram et al. 2017). Thus, there is stagnation at entry and middle-career levels and the gender gap widens over the years significantly. Among the companies surveyed, 88.5 per cent reported that less than 10 per cent of their C-Suite is female and 80 per cent companies had less than 20 per cent at the senior management levels (NASSCOM 2018). As per the same source, more than 50 per cent companies have stagnated at the same level of women in senior management (4%) in 2017 as in 2012. In 2006, women constituted 26 per cent of the professionals in the technical segments of the IT industry, which employ a large number of engineers. However, the ratio of males to females is reversed (i.e., 31: 69) in the BPO sector (Gupta 2015), which is mainly a non-technical segment of the IT industry. This is affirmed by a recent survey[8] which found 26 per cent women in engineering roles; that 45 per cent women move out of core engineering jobs after 8 years of experience to marketing, product management or consulting; that more women are in software testing jobs (34:66 as men–women ratio) which are less sought after than hard-core programming roles (men–women ratio at 75:25). This indicates that a growth in numbers of technically trained women does not imply a consecutive decline in gender segregation in the labour market.

There are further evidences of gender inequalities in the profession. A survey found that the years of work experience are almost exactly the same for male and female employees at the different career levels (Raghuram et al. 2017). However, while men and women start their careers in IT companies in India at similar ages, men at senior positions are often younger than women at a similar level. This indicates that women with career breaks or part-time work take longer to move up. Majority of women working in the industry are aged 30 years or below and are usually single (Raghuram et al. 2017). A large proportion of women tend to exit from the industry after the first five years of employment.[8]

IT companies face a significant problem of retention following maternity leave and are concerned about the levels of women not returning to work; the two most common constraints perceived by IT companies in employing women are: they wonder whether women can combine work with family commitments; and the challenge of dealing with government's regulations on working hours and parental leave (Raghuram et al. 2017). These findings are striking and reflect on the general status of women in STEM workforce in the private sector. First, work–family balance issue is significant for the recruiters; second, government regulations on work-life balance are perceived as a burden by companies; third, high attrition among women following maternity leave bothers the companies but remains an unresolved issue for the most.

The work-life balance policies encounter hurdles at the implementation stage. Nearly half of the respondents (47%) to PricewaterhouseCoopers Private Limited (PwC 2016) survey of female millennials said that although flexibility and work-life balance programmes existed in their organization, they were not readily available to them in practice. More than half (53%) believed that taking advantage of flexibility and work-life balance programmes would have negative consequences for their careers. There is a difference between the perspective of individuals and companies as the proportion of individuals who are able to work flexibly and work from home is lower than the proportion of companies who say they are offering this provision (NASSCOM 2018). Thus, there is a gap between policymakers and those who implement those. There is considerable evidence of such implementation gap between policy and practice elsewhere also (Gambles, Lewis and Rapoport 2006; Holt and Lewis 2009). Policies are often undermined by non-supportive managers (Lewis, Brannen and Nilsen 2009) and gendered workplace cultures (Haas and Hwang 2007); there is a gap between the discourse of supporting women and the reality of cultural and structural barriers (Lewis and Humbert 2010).

Apart from the implementation gap, certain issues affecting women remain unaddressed. International assignments, which offer an opportunity for skill development and career progression, are reported more for women than men (55%–62% women and 42%–50% men: NASSCOM 2018)[9] but they are usually undertaken by younger women indicating difficulties in combining them with childcare commitments (NASSCOM 2018). The maternity leave policies are well established but the post-maternity leave phase lacks support which is critical to retain talent (NASSCOM 2018).

Studies have found that gendered assumptions are also built into competencies required for work in the IT sector. For instance, assumptions such as men have greater 'working flexibility' and potential for 'working under pressure' are built into the appraisal system, so that women find evaluation biased and stressful (Arun, Heeks and Morgan

2007). The top management in IT inadvertently deny equal opportunities to women as the definition of 'merit' continues to hold masculine attributes (Chakraborty 2019). Nature of organization also impacts women. Gupta, Raychaudhuri and Haldar (2015) found that a small company may provide its women employees a better work environment than a big organization. This is also indicated in a NASSCOM report (Raghuram et al. 2018) according to which the size of company matters and the smallest companies are most gender diverse.

Some studies, however, report more positive outcomes for women in the IT sector. Kelkar, Shrestha and Veena (2002) in a study of Bangalore and Delhi found that the nature of work in the IT industry, with its networking capacities, tools (such as e-mail, the Internet) and individuation of these capacities, has resulted in greater women's capacity to take decisions and thereby enhance their agency. Further, prestige attached to the IT industry allows young women to work night shifts, live alone in cities and control their incomes. The high salaries of women software engineers lead to an accumulation of 'symbolic capital' in terms of greater respect from their husband than they would otherwise have, making parents more proud to have a working daughter, who can often support them just as well as a working son (Radhakrishnan 2008). The wife supporting her parents challenges the patriarchal norm of a woman being of peripheral status to her parental family upon her marriage as she shifts residence and allegiance to her husband's family (Mukhopadhyay and Seymour 1994).

Thus, the situation is riddled with contradictions. On the supply side, gender segregation in the labour market does not seem to deter young women engineers from pursuing a degree in STEM and subsequently a job in IT industry. While acquiring a job is important, a high degree of career orientation is not. Most career women at IT firms do not aspire to rise beyond a certain point in the company hierarchy (Radhakrishnan 2009). However, for many women, lower aspirations at job might be a product of organizational conditions. According to Hoobler, Lemmon and Wayne (2011), when women do not get critical on-the-job development opportunities, they may report a lower desire to pursue the top jobs.

From demand side, the supply of engineers and acquiring talent is critical for business and innovation which requires gender diversity. Yet the workplace essentially remains gendered in terms of the nature of jobs performed and career advancement opportunities available. Women hit invisible barriers (the glass ceiling), such as stereotypes, that affect their career progression. These are reflected, for instance, in the employers' perception that women employees might not be able to combine work with family/childcare commitments (Raghuram et al. 2017) and in stressful evaluations (Arun et al. 2007). Organizations falter in hitting at the real challenges for women, such as need for a good childcare centre; eldercare/day care structures; mobility and talent development opportunities at different stages of a woman's career and, more importantly, greater integration of women's concerns with the opportunity structure. As a result, D&I initiatives fall short of women's representation at all levels in the organizations.

Further, Chakraborty (2019) found that the discourse on business case for gender diversity uses gender stereotypes such as valuing diversity for women's different leadership style. Often initiatives for inclusivity themselves demonstrate or digress into gendered measures. A recent survey (Singh 2018) found that replacement of a male incumbent as HR head by a female was part of D&I strategy of the companies (in various sectors); that targets for inclusivity in leadership positions find route through HR departments since women are believed to have feminine qualities of empathy, emotional intelligence and interpersonal skills.

WOMEN IN MEDICINE

Density of physicians in India has increased from 0.2 per 1,000 population in 1960 to 0.5 in 2001 to 0.8 in 2016. Yet it falls short of the world average of 1.49 (World Bank 2018). All those who call themselves allopathic doctors do not have a degree in medicine; hence, according to another estimate, the ratio of 6.07 doctors per 10,000 population as per 2001 census data falls to 3.8 per 10,000 population (Rao 2013: 6). There are gross disparities related to health manpower. The number of allopathic doctors in urban areas is four times that in the rural areas. Of the graduate doctors, 74 per cent live in urban areas, serving only 28 per cent of the national population (Thayyil and Jeeja 2013).

The growth of women in medical profession albeit as a peculiarly zenana creation during the colonial period led to an acceptance of women in medicine in post-colonial India. Based on the available statistics (based on the 2001 census), the total health care workforce (Rao et al. 2011) consists of allopathic doctors (31%), nurses and midwives (30%), pharmacists (11%), practitioners of Ayurveda, yoga and naturopathy, Unani, Siddha and homoeopathy (9%) and others (9%). In this section, we refer to allopathic doctors. At present, there are about 9.88 lakh allopathic doctors registered in India.[10] According to a study (Rao et al. 2011), only 17 per cent of all allopathic doctors are women. According to another report (also based on the 2001 census), men doctors are 5.1 times the women doctors (i.e., women as 16.39%; Anand and Fan 2016: Figure 2.2.3). This is an astoundingly low figure considering the proportion of women enrolled in MBBS and PG courses in allopathic medicine. In 2011–2012, women constituted 46.8 per cent of total enrolled in the MBBS programme, a ratio of 88 women to 100 men (Ministry of Human Resource Development 2016: 49). At present, in 2017–2018, the enrolment has achieved parity, 101 women for 100 men (Ministry of Human Resource Development 2018: 41). In PG course in general medicine, for instance, women constitute 36 per cent of the enrolment (3,225/8,945) in 2017–2018 (Table 13). Further, most women doctors are concentrated in the urban areas. According to Rao et al. (2011), only 6 per cent of the allopathic doctors in rural areas are women.

This shows that a large proportion of women that graduate do not practice. There is a dearth of studies that have researched this aspect. However, this lends evidence to the point discussed earlier that while education of women is encouraged, a successful career is not; that women in S&T are essentially an urban middle-class phenomenon. The bottlenecks in a medical career are related to both the issues of work-life balance and workplace discrimination.

The long work hours and juggling work–home responsibilities could be daunting in a medical career. Women physicians in public sector are granted maternity leave/childcare leave as per the GOI rules. Reliable day care is available in few hospitals/medical colleges for toddlers but none for the school-going children. There is a lack of opportunity for flexible training, creative scheduling of job or training if women want to come back to academic or professional life after a gap in career (Sood and Chadda 2010).

Sood and Chadda (2010) show that medicine is male dominated through hegemony over positions of power and structural dominance. Thus, the situation is not very different in India compared to many other countries (Ramakrishnan, Sambuco and Jagsi 2014).[11] In the statistics available in NIRF (2018; but not in NIRF 2019), women constitute 26.7 per cent of the faculty at the reputed AIIMS, about 31 per cent in Postgraduate Institute of Medical Education & Research at Chandigarh. This is not a very low percentage given the fact that the national percentage of allopathic doctors is less than 20 per cent. An analysis was made of participation of women scientists (mostly doctorates) in biomedical research in the ICMR, a premier research organization in the country working under the Department of Health Research (Desai-Gorakshakar, Padwal and Ghosh 2011). Under the umbrella of ICMR, there are 21 permanent centres and 7 Regional Medical Research Centres (RMRCs) in the country. Overall 26 per cent of the total scientific manpower in ICMR are women, but there is considerable heterogeneity across various institutes; seven RMRCs situated in remote areas of the country employ only 19 per cent of the women scientists. Women scientists in the four ICMR institutes in Delhi and Mumbai represent 45 per cent of the scientists employed there. Thus, women in medicine/medical research tend to cluster in metro cities. This, as authors argue, could be because RMRCs located in remote areas would require localizing their research problems, and working in them might require extensive fieldwork. ICMRs working with highly infectious diseases are also under-represented.

There are few women physicians in senior positions. Sood and Chadda (2010) found 36 per cent of the women faculty in AIIMS in senior faculty positions compared to 64 per cent in junior faculty positions. Eight per cent held the post of departmental chairs and less than 5 per cent in the then Medical Council of India (chief regulatory body for medical education). AIIMS has had only one woman director since the last 60 years and ICMR only two women director-generals till the last 80 years (Indian Academy of Sciences, National Academy of Sciences and Indian National Science Academy 2016). There is horizontal segregation and by excluding obstetrics, gynaecology and ophthalmology from surgical branches, only 5 per cent of faculty positions in surgery were occupied by women in the institute. Further, barring obstetrics and gynaecology, women appear to join those medical/surgical branches, which are less demanding in terms of time spent on administrative and emergency duties (Sood and Chadda 2010).

Surgery is male dominated and is construed as a masculine profession (Bhadra 2011). The encounter with male bodies required in surgery has been culturally disliked and therefore women tend to take up those branches of surgery that require no or minimal contact with the adult male body (Bhadra 2011). Further, surgery is believed to be physically demanding and there are few role models in specialties such as cardiology. For female physicians, the prospect of combining their professional career with family responsibilities is a key issue in the process of specialty choice (Sood and Chadda 2010). The workplace discrimination in medicine extends to the woman physician and patient relationship. According to Kumari et al. (2015), a majority of the women doctors feels that patients discriminate between male and female doctors with men being preferred for consultation. Thus, male doctors are perceived as superior to women doctors similar to findings elsewhere.

In India, medical education has been found to be divorced from the gender perspective and gender biases are actively promoted in medical textbooks used for teaching (John 2016). Gender sensitization is essential in curriculum because it has consequences for diagnosis and treatment.

Is there a feminization of the profession in India? In the West, a dramatic increase of women in medical schools and residency programmes has spurred the discourse on feminization of the profession. While it is seen to have positive consequences for the delivery of care, its negative consequence of lowering the status of the profession itself has also been a subject of speculation (Levinson and Lurie 2004). In India, the proportion of women in medical education has been high and even rising; however, this does not seem to have lowered the attraction for the profession. The studies continue to indicate the prestige of the profession (Sood and Chadda 2010) and numbers of those entering medical education has increased for both men and women (as discussed in Chapter 2). However, a high representation in medical education has not translated into a high representation in career; medicine continues to be male dominated and masculine.

WOMEN IN SCIENTIFIC ENTREPRENEURSHIP

One might conceive two strands of scientific entrepreneurship; first, enterprise or start-ups involving scientific products or knowledge but not necessarily innovation, and second, commercialization of academic research. The first case is related to the general business climate, and the second one involves the issue of academia–industry interaction and patenting activity.

India has a large presence of technical start-ups and is in fact the third largest tech-based start-up hub in the world with over 5,200 start-ups in the country (IT & ITES 2018b). There are encouraging signs in the recent years with more women starting companies in India. According to Sudha (2012), the participation of females in the formal entrepreneurship sector in the country was less than 10 per cent. This figure excludes women engaged in small and micro-enterprise and livelihoods activity. In 2018, women founders of start-ups have grown to 14 per cent according to the president of NASSCOM (Sharma 2018b). Indian Angel Network (IAN), one of the largest angel investor clubs in the country, has seen ideas from women increase from 10 per cent four years ago to 30 per cent currently; LetsVenture, a Bengaluru-based platform for raising funds, has seen 100 per cent growth in women-funded start-ups, with one-fifth of the companies that the platform has funded in the last 12 months having women founders or co-founders (Singh 2018).

Also, there are more companies being founded by women in the fields earlier seen as men's domain, such as, stem cell research and drug trials (Sharma 2018b; Singh 2018). According to Ruparel, President, IAN, there is quite a shift since 2013–2014, when women founders were frequently overlooked (Singh 2018). The reason for this change is due to changes in the workplace environment in the last few years. Anuradha Mittal, who worked at technology companies including IBM and Cisco before turning an angel investor believes that although there are disruptions for women due to marriage and motherhood, there are also professionally run crèches, women-friendly workplaces and changing attitudes that are contributing to a shift. However, this change in environment is greater in huge metro cities such as Delhi, Mumbai or Bengaluru (Sharma 2018b; Singh 2018).

Government encouragement to women has become pronounced. In 2014, India introduced a quota of at least one woman on every board of listed companies. India is the first developing country to introduce a quota for women on boards. Women technology start-ups are also being encouraged by NASSCOM through discounts and provisions of infrastructure.[12]

However, the challenges to women's entrepreneurship persist. The number of women-founded companies has increased but is still small. The angel investing community is still male dominated. Women find it difficult to network, build business relationships, getting customer leads and accessing talent. While presence of women in start-ups, as indicated earlier, is about 14 per cent, it is lower in the STEM fields. According to a report, 'Women and Men in India—2017' (MOSPI 2018) by the Indian government, women are about 6.5 per cent (30,681 out of 472,287: Table 4.28) of the owners of proprietary establishments related to 'professional, scientific and technical activities'.

Women's scientific entrepreneurship is related to the business climate in the country for women. Overall, as per Mastercard Index of Women Entrepreneurs (MIWE 2018), women as percentage of total business owners in India are 11 per cent and rank 48th out of 57 countries in the list. Further, in women's advancement as entrepreneurs, India is 52nd and above just five countries: Iran, Saudi Arabia, Algeria, Egypt and Bangladesh. India falls among the countries where women have very low opportunities to become business leaders/professionals, to engage in businesses and enter the workforce. In such countries, women show less inclination for business. The Report MIWE (2018) indicates that India's underlying conditions for women entrepreneurs are less favourable when compared to countries that obtained a high index score; that the cultural bias against women business owners, leaders or professionals are more pronounced; that women are less driven or able to grow their business and are more likely than other regions to discontinue their businesses for reasons such as unprofitability or lack of finance (53, 58).

Women's participation in science entrepreneurship and in entrepreneurship in general is an extension of the women's position in the labour force. First, women's status as primary caregivers interferes in obtaining funding. Many have said that during fundraising meetings, they often get asked questions that are personal and usually not related to their respective businesses (Balaji 2017). For instance, Vaishali Neotia, co-founder of award-winning AR and VR start-up Merxius says:

> Men are questioned about ambition, growth and prosperity, while women are questioned about stability, safety and security. The bias is more prominent if the woman is married and/or has children. It is assumed that women with familial responsibilities aren't serious about business and this makes investors wary. (Balaji 2017)

However, capital alone is not a problem. According to Poornima Parameswaran Batish, founder of *Woman at Work* magazine, 'the problem for female entrepreneurs in India is not starting a business but sustaining and scaling it up because the ecosystem is still heavily male dominated' (ACG Inc. 2015: 15). The report indicates that the entrenched gender bias in India holds back women. In this report, countries are ranked on the basis of composite index comprised of 21 indicators that highlight important aspects of a country's institutional and business environment, gendered access issues and individual-level entrepreneurial characteristics, in which India is ranked almost at the bottom at 29 out of 31 countries (with a score of 17 out of 100) surveyed on the ease of doing business for women (ACG Inc. 2015).

Second strand of scientific entrepreneurship relates to industry–academia interaction and commercialization of academic research through patents. Academia-based innovation and its patents are a relatively less researched field in India, possibly because of the low density of institutional linkages. Research elsewhere shows generally gendered nature of entrepreneurship, that women in knowledge-based sectors usually comprise very few academic entrepreneurs, commercializing their research less frequently than their male counterparts and (Lawton-Smith et al. 2017) particularly in academic STEM disciplines (Schiebinger 2008).[13]

India's industry–academia linkages are limited. Not many industries support university-driven research projects and they still have a conventional mindset of viewing universities as just teaching and research schools (Shanker 2015). Even if there were some collaboration for consulting, it would involve small- and medium-sized projects. In the recent years, IITs and IISc have incubated new ideas as business ventures through involvement of venture capitalists and angel investors, and Department of Science and Technology (DST) has supported application-oriented research projects in universities. The network of industry–academia linkages is particularly weak for the IT industry due to a particular type of an export-oriented model, which is based on offshore development of software services, targeted mainly to the USA (D'Costa 2006).

In the recent years, private companies have sponsored the creation of private higher education initiatives in order to obtain more of the skilled personnel they require; corporations such as Infosys have well-established corporate universities/learning centres. These may not be corporate universities in a precise sense, but they are another form of hybrid institution (Baporikar 2014).

Scientific entrepreneurship for women researchers is impacted by the research ecosystem apart from the factors affecting all women entrepreneurs. Lack of interdisciplinary education, for instance, Krishnan's (principal scientist, GE Global Research) background in theoretical physics would have been inadequate in running business had she not gained experience in industrial physics in a family company; lag in the educational system which fails to inculcate creativity and curiosity; few role models in the field of women scientific entrepreneurship and a lack of strong innovation networks for women entrepreneurs are some of the aspects that hamper scientific entrepreneurship (Chatterjee and Ramu 2018).

Patent analysis is generally used to understand women's participation in S&T innovation. India's share of Patent Cooperation Treaty (PCT)[14] applications with women inventors for the top 20 origins is 28 per cent in 2016 (Figure A37).[15] This percentage is not far behind many developed countries considering the share of the USA at about 31 per cent and the UK at 22.3 per cent. India shows annual growth rate of 5.7 per cent of such applications with women inventors. As per World Intellectual Property Organization (WIPO 2016), India is ranked at 10th position in terms of resident patent filing activity. However, it does not figure among the top 20 countries for the resident patent applications per million population.

Most studies on patents suffer from the problem of gender attribution to authors/inventors, which remain most problematic for India (Sugimoto et al. 2015; WIPO 2016). In a unique study of patents of Council of Scientific & Industrial Research (CSIR) labs (Lemoine 1992), it was found that only 1,222 (17.4%) out of 7,029 CSIR researchers have produced patents; 18.1 per cent of the male and 10.4 per cent of the women population are patent holders; that Indian male and female inventors seem to be equally productive: the median is two patents for both sexes. However, more research and recent data are needed for definite conclusions.

Part II
Women in S&T Academia and Research Laboratories

Although India's research output is growing, it is still a relatively small player on the global scientific stage. India is third among the countries in awarding doctorates in S&T and occupies sixth position in scientific publications (its share in publications at 3.7% or 4.4% in 2013 according to SCI and SCOPUS database, respectively; Ministry of Science and Technology 2017) with publications growing at the rate of 14 per cent, much above the world average growth rate of 4 per cent. Its share of top cited papers is only 3 per cent in 2013 as per SCOPUS database (Ministry of Science and Technology 2017). Compared to the population of the country, India has a low research population. As per the latest statistics, in 2015, India had only 218 researchers per million population (NSTMIS 2017), although the number has grown by more than 100 per million since 2000 (at 110 in this year); in 2015, China had 1,176 researchers per million population (World Bank 2019). Surely, there is a case for enhancing the number of good quality researchers in the country and the need for tapping the talent of women doctorates for research.

DOCTORATES AND POSTDOCTORATES IN S&T

The women scientists in the first half of the 20th century had to grapple with conservative social conditions in the society and the academia while pursuing doctoral studies. The social prejudices are evident even now for the female doctoral students in S&T. These prejudices manifest themselves in the lower expectations of parents, biases against the capabilities of women and tensions in the informal milieu affecting their social capital.

Historically, as noted in Chapter 2, women were not expected to seek employment after education. This led to their exclusion from science and mathematics in the first half of the 20th century. It is therefore remarkable that a few women scientists emerged in this period. These included Janaki Ammal in plant sciences (DSc in 1931 from University of Michigan) from Kerala; Asima Chatterjee in organic chemistry, who was the first woman scientist to be awarded DSc by an Indian university (in 1944, Calcutta University) and Anandibai Joshi, one of the first two women doctors (medical degree from the USA in 1886) at the end of the 19th century (Godbole and Ramaswamy 2008). The only other woman physician in the period was Kadambini Ganguly; she was the first woman to graduate from Medical College, Bengal, (later called the Calcutta Medical College) in 1886. They belonged to middle-class families and were encouraged by their fathers or husbands (Godbole and Ramaswamy 2008). According to Sur (2009), all three women in C. V. Raman's lab (Nobel laureate in Physics in 1930) at IISc Bangalore, Lalitha Chandrasekhar, Anna Mani and SunandaBai, belonged to middle- or upper-class families of the time that valued education of women. Yet the supportive men were unable to counter their own prejudices at times. For instance, Anandibai, whose husband supported her initially, reportedly said (Thakkar 2008: 15):

> He (Anandi's husband) kept on taunting me (Anandi) that I was a free bird in a foreign land and that I had probably forgotten my 'poor', 'uncivilized' and 'incapable' husband who wasn't as 'great' as me. On seeing an innocent photograph I had sent him, he made a remark that I appeared to have forgotten my tradition and culture as my pallu was askew.

Conservatism in Indian society was reproduced for the women scientists in the structures, processes and interactions. Sur (2009) writing on the three women scientists in Raman's lab noted that survival in science demanded from women social conformity and conservatism. The informal environment in the lab reproduced gender. For instance, the heightened visibility brought an intense scrutiny of their actions; the male colleagues questioned their academic credentials; ridicule in the guise of humour (as in giving nicknames to every female student) enacted gendered relations. The sociocultural norm of gender segregation was strictly followed by Raman within his lab who frowned upon any interaction between men and women. Conditions of work were particularly difficult due to such norms which also constricted physical spaces available to them. Apart from the gendered interactions, the scientific institutions and their processes 'perpetuated their own gender biases' (Sur 2009: 119). Anna Mani and SunandaBai were denied doctoral degree on flimsy pretexts though they truly deserved it and their dissertations lie in the library of the Raman Research Institute among other dissertations that were awarded degrees. Just before departure to Sweden for postdoctorate, Sunanda Bai committed suicide which remains a mystery till date.

Although there are considerable differences in the sociocultural milieu in the present as evidenced in more women entering science, the caste–class composition and construction of gender in the doctoral programme indicates continuities. Studies of women scientists since the 1990s show (Gupta 2007; Jaiswal 1993; Kumar 2001; Subrahmanyan 1998) that women in science belong to a better socioeconomic stratum than men. This indicates a selective access of women to higher education. Families with a higher income and educational background are more willing to send their daughters for higher education in science; and such a background ensures a positive environment for the academic growth of girls. In a study of IITs (Gupta 2007), about three-fourth of women and only half of men surveyed said that parents encouraged questioning rather than blind obedience. However, parental expectations from daughters are lower even among this socio-economic stratum. As many as 61 per cent men (and only 40% women) reported that their parents would like them to be 'highly successful'. While the expectations for the sons are in terms of professional career advancement, the daughters are expected to use their education for being 'independent'.

There is a rise in the percentage of women doctorates from the IITs/IISc with women PhD scholars in such institutes growing since 2003–2004 (Gupta 2007) from about 11–17 per cent to about 30 per cent in a decade (Vasudevan 2015). Overall, the proportion of women enrolled in PhD in the institutes of national importance, such as the IITs, NITs, AIIMS, IIITs and IISERs is 31.2 per cent; the proportion is higher in central universities at 44 per cent and in the state public universities at 45 per cent (Ministry of Human Resource Development 2018: Table 26). Although studies are lacking, there are various reasons for this rise in this period. One, it reflects that women's education is becoming increasing important among the middle classes. Second, with growth in number of colleges, respectable UG teaching position becomes a possibility. In a survey of women doctorates in science, engineering and medicine, a majority of those who were not engaged in research were doing UG teaching (Kurup et al. 2010). The doctoral research environment is gendered and affects careers of women in scientific research.

GENDER AND DOCTORAL
RESEARCH ENVIRONMENT

Informal communication and interaction are integral components of the practice of science, including the doctoral process. It is a period when a doctoral student acquires training in 'tacit aspects' of research such as learning to grapple with vagaries of experiments (Delamont and Atkinson 2001) and learning to design research, write grant proposals, co-author publications and organize people (Fox 2000). As in the West, women in India are disadvantaged in this informal learning process since women lack the same rapport as men do with their advisor, thus losing out on mentoring. A lack of interaction with colleagues and seniors leads to isolation and a dependence on their merit and hard work. These issues are compounded by the institutional indifference to the problems of women. However, this general subordinate position of women in science in India assumes a different form and varies in content. The problems in the informal milieu assume a specific form derived from the position of women in society and the impact of the particular sociocultural milieu.

In the IIT study (Gupta 2007), a majority of the women (60%) interacted formally with the supervisor for thesis work in his/her office only, while about 64 per cent men interacted informally with the supervisor within and outside the department. According to a woman respondent in the study (maths, IIT1), 'Boys [sic] are more comfortable in interaction with the supervisor. They can approach him anytime. I have to think twice not because of the supervisor but because of my sex'. Another respondent (maths, IIT2) said, 'Not only male scholars interact more with the supervisor, the supervisor also interacts more with them. It helps in both ways'. A lack of informal interaction with the supervisor affects the level of mentoring received from the advisor. A research scholar may have to perform extra work for the advisor, such as preparing conference presentations, writing reports and performing experiments that have no relation to the thesis. Such work may provide a good learning experience and is important in building an informal interaction with the advisor. However, women are usually given fewer of such extra tasks, implying a lack of mentorship.

There is a belief in the intellectual superiority of men. In the same study (Gupta 2007), while women researchers clearly reject stereotypes about a woman's ability to pursue science, men researchers do not reject these stereotypes with the same vehemence as women. About 30 per cent male (and only 8% female) scholars agreed that science and engineering require intellectual abilities more suited to men than women. Similarly, about one-third of the male researchers believed that men are better teachers and researchers, while only about one-tenth of the women think so. This social prejudice against women in science is also reflected in women's interaction with the supervisor. According to a woman doctoral student in chemistry:

> Even if the non-thesis work is given to girls [sic], boys [sic] get appreciated more. If girls [sic] do well in such tasks, guides often say, 'you must have done this with the help of boys [sic]. You girls [sic] can't do this'.

Some women respondents reported faculty members were 'preferring boys [sic] in the laboratory' since they can work at odd hours and are seen to be 'more intelligent'. A woman respondent about to complete her doctorate in chemistry remarked, 'girls [sic] might get scolded much more which puts them into depression and brings down their research level'. Male research students are preferred when work involves travel or is heavy (Subrahmanyan 2009). Women doctoral students are seen as a 'waste' to the doctoral programme and the advisor as they might leave the programme to get married or they might not practise their profession after marriage (Subrahmanyan 2009).

Male scholars also have unpleasant interactions with their advisors. However, failings of women might be equated with their lack of competence and gender, affecting their self-esteem (Gupta 2007). Women scientists might suffer loss of self-esteem during doctoral period due to a dismissive and apathetic interaction with the adviser and blatant sexism (Subramanian 2017). Casteism plays a huge role in one's gendered experience; Dalit and Adivasi female students are even more vulnerable to an advisor's frustrations simply because they face more severe costs to speaking out (Kondaiah et al. 2017).

These experiences are a manifestation of an unequal power relation existing between an advisor and student coupled with gender hierarchy. Advisors are extremely powerful since they have the sole authority to decide whether sufficient quantity and quality of work have been accomplished to merit the degree (Gupta 2007); their organizational position and networks lend them leverage over a doctoral student's future as the student requires advisor's recommendations for career moves after the degree. This leads to harassment of a doctoral student at times and might translate into sexual harassment in the case of a female student. The power and patriarchy are enmeshed in the persona of a male advisor. Power makes individuals less inhibited (Keltner, Gruenfeld and Anderson 2003). Studies on sexual harassment are few and Subrahmanyan (2009) found in the study of Madras University that cases of sexual harassment of female doctoral students by male advisors are common. Although common in academia worldwide, its reports were muted in India until the newspaper reports on sexual harassment of female doctoral students in central and state universities started emerging since the start of the millennium (Thomas 2015). The reports of harassment from premier institutes such as the IITs/IISc are only now emerging,[16] suggesting a greater confidence among women in getting justice at present. This growing confidence is mainly due to the law against sexual harassment which was enacted as late as 2013 and the 'Me Too' movement that has emerged across the various sectors in the country, including academia, since 2017.[17] It is significant that feminists themselves have objected to this movement in academia in India as in the West.[18] Women in leadership positions in science have not always supported the victims.[19] This exemplifies how women leaders might 'do gender' as they succumb to a masculine culture at the workplace.

There are systemic disadvantages for female doctoral students as also noticed for women UGs in the IITs (Chapter 2). For instance, a unit of lab in an IIT was situated in a men's hostel where female students were not allowed after certain time (Gupta 2007). Men get their administrative work done through the clerical staff (mostly male) more easily than women; Women are less aware of the procedures and formal rules compared to men due to absence of a large peer group (Gupta 2007).

Considering the disadvantages for women doctorates, it is not surprising that in Gupta's study (2007), while about half of the male doctoral students strongly agreed that they were confident of producing good results in their present research efforts, only one-third women could strongly agree with it. Large numbers of PhD students seem to quit doctoral programme even from the IITs either due to taking up jobs, personal problems or harassment from guides (Mohanty 2017). The attrition of women PhDs from science is about 11 per cent in one survey (Kurup et al. 2010).

In a survey of those women who dropped out of careers after PhD in S&T said that they had left because they did not find appropriate job or support and not because of family reasons (Kurup et al. 2010). Also, being married to scientists does not necessarily give fillip to careers as 43 per cent of 'women not working' in the same study, and 40 per cent among those pursuing careers in scientific research were married to scientists engaged in research, teaching or consultancy. Nevertheless, most women scientists married to men scientists and pursuing careers find moral support from spouses (Gupta and Sharma 2002).

A positive mentoring by advisors can drastically enhance women's careers. For instance, Rosy Mondal, a cancer biologist, attributes her ability to deal with the issues of lost data and scarce samples during her degree to her advisor at Assam University (Jayaraj 2017). She went on to obtain the prestigious DST INSPIRE Faculty Award. Similarly, the only woman HOD of a CSIR lab at the time of a survey (Gupta 2013) was mentored by her PhD advisor. Her career at an early stage was aided by her advisor's handing over to her the responsibility of writing research proposals to DST and other government funding agencies, defending those proposals, writing reports and working on high-profile assignments. This gave her the necessary experience and visibility for independent research.

In pure sciences and mathematics, one usually requires postdoctoral studies for appointment as a permanent faculty in a reputed institute. Various institutes including the IITs and IISc offer postdoctoral studies. However, postdoctoral fellowships (PDFs) in India are few; for instance, at IISc, faculty–postdoc ratio is 2.8:1 and at Stanford it is 1:1. IIT Madras has a specific scheme for PDF of one year for women with break in career.[20] There are little data on women postdoctorates and studies are few. A report based on the sample from premier institutes under eight ministries and autonomous departments under the Government of India notes that male postdoctoral fellows are 2.5 times their female peer group, whereas at the PhD level male enrolment is less than twice the female enrolment (SSESS 2017: 30). Thus, there is probably considerable attrition of women from PhD to postdoctoral research. The 'pipeline' tends to next 'leak' in moving from postdoctorate to permanent position. This is due to various factors. For instance, in biosciences, according to Bal (2005), postdoctoral studies usually take up 2–10 years. This leads up to age beyond 30 years at which both men and women tend to get married. However, with domestic roles/childbearing, women end up with having poorer professional achievements compared to men of the same age and basic qualifications. Hence, fewer women are likely to apply or are able to compete with the men.

DOCTORATES/POSTDOCTORATES FROM ABROAD

Elite institutes such as the IITs seem to prefer doctorates from abroad. A survey of faculty across select new and old IITs shows that two of them, Delhi and Powai, hired over 75 per cent of their new faculty across three departments—EEE, CS and ME—with foreign PhDs. Many other well-established Indian universities and other higher education institutions such as the IIITs have attracted and hired a significant number of foreign PhDs (Pushkar 2015). Women are less likely to travel abroad for PhD compared to men due to family and security reasons (Campion and Shrum 2004). The value attached to a doctorate from abroad is a product of India's developing country status. Few Indian institutes fall in top 100 of the world rankings; good quality research occurs only in top IITs/IISc and they have among their faculty a large proportion of foreign PhDs. The general belief that doctorate from India is lower in quality than the one abroad might not always be true but the system favouring foreign PhDs create an automatic advantage at the outset of the career (Pushkar 2015).

Also, the perception of India-trained postdoctorates is low in academia and students are strongly advised by their PhD mentors to pursue a postdoctorate overseas (Naik and Megha 2018). This is further substantiated by the fact that prominent research and educational institutes usually prefer foreign-trained postdoctorates for faculty positions. Thus, 70 per cent of students in a survey (Naik and Megha 2018) felt a need to train overseas for a faculty position in Indian academia. There is absence of data on Indian men and women in postdoctoral programme in India and abroad. It might be assumed that it is tougher for women to obtain postdoctorates abroad as it is likely to involve greater social pressures than for men to remain in the country either to get married, thereby moving to a patrilocal residence (or husband's place) or to stay put, if already married. Women scientists in developing countries including India are subject to 'educational localism' (Campion and Shrum 2004), that is, men are more likely than women scientists to have at least some training in developed countries, and to spend more time abroad for training and education. This restricts career opportunities for women as discussed in Chapter 4.

WOMEN IN ACADEMIC/RESEARCH CAREERS: REPRESENTATION AND SEGREGATION

As noted in Chapter 2, women constitute about 40 per cent of the doctorates in science and about 30 per cent in engineering. However, women scientists in academic and research careers continue to be under-represented at elite institutes. Even in the new IITs, their proportion is around 11–12 per cent; for example, 11.2 per cent at IIT Indore; 11.5 per cent at IIT Hyderabad and 12 per cent at IIT Ropar according to NIRF (2018).

According to DST statistics (NSTMIS 2017: Tables 6 and 7), as on 1 April 2015, there were 13.9 per cent (39,388) women out of total 2.82 lakhs R&D personnel (full-time equivalent of manpower) directly engaged in R&D activities in various sectors. They constitute 13 per cent (14,700 out of 113,074) in the higher education sector;

15.5 per cent (13,313 out of 85,811) in the institutional sector (major scientific agencies, central and state governments) and 13.5 per cent (11,376 out of 84,109) in the industrial sector (public sector/joint sector; private sector and silo). Women in private sector constitute 62.3 per cent (7,089/11,376) of the women in the industrial sector, implying more women in the private R&D than in public/joint sector. However, within the private sector R&D, women constitute only 11 per cent (7,089 out of 64,446) of the total in this sector R&D (excluding small-scale industries).

Despite the fact that India produces third largest number of doctorates in S&T in the world after China and the USA (Ministry of Science and Technology 2017),[21] there are considerable faculty shortages in the country in most universities, technical institutions and elite academic institutes including the IITs.[22] In the newly opened central universities, it is as high as 80 per cent (Sharma 2018a). The reasons are remote locations of some universities, preference of universities for ad hoc/temporary teachers as less salaries need to be paid since universities are cash strapped; private universities/institutes tend to employ the bare minimum to maximize profits; elite technical institutes such as the IITs face shortage due to lack of availability of qualified academics.[22] The shortage of faculty is accompanied by a surplus of doctorates which is compounded by a lack of industrial R&D and therefore low capacity to absorb PhDs (Pradeep 2018). In all of this, there appears to be a huge wastage of doctorates in the country both as underemployed/unemployed.

Some of the significant factors in this wastage of trained scientific personnel are lack of funds with the public sector universities and the quality of education imparted in most universities/institutes barring the few elite ones (higher education sector accounting for only 4% of GERD). While lack of funds with the universities affects the numbers hired, poor quality of doctoral programmes render the doctorates unemployable by well-known academic/research institutions. According to Krishna (2014), just about 10–12 per cent of the universities and colleges are research intensive; the rest, nearly 88 per cent of the universities, are only teaching institutions. Among the engineering and technological institutes, the IITs/IISc lead in research quality and quantity, and NITs are lower performers compared to the older IITs and some of the universities (Prathap and Gupta 2009).

In this system, gender inequality is manifested through lower career outcomes for women than men. The proportion of women declines with the rise in the institutional hierarchy and academic hierarchy within the institutes. There are a higher number of women teaching science and mathematics in colleges than universities according to most reports, although specific data are lacking (Indian Academy of Sciences, National Academy of Sciences and Indian National Science Academy 2016). The number of total teachers at the *university level* is around 1.58 lakh out of which about 64 per cent are males and 36 per cent are females. At the *college level*, the number of teachers is 10.55 lakh with 43 per cent female teachers. The ratio of women to men also declines with rise in academic position, from 74:100 at assistant professor position to 58:100 and 37:100 at associate professor and professor positions, respectively (Ministry of Human Resource Development 2018: 21). According to this report, the number of women to men as temporary teachers is near parity, at 101 women per 100 men, and exceeds men as tutors/demonstrators (189 women to 100 men).

More than half of the R&D personnel are employed in the government sector (including institutional sector, public sector industries and elite educational institutes funded by the government). About 81 per cent of the central government funding is incurred on the eight major scientific agencies such as CSIR, DRDO, DST, etc. (Ministry of Science and Technology 2017). Women, however, constitute an overall 15.5 per cent in the institutional sector (including centre and state) as mentioned earlier.

The proportion varies for different fields, with higher proportion in biological sciences than for physics. For instance, at DBT and ICMR, the percentage is 27 and 29, respectively, in 2008 (Ministry of Science and Technology 2010). Women in physics at eight universities and elite teaching institutes are about 19.4 per cent, while those at the 10 research institutes surveyed (Resmi et al. 2019) are a mere 11 per cent; the number of women fellows in physics in the Indian Academy of Sciences is 12 (out of 209, i.e., 5.7%); and proportion in governing councils of 14 elite institutes is 3.5 per cent (3/86; Resmi et al. 2019).

The fraction of women scientists as project heads and division heads is higher (at 30%) in agencies that do not require application for grants, as in DRDO, ISRO and DoS than in others such as DST and DBT (Indian Academy of Sciences, National Academy of Sciences and Indian National Science Academy 2016). The project director of 'Agni-IV' in ISRO is a woman, and women scientists' role in the launch of Chandrayaan mission is well known. DRDO has its first woman director-general (R&D-Electronic and Communication Systems). At present, in DRDO, four director-generals (a dozen in DRDO), five directors of laboratories (network of more than 52 labs) and a couple of project director positions are held by women, according to the available information (Somasekhar 2018). There are two aspects of this rise of women in powerful positions in some organizations and labs: first, though the proportion of women scientists is rising, it still remains low. For instance, ISRO has 16.08 per cent women in S&T category (ISRO 2017–2018) and DRDO has about 15 per cent (*Deccan Chronicle* 2017), and second, in most labs and in academia, proportion of women remains low in leadership positions.

There is some improvement in the proportion of women faculty at most of the older IITs. Gupta and Sharma (2003) found the percentage of women faculty at about 7 per cent in science and engineering and at present figures show 15 per cent including Humanities and Social Sciences (HSS) departments (NIRF 2018). Excluding the HSS department of the IITs from faculty counts lowers the percentage of women. By counting women faculty from faculty page of HSS website, at IIT Delhi, the percentage falls from 15.2 per cent to 11.9 per cent (55/463); at IIT Madras from 12.8 per cent to 11.1 per cent (66/595). The proportion at IISc Bangalore remains unchanged in 2018 (7.4%; NIRF 2018) compared to 2008 (7.5%; Indian Academy of Sciences, National Academy of Sciences and Indian National Science Academy 2016).

On the basis of the data of NIRF (2018), the percentage of women as faculty in different types of elite academic institutes are as follows:

Women faculty strength in IITs (including HSS):
IIT Kharagpur: 66/644 (10.2%)
IIT Bombay: 61/528 (11.5%)
IIT Madras: 78/607 (12.8%)

IIT Kanpur: 34/418 (8.13%)
IIT Delhi: 73/481(15.2%)
IISc = 32/430 (7.4%)

Vertical segregation is indicated in various surveys and studies. The figures as per the Indian Academy of Sciences, National Academy of Sciences and Indian National Science Academy (2016) are given for the year 2008 as follows:

IISc: Women scientists = 7.5 per cent (25/330)
    Assistant Professor = 9.9 per cent
    Associate Professor = 5.5 per cent
    Professor = 8.3 per cent
Delhi University: Women faculty (Sciences) = 20 per cent (58/291)
    Lecturer = 37 per cent
    Reader = 6 per cent
    Professor = 10 per cent

Kumar (2001) found in her study of physical scientists at four universities and four national laboratories that higher the rank, lower is the proportion of women; women as assistant professors, associate professors and professors were 60.7, 35.7 and 3.6 per cent, respectively, in the sample. In a study of two universities and two IITs, Gupta and Sharma (2003) found half of the women faculty as assistant professors. There is horizontal segregation as well. The women faculty in ME departments were nil in the four institutes studied (Gupta and Sharma 2003). Websites of IIT Kharagpur and IIT Kanpur show no woman faculty in ME; at IIT Madras, about 3 out of more than 60 faculty are women. Even in the biological sciences, where women constitute 56 per cent of the doctorates, senior women scientists in national labs are usually 8–25 per cent and junior constitute 34–56 per cent; vertical segregation exists in universities also (Bal 2005).

The CSIR, India's largest R&D organization with a network of 38 labs and 4,600 active scientists (as per their website), also exhibits dominance of men in numbers and in higher positions. Women constitute only 16 per cent of the total scientific community in the CSIR labs according to a government report (Ministry of Science and Technology 2010). Women's presence as the HODs is miniscule (Gupta 2016). Although there has been an improvement since 1975 when women at the 'Scientist F' level were nil and were miniscule in number at the 'E' level in any CSIR lab (Gurnanai and Sheth 1984), in the two CSIR labs surveyed in this study (Gupta 2016), there was only one woman scientist heading an institute-level committee at CSIR1 and two women out of 12 HODs, while in CSIR2 there were only two women in administrative positions and 1 (out of 8) was an HOD. In the entire CSIR group, there is only one woman scientist at the Scientist H level (which is the highest level, introduced in 2008 and is a tenured appointment for five years to an outstanding scientist), while within CSIR2 itself there were three men at that level. The lone woman ever to head a CSIR lab was appointed in 2013. The hegemonic position of men in these institutes translates into an overall greater representation in positions with higher pay, more status and more formal organizational, political and institutional power (Gupta 2016).

There are few women as directors and chairmen. There are as few as three women directors in the S&T institutions in India (Ministry of Science and Technology 2010). Women are seldom appointed as chairman of institute-level committees or as the heads of departments. Of 300 government-run universities, only 6 per cent have women vice chancellors and these are mostly women universities; IIT Council has had only one woman member till date (Indian Academy of Sciences, National Academy of Sciences and Indian National Science Academy 2016). There have been no women chairmen of JEE and GATE examination bodies of the IITs.

Women scientists lack recognition. For instance, women recipients of the prestigious Bhatnagar Award for young scientists are only 3.38 per cent of the total (15/447) between 1958 and 2014, and the proportion of women as fellows of national science academies constitutes not more than 10 per cent (Indian Academy of Sciences, National Academy of Sciences and Indian National Science Academy 2016). At present, there are 820 Indian fellows of the Indian National Academy of Engineering (INAE), who are selected from industry, academia and R&D,[23] and as per the Indian Academy of Science website, about 15 are women, a miserly 1.8 per cent.[24] Women's lack of recognition and a lower status in science partly stems from the institutional context of science which reflects a lack of 'universalism' in judging merit, as discussed further.

THE INSTITUTIONAL CONTEXT:
GENDERED NOTION OF MERIT

Universalism in science or that the scientific contributions are judged objectively and careers are open to talent with evaluations based on merit is one of the important norms in the Mertonian ethos of science. However, 'merit' in science is a notion that has been highly contested. For instance, Moss-Racusin et al. (2012) concluded after an experiment that the science faculty rated the assumed male applicants higher than the identical application materials of the assumed female candidates. The male and female science faculty were equally likely to favour a male candidate which, according to the authors, suggests that the bias is likely unintentional, generated from widespread cultural stereotypes rather than a conscious intention to harm women. Similar results, showing preference for male candidates, have been reported by Steinpreis, Anders and Ritzke (1999), and Castilla and Benard (2010). Further, a myriad of decisions and activities take place outside the formal channels of authority in which friendship cliques and tacit workplace norms play a part (Smith-Doerr and Powell 2005). Role of networks and contacts in recruitment and promotions, and women as disadvantaged (Etzkowitz, Kemelgor and Uzzi 2000), the bar being set higher for women than for men so that women have to excel at each and every qualification for selection (Brink and Benschop 2011), challenge the notion of 'merit'. Studies have found that women scientists are less likely to be selected for prominent awards reflecting 'Matilda effect' or bias against acknowledging achievements of women scientists whose work gets attributed to their male colleagues (Lincoln et al. 2012). Various researchers have examined different elements of academic excellence, such as, journal rankings, citation indexes, peer review systems and grant applications, in order to demonstrate that hegemonic structures of inequality based on gender, race and class are being reproduced in judging merit (Adler and Harzing 2009; Hearn 2004; Laudel 2006; Nkomo 2009; Özbilgin 2009; Wanneras and Wold 1997).

Subramanian (2007) found that scientists in India equate merit with talent for doing science which is believed to be inherent in a person and will manifest itself irrespective of the external conditions.

She discusses how such a notion is flawed and that academic merit is a product of the opportunities available which for women are circumscribed by the structure, processes and behaviours at the workplace.

Merit at the entry-level faculty positions in academia is judged in terms of linear progression of obtaining academic credentials with minimum breaks. Thus, most appointments to the starting-level faculty positions prefer candidates below the age of 35 years (e.g., at IIT Kharagpur/IIT Bombay).[25] This disadvantages women for whom the early 30s coincides with marriage and childbearing. Early achievement is taken as a sign of brilliance and is celebrated. For instance, the INAE young engineers' award and the INSA medal for young scientist specify age limit at 35 years. One of the most prestigious awards for sciences (including engineering), Shanti Swarup Bhatnagar Award, is given for achievements up to the age of 45 years. Gupta and Sharma (2002) found that women scientists are most productive researchers in their 50s. A higher age is associated with greater funding, greater collaborations, networks and more students which lead to higher research productivity. For women, age of 50 and above also implies a reduction in commitments in 'private' (domestic) sphere. In a study of speech and hearing faculty (Subramanian and Nammalvar 2017), while the peak productivity was observed for the female teaching faculty at >55 years (with a rising trend in the 50s), the peak productivity for the male teaching faculty was observed at less than or equal to 30 years (although increase in the 50s is steady). Saha and Ray (2015) conclude that Indian academic scientists tend to become not only more active but also more productive in research over their lifetime. Hence, raising age limits for recognitions while benefitting women will help male researchers also.

Fellowships of national academies require that the scientist be nominated by the existing fellows and the application is then screened by sectional committees. It is an unwritten fact that knowing the decision-makers and members of various committees helps in nomination and then selection (Bal 2005). Given the lack of social capital, women lose out in terms of recognition. Lack of recognition excludes women from powerful positions in decision-making bodies of the government. Absence of open democratic approach in science institutions vests power in few. Thus, such institutions cannot be 'universalistic' in rewarding merit (Subramanian 2007).

The research publications are the prime criteria for judging contributions of scientists. This makes it imperative to examine the relationship between women's lack of status in science and their research productivity.

PRODUCTIVITY

Contrary to the Western studies, women's publications in India do not seem to lag behind the men. In the West, there is a vast literature that documents the fact that the measured productivity is lower for female than for male scientists, almost in any discipline and whatever the productivity measure considered (Lee and Bozeman 2005). Lower research productivity appears to account for the lower status of women in science in the West.

However, in India, most studies report that there is no significant gap in research productivity. Gupta, Kumar and Aggarwal (1999) found that the average productivity of Indian female and male scientists in the physical sciences, biology and engineering sciences was not significantly different. Hasan et al. (2012), analysing SCI publications of research scholars from CSIR labs between 2004 and 2009, concluded that research output of female research scholars is at par with male research scholars and commensurate with their numerical strength in academic and R&D institutions. Lemoine (1992) found in study of CSIR scientists that the proportion of less productive scientists was slightly greater for men than for women. In an analysis of publications of scientists at Bhabha Atomic Research Centre (BARC) for the period 2006–2010, while women formed 16 per cent of the total number of the scientists at BARC, they contributed about 36 per cent of the technical journal publications (Upadhye et al. 2014).

A few Indian studies have reported a lower productivity of women compared to men particularly in the field of biological sciences/life sciences. Bal (2005) examined 669 publications indexed by PubMed during January 1994–April 2004 to study the scientific productivity of female biologists and found that women contributed 14.5 per cent of all publications with high impact factor values (IF > 5). She concluded that quality of productivity is not commensurate with their proportion in employment and attributed this to women-specific environmental factors. Using the publication and citation data in the 12 sub-disciplines of life sciences in journals indexed by Web of Science (WoS) database of Thomson Reuters for 2008–2009, Garg and Kumar (2014) also found that women publish less in this field and publish in low-impact factor and domestic journals; they work in small teams and have very less international collaborative papers. Thelwall et al. (2019) found that compared to the USA, India has a much lower share of female first authors but smaller variations in gender differences between broad fields. Dentistry, economics and mathematics are all more female in India, but veterinary is much less female than in the USA. These differences, according to the authors, are probably an extension of subject choices at the tertiary education level.

Whether women scientists publish less or more than men is not important to women's position in science. The fact remains that neither a strong female doctoral pipeline nor a comparable scientific productivity is able to influence the under-representation of women at the top ranks of academic/research institutes. This is confirmed through other studies (e.g. D'Amico, Vermigli and Canetto 2011). Women scientists have a lower status in India despite the evidence of a comparable productivity in several S&T fields. Kumar (2001) found no significant difference in the research productivity of men and women scientists, yet there were significant differences in academic ranks of men and women with women at lower ranks. 'Universalism' falters in science and women are less able to translate their productivity into resources and recognition (Long and Fox 1995). A lower publication rate among women scientists in the West, as several studies show, is a product of several institutional and individual-level reasons (Fox 1983; Zainab 1999) and is both the cause and effect of gender disparity in career attainments in science (Fox 2006: 23). This affirms Fox (2004) that the publication gap is not a significant factor in women's lower position in science.

Gender-based citation differences are particularly marked in India. In a study of gender differences in research impact through SCOPUS citations and Mendeley readers in five countries including India, for articles published in 2014, Thelwall (2018) found that female-authored research is less cited in India compared to the USA, UK and Spain and has least Mendeley readers (suggesting low audience for research) among countries surveyed. As per the author, there could be various reasons for this including sociocultural biases, lack of resources, of mobility to attend prestigious institutes and lack of networks among women, older scientists (mostly males) producing more visible research and women in lower citation specialisms.

In sum, literature shows a high proportion of women as doctoral students but low proportion as faculty; comparable productivity but less recognition in terms of low position in hierarchy, awards and recognition. The hegemony of men in science institutions and a lack of universalism in science imply that a lower status of women in science is related to sociocultural and organizational environment factors coupled with a masculine ethos of science rather than with a fair assessment of one's scientific contributions.

RESEARCH BEYOND THE PREMIER INSTITUTES/LABS

As mentioned earlier, India has few high-quality universities, and most state universities are cash-strapped, although the number of PhD students produced is largest in the state public universities. The hierarchy of institutes maps on to gender hierarchy. Women account for a much higher proportion of doctoral students (45%) in state universities than in the Institutes of National Importance (31%; Ministry of Human Resource Development 2018: Table 26). While this proportion includes all branches of learning, the proportion should roughly apply to those in S&T also.

In many state universities, there is a lack of facilities and of mechanisms to utilize expensive resources/materials/machines available with other NITs or the nearby IITs.[26] At MDS University, Rajasthan, for instance, the research departments lack funding and all but two of them cannot even afford to run UG courses. The researchers are offered little help by the system to patent their work, to reach out to industries or collaborate with other research groups.[26] Geographically, research in the north-eastern states is hampered by a lack of accessibility through roads because of which chemicals and machinery take a long time to reach, poor governance and lack of adequate manpower as most doctoral researchers move to metro or big cities.[27]

Lack of facilities is there for men also in such universities. However, discriminatory structures and lack of funding in state universities enhances the segregation (Kurup, Mathew and Singh 2017). Further, given women's lack of geographical mobility after marriage, it is likely that the talented women are unable to move to better universities/ institutes and use their potential. Also, movement after marriage creates recruitment hassles at the new location. Often state-funded universities and research labs in India follow 'son of the soil' policy, recruiting majority of the personnel from within the state. A woman moving outside the home state due to marriage might find it difficult to find a job. Thus, Amarnath (2011) recommended 25 per cent seats for men and women in such institutes for meritorious candidates of other states. Many national level institutes, such as the NITs, fill up 50 per cent seats during faculty recruitment from domicile of the state.[28]

Private research sector is a relatively new phenomenon in India which received considerable impetus with the liberalization in the 1990s. Private expenditure on R&D (in rupees) was about 3,292 crores in 2001–2002, which has increased to 32,538 crores in 2014–2015. As a percentage of national expenditure, this has increased from 19.3 per cent to 38.1 per cent (NSTMIS 2017: Table 1); the sector employs 26 per cent of the total R&D personnel in the country (Table 6) and two-thirds of the women in R&D in industrial sector.

There is a paucity of studies on women researchers in private sector. A study (Gupta 2017) of women scientists was conducted at two reputed Indian pharmaceutical private sector companies with a global clientage (referred to as Private1 and Private2 to honour the confidentiality contract). These companies are among the top 10 research labs in patenting activity and are located in metropolitan cities. The pharmaceutical industry is one of the few industries in India that has demonstrated R&D capabilities in the private sector.

It has been a rapidly advancing sector in the country both in terms of production and technological capabilities (Krishna and Chandra 2009). These R&D labs are elite in terms of their reputation as the best private research labs in the country, employment of a highly educated workforce, high salaries, plush organizational setting and international reach. Most employees are Hindu upper caste and the average age of the researchers was less at 34.91 years, compared to those in CSIR labs, for instance, which was 47.64 years (Gupta 2016). This indicates a younger population in private R&D which might be due to a late beginning of research in the sector, mainly at the turn of this millennium.

The percentage of women in these labs varies from 6–14 per cent in their various R&D units indicating representation of women similar to those in government sector and represents severe lack of critical mass. Similarly, men tend to occupy most of the leadership positions with women as managers in scientific teams being 5 per cent to 30 per cent in these units and those at higher management as miniscule or none (Gupta 2017). Although, scientists in private sector identify themselves more as employees of the company rather than with the professional community of scientists, various issues facing women in these labs resemble women scientists in academia and public sector in various ways. These are discussed in Chapter 4.

CONCLUSIONS

There are certain issues common to women in the various S&T professions. Women in S&T careers encounter gender inequalities in the form of vertical and horizontal segregation. Few women rise to the leadership positions and women tend to cluster in lower status jobs or excluded from certain fields. Partly, this is a product of the gendering of the professions with certain tasks/fields considered as more 'male appropriate' and high in status while others, usually lower status ones, find more proportion of women; for instance, hard-core programming is regarded as masculine and superior compared to software testing and more women cluster in the latter. In medicine, surgery-related branches (excluding a few such as obstetrics, genecology and ophthalmology) are considered masculine and find more men in these fields. In engineering, few women faculty are found in ME.

Notions of merit are gendered in these professions. For instance, in IT, gendered assumptions are built into competencies required for job performance. In research/academia, consideration of gender enters in judging 'merit'; 'merit' is associated with factors (such as early achievement) that suit men more than women, accumulation of merit itself is a gendered process (e.g., significance of contacts/networks). While research productivity is believed to be a prominent yardstick for judging merit, similar research performance does not yield similar career outcomes for men and women.

Specifically, women in the private sector face gender pay gap with the rise in experience, widening career gap with male colleagues beyond mid-career levels, gap between work-life balance programmes and their implementation; in IT, the issue of high attrition levels among women post-maternity leave remains an unresolved issue. Women's careers often believed to be held up by family issues actually fall victim to a lack of supportive organizational systems.

The second part, which focused on scientific research, showed how lacunae in our scientific and education systems and the developing country status of India impacts women scientists. Low funding and poor quality of higher education in most universities render doctorates unemployable by top institutes. Women faculty tends to cluster in colleges and state universities and very few find employment in elite institutes. The prestige attached to postdoctorates/doctorates abroad by the elite institutes, women's constrained mobility for acquiring experience abroad and lack of mentoring and of social capital combine to reduce their chances for position in the elite institutes.

Within academic/research system, there is a gender hierarchy in terms of positions, rewards and recognitions. Women find it difficult to rise due to a male hegemony in numbers and position and due to the structures and processes that support a masculine culture. Beliefs about gender are reproduced at the workplace through various processes that lead to the reproduction of gender in organizations. This is dealt with in Chapter 4 on women scientists.

NOTES

1. As per MOSPI (2018: Table 4.15), in 2011–2012, women in urban areas of age 15–59 years that are graduate and above were earning ₹623.82 and men ₹809.79, which is, 23 per cent less than men on an average. See http://www. mospi.gov.in/publication/women-and-men-india-2017 (accessed on 7 August 2019). For graduates and above, the wage gap is high at 24 per cent in urban areas (Ghai 2018: 17).

   According to Korn Ferry (2018; the index is an analysis of gender and pay for more than 12.3 million employees in 14,284 companies in 53 countries across the globe), women in India are paid on an average 16.1 per cent less than men, which is similar to the global average. See https://www.kornferry.com/press/korn-ferry-global-gender-pay-index-analyzes-reasons-behind-inequalities-in-male-and-female-pay (accessed on 7 August 2019). Based on six sectors (construction, technical consultancy; education, research; financial services, banking, insurance; health care, caring services, social work, ICT services; legal, market consultancy, business activities; manufacturing; transport, logistics, communication), the pay gap is about 25 per cent in 2016 (Monster India 2016). Also, see https://media.monsterindia.com/logos/research_report/MSI_Full_Report_2016_July_2017.pdf (accessed on 7 August 2019).

2. Available at https://jobs.newscientist.com/article/how-the-gender-pay-gap-permeates-science-and-engineering (accessed on 7 August 2019).

3. Available at https://media.monsterindia.com/logos/research_report/MSI_Full_Report_2016_July_2017.pdf (accessed on 7 August 2019). See pages 22–23.

4. IT–BPM: The acronym change was designed to lift the public image of the BPO industry. It has moved from call centre work to business processes.

   Read more at http://timesofindia.indiatimes.com/articleshow/22734976.cms?utm_source=contentofinterest&utm_medium=text&utm_campaign=cppst (accessed on 7 August 2019).

5. World Bank (2018). See https://data.worldbank.org/indicator/ny.gdp.mktp.kd.zg?end=2017&start=2013 and http://meity.gov.in/content/performance-contribution-towards-exports-it-ites-industry (accessed on 7 August 2019). The bulk of these revenues are accounted for by exports (57%). Among the various sectors of IT & ITES, IT services account for half of the revenues, followed by ER&D and software, and BPO (Ministry of Electronics & Information Technology: http://meity.gov.in/content/performance-contribution-towards-exports-it-ites-industry [accessed on 7 August 2019]).

6. Available at http://meity.gov.in/content/performance-contribution-towards-exports-it-ites-industry (accessed on 7 August 2019).

7. Available at https://www.thehindu.com/news/national/tamil-nadu/Number-of-unemployed-women-engineers-in-India-is-as-high-as-40/article14590448.ece (accessed on 7 August 2019).

8. Available at http://blog.belong.co/gender-diversity-indian-tech-companies (accessed on 7 August 2019).

9. Available at https://www.nasscom.in/sites/default/files/media_pdf/indian-it-industry-soars-towards-gender-parity-with-a-rising-number-of-women-in-leadership-roles.pdf (accessed on 7 August 2019).

10. Available at http://www.indiamedicaltimes.com/2017/02/04/over-9-8-lakh-allopathic-doctors-registered-in-india/ (accessed on 7 August 2019).

11. Although there has been considerable growth in proportion of women physicians in several countries comprising more than 40 per cent in Scandinavia and about 70 per cent in Russia, they may continue to be under-represented in positions of leadership and prestige; that workforce policies, environments and cultural views of gender roles are significant in women's status in profession (Ramakrishnan, Sambuco and Jagsi 2014).

12. Available at https://www.nasscom.in/sites/default/files/NASSCOM_signs_MOU_with_Niti_Aayog_to_accelerate_Women_Entrepreneurship.pdf (accessed on 7 August 2019).

13. Note on patents: Research in the West shows that women file proportionately fewer invention disclosures and patents, launch fewer start-up companies and are less successful in attracting venture capital and angel funds. This is due to a lower access to networks and R&D for commercializing research and lack of institutional support (see for e.g., Smith et al. 2017).

14. Note on WIPO: An international treaty administered by WIPO, the PCT allows applicants to seek patent protection for an invention simultaneously in a large number of countries by filing a single PCT international application. The granting of patents remains under the control of national and regional patent offices and is carried out in what is called the 'national phase' or 'regional phase'.

15. World Intellectual Property (WIPO) Indicators 2017. Available at http://www.wipo.int/edocs/pubdocs/en/wipo_pub_941_2017-chapter2.pdf (accessed on 7 August 2019).

16. Available at http://eklavyajee06.blogspot.com/2014/06/harassment-at-edu-work-place.html and https://thewire.in/the-sciences/iisc-sexual-harassment-metoo (accessed on 7 August 2019).

17. List of sexual harassers in academia (LoSHA) was first released on 24 October 2017 on social media as a caution for students to avoid those harassers (the professors and academics). 'The List' initially included the names of about 60 highly respected academic men. The List was posted on 24 October 2017 by activist Inji Pennu and an Indian student in California named Raya Sarkar, who alleged they personally confirmed every incident. A second list came out a week later that was made by women from lower caste backgrounds and included more names, bringing the total up to around 70. Available at https://en.wikipedia.org/wiki/Me_Too_movement_(India) (accessed on 7 August 2019).

18. Twelve Delhi-based feminists published a statement expressing dismay at the use of social media to 'name and shame', arguing that there can be no substitute to the due process of law in order to get justice in cases of sexual

harassment. Sociologists (https://www.epw.in/engage/special-features/power-relationships-academia [accessed on 7 August 2019]) have pointed out that rather than looking at the list and the statement as binary positions, it is more pertinent to assess the reasons for students' lack of confidence in the complaints committees in their colleges and universities. See https://www.epw.in/engage/special-features/power-relationships-academia (accessed on 7 August 2019). In the West, complaint of sexual harassment against New York University professor Avital Ronell aroused defence for Ronell by feminists. See https://thewire.in/rights/feminism-me-too-avital-ronell-nyu-academia-sexual-harassment (accessed on 7 August 2019).

19. Available at https://www.americanbazaaronline.com/2015/10/08/drdo-junks-sexual-harassment-complaint-against-senior-scientist/ (accessed on 7 August 2019).

20. Available at https://www.iitm.ac.in/content/post-doctoral-fellowship-women-break-career (accessed on 7 August 2019).

21. Note on no. of doctorates: Out of the total 27,327 doctorates in the country, 15,246 (56.4%) doctorates were from S&T discipline during 2014–2015. India occupies third rank in terms of number of PhD's awarded in S&T after China (30,017) and the USA (26,520). See http://www.nstmis-dst.org/statistics-Glance-2017-18-2.pdf (accessed on 7 August 2019).

22. Available at https://www.telegraphindia.com/india/faculty-shortage-in-eight-iits/cid/1677438, https://timesofindia.indiatimes.com/city/bengaluru/34-faculty-shortage-hits-iits-across-india/articleshow/63552686.cms and https://thewire.in/education/like-it-or-not-faculty-shortages-in-indian-universities-are-now-permanent (accessed on 7 August 2019).

23. Available at http://inae.in/fellowship-profile/ (accessed on 7 August 2019).

24. Available at https://www.ias.ac.in/Initiatives/Women_in_Science/Women_Fellows_of_INAE (accessed on 7 August 2019).

25. Available at https://erp.iitkgp.ac.in/FacultyCareer/advtFacultyRecruitment.jsp under 'General Information' or at http://www.iitb.ac.in/sites/default/files/jobs/2016-11/B-9%20Advertiise.pdf (accessed on 7 August 2019).

26. See interview by Jayaraj at https://thelifeofscience.com/2017/11/22/life-cycle-shanti-stars/; also see https://thelifeofscience.com/2016/04/18/monica-algologist/ and https://www.currentscience.ac.in/Volumes/112/10/1986.pdf (accessed on 7 August 2019).

27. Available at https://www.news18.com/news/tech/science-technology-in-northeast-suffers-from-poor-infra-lack-of-good-governance-1354497.html (accessed on 7 August 2019).

28. Available at https://www.nitt.edu/home/Faculty%20recruitment%20notifica-tion-%207-10-2014%5B1%5D.pdf (accessed on 7 August 2019).

REFERENCES

ACG Inc. 2015. *2015 Global Women Entrepreneur Leaders Scorecard: Executive Summary*. Available at https://i.dell.com/sites/doccontent/corporate/secure/en/Documents/2015-GWEL-Scorecard-Executive-Summary.pdf (accessed on 7 August 2019).

Adler, N. J., and A. W. Harzing. 2009. 'When Knowledge Wins: Transcending the Sense and Nonsense of Academic Ranking'. *Academy of Management Learning and Education* 8 (1): 72–95.

Amarnath, V. 2011. 'Dilemma of Women Scientists'. *Current Science* 101 (3). Available at https://www.currentscience.ac.in/Volumes/101/03/0259.pdf (accessed on 3 August 2019).

Anand, Sudhir, and Victoria Fan. 2016. 'The Health Workforce in India'. Human Resources for Health Observer Series No. 16. Geneva: WHO. Available at https://www.who.int/hrh/resources/16058health_workforce_India.pdf (accessed on 7 August 2019).

Arun, S., R. Heeks, and M. Morgan. 2007. 'ICT Initiatives, Women and Work: Reproducing or Changing Gender Inequalities?' In *Urban Women in Contemporary India: A Reader*, edited by R. Ghadially, 297–308. New Delhi: SAGE Publications.

Ashcraft, Catherine, Brad McLain, and Elizabeth Eger. 2016. *Women in Tech: The Facts*. Available at https://www.ncwit.org/sites/default/files/resources/womenintech_facts_fullreport_05132016.pdf (accessed on 7 August 2019).

Bagchi, S. 1999. 'India's Software Industry: The People Dimension'. *IEEE Software* 16 (3): 62–65.

Bal, Vineeta. 2005. 'Women Scientists in India: Nowhere Near the Glass Ceiling'. *Current Science* 88 (6): 872–878.

Balaji, S. 2017, 14 December. 'Women-Led Startups Could Grow India's Economy by 60%, But Obstacles Remain for Female Founders'. *Forbes*. Available at https://www.forbes.com/sites/sindhujabalaji/2017/12/14/india-needs-more-women-led-startups-it-makes-economic-sense/#5334ef9c7e58 (accessed on 3 August 2019).

Baporikar. 2014. 'Corporate University Edification in Knowledge Society'. *International Journal of Strategic Change Management* 5 (2).

Bhadra, M. 2011. 'Indian Women in Medicine: An Enquiry Since 1880'. *Indian Anthropologist* 41 (1): 17–43.

Brink, Marieke van den, and Yvonne Benschop. 2011. 'Gender Practices in the Construction of Academic Excellence: Sheep with Five Legs'. *Organization* 19 (4): 507–524. Available at https://doi.org/10.1177/1350508411414293 (accessed on 3 August 2019).

Buddhapriya, Sanghamitra. 2013. 'Diversity Management Practices in Select Firms in India'. *A Critical Analysis Indian Journal of Industrial Relations* 48 (4): 597–610. Available at https://www.jstor.org/stable/23509817 (accessed on 3 August 2019).

Campion, P., and W. Shrum. 2004. 'Gender and Science in Development: Women Scientists in Ghana, Kenya and India'. *Science, Technology and Human Values* 29: 459–485.

Castilla, Emilio J., and Stephen Benard. 2010. 'The Paradox of Meritocracy in Organizations'. *Administrative Science Quarterly* 55 (4): 543–676. Available at https://doi.org/10.2189/asqu.2010.55.4.543 (accessed on 3 August 2019).

Chakraborty, S. 2019. 'The Business Case for Gender Diversity in the Indian Information Technology Industry'. In *Inequality and Organizational Practice. Palgrave Explorations in Workplace Stigma*, edited by S. Nachmias and V. Caven, 211–233. Cham: Palgrave Macmillan.

Chatterjee, C., and S. Ramu. 2018. 'Gender and Its Rising Role in Modern Indian Innovation and Entrepreneurship'. *IIMB Management Review* 30: 62–72. Available at https://reader.elsevier.com/reader/sd/pii/S0970389617305694 ?token=454EA77E15044CDFAA6A9AA040F9346CF58F84E10F7BE5A63 FEBDAA759BE56B91896D3E89DF1B2EA6CC0FC647A0238B3 (accessed on 3 August 2019).

D'Amico, Rita, Patrizia Vermigli, and Silvia Sara Canetto. 2011. 'Publication Productivity and Career Advancement by Female and Male Psychology Faculty: The case of Italy'. *Journal of Diversity in Higher Education* 4 (3): 175–184.doi:10.1037/a0022570

D'Costa, Anthony P. 2006, April. 'Exports, University–Industry Linkages, and Innovation Challenges in Bangalore, India'. World Bank Policy Research Working Paper No. 3887. Available at https://openknowledge.worldbank. org/bitstream/handle/10986/8725/wps3887.txt (accessed on 3 August 2019).

Deccan Chronicle. 2017. Women scientists at Defence Research and Development Organisation Up 5-Fold. Available at https://www.deccanchronicle.com/ nation/current-affairs/090317/women-scientists-at-defence-research-and-development-organisation-up-5-fold.html (accessed on 3 August 2019).

Delamont, S., and P. Atkinson. 2001. 'Doctoring Uncertainty: Mastering Craft Knowledge'. *Social Studies of Science* 31 (1): 87–107.

Desai-Gorakshakar, Kala A., Vijay G. Padwal, and K. Ghosh. 2011. 'Women Scientists in India Are Marching Ahead'. *Current Science* 101 (3): 259–261.

Duttagupta, I. 2010. *Indian Companies Started to Believe in Diversity of Workforce.* Available at https://economictimes.indiatimes.com/articleshow/6538780. cms?utm_source=contentofinterest&utm_medium=text&utm_ campaign=cppst (accessed on 3 August 2019).

Etzkowitz, H., C. Kemelgor, and B. Uzzi. 2000. *Athena Unbound: The Advancement of Women in Science and Technology.* Cambridge: Cambridge University Press.

Fox, M. F. 1983. 'Publication Productivity among Scientists: A Critical Review'. *Social Studies of Science* 13 (2): 285–305.

———. 2000. 'Organizational Environments and Doctoral Degrees Awarded to Women in Science and Engineering Departments'. *Women Studies Quarterly* 28: 47–61.

———. 2004. 'Women in Scientific Fields: Doctoral Education and Academic Careers'. Workshop on Women's Advancement, American Political Science

Association. Available at http://209.235.207.196/imgtest/maryfrankfox.pdf (accessed on 3 August 2019).

Fox, M. F. 2006. 'Women and Academic Science: Gender, Status, and Careers'. In *Dissolving Disparity, Catalyzing Change: Are Women Achieving Equity in Chemistry?* edited by C. Marzabadi, V. Kuck, S. Nolan and J. Buckner, 17–27. New York, NY: Oxford University Press.

Gambles, R., S. Lewis, and R. Rapoport. 2006. *Work–Personal Life Harmonisation*. Chichester: Wiley.

Garg, K. C., and Suresh Kumar. 2014. 'Scientometric Profile of Indian Scientific Output in Life Sciences with a Focus on the Contributions of Women Scientists'. *Scientometrics* 98 (3): 1771–1783.doi:10.1007/s11192-013-1107-4

Ghai, S. 2018. 'The Anomaly of Women's Work and Education in India'. Working Paper No. 368. ICRIER. Available at http://icrier.org/pdf/Working_Paper_368. pdf

Godbole, R., and R. Ramaswamy, eds. 2008. *Lilavati's Daughters: The Women Scientists of India*. Bangalore: Indian Academy of Sciences.

Gupta, B. M., Suresh Kumar, and B. S. Aggarwal. 1999. 'A Comparison of Productivity of Male and Female Scientists of CSIR'. *Scientometrics* 45 (2): 269–289. Available at http://link.springer.com/article/10.1007%2FBF0245 8437?LI =true#page-20 (accessed on 3 August 2019).

Gupta, Namrata. 2007. 'Indian Women in Doctoral Education in Science and Engineering: A Study of Informal Milieu at the Reputed Indian Institutes of Technology'. *Science Technology and Human Values* 32 (5): 507–533.

———. 2013. *Women in Scientific Research in Government and Industrial Laboratories: A Comparative Study of Work Environment and Socio-Cultural Milieu*. A Report submitted to ICSSR under the Senior Fellowship scheme, ICSSR. vide Fellowship no. F.No. 2–11/10/S.Fel. New Delhi: ICSSR.

———. 2015. 'Rethinking Relationship between Gender and Technology'. *Work, Employment and Society* 29 (4): 661–672.

———. 2016. 'Perceptions of the Work Environment: The Issue of Gender in Indian Scientific Research Institutes'. *Indian Journal of Gender Studies* 23 (3): 437–466.doi:10.1177/0971521516656079

———. 2017. Gender Inequality in the Work Environment: A Study of Private Research Organizations in India, Equality, Diversity and Inclusion'. *An International Journal*.doi:10.1108/EDI-04-2016-0029

Gupta, N., and A. K. Sharma. 2002. 'Women Academic Scientists in India'. *Social Studies of Science* 32 (5–6): 901–915.

———. 2003. 'Gender Inequality in the Work Environment at Institutes of Higher Learning in Science and Technology in India'. *Work, Employment and Society* 17 (4): 597–616.

Gupta, Sangita Dutta, Ajitava Raychaudhuri, and Sushil Kr. Haldar. 2015. 'Information Technology Sector in India and Gender Inclusivity'. *Gender in Management: An International Journal* 30 (2): 94–108. Available at https://doi. org/10.1108/GM-04-2013-0046 (accessed on 3 August 2019).

Gurnanai, S., and M. Sheth. 1984. 'Women Scientists in India: Their Position and Role'. *Interdisciplinary Science Review* 9 (3): 259–270.

Haas, L., and C. P. Hwang. 2007. 'Gender and Organizational Culture: Correlates of Companies'. *Responsiveness to Fathers in Sweden, Gender & Society* 21 (1): 52–79.

Hasan, S. A., Mahender Kumar Sharma, Sushila Khilnani, and R. Luthra. 2012. 'Research Productivity of Female Research Scholars and Their Migration Pattern in Pursuit of Higher Education and Research'. *Current Science* 103 (6): 611.

Hearn, Jeff. 2004. 'From Hegemonic Masculinity to the Hegemony of Men'. *Feminist Theory* 5 (1): 49–72.

Hewitt, Aon. 2016, 21 July. 'Gender Pay Gap: Is It Deliberate?' *India Forbes*. Available at http://www.forbesindia.com/blog/business-strategy/gender-pay-gap-is-it-deliberate/ (accessed on 3 August 2019).

Holt, H., and S. Lewis. 2009. 'You Can Stand on Your Head and Still End Up with Lower Pay': Gliding Segregation and Gendered Work Practices in Danish "Family-Friendly" Workplaces'. *Gender, Work and Organization* 18 (s1): e202–e211.

Hoobler, Jenny M., Grace Lemmon, and Sandy J. Wayne. 2011. Women's Managerial Aspirations: An Organizational Development Perspective. *Journal of Management* 40 (3): 703–730. https://journals.sagepub.com/doi/abs/10.1177/0149206311426911

Indian Academy of Sciences, National Academy of Sciences, and Indian National Science Academy. 2016. *Women in Science & Technology: A Vision Document*. Available at http://www.nasi.org.in/Report%20-%20Women%20in%20Science%20&%20Technology%20-A%20Vision%20Document.pdf (accessed on 7 August 2019).

ISRO. 2017–2018. *Annual Report 2017–2018*. Available at https://www.isro.gov.in/annual-report-2017-18-english (accessed on 3 August 2019).

IT & ITES. 2005–2006. *Department of Information Technology*. Available at https://www.indiaservices.in/it-ites/ (accessed on 7 August 2019).

———. 2018. *India Services: IT & ITES Services*. New Delhi: Ministry of Commerce and Industry, Government of India. Available at https://www.indiaservices.in/it-ites/ (accessed on 7 August 2019).

Jaiswal, R. P. 1993. *Professional Status of Women: A Comparative Study of Women in Science and Technology*. Jaipur: Rawat Publications.

Jayaraj, Nandita. 2017. *Rosy's Red Alert to the North-East*. Available at https://thelifeofscience.com/2017/11/29/rosys-red-alert-north-east/ (accessed on 3 August 2019).

John, P. 2016. 'Gendered Medicine: A Study among Medical Educators in Maharashtra'. *BMJ Global Health* 1: A37–A38. Available at https://gh.bmj.com/content/1/Suppl_1/A37 (accessed on 3 August 2019).

Kanter, R. 1977. *Men and Women of the Corporation*. New York, NY: Basic Books.

Kelkar, G., G. Shrestha, and N. Veena. 2002. 'IT Industry and Women's Agency: Explorations in Bangalore and Delhi, India'. *Gender, Technology and Development* 6 (1): 63–84.

Keltner, Dacher, Deborah H. Gruenfeld, and Cameron Anderson. 2003. 'Power, Approach, and Inhibition'. *Psychological Review* 110 (2): 265–284. doi:10.1037/0033-295X.110.2.265

Kondaiah, Bittu Karthik, Shalini Mahadev, Maranatha Grace, and Tham Wahlang. 2017. 'The Production of Science Bearing Gender, Caste and More'. *Economic & Political Weekly* 52 (17): 73–79.

Korn Ferry. 2018. *Korn Ferry Gender Pay Index Analyzes Reason Behind Inequalities in Male and Female Pay*. Available at https://www.kornferry.com/press/korn-ferry-global-gender-pay-index-analyzes-reasons-behind-inequalities-in-male-and-female-pay (accessed on 7 August 2019).

Krishna, V. V. 2014, 26 July. 'A Disappointment for Scientific Community'. *The Hindu*. Available at https://www.thehindu.com/opinion/op-ed/a-disappointment-for-scientific-community/article6250153.ece (accessed on 3 August 2019).

Krishna, V. V., and N. Chandra. 2009. 'Knowledge Production and Knowledge Transfer: A Study of Two Indian Institutes of Technology (IIT Madras and IIT Bombay).' ARI Working Paper No. 121. Asia Research Institute, National University of Singapore. Available at http://www.ari.nus.edu.sg/docs/wps/wps09_121.pdf (accessed on 3 August 2019).

Kumar, Nagesh. 2001. 'Indian Software Development: International Perspective'. *Economic & Political Weekly* 36 (45): 4278–4290.

Kumar, Neelam. 2001. 'Gender Stratification in Science: An Empirical Study in the Indian Setting'. *Indian Journal of Gender Studies* 8 (1): 51–67.

Kumari, J. S., S. G. Lakshmi, P. A Chandra Shekharan, and C. Bindu. 2015, November. 'Work Place Issues and Challenges Faced by Women Doctors in Clinical Departments'. *IOSR Journal of Dental and Medical Sciences (IOSR-JDMS)* 14 (11) (Ver. V): 51–61.

Kurup, Anitha, R. Maithreyi, B. Kantharaju, and Rohini Godbole. 2010. *Trained Scientific Women Power: How Much Are We Losing and Why?* IAS–NIAS Research Report. Available at http://eprints.nias.res.in/142/1/IAS-NIAS-Report.pdf (accessed on 3 August 2019).

Kurup, Anitha, L. Mathew, and T. Singh. 2017. 'Women in STEM Disciplines. Meeting Report'. *Current Science* 112 (10): 1986–1987. Available at https://www.currentscience.ac.in/Volumes/112/10/1986.pdf (accessed on 3 August 2019).

Laudel, G. 2006. 'The "Quality Myth": Promoting and Hindering Conditions for Acquiring Research Funds'. *Higher Education* 52 (3): 375–403.

Lawton-Smith, H., H. Etzkowitz, V. Meschitti, and A. Poulovassilis. 2017. 'Female Academic Entrepreneurship and Commercialisation: Reviewing the Evidence and Identifying the Challenges'. In *The Routledge Companion to Global Female*

Entrepreneurship, edited by C. Henry, T. Nelson and K. Lewis, 78–92. London: Routledge.

Lee, S., and B. Bozeman. 2005. 'The Impact of Research Collaboration on Scientific Productivity'. *Social Studies of Science* 35: 673–702.

Lemoine, W. 1992. 'The Frequency Distribution of Research Papers and Patents According to Sex. The Case of CSIR, India'. *Scientometrics* 24 (2): 449–469.

Levinson, W., and N. Lurie. 2004, 21 September. 'When Most Doctors Are Women: What Lies Ahead?' *Annals of Internal Medicine* 141 (6): 471–474. Available at https://www.ncbi.nlm.nih.gov/pubmed/15381521 (accessed on 3 August 2019).

Lewis, S., J. Brannen, and A. Nilsen. 2009. *Work, Families and Organisations in Transition. European Perspectives*. London: Policy Press.

Lewis, Suzan, and Anne Laure Humbert. 2010. 'Discourse or Reality?: "Work-Life Balance," Flexible Working Policies and the Gendered Organization'. *Equality, Diversity and Inclusion: An International Journal* 29 (3): 239–254. Available at https://doi.org/10.1108/02610151011028840 (accessed on 3 August 2019).

Lincoln, A. E., S. Pincus, J. B. Koster, P. S. Leboy. 2012. 'The Matilda Effect in Science: Awards and Prizes in the US, 1990s and 2000s'. *Social Studies of Science* 42 (2): 307–320. Available at https://journals.sagepub.com/doi/10.1177/0306312711435830 (accessed on 3 August 2019).

Long, Scott J., and Mary F. Fox. 1995. 'Scientific Careers: Universalism and Particularism'. *Annual Review of Sociology* 21: 45–71.

Ministry of Human Resource Development. 2016. *All India Survey on Higher Education 2015–16*. New Delhi: Department of Higher Education, Government of India. Available at http://aishe.nic.in/aishe/viewDocument.action;jsession id=599E34E12A31E35C9F1E8B96E025E750?documentId=227 (accessed on 7 August 2019).

———. 2017. *All India Survey on Higher Education 2016–17*. Available at http://aishe.nic.in/aishe/viewDocument.action;jsessionid=429CC9A01D7DBD3DA F701BFAB10B86C1?documentId=239 (accessed on 7 August 2019).

———. 2018. *All India Survey on Higher Education 2017–18*. Available at http://aishe.nic.in/aishe/viewDocument.action;jsessionid=599E34E12A31E35C9F1 E8B96E025E750?documentId=245 (accessed on 7 August 2019).

Ministry of Science and Technology. 2010. *Evaluating and Enhancing Women's Participation in Scientific and Technological Research: The Indian Initiatives*. Available at https://www.ias.ac.in/public/Resources/Initiatives/Women_in_ Science/taskforce_report.pdf (accessed on 8 August 2019).

———. 2017. *Research & Development Statistics at a Glance 2017–18*. New Delhi: Department of Science & Technology, Government of India. Available at http://www.nstmis-dst.org/statistics-Glance-2017-18-2.pdf (accessed on 7 August 2019).

MIWE. 2018. *Mastercard Index of Women Entrepreneurs.* Available at https://newsroom.mastercard.com/wp-content/uploads/2018/03/MIWE_2018_Final_Report.pdf (accessed on 3 August 2019).

Mohanty, B. K. 2017. *Jobs, Harassment Push Up PhD Dropouts.* Available at https://www.telegraphindia.com/india/jobs-harassment-push-up-phd-dropouts/cid/1521829 (accessed on 7 August 2019).

MOSPI. 2018. *Women and Men in India—2017. Ch 4. Participation in Indian Economy.* Ministry of Statistics & Programme Implementation. GOI. Available at http://www.mospi.gov.in/publication/women-and-men-india-2017 (accessed on 3 August 2019).

Moss-Racusin, C. A., J. F. Dovidio, V. L. Brescoll, M. J. Graham, and J. Handelsman. 2012. 'Science Faculty's Subtle Gender Biases Favor Male Students'. *Proceedings of the National Academy of Sciences of United States of America* 109 (41): 16474–16479. Available at https://www.pnas.org/content/109/41/16474

Monster India. 2016. *Monster Salary Index.* Available at https://media.monster-india.com/logos/research_report/MSI_Report_Low_IT_2016_.pdf (accessed on 7 August 2019).

Mukhopadhyay, C. C., and S. Seymour. 1994. 'Introduction and Theoretical Overview'. In *Women, Education and Family Structure in India,* edited by C. C. Mukhopadhyay and S. Seymour, 1–33. Boulder, CO: Westview Press.

Naik, S., and Megha. 2018. 'The Curious Case of the Missing Indian Postdoc'. *IndiaBioscence.* Available at https://indiabioscience.org/columns/opinion/the-curious-case-of-the-missing-indian-postdoc (accessed on 7 August 2019).

NASSCOM. 2001, February 22. NASSCOM press release. At the Workshop on IT Enabled Services for Women Entrepreneurs, jointly organized by NASSCOM and Government of NCT of Delhi, New Delhi.

NASSCOM. 2018. *Women and IT Scorecard—India.* Milton Keynes: The Open University. Available at http://gsm-it.com/userassets/Publications/GSM-IT_SCORECARD-INDIA_2018_Final.pdf (accessed on 7 August 2019).

NIRF. 2018. *India Rankings 2018.* Available at https://www.nirfindia.org/2018/Ranking2018.html (accessed on 7 August 2019).

———. 2019. *National Institutional Ranking Framework.* National Rankings 2019 and ARIIA 2109, MHRD. Available at: https://www.nirfindia.org/2019/Ranking2019.html

Nkomo, S. M. 2009. 'The Seductive Power of Academic Journal Rankings: Challenges of Searching for Otherwise'. *Academy of Management Learning and Education* 8 (1): 106–112.

NSTMIS. 2017. *Research and Development Statistics 2017–18.* Available at http://www.nstmis-dst.org/SnT-Indicators2017-18.aspx (accessed on 7 August 2019).

OGD. 2012–2015. *Employment in Organised Sectors—Public and Private.* Government of India. Available at https://data.gov.in/catalog/employment-organised-sectors-public-and-private (accessed on 7 August 2019).

Özbilgin, M. 2009. 'From Journal Rankings to Making Sense of the World'. *Academy of Management Learning and Education* 8 (1): 113–121.

Pal, J. 2010. 'Of Mouse and Men: Computers and Geeks as Cinematic Icons in the Age of ICTD'. iConference 2010 papers (2010-02-03). IDEALS. Available at https://www.ideals.illinois.edu/bitstream/handle/2142/14931/of%20mouse%20and%20men.pdf?sequence=2 (accessed on 7 August 2019).

Parikh, P. P., and S. P. Sukhatme. 2004. 'Women Engineers in India'. *Economic & Political Weekly* 39 (2): 193–201.

Pradeep, T. 2018, 20 September. 'How Far Does a PhD Go? *The Hindu*. Available at https://www.thehindu.com/opinion/op-ed/how-far-does-a-phd-go/article24988294.ece (accessed on 3 August 2019).

Prathap, Gangan, and B. M. Gupta. 2009. 'Ranking of Indian Engineering and Technological Institutes for Their Research Performance During 1999–2008'. *Current Science* 97 (3): 304–306.

Pushkar. 2015, 13 December. 'Should India's Elite Universities Be Partial to Foreign PhDs in Faculty Hires?' *The Wire.* Available at https://thewire.in/education/should-indias-elite-universities-be-partial-to-foreign-phds-in-faculty-hires (accessed on 7 August 2019).

PwC. 2016. *Making Diversity Work. Key Trends and Practices in the Indian IT–BPM Industry.* Available at https://www.pwc.in/assets/pdfs/publications/2016/making-diversity-work-key-trends-and-practices-in-the-indian-it-bpm-industry.pdf (accessed on 7 August 2019).

Radhakrishnan, S. 2008. 'Examining the "Global" Indian Middle Class: Gender and Culture in the Silicon Valley/Bangalore Circuit'. *Journal of Intercultural Studies* 29 (1): 7–20.

———. 2009. Professional Women, Good Families: Respectable Femininity and the Cultural Politics of a "New" India'. *Qualitative Sociology* 32 (2): 195–212(18).

Raghuram, Parvati, Clem Herman, Esther Ruiz Ben, and Gunjan Sondhi. 2017, February. *Women and IT Scorecard—India, A Survey of 55 Firms.* Report No. 1. Milton Keynes: The Open University.doi:10.13140/RG.2.2.10118.98882

Raghuram, Parvati, Clem Herman, Gunjan Sondhi, Esther Ruiz Ben, and Helena Carreira. 2018. *Women in IT leadership: Moving towards Gender Parity. Top Tips for Increasing Women in Leadership-Industry.* Available at https://www.researchgate.net/publication/328603332_WOMEN_IN_IT_LEADERSHIP_Moving_towards_gender_parity_Top_tips_for_increasing_women_in_leadership-Industry (accessed on 7 August 2019).

Ramakrishnan, Aditi, Dana Sambuco, and Reshma Jagsi. 2014. 'Women's Participation in the Medical Profession: Insights from Experiences in Japan, Scandinavia, Russia, and Eastern Europe'. *Journal of Women's Health (Larchmt)* 23 (11): 927–934.doi:10.1089/jwh.2014.4736

Rao, Krishna D. 2013. 'Situation Analysis of the Health Workforce in India'. Human Resources Background Paper No. 1, Public Health Foundation of India (PHFI), New Delhi. Available at http://uhc-india.org/uploads/SituationAnalysisoftheHealthWorkforceinIndia.pdf (accessed on 3 August 2019).

Rao, Mohan, Krishna Rao, A. K. Shiva Kumar, Mirai Chaterjee, and Thiagarajan Sundararaman. 2011. *Human Resources for Health in India*. Available at https://www.thelancet.com/journals/lancet/article/PIIS0140-6736(10)61888-0/fulltext (accessed on 7 August 2019).

Resmi, Lekshmi, Prajval Shastri, Srubabati Goswami, Pragya Pandey, Vandana Nanal, Preeti Kharb, Urbasi Sinha, Tanusri Saha-Dasgupta, Suratna Das, and Suchetana Chatterjee. 2019. 'Gender Status in the Indian Physics Profession and the Way Forward'. AIP Conference Proceedings 2109, 050019 (2019). https://aip.scitation.org/doi/abs/10.1063/1.5110093.

Saha, S., and A. S. Ray. 2015. *Science Research and Knowledge Creation in Indian Universities: Theoretical Perspectives and Econometric Evidence*. Available at https://www.jnu.ac.in/sites/default/files/DP10_2015.pdf (accessed on 7 August 2019).

Schiebinger, L. L. 2008. *Gendered Innovations in Science and Engineering*. Stanford, CA: Stanford University Press.

Shanker, Deepika. 2008. 'Gender Relations in IT Companies: An Indian Experience'. *Gender, Technology and Development* 12 (2): 185–207.

Shanker, Deepthi. 2015, 2 July. 'Education and Academic Entrepreneurship in India'. IIM Bangalore Research Paper No. 494. Available at http://dx.doi.org/10.2139/ssrn.2625903 (accessed on 3 August 2019).

Sharma, K. 2018a, 29 May. 'These Universities Are Less than a Decade Old But Are Facing a Severe Shortage of Teachers'. *The Print*. Available at https://theprint.in/governance/these-universities-are-less-than-a-decade-old-but-are-facing-a-severe-shortage-of-teachers/63729/ (accessed on 3 August 2019).

———. 2018b, 26 October. 'How Healthy Is India's Start-Up Industry? NASSCOM Says It Is Doing Fine, But'. *NDTV Profit*. Available at https://www.ndtv.com/business/how-healthy-is-indias-start-up-industry-nasscom-says-it-is-doing-fine-but-1937706 (accessed on 3 August 2019).

Singh, Namrata. 2018. *Women Replace Men as HR Heads in 60% Companies*. Available at http://timesofindia.indiatimes.com/articleshow/67237898.cms?utm_source=contentofinterest&utm_medium=text&utm_campaign=cppst (accessed on 7 August 2019).

Singh, Shelly. 2018. How More and More Women Are Turning Entrepreneurs While Managing Family Along the Way. Available at https://economictimes.indiatimes.com/small-biz/startups/features/how-more-and-more-women-are-turning-entrepreneurs-while-managing-family-along-the-way/articleshow/63179713.cms (accessed on 7 August 2019).

Smith-Doerr, L., and W. W. Powell. 2005. 'Networks and Economic Life'. In *The Handbook of Economic Sociology*, 2nd edition, edited by N. J. Smelser and R. Swedberg, 379–402. Princeton, NJ: Princeton University Press.

Somasekhar, M. 2018. *From Manning Missiles to HR, Women Power Rising in Defence R&D, Production*. Available at https://www.thehindubusinessline.com/news/variety/from-manning-missiles-to-hr-the-rising-women-power-rising-in-defence-rd-production/article22970516.ece (accessed on 7 August 2019).

Sood, Mamta, and R. K. Chadda. 2010. 'Women in Medicine'. *Indian Journal of Gender Studies* 17 (2): 277–285.

SSESS. 2017. *Status of Women in Science among Select Institutions in India: Policy Implications*. Kolkata: SSESS. Available at http://niti.gov.in/writereaddata/files/document_publication/Final_Report_Women_In_Science_SSESS.pdf (accessed on 7 August 2019).

Steinpreis, R. E., K. A. Anders, and D. Ritzke. 1999. 'The Impact of Gender on the Review of the Curricula Vitae of Job Applicants and Tenure Candidates: A National Empirical Study'. *Sex Roles* 41: 509. Available at https://doi.org/10.1023/A:1018839203698 (accessed on 7 August 2019).

Subrahmanyan, Lalita. 1998. *Women Scientists in the Third World: The Indian Experience*. New Delhi: SAGE Publications.

———. 2009. 'Women in Science in India. Has Feminism Passed Them By?' In *Women and Science in India*, edited by Neelam Kumar, 178–205. New Delhi: Oxford University Press.

Subramanian, J. (2007). 'Perceiving and Producing Merit: Gender and Doing Science in India'. *Indian Journal of Gender Studies*, 14 (2): 259–284.

———. 2017. 'Mathematics to Mathematics Education: A Telling Trajectory'. *Economic & Political Weekly* 52 (17): 52–60.

Subramanian, R., and N. Nammalvar. 2017. 'Age, Gender and Research Productivity: A Study of Speech and Hearing Faculty in India'. *Journal of Scientometric Research* 6 (1): 6–14.

Sudha, Nair. 2012. *National Assessments on Gender Equality in the Knowledge Society. Country Results: India*. WISAT. The Elsevier Foundation. Available at http://wisat.org/wp-content/uploads/National_Scorecard_India_Reduced.pdf (accessed on 7 August 2019).

Sugimoto, Cassidy, Chaoqun Ni, Jevin D. West, and Vincent Larivière. 2015. 'The Academic Advantage: Gender Disparities in Patenting'. *PLOS One* 10 (5): e0128000. Available at https://www.ncbi.nlm.nih.gov/pmc/articles/PMC4446102/ (accessed on 3 August 2019).

Sur, Abha. 2009. 'Dispersed Radiance. Women Scientists in C. V. Raman's Laboratory'. In *Women and Science in India*, edited by Neelam Kumar, 98–136. New Delhi: Oxford University Press.

Thakkar, Pooja. 2008. 'Anandi Gopal. Anandibai Joshi'. In *Lilavati's Daughters: The Women Scientists of India*, edited by R. Godbole and R. Ramaswamy, 13–16. Bengaluru: Indian Academy of Sciences.

Thayyil, J., and M. C. Jeeja. 2013. 'Issues of Creating a New Cadre of Doctors for Rural India'. *International Journal of Medicine and Public Health* 3 (1): 8–11.

Thelwall, Mike. 2018, November. 'Do Females Create Higher Impact Research? Scopus Citations and Mendeley Readers for Articles from Five Countries'. *Journal of Informetrics* 12 (4): 1031–1041.

Thelwall, Mike, Carol Bailey, Meiko Makita, and Devika P. Madalli. 2019. 'Gender and Research Publishing in India: Uniformly High Inequality?' *Journal of Informetrics* 13 (1): 118–131.doi:10.1016/j.joi.2018.12.003

Thomas, Anju. 2015. 'Incidents of Sexual Harassment at Educational Institutions in India: Preventive Measures and Grievance Handling'. *International Journal of Recent Advances in Multidisciplinary Research* 2 (3): 317–322.

Upadhya, Carol. 2006.'Gender Issues in the Indian Software Outsourcing Industry'. In *Gender in the Information Society: Emerging Issues,* edited by Anita Gurumurthy, P. J. Singh, A. Mundkur and M. Swamy, 74–84. UNDP-APDIP (Elsevier).

Upadhye, Rekha P., Priya Vijay Girap, Shalini Tewari, Tara Ashok, K. Bhanumurthy, and Ratan Kumar Sinha. 2014. 'Journal Publication Productivity of Women Scientists at Bhabha Atomic Research Centre, India'. *International Journal of Nuclear Knowledge Management* 6 (3). Available at https://doi.org/10.1504/IJNKM.2014.058939 (accessed on 3 August 2019).

Varma, R. 2010. 'Computing Self-Efficiency among Women in India'. *Journal of Women and Minorities in Science and Engineering* 16 (3): 257–274.

Vasudevan, S. 2015. *Number of PhD Scholars at IIT-Madras Rises to 270.* Available at https://timesofindia.indiatimes.com/home/education/news/Number-of-PhD-scholars-at-IIT-Madras-rises-to-270/articleshow/50383462.cms (accessed on 7 August 2019).

Wenneras, C., and A. Wold. 1997. 'Nepotism and Sexism in Peer-Review'. *Nature* 387: 341–343.

WIPO. 2016. *Special Section Measuring Women's Participation in International Patenting.* Available at https://www.wipo.int/edocs/pubdocs/en/wipo_pub_941_2016-chapter1.pdf (accessed on 7 August 2019).

Women's Bureau. 2015. *Computer and Information Technology Occupations.* Available at https://www.dol.gov/wb/stats/Computer_information_technology_2014.htm (accessed on 7 August 2019).

World Bank. 2018. *Physicians (per 1,000 People).* Washington, DC: World Bank. Available at https://data.worldbank.org/indicator/SH.MED.PHYS.ZS?end=2016&start=1960 (accessed on 7 August 2019).

———. 2019. Researchers in R&D (per Million People). Washington, DC: World Bank. Available at https://data.worldbank.org/indicator/SP.POP.SCIE.RD.P6 (accessed on 7 August 2019).

Zainab, A. N. 1999. 'Personal, Academic and Departmental Correlates of Research Productivity: A Review of Literature'. *Malaysian Journal of Library & Information Science* 4 (2): 73–110.

Gender in S&T Organizations

INTRODUCTION

Scientific research is conducted in organizations and the latter are believed to be rational and gender-neutral. However, this belief masks a gender culture that hinders full utilization of the potential of women scientists. Although there is men's dominance in the scientific research organizations, this dominance is not a simple function of a lack of critical mass of women but a product of patriarchal relations in society woven with the context of practice of science and the organizational milieu. This chapter first focuses on the *structural and normative factors that favour men in science* and then shows how certain sociocultural *norms that devalue women in public spaces* lead to a gendered position of women in science. The 'structural and normative factors that favour men' differ from profession to profession in details. Therefore, issues that discriminate women scientists are different compared to those in other professions. However, the second part, the 'norms that devalue women' are common to women in most organizations that are both male dominated and 'masculine'. These norms, behaviours and practices lead to marginalization of women at the workplace. Although these practices might be found elsewhere in the world, the manner in which they are enacted reflects national institutional system of science and national cultural norms.

Gender inequality is experienced as 'tokenism' particularly in the male-dominated professions (Kanter 1977). A low proportion of women in organizations (usually less than 15%) create performance pressure to overachieve or involves attempts to limit their exposure (heightened visibility), creates barriers in informal socialization (boundary heightening) and casts women in stereotyped roles (role encapsulation). Dresselhaus (1986), a physicist, believed that women will experience lower career obstacles if their numbers reach 10–15 per cent. However, the consequences of tokenism are not merely due to low proportions but an overlap with a low social position of the minority group. Studies of men in female-dominated professions show that men encounter enhanced career opportunities or glass escalator (Williams 1992) rather than glass ceiling which indicates sexism as the root cause of consequences of 'tokenism'. Further, these consequences of tokenism reflect, reproduce and maintain differences in power (Lewis and Simpson 2012). A masculine culture in science is a product of an issue of lower proportion of women coupled with an unequal power relation evident in the hegemony of men in positions of power and dominance of men's practices.

Studies on organizations show that gender stereotypes and schemas, such as beliefs about women's 'appropriate' roles, public–private dichotomy, perceived lack of fit between women's appropriate roles and traits required for success at workplace, construct gender at workplace (Bobbitt-Zeher 2011; Heilman 2012; Ridgeway 2009). These gendered beliefs are manifested through interactions and processes in the organizations creating gender inequalities (Acker 2006; Ridgeway and Correll 2004). Perceived incongruity between female gender role and leadership lead to perceiving women less favourably than men as potential occupants of leadership positions and also to evaluating women's leadership less favourably (Eagly and Karau 2002). These inequalities are more pronounced in the male-dominated professions, such as science, which are believed to be traditionally masculine (Ridgeway 2009).

The workplace is embedded in the larger sociocultural context and reproduces the national cultural norms. Patriarchy and hierarchy are significant aspects of the Indian society. They contribute to a masculine environment at the workplace. While a professional woman is increasingly appreciated, the middle-class construction of the cultural domain continues to construe the inner world, that is, home, as being woman-centred (Thapan 2007). A separation of spheres continues to exist in the minds of employers and male colleagues at work (Patel and Parmentier 2005). Organizations typically assume that a working woman is placing family before work and the 'dual burden' is a woman's problem. As a result, even in multilateral organizations and universities, which are liberal spaces, dual income couples face the daunting task of childcare and eldercare (Grover, Samantroy and Paiva 2015). On the one hand, there is a prevalence of traditional gender role ideologies and people do not think that women need support in managing the dual responsibilities. On the other hand, there is a lack of organizational support for family responsibilities (Ramadoss and Rajadhyaksha 2012).

'Hierarchy' has been a prominent feature of the traditional Indian social structure dominated by caste hierarchy. Although public spaces are open to all, India exhibits a high 'power distance' scoring high on this dimension, 77 (compared to the world average of 56.5). Power distance is the degree to which members of an organization or society expect and agree that power should be shared unequally. A high power distance indicates an appreciation for hierarchy and a hierarchical structure in society and organizations. Studies of hierarchical patterns in Indian industrial firms indicate that Indian business culture is hierarchical, with boss subordinate relations which are highly valued (Heuer 2006; Sinha and Kanungo 1997). India's red tape is an 'epidemic'; its bureaucratic morass impedes research and innovation (*Nature* 2015). Research has shown that women in science benefit from formalized structures specifying duties, expectations and criteria of performance evaluation and disseminating information evenly (Long and Fox 1995); that hierarchy and bureaucratic structure by themselves are not detrimental to gender equity (Roth and Sonnert 2011). However, as shown in a study (Gupta 2016) and in this chapter, inefficiencies of the procedures, a hierarchical culture which values contacts with those in power, combined with Indian segregation norms affect women scientists adversely and help perpetuate the male dominance in the system.

Since the Nehruvian days, the 'power elite' in science or the scientists close to political establishment (for instance, Advisory Council to the Prime Minister or Secretary, DST) was drawn or constituted from the mission-oriented science agencies (MOSA, such as the CSIR, the Department of Atomic Energy, the Defence Research and

Development Organisation, etc.) rather than from the academic settings or the universities' (Krishna 2001: 244). However, it is often alleged that 'most scientists at the national laboratories merely consider themselves as just any other government employee with a desire to wield bureaucratic power' (Pandey 2007: 7). In the recent times, the power elite are also being drawn from IISc and the older IITs. The bureaucratic nature of science institutes in post-colonial India and the fact that traditionally the Indian society has been a caste society and has a hierarchical culture renders the system, composed of both scientific and non-scientific members, excessively respectful of those in power with members seeking contacts with the powerful. Indian scientists (Joseph and Robinson 2014) and scholars (such as Kumar [2009]) agree that science and its institutions are not free from feudal, authoritarian values prevalent in the Indian society.

The following sections attempt to understand how gender is constructed in the specific sociocultural and organizational context in which women scientists work. Broadly, construction of gender occurs through practices and norms that favour men and devalue women in public spaces, producing a work climate that adversely affects careers of women scientists and their rise to higher positions.

MASCULINE ENVIRONMENT AT SCIENTIFIC WORKPLACE

Masculine environment implies a workplace climate which produces a greater sense of belonging and an enabling environment for men than for women. It is marked by men's privilege and dominance resulting in women's marginalization. As seen earlier, women constitute less than 15 per cent in many reputed government sector research institutes and organizations. Further, even in professional fields such as biological sciences where percentage of women is higher, men occupy most positions of power. This is to a large extent due to norms and practices that construct privileges and power for men in science organizations. These norms and practices include gendered networking, the concept of an ideal worker/scientist and organizational preferences. Masculinity is also constructed through interpretation of incidents of discrimination as unrelated to the formal system and of special policies for women as 'privileges'. The section also looks at two other aspects: the working of caste and masculinity, and construction of masculinity in private labs as a case study.

Gender and Networking

Mentoring, networking and contacts are significant in professional development in science academia (Etzkowitz, Kemelgor and Uzzi 2000; Levinson 1978; Reskin 1978). This is because such 'who you know' web of contacts and relationships creates social capital. This capital is a vital source of information on sources of materials, data or services. Networking within and outside one's workplace helps to acquire tacit knowledge on how to get ahead, for instance, tips about funding/award opportunities, potential employees or job prospects, current research of other scientists. Further, it makes possible an exchange of ideas, resources and collaborations. A scientist, through networks outside the workplace, introduces his/her doctoral/ postdoctoral students to each other or to other scientists for future employment or research. Social capital, as shown in research elsewhere, establishes credibility of a candidate in hiring, promotions, awards, etc. (Cabrera and Thomas-Hunt 2007). Wennerås and Wold (1997) found that the distribution of fellowships was made to persons known by the committee members (at least one member).

Research elsewhere shows that women lack networking both within and outside their workplace. This is due to two reasons: first, women are less incorporated into informal chat groups, tea clubs, old boys' networks due to a 'boundary heightening' which lead to exclusion of the minority in socialization (Kanter 1977). Second, in forming network ties, individuals tend to interact with those who have similar attributes such as race, gender and religion (McPherson, Smith-Lovin and Cook 2001). So men tend to network with men. This is also called gender homophily. Belle, Smith-Doerr and O'Brien (2014) in research on networks of STEM faculty found gender homophily with men reporting more ties with men and women reporting more ties with women; further, this homophily is greater with lack of critical mass; and women in departments with critical mass (15% or more) reported greater satisfaction with collaboration opportunities. A lack of networking creates a deficit of information, collaboration and mentors, and an excessive dependence on human capital, that is, dependence on their own merit/skills (Didion 2009; Etzkowitz et al. 2000). Through exclusion from powerful male networks, women are relegated to the periphery of scientific activity which enhances masculine character of the institutions.

In India, gender homophily and tokenism are enhanced due to interaction norms (upper-caste patrifocal restrictions on male–female interaction) which create barriers for women. For instance, in engineering departments at the elite institutes which lack critical mass of women doctoral students, seeking help of male colleagues is difficult due to a lack of interaction with them. Further, men do not seek help of women due to their own large network. As a result, it takes longer for women to finish their work (Gupta 2007). Due to interaction norms, availability of critical mass of women does not necessarily lead to a healthy interaction; this is either because gender-based grouping in departments comes up or a large number of women students in a department gets divided into labs (Gupta 2007). Further, as mentioned in Chapter 3, women doctoral students, as compared to their male counterparts, lack interaction with their male supervisors. This further translates into lack of mentorship and of career opportunities for them.

Networking within one's institute helps in creating opportunities for mentorship. This is more important for the women scientists at junior level who need help in understanding the system and the opportunities available for research and information on how to move ahead in career. Social capital at the workplace generates a host of other opportunities, such as, being asked informally for nomination in an institute committee. While e-communications help to circumvent patrifocal restrictions and facilitate contacts abroad, women have fewer contacts within their institute (Gupta and Sharma 2003) and even within their departments (Palackal et al. 2007) compared to men scientists. Segregation norms aggravate tensions of low numbers, particularly in departments with a lack of critical mass (Gupta 2016; Gupta and Sharma 2002, 2003). Thus, according to a study of two CSIR labs, referred to as CSIR1 and

CSIR2 (Gupta 2016), a (female) scientist, Scientist E2 at CSIR2 said, 'informal interaction is there but mostly with women colleagues....' Another scientist (female, Scientist E2, CSIR1) remarked, 'you can't be pally with men scientists...'. Jayaraj (2017) found that where the boss is male, women tend to be excluded from after-work hangouts, smoking breaks, outstation field trips, etc.; as a result, the front runner for most opportunities, whether promotion or the chance to attend an international conference, ends up being male. Working with a male boss could be hazardous. A woman academic who was a dean at Banaras Hindu University found the initial vice chancellor supportive and 'work was going really fast for me (sic). If I needed to see him, I would call his office and if he was busy, he got back to me later'. But things got ugly when the vice chancellor changed and it emerged that some people had been very envious of her. 'I got some letters that claimed I had an affair with the previous vice chancellor' (Jayaraj 2017). Thus, norms against mixed interaction could be easily misused to damage a woman's reputation.

On the other hand, men scientists usually interact informally at tea sometime during the day and they also tend to stay beyond office hours. A scientist (male, Scientist C, CSIR1) said, 'In the Indian scenario more than professional contacts, informal contacts are likely to help you. I interact informally in the Institute mainly at tea' (Gupta 2016). Informal contacts within the institutes lead to interpersonal relations that often take the form of 'pull', 'prejudice' and 'favouritism'. An overwhelming proportion (more than 70%) of women scientists admitted in a study that there were powerful groups in their department who influenced decisions and that they (these women) were not part of any group (Gupta and Sharma 2003). Groupism could be based on specialization, seniority, vested interests and could also be on the basis of gender, caste or institution of graduation.

Networking also counters hierarchical culture for scientists. It creates rapport with seniors/influential which provides a faster movement in the institute hierarchy. A lack of such rapport with seniors might lead to delay in promotions. A scientist in a study (Gupta 2016) remarked, 'It is easier if you have a godfather; otherwise you might be late (in getting promotion) by 3–5 years' (male, Scientist F in CSIR2).

Without contacts with the seniors, a junior scientist is vulnerable to the 'politics' of those in higher positions (Gupta 2016). This is more so in case of women due to an overlapping of gender with lack of social capital. For example, in CSIR2, a woman scientist (Scientist F), who said, 'I am not a member of any committee and have never been; I was always isolated...', was caught between two HODs when she was to be promoted from E2 to F. 'It took several years because one HOD left and the new one wanted to get his own back on the first one; I was the soft target. I could not trouble strong people; I don't fight back' (by which she meant that she did not have the courage to fight strong people like the HODs).

Lack of networking strengthens glass ceiling due to low credibility, low visibility, slower promotions and advancement, and vulnerability to politics; and this glass ceiling, due to being trapped at lower positions, strengthens dual burden assumptions that due to lack of time and family duties of a woman, she cannot do 'good' science.

Age and seniority act positively in terms of interaction and networking for the women scientists. Women scientists aged 50 years or more are more mobile as they reported higher participation in seminars and conferences (due to higher research activity, less family responsibilities) than their younger counterparts (Gupta and Sharma 2003). Further, a higher age and rank lowers the socio-normative emphasis on sex segregation providing greater leeway for mixed interaction. As a woman scientist (Scientist G, CSIR2), who is 57 years old, remarked, '...Now I have become senior; I don't mind barging into a group of drinking people (male colleagues), but it was difficult until a few years ago'. However, whether such late networking helps in catching up with career lags encountered earlier is doubtful and does not explain why only a few older women scientists reach senior/leadership positions or obtain recognition.

Social capital is considered significant by the women scientists and its deficit affects career opportunities. Almost all the women scientists interviewed in a study (Gupta and Sharma 2003) reported that merit alone is insufficient for success in scientific career; that geographical mobility, and contacts and networking with other scientists is important. Interactional norms, family constraints and structural constraints in travelling due to security reasons constrain women in networking through participation in professional gatherings outside the workplace (Campion and Shrum 2004; Gupta and Sharma 2003). Women scientists often find themselves excluded from informal socialization and male informal networks outside the workplace as well. There are few women in professional gatherings. A lesser networking of women with men who form the bulk of the scientific community leads to lesser visibility and lesser recognition than men, which, in turn, implies lesser contacts and so the vicious circle continues (Gupta and Sharma 2003).

Gender, 'Scientist' and 'Ideal Worker'

The pervasive stereotype of a 'scientist' is a male, and a 'male model' in science is a norm that women must conform to; it requires, for instance, devoting long hours to lab or research (Etzkowitz et al. 2000). This overlaps with the notion of a universal/ideal worker in organizations which is a male unencumbered by familial responsibilities (Acker 1990; Brumley 2014; Collinson and Hearn 1996). It is premised on the ideology of separate spheres with public sphere as the man's domain.

The masculine norm of long working hours is prevalent in the Indian research institutes reflecting the notion of a 'male model' of science. This is evident in the following statement of a scientist (male, Scientist F) at a CSIR lab (Gupta 2016): 'A capable scientist is one who has more recognition. Actually, the time period that man can devote is more because a woman cannot. This affects her work and it takes a long time to complete the same work'.

This statement highlights the relationship between the notion of time required for doing good science and success. Further, since women are perceived as devoting less time, their research is assumed to be below par as reflected in the following statement of a senior scientist (male, Scientist G, CSIR2) (Gupta 2016): 'Research of women is mediocre; you need to be immersed in research. Women are family oriented because in India it's given that women sacrifice more'.

That women's 'research is mediocre' was probably a generalization based on a limited sample, that of two women scientists in his department who happened to be average researchers. Thus, women's failures are magnified due to a 'heightened visibility'. Also, there is a lack of recognition for women's achievements. Further, the belief that the scientific research of women is not at par with that of men is negated by the evidence (Gupta, Kumar and Aggarwal 1999; Hasan et al. 2012).

An underestimation of women's performance, also referred to as 'professional diminution' or questioning a woman faculty member's professional authority, is one of the most common micro-inequities in the academic profession (Collins, Chrisler and Quina 1998: 8). In a study of the women faculty at the academic science institutes (Gupta and Sharma 2002), about 40 per cent of the respondents believed that male colleagues are not able to accept women as equals. Only about 34 per cent of women academics could say that their male colleagues correctly evaluate their work, and that the performance of a woman is not underestimated. This is brought out in the statements of women scientists (Gupta and Sharma 2003) that 'men colleagues take a long time to see that a woman is equally competent'; 'men are unable to accept that a woman of the same designation can do better than them'.

The reason for diminution is often dual burden assumptions of the male colleagues as reflected in the phrase 'family oriented' in the earlier statement and because 'men feel that women are less committed … they have to be two and a half times better than men to achieve similar recognition' (a woman scientist in Gupta and Sharma [2003]). Women's capabilities are doubted, at least initially, so that the time required to prove that they are equally capable may be quite long. 'The colleagues initially questioned my professional competence and tried to put me down in meetings and general talks. I had to be on my guard. Lot of professional energy was dissipated in that, otherwise I could have done much better' (Dr Rita Gupta, Associate Professor, Gupta and Sharma [2003]).

That women scientists devote less time to research compared to men might also be a myth. In a survey conducted in 2010 on 312 women and 161 men in research by the Indian Academy of Science along with the National Institute of Advanced Studies showed that women often work harder than men with 62.8 per cent women spending 40–60 hours a week at work as compared to 46 per cent men. About 25.5 per cent men reported less than 40 hours compared to 16.5 per cent women; and 28.6 per cent men worked more than 60 hours compared to 20.5 per cent women (Kurup et al. 2010: Table 41).

The notion of a scientist as a male encompasses not only a 'male model' but also a perception of science/engineering as more suitable for men. For instance, studies on elite Indian academic institutes have found stereotypes such as women would find it difficult to handle field work; women cannot teach boys effectively (Gupta and Sharma 2002); women are incapable of handling certain engineering sections as seen in this statement of a woman faculty (Gupta and Sharma 2003):

> A problem occurred when I was given the charge of the PQR engineering section in our department four years ago. Some seniors thought that a woman could not run the section and raised the issue in the departmental meeting. Though the section has continued to be under my charge, the rules related to its running have been flouted. Till date, I have not been given peons and technical assistants.

The concept of an 'ideal worker' (such as the scientist as an employee in an organization) as always available and visible for the organization is a male (Lewis and Humbert 2010). This is manifested in meetings scheduled beyond the office hours, which affects women's participation due to work-life balance issues (Gupta 2016, 2017). However, this notion of men as ideal worker remains unimpaired when men alter practices to create work-life balance. Men wanting to pick up kids from day care in Tata Institute of Fundamental Research (TIFR) led to rescheduling of the meeting time.[1] The primacy of man in public sphere is further reflected in the contradictory assumptions about similar actions of men and women as is brought out in observations of women scientists such as, 'if I am late in coming to the department, it is attributed to domestic duties at home, while if a man is late, he is considered to be busy in some legitimate work' (Gupta and Sharma 2003).

Practices in science workplaces reflect a masculine culture. For instance, women do not form part of the informal meetings after the office hours when names for various committees are decided

(Gupta and Sharma 2002). Further, men usually appoint men as committee heads (Gupta 2013) suggesting 'homosocial' reproduction (Connell 2000). That a worker is a male is further enhanced through application of a gendered decorum of behaviour that marginalizes women. It is supposed that to be womanly is to be submissive (Mukhopadhyay and Seymour 1994). As a woman scientist stated, 'Some men colleagues initially wanted to force their views on me; they thought that being a woman I should simply agree to their viewpoint' (Gupta and Sharma 2002). The problem is greater in the traditional engineering departments, or in those departments that have relatively older faculty members or in those with very few women (Gupta and Sharma 2002).

Another consequence of male hegemony is condescension reflected in men faculty members being sometimes too appreciative of the small achievements of women faculty (Gupta and Sharma 2002), 'even if I do something of little merit, men faculty show a lot of appreciation' (Dr Savita Jain, Assistant Professor, physics), or 'the men colleagues are extra polite towards us which is quite irritating' (Dr Sheela Roy, Assistant Professor, EE). A woman faculty in Subrahmanyan's (2009: 188) study recounted how her HOD when convening a committee for administrative purposes that had no man in it, would ask her, 'can you manage?' or 'You are all ladies. Shall I put a man along with you?' This reflects the sense of male entitlement at the scientific workplace and translates into gender illiteracy as remarked by a woman professor, 'More often than not, men don't even realize that something they have said or done was offensive or threatening to women colleagues or students' (Masoodi 2016).

Organizational Preferences/Gendered Logistics

Organizational preferences and logistics construct gender in various ways which affects women's careers. One, women are unable to capitalize on the opportunities that lead to an accumulation of certain forms of 'career capital'. Acquisition of such career capital is enmeshed with the normative context of women's centrality in the domestic sphere. Women whose marriage coincides with the completion of the doctorate degree program would find it difficult to capitalize on their degree and obtain a position if they take a break in career. Those who continue to do research through research projects (after doctorate) are at a disadvantage compared to those with teaching/industrial experience for a faculty position (Gangopadhyay and Das 2016); further, returning to position in academia through entry-level positions after a break is also difficult because institutes do not prefer candidates above 35 years of age for such positions (as indicated in Chapter 3). On the other hand, senior positions are usually filled by internal promotions rather than through lateral hiring (Joseph and Robinson 2014). This would filter out women researchers that manage to do well (either in lesser institutes or through research projects) and apply later to the elite institutes. Thus, career trajectories off the beaten path, more common in case of women, are discouraged. Further, elite institutes prefer doctorates or postdoctorates from abroad which disadvantages women as they are less likely to travel abroad for these degrees than men (also discussed in Chapter 3). Many government institutes/labs do not prefer to hire couples (Gupta 2002; Jayaraj 2017) due to which either a woman compromises or the couple has a tough time in obtaining jobs, also referred to as the 'two-body problem'.

Accumulation of career capital is also affected by allocation of tasks and resources in the departments that can become gendered. No institute makes a distinction between men and women regarding the allotment of various resources such as laboratory equipment, materials, space, etc. However, in practice, resources seem to be less available for women (Gupta and Sharma 2003). Women faculty at times face problems in obtaining research scholars. While student choice of an advisor is considered for allotting advisors in most elite institutes, the weightage given to their choice varies from institute to institute and even department to department. Both student prejudices and department policies could marginalize women faculty. Women are usually junior and are seen by the students as having less time and low contacts (Gupta and Sharma 2003). In a study of doctoral students at IITs (Gupta 2007), it was found that about one-third of the male doctoral students believed that men are better teachers and researchers, while only about one-tenth of the women thought so. In some institutes/universities where departments play a major role in the decision on who takes which scholar, such decisions are usually influenced by the seniors and politics, and favouritism plays a role (Gupta and Sharma 2003). This is true for some CSIR labs also; a scientist (female, Scientist C, CSIR2) explained that the requirement for students in their institute was more than the intake and students are given a choice to join any faculty. So some faculty might have none.

> There is domination of seniors in research; if you are in a committee, you favour yourself; there is no transparency; they have better access to instruments, they take students; students go to the faculty that already has students; I receive e-mails from scholars interested in working with me, but they are filtered down by the system; the system should identify those who don't have research scholars. (Gupta 2013: 100)

Practice of science requires dealing with the administrative staff. In India, the lower administrative personnel in academia/labs are often male. According to the report on higher education (Ministry of Human Resource Development 2018), total male non-teaching staff is 68.1 per cent as compared to merely 31.9 per cent women staff. As a result, an inefficient system ridden with red tape and a hierarchical mindset combine with gender biases in professional practice of science for women scientists. For instance, in universities, appointments as external examiners are decided at the lower administrative level and these appointments are a source of greater visibility to the faculty in their discipline. In the study of Madras University, Subrahmanyan (2009) found that women faculty were not usually appointed as external examiners because women do not fraternize with the staff, while male faculty would go to them and ask their name to be put down for it. A recurring theme in the interviews in a study of CSIR labs was that the CSIR system is slow moving and that contacts and a high position in the hierarchy ease the pressures of bureaucratic procedures. As a senior scientist (male, Scientist G, CSIR2) commented, '...lethargy of the system is there at all levels [in] procurement, recruitment, getting funds, paper work.... Person who is well connected, things move for him'. The term 'well connected' here implies contacts with those in higher positions. Interpretation of rules might vary and the administrative staff which usually implements the rules tends to favour those with higher status in the institute hierarchy. For instance, according to a scientist (male, Scientist C, CSIR1), 'The administrative staff is not very helpful. Their help depends on what kind of relation you have with them or how senior you are; …"Show me the face I will show you the rules"'.

As stated earlier, there are few women in high positions. Also, routine procedural matters of purchase and funding involve non-scientific staff which is usually male. Women scientists of junior rank face problems that combine rank with gender. For instance, according to a scientist (female, Scientist C, CSIR1), 'Sometimes it is very difficult to speak to a male staff member, they feel offended…. Lower staff is very adamant; they will not listen to you because of your (younger) age and gender'.

Although research in leading institutes is well funded, obtaining funds for seminars and conferences might also involve bureaucratic hurdles, and some women scientists in academia (Gupta and Sharma 2003) might not apply for funds at all, because the application requires a great deal of 'running around' and decisions suffer from favouritism. A respondent in this study (Gupta and Sharma 2003) overheard a clerical staff member saying 'lagaane do isko chakkar' (let her keep running around). Research grants also require lobbying with the officials in funding agencies in Delhi when their proposals are evaluated by those agencies. Women usually engage in formal communication in such situations as informal interaction which is more helpful is limited for women both due to inappropriateness of interacting with men after official hours and of manipulation as unbecoming of women (Subrahmanyan 2009).

Logistics of research requires funding from external agencies. Percentage of women receiving extramural grant for R&D by central R&D agencies has increased to 29 per cent in 2014–2015 from 13 per cent in 2000–2001 due to various initiatives of the government (Ministry of Science and Technology 2017). DST and Department of Biotechnology (DBT) are two main players in extramural grants. However, the gender gap in the extramural grants has remained stagnant since 2009–2010 with male–female participation as 69–31 per cent in 2009–2010 to 71–29 per cent in 2014–2015 (Ministry of Science and Technology 2017). An analysis of Scheme-wise Extramural Research And Development Projects Approved During 2009–2010 shows that about 16 per cent of the DST projects (236/1,476) were awarded to women under women scientists' schemes of the DST initiated in 2002–2003 (OGD 2012–2015). Thus, it seems that this increase (from 13% to 29%) might be mostly owing to the special schemes for unemployed women scientists with a career break (WOS-A, WOS-B and S&T for women). Proportion of such research grants or its increase for women in regular positions is not known.

Interpretation of Discrimination as 'Individual'/Informal

Women scientists at times encounter overt discrimination in day-to-day interaction which may affect their career. However, studies show that incidents of discrimination are seen as isolated incidents and blamed on individuals (Gupta 2013, 2016). They are not seen as organizational discrimination and this discounting of the gendered practices at the informal level add to the masculine nature of the work environment. For instance, a scientist (E2) at CSIR1 (Manya, a psuedonym), who was the only woman in her department for 15 years, was denied promotion due to biased reports of her HOD. She said (Gupta 2016):

> My institute, my director and most of my colleagues are lovely. Gender bias occurs usually because of one person. It occurred because of the bad mentality of my HOD. Then there are two other colleagues. HOD doesn't publish. He is an HOD by age/seniority. Scientifically he is very weak. So there is professional jealousy....

She believed that gender equality 'is respect, which I am not getting from my male colleagues; but there was gender equality in her organization' '...my gender discrimination is personal, it is nothing professional'. Another scientist, Maansi (a pseudonym), in the same study (Gupta 2016), who joined as a Scientist B (CSIR2) in 1987, was not independent and had to work under the supervision of the HOD. She encountered serious difficulties from her HOD until he retired in 2005. However, when asked if she thought there was gender equality, she said 'yes' because 'the system provides equal opportunities to both men and women'. Further, she remarked, 'I have patience and mental strength; hence, I was able to fight him'.

Although narrated as discrimination by individuals, the discrimination faced by Manya and Maansi was organizational. The perpetrators belonged to the same organization as the victims and held senior positions in the system. In Manya's case, a few male colleagues were colluding with the HOD while some others were mute spectators. Maansi hinted at systemic fault for not removing the erring individuals when she remarked that 'If middle manager is notorious he should be removed'. Thus, gender biases are widespread and Manya had to fight for even the basic facilities, such as lab space. Further, the discrimination occurred over a long period of time and could recur if the discriminating HODs were still around. Yet Manya and Maansi perceived no discrimination in organization since they did not recognize any problem with the 'system' which as Maansi said provides 'equal opportunities'.

The earlier incidents indicate that the system is equated with formal rules, and by blaming discriminatory individuals or men as a group, women uphold the assumption of gender equality in their organization. This is further seen in another statement of a woman scientist (Scientist G, CSIR1), 'Yes, equality exists; during selection, the system never thinks of male or female'; however, in response to question: 'Do you think women in everyday life face specific situations because they are women?' she replied, 'when more men are there and so few ladies, naturally men decide what they want and women's voice may not be heard' (Gupta 2013). Thus, the male predominance in numbers translating into the hegemony of men's practices with the latter being perceived as 'natural' and therefore not as systemic inequality.

In perceiving the individual incidents of discrimination independent of the system, the latter is perceived as rational and gender-neutral; second, the system is equated with formal rules but not with the formal practices. As a result, biases in meetings, selections, and official day-to-day interactions are seen as processes unrelated to the formal system. Finally, a lack of critical mass creates a climate of acceptance of male practices and leaves little scope for dissent from the minority.

In constructing discriminatory incidents as individual, women exhibit 'individualization' in the Western sense that individuals assume responsibility for their life and for all their choices (Kelan 2009). However, this process of 'individualization' overlaps with traditional social forms (such as family) in post-colonial societies (Belliappa 2013). This is evident in the dual burden assumptions that construct gender inequality as 'social' as discussed in the section on 'norms that devalue women'.

Women as Privileged

In a study of doctoral students, men and women had contradictory gender perceptions (Gupta 2007, 2010). It was found that male students believed that women did not face any constraints or minor constraints and were even privileged. The privilege was perceived in terms of women getting more cooperation, being graded softer by faculty members or being given undue favours. They were overwhelmingly unaware of women's problems relating to interaction, prejudices and lack of academic help.

The notion of women's 'privilege' carries over to faculty level. Government schemes convey the impression that women get 'things' easily as, for instance, in a study (Gupta 2016), a scientist (male, Scientist F, CSIR1) said, 'Actually women get more opportunities and get things more easily than men ... because government is encouraging them ... if there is some award, women being few at high positions, face less competition and get it easily'.

Women scientists are perceived as having a less rigorous professional life and therefore advantaged. For instance, a scientist (male, CSIR2, Scientist G) in this study (Gupta 2016) said, 'there is no bias here. On the contrary women are *privileged*. They come late (to the lab), go back early'. Some male scientists perceived bias *against men* since men were given more responsibilities as, for example, when women were 'let off' certain tasks (Gupta 2016). However, more responsibilities for men also imply denial of opportunities for women as, for instance, in being 'let off' the charge/membership of a departmental committee. In perceiving women as privileged, women scientists are seen as negating the ideal/universal worker concept of

devoting long hours to the lab and being available to the organization. The concept 'excludes and marginalizes women who cannot ...
achieve the qualities of a real worker because to do so is to become
like a man' (Acker 1990: 150).

Masculinity and Caste

As mentioned in the Introduction, women and men scientists overwhelmingly belong to the upper castes. As a result, women scientists of
lower castes face issues that magnify the consequences of masculinity
when it intersects with upper-caste institutions and marginalize them
even further in the scientific community. In a study on scientists at
CSIR labs (Gupta 2013), a Scheduled Caste woman scientist, Scientist
C at CSIR2, narrated, 'even though I had credentials, and had more
papers than the other person who was taken under open category, I
was not taken (appointment) under open category but under reserved
category and given the position of Scientist B'. She feels quite bitter
about this initial appointment saying, 'Scientist B was not where I
should have joined; we are forced to write caste on application forms
and then denied what should be given to us as an equal'. This indicates
a process of labelling or stigma-based categorizations which consolidates gender-based disadvantages.

After her promotion to Scientist C, when she became independent,
she started writing projects for funding.

> I applied many times to agencies outside this lab, but failed to get any
> project. I have been called for presentation, but was not given any reason
> for their refusal. However, I have been working on a couple of joint projects
> and have one from this institute.

She has also failed to get PhD students till now without which research
is difficult. She has project trainees but they are supposed to be
employed only for 6 months. She has not been part of any committee. No one has approached her for this. She does not see it as caste
issue but feels that 'men tend to involve men more in committees and
meetings; women don't say that they want to be a part of it'. Thus, the
problems faced by women scientists of lower castes reveal an overlap
of caste, gender and systemic inefficiencies.

Caste discrimination, although outlawed in the Indian Constitution, exists tenaciously in all walks of life from schools to university in subtle forms. The assumptions of neutrality and rationality in science institutions preclude discourse on caste biases. Caste is a case of acquisition of cultural capital depending upon one's location in the caste position. As Shalini Mahadev, a doctoral student at the University of Hyderabad, narrates her experience of how she 'stood out' in masters in a university even though no one asked about caste, because of the clothes, mannerisms, accent; colleagues had a better education and more comfortable life, having better knowledge and talking better; further, performance expectations from the lower castes in general are low; these aspects overlap with gender as women are pressurized into being docile and are constantly judged. In the seemingly casteless institution, caste is visible in surnames, language and culture, and the biases are extremely difficult to pinpoint, leading Kondaiah et al. (2017) to label science institutions as 'castelessly' casteists (77).

Masculine Culture at Private Sector Research Labs: A Case Study

The case of private research labs[2] provides a glimpse into a masculine culture that is shaped by the specific exigencies of a profession and yet impacted by similar sociocultural norms (such as hierarchy). The scientists in private labs identify themselves more as employees of the company rather than with the professional community of scientists. In the pharma labs studied (Gupta 2017), the scientists are mostly PhDs or doing PhD. The research problems of the scientists are decided by the company which also maintains control over data, materials, tools and results. They prefer to patent new findings rather than disseminate them in journal. Research in these labs is governed by commercial interests. The scientists work on the target-oriented modules set by the management. Delivery of timelines as per these targets is of prime importance.

The project manager along with the company bosses decides the timelines for a research project and the team has to work accordingly. The actual working is left to the scientists in the team. The team is composed of scientists in a hierarchical arrangement from junior to senior scientists. In both types of research labs, there is not only a preponderance of men in numbers, but men occupy most of the higher positions reflecting greater formal power.

In private research labs, an 'ideal worker' is visible and available, as elsewhere (Lewis and Humbert 2010). An informal practice of judging employees' contribution in terms of hours spent at work irrespective of the amount or quality of work accomplished is widely prevalent which affects women adversely (Gupta 2017). As Jhanvi (female, a Junior Scientist in Private1) remarked:

> when a man and a woman are at the same level but only one has to be marked for promotion, the superiors see who has worked hard and this is judged by the number of hours given to work…. I may finish my day's task and still go back on time. But this is not recognized by the superiors.

The long-hours culture is aggravated in the Indian hierarchical cultural context. If the boss stays late, the juniors are unable to leave early reflecting a high power distance. A hierarchical culture in India heightens the need for visibility for the benefit of bosses. Visibility is required not only in terms of long hours but also in the form of interpersonal interaction and rapport with the seniors. Interaction norms that inhibit networking with men, meetings kept beyond office hours (sometimes without much agenda and, therefore, wasteful) impact women in these labs also. Informal contacts and networks for women scientists in private labs are further restricted by the inflexibility of the work schedule that requires presence at the workplace in the office hours and gendered practices. For instance, the requirement for plant visits in pharma labs which provide networking opportunities are structurally unfriendly and unsuitable for women (Gupta 2017).

In private research labs, companies have certain preferences in recruitment as well as during promotions that act as an advantage for men. For instance, more value/preference is attached to the worker who has gained experience in similar companies. Constrained by family, women most often do not change companies as it usually requires relocation to a different city. The preference for outside experience is not a part of formally written rules but practised informally.

It leads to a lower position for women in the company than a man who has the same experience as her but might have worked at various other companies. Such informal practices disadvantaging women exemplify 'gliding segregation' (Holt and Lewis 2009), that is, the process of women and men starting at the same place with the same level of education ending up with different opportunities for development due to gender. Plant visits, as mentioned earlier, are important for promotions also, but extremely difficult for women due to lack of facilities. This exemplifies how organizational 'gender neutrality' translates into facilities favouring only men.

The women in most male-dominated professions face similar norms that devalue their status at workplace. These are discussed with reference to women in the academia and public/private research labs further.

NORMS AND PRACTICES DEVALUING WOMEN SCIENTISTS AT WORKPLACE

The idea of women's primary domestic role gives rise to norms and practices that devalue women in public spaces leading to inequality for women in science. These include beliefs and practices reflecting the dual burden assumptions of male colleagues, biased treatment of pregnant employees, the manner in which men distance themselves from work-life balance policies and the gendered assumptions about leadership roles. The denial of gender inequality at the workplace precludes any discussion about gender within the organizations. These norms and practices consolidate institutions as the 'natural preserve of men' (Srivastava 2018: 42).

Assumptions of Men about Dual Burden

An ideological belief in women at the centre of the domestic sphere is coupled in recent decades with the growth of Hindu nationalism and a consequent reassertion of the notion of family and family values as the fulcrum of Hindu identity among the urban middle classes (Radhakrishnan 2011). Studies elsewhere show that women are not looked upon as flexible workers, or considered flexible to the needs of the workplace, which is construed as a lack of commitment to work (Holt and Lewis 2009). The examples here indicate how assumptions of women's family roles result in loss of opportunities and compromise women's position in the organizational hierarchy. Although many examples resonate with studies in other parts of the world, they also go beyond those studies to indicate a more entrenched belief in separation of spheres.

The belief in separation of sphere is primarily manifested through the assumptions of men that women are constrained at work due to their devotion to their family. For instance, women faculties at national institutes have reported facing interview committees for appointment that ask gender-based questions (Gupta and Sharma 2002) such as, 'why do you want a job?' or 'how will you take care of your family?' The interview committees (for the appointment of faculty) reflect various social prejudices, such as the fear of an unmarried woman candidate getting married and losing commitment, or of a married woman leaving the job to join her husband working elsewhere. In the study on CSIR labs (Gupta 2016), a junior woman scientist (Scientist E1, CSIR2) said, 'awareness of a dual burden on women affects hiring. The woman has to prove that she is better than a man for any job'; a senior male scientist, also an HOD at a CSIR lab, on the one hand, remarked, 'whosoever is qualified should be appointed', but on being asked what if both male and female candidates are equal, he replied, 'the male is preferred because he can work for longer hours, as compared to a female'. The scientists featured on The Life of Science reported being asked personal questions during job interviews like 'you have applied for a job in this city but your husband is in another city or country so how will you manage?' (Thite 2017). There are stereotypes that a woman, by being appointed as a faculty member, is taking away a man's seat (Gupta and Sharma 2003). These questions reflect the public–private dichotomy with the assumption that domestic roles are women's domain; the absence of public care system/organizational infrastructure for childcare, etc., strengthen the uncertainty surrounding women's management of a dual burden. There are no studies on various stages of recruitment, such as screening of the biodata, seminars and interviews. The selection process lacks transparency and the institutes maintain a strict confidentiality.

The assumption of women's domestic role is often used as an instrument to promote a male candidate or to isolate women scientists in organizations from important tasks/committees (even though a woman might be willing or capable of handling). For instance, a senior woman scientist at a CSIR lab remarked (Gupta 2016):

> Whenever something important is going on in the division and someone has to take charge of it, they automatically think of men. For a long time I was the only woman in this division. It was assumed that I have a lot of work at home. In the guise of helping, they sideline.

This exclusion often takes the form of 'letting off', that is, allowing a woman colleague to opt out of important tasks, usually administrative and non-academic, requiring long hours. A woman is not always consulted for those tasks as apparent from the earlier statement. At times, women themselves request being let off. However, such request might imply structural constraints and lack of support (Gupta 2016). This 'letting off' assumes that family role of women is part of the 'Indian culture'. There is also a lack of confidence in the abilities of a woman. For example, in the same study, a senior male scientist said:

> For a particular task, if (we are) selecting people you are avoiding women, may be you have more confidence in men, or woman may have to work at odd-hrs or have small kids, so it's a human thing that o.k. go early, it's our Indian culture....

This identification of women's family roles with 'Indian culture' masks the glass ceiling effects. The use of dual burden assumptions by men colleagues for excluding women is reported by various women scientists as, for instance, 'men want to make men as committee heads because men say that a woman would spend more time on domestic front'; 'sometimes opportunities suffer because they (men colleagues) calculate that women can't devote time; only when there is no option, opportunities are given to women' (Gupta 2016). These opportunities are 'participation in seminars, consultancy, in any difficult work, in going abroad or taking part in decisions'. Hence, on the one hand, there is an assumption that dual burden on women renders them unavailable for significant tasks and, on the other hand, there is a sense among women scientists of being left out. While there are women scientists who themselves do not wish for an administrative position or committee headships, but, as a woman scientist, at a CSIR lab, commented (Gupta 2016), '70 per cent of women will not go after leadership position, but if it comes to them, they will not say "no".... Men lobby for it....'

Thus, the repertoire of 'Indian culture' in terms of assumptions of women's devotion to family enacts a gendered system in organizations through 'automatic sex categorization' (Ridgeway 2009). This assumption in India is so strong that a woman committing extra hours to work might be perceived by the colleagues as compromising her primary domestic role. For instance, a woman scientist overheard a male colleague saying, 'she always comes at nine in the morning; she does not seem to have any work at home', and she felt that it was expected of her to go home at five in the evening (Gupta and Sharma 2003).

In the study of private labs (Gupta 2017), dual burden perceptions of seniors affected promotions of women scientists. The latter were often given less important tasks. They were denied promotions because of the perception that as mothers they might not be able to handle the enhanced duties; if promotion required mobility or transfer, her non-availability was assumed without asking her.

Biased Treatment in Pregnancy

The masculine image of a scientist is incompatible with a woman scientist, even more so when she is pregnant. Martin (1990) suggests that in the male-dominated organizations, a pregnant employee is an alien. This is reflected in the situations faced by the women scientists, as, for instance, a scientist (female, Scientist F, CSIR2) said:

> (During) First time (pregnancy), my seniors troubled me by giving difficult job; second time, they ignored me; they thought that I should go home, why am I coming here, my husband is earning; that two years she will not do any work. They used to tell me that I should leave the job and go home. (Gupta 2013)

The feeling of hostility for a pregnant woman scientist occurs as pregnancy seems to be an intrusion of the 'private' (or domestic) sphere in the 'public' (or economic) domain. Socialized in the Indian patriarchal system, many women believe that family/child-care issues are women's problems. For instance, justifying the negative feelings of the male colleagues, a woman scientist (Scientist G, CSIR1) said:

> In pregnancy, *thoda sa to dekhiye hota hai, ab chhuti pe chhale jayenge* (see, colleagues do have some negative feelings, they feel you would go on a holiday). But one has to understand their state of mind. I will feel the same way. I will also tell my student—*jaldi kar lo nahin to phir chhe maheenein nahin kar paogi* (do it fast otherwise you will not be able to do it for the next six months). (Gupta 2013)

However, there is a subtle difference in male colleagues reflecting on pregnancy as a holiday and a woman supervisor persuading her student to try to finish some work. The first one is a belief that pregnancy is a systemic loss, while in the latter the student herself would be a loser.

In the private labs, the bosses might be considerate during the pregnancy of a woman scientist, but this has its own price (Gupta 2017). If a woman is pregnant, bosses usually might not allow her to do heavy work and give her a reduced workload. However, the work diminishes her career and even after pregnancy leave, she is not given important work. The male colleagues in the team might be hostile. Pregnancy leave is often seen as time off as, for instance, in the statement 'women can take off for more than 4 months' (Gupta 2017). The statement reflects a lack of respect for women and reflects how women's innate inability to be an 'ideal worker' or a full-time, available and visible worker devalues them in the public sphere.

Work–Life Balance Policies and Practices

Work–life balance structures, while actually aiding work-life balance, can play a major part in diluting the male perception that women find work role difficult to manage along with the domestic role. However, typically, organizations in India lack childcare and day care infrastructure compared to the West and it is coming up mostly in response to globalization and the need to attract and retain the best talent to the organization, and not because of an intrinsic belief in them (Gupta 2017; Rajadhyaksha 2012). Leave benefits provided by the government institutes are more than in private as, for example, the childcare leave for women up to 2 years (recently extended to single men with children) which is absent in private sector; similar is the case with leave travel concession (LTC) and sabbatical leave of one year for advanced study or research. Some organizations (public and private sector) have better work-life balance policies and infrastructure than others.

Work-life balance policies in practice seem to contribute to hegemonic masculinity at the workplace. As mentioned earlier, these policies are treated as privileges for women by the male employees and the pregnancy period is often seen as time off. Men rarely avail flexible timings existing in private sector; according to Rajan (male), principal scientist at a private lab, 'organization has flexi-time policy in which one can come late (at 11 a.m.) and go back early. I have availed it only once or twice (due to family requirement). It is basically for women. Women avail of it more' (Gupta 2017).

The study (Gupta 2017) found that those who use such flexi timings are viewed unfavourably and by implication, men are viewed as more regular and therefore more committed to work. Although work–life balance policies have their strengths, researchers have found that they fail to tackle the male model of working (Lewis, Gambles and Rapoport 2007) or the structures of patriarchy that necessitate such interventions (Rajadhyaksha 2012). The perception that such policies are for women reflects both the masculine notion of worker as a full-time committed worker and women's centrality in domestic sphere strengthening the idea of separation of spheres.

Pregnancy period results in career loss to a woman. In academia/ research, the period lost to a woman in pregnancy lowers her research publications and reduces chances of promotions along with her batch of recruits (Ananth 2014). In the private organizations, at the time of promotions, the period of pregnancy leave is not counted as part of 'experience' and is compared to a man who has worked for the entire 12 months. The pregnancy leave period deprives women of career growth in an important phase of their life when they are still at the junior level (Gupta 2017).

Company/organization considers the pregnancy period as a loss to itself. This was recently witnessed in the consequences of a recent policy. A recent amendment to the Maternity Benefit Act of 1961, passed in 2017, has brought maternity leave of public and private sector at par (to 26 weeks). However, many companies, both in the government and private sector, were reluctant to hire pregnant women due to this extension of maternity leave and some were even firing women employees. Hence, government had to intervene and announce that it will give employers the salaries for 7 of the 26 weeks of maternity leave for women earning more than ₹15,000 a month.[3] As per an amendment to maternity leave rules in 2017, employers with 50 employees have to provide crèche facilities.[4] While such facilities have yet to come up at all such places, their quality remains unregulated; the lack of day care centres for grown-up children and eldercare facilities remain poor.

Can women manage dual burden and do well professionally? What is the relationship between the marital status and research productivity? Xie and Shauman (1998) found both men and women married scientists to have significantly higher (by 7%–11%) rates of productivity than unmarried scientists. Research from various parts of the world indicates contradictory evidences on relationship between motherhood and scientific productivity. Some research shows that motherhood could have positive effect on productivity (Fox and Faver 1985). Still others have found that married women with children have lower research productivity (Hargens, McCann and Reskin 1978). According to Stack (2004), only women academics with young children publish less than other women with children; academia's flexitime facilitates balancing childcare and academic work.

In India, such research regarding impact of marriage and motherhood on women's research productivity is negligible. In most of the elite academic institutes and the government research labs, there is considerable freedom to the scientists to decide their work schedule. Hence, the issue is not of flexi hours but of time management for women in such organizations. For those who now have grown-up children, there are different sets of problems compared to those with younger children, as a woman scientist in a CSIR lab remarked, 'Flexi-hrs is there. But it is horrible in the first 2–3 years when kids are small. Even now if an elderly at home is not well, you have to take care' (Gupta 2013). Women in institutes lacking in campus residence for scientists have greater time management issues due to commuting. Also, in such cases, the presence of crèche alone is insufficient as a day care centre is required for school-going children.

Responsibilities of childcare and eldercare are often the primary reason for the breaks in career (Kurup et al. 2010). Such breaks tend to lower women's position in science as they are left behind in research and in organizational hierarchy. Family roles have an impact on opportunities for women in terms of fellowships abroad, position as visiting scientist and travelling for conferences and workshops (Gupta and Sharma 2002). As pointed out in Chapter 3, women scientists show highest level of research activity in their 50s. In general, a greater networking, collaborations and availability of resources might account for a late boost in publications for women; and the age of post-50 also coincides with greater freedom from a dual burden.

In the absence of infrastructural facilities, women receive assistance from non-institutional sources (spouse, in-laws, parents, paid help) for childcare as per IAS-NIAS report (Kurup et al. 2010). Such sources of assistance, such as parents-in-law, have their own complications arising from gendered expectations (Gupta and Sharma 2002). The support of spouse in professional matters and his help in domestic roles has been critical for a majority of women scientists in this study, which illustrates how individual families might be changing. However, working status continues to have a differential impact on men and women. Research on work–family conflict (Rajadhyaksha and Velgach 2015) of working women found that although working status tends to create more egalitarian gender role ideology (GRI; refers to an individual's attitudes and beliefs about the proper roles of men and women), *working women seem to lean towards a more egalitarian GRI relative to working men*. Higher family interference in work roles and higher mean levels of childcare hours, eldercare hours and house work hours for women suggested that men may be taking on family roles at a slower rate than women maybe embracing a work identity. Thus, as the authors argue, this creates rationale for *greater institutional rather than family-based support* for family demands such as childcare centres, eldercare centres, assisted living and hospice care.

Careers in scientific research seem unfriendly to women through another statistic. There is a higher proportion of 'single' women than men in science. In a survey among women in research, those who never married constituted about 14 per cent; among the men in research, only 2.5 per cent were unmarried (Kurup et al. 2010). Although this proportion is smaller compared to National Science Foundation (NSF) statistics of 34 per cent women and 17 per cent men doctoral scientists and engineers as unmarried,[5] it is high in the Indian context with marriage regarded as a sacred duty. Single women scientists (including divorced/widowed/never married) do not necessarily demonstrate higher research activity than married women in terms of research publications and participation in conferences. Social isolation and higher difficulties in collaboration and interaction with men colleagues possibly lead to being a less prolific researcher than a married woman (Gupta and Sharma 2002). This is also found in research in other countries (Aiston and Jung 2015) and the authors suggest that family-related variables are overrated in their relationship to productivity.

A gendered work environment and multiple role management, efforts at time management and self-discipline extract their cost leading to exhaustion for women scientists, at least physically at the end of the day (Gupta and Sharma 2002). Women scientists have to work twice as hard as men due to workplace and institutional barriers (Gupta and Sharma 2002, 2003). In attempting to balance multiple roles, they compromise on opportunities and are unable to use their potential fully which lead women to scale down their expectations from their career.

It is essential to note here that publication productivity of women does not vary substantially from men in most fields (as discussed in Chapter 3). Research activity of married women is higher than of single women. Even if research productivity of women is less than men, as in the USA, for instance, it is more due to systemic factors. The focus on familial burdens of women takes away the focus from the systemic and organizational biases that impact women's position in science. Absence of work-life balance structures/policies are symptoms of the biases. A dual burden on women scientists becomes significant mainly due to these biases and systemic lacunae that discourage work-life balance. As Padavic, Ely and Reid (2019) remark that the work–family explanation has become a 'hegemonic narrative' or a pervasive, status quo preserving story that prevails despite countervailing evidence.

Leadership Positions

While there are various challenges to women in junior positions as discussed earlier, those women, who do manage to counter barriers and move ahead in research and the organizational hierarchy encounter further obstacles in leadership positions.

The leadership is associated in South Asian countries such as India with particular types of masculinity, competitive, ruthless and politically networked (Morley and Crossouard 2015). Socialized to believe that women are obedient and docile, some men and women scientists in a study (Gupta 2017) felt that women were less capable in managing or were softer in making decisions compared to men. There are stereotypes 'because of which they (men colleagues) would like to keep women away from administrative responsibilities. They would say, "that poor thing; she would have no idea how crooked people could be" and start patronizing' (Gupta 2016). Leadership is not only masculine but is also visualized as a 'male' domain. There are constraints in giving higher positions to women 'in minds of people, if she is a mother, she can't handle' (Gupta 2013). There is a lack of respect for the leadership abilities of women, and male colleagues find it difficult to work under a female boss (Gupta 2016).

There are also women scientists who themselves do not wish for an administrative position or committee headships. While most of them will not lobby for such positions, they will not refuse if offered (Gupta 2016). In a study of four academic institutes (Gupta 2003), two women were offered a deanship and they refused because of their perception that their research would suffer due to the time taken up by administrative duties. But there are also two cases of senior women academics who were eligible and willing to accept the position but were not offered the post. In general, the reasons given by the women scientists for a lack of women deans were there being very few women faculty at the senior level; gendered notions such as a respondent was told that women could not work at night; or that 'men do not like to be bossed around by a woman' or that the 'institute will not prefer women deans'; such positions require politicking and *chamchagiri* (ingratiation), which women academics tend to avoid. The other reasons stated included a lack of ambition on the part of women, family constraints and lack of time—reasons which are also a reflection of successful internalization of gendered norms by women (Gupta 2003).

Women bosses have to grapple with the stereotyped assumptions of those junior to them. In a study on private labs, a woman scientist at the second-most senior level in her R&D division (Private2) recounted how a new male entrée, a junior scientist, had apprehensions that being a woman boss, she would devote less office hours and so would give away all the work to others so that they (the juniors) would be overburdened (Gupta 2017). She remarked that the earlier group she headed consisted mainly of women but she never heard of this there.

Some women scientists that move up in leadership positions might adopt 'masculine' behaviour such as being aggressive. This might be because of their desire to be seen as fair or as capable as men. Female leaders often face the paradox of whether to emulate a masculine leadership style or a stereotypically warm and nurturing feminine style. In the first case, their male subordinates will dislike them and in the second, they will be liked, but not respected (Kawakami et al. 2000). A male scientist in a CSIR lab remarked that women in higher administrative positions are harsh to junior women scientists (Gupta 2013). A woman scientist in a senior position in a private lab had noticed that when women came to power, some of them adopted very aggressive behaviours 'probably because they had struggled so much in the process of rising, which is tough in corporate, they have build up their defences; becoming offensive is a part of that defence' (Gupta 2017). Through aggressive behaviours, women fulfil masculine script in leadership work and end up 'doing gender' (Kelan 2010).

Denying Gender Inequality and Blaming Women

Research on gender and organizations show that despite gender inequalities, workers/employees tend to deny those due to the assumption of gender-neutrality of organizations (Acker 1990; Kelan 2009; Korvajärvi 2011). Additionally, the norm of 'universalism' in judging merit (Merton [1942]1973) in science tends to override practices which invisibilize gender inequalities to scientists (Etzkowitz 2007). Even the earliest women scientists in India, who encountered greater patriarchal rigidities than one would today, refused to accept that there is any gender issue in being a scientist. Thus, Sur (2009) found Anna Mani dismissive and derisive of any gender-related problems in her career as a scientist. According to the author, the notion of science as gender-neutral and influence of Indian nationalism that asserted Indian pride dissolving caste, class and gender differences perhaps accounted for such denial.

As indicated earlier, while women scientists acknowledge discrimination by some men colleagues, they usually separate their gendered experiences from the system which is believed to be gender-neutral. Gendered experiences usually arise outside the formal system of rules and regulations which are not discriminatory. The biases in informal practices that surround the application of formal rules are not considered systemic issues.

Further, many women and men either tend to blame women for their lower status (e.g., women's choice to devote more time to family) or see it as a product of 'social' issues arising out of women's domestic role. For instance, statements by scientists in a study (Gupta 2013) included: 'gender equality means when both men and women use their full potential; ... no, it (gender equality) does not exist (in this institute) because *women* are not stretching their full potential ... they do not give their 100 per cent (due to family roles). It's their decision and you can't blame others'; 'Lot of time *women* scientists go into backseat; it is their choice not organizations'; sometimes they prefer home more than career'.

In the exercise of women's 'choice', national culture plays a major role (Hakim 2000). Also, the very existence of such cultural beliefs at the workplace creates conditions of gender inequality. Further, the 'choice' is constrained not only by cultural norms prevailing in society and the institutions but also by a lack of structural and systemic support at the workplace.

In the West, denial of gender inequalities by employees is a product of a weariness of having dealt with gender, summed up as 'gender fatigue' by Kelan (2009) and that there is a lack of energy to tackle afresh something no longer perceived as a problem. In India, there is a lack of gender awareness, and the thinking about discrimination at workplace is still at a preliminary stage.

DISCUSSION AND CONCLUSIONS

To conclude, various norms and practices construct privileges and power for men in science organizations. These norms and practices affect women scientists' careers in several ways, For instance, as illustrated in this chapter, they affect internal networking for countering hierarchy and finding mentors which in turn affects visibility and promotions. Organizational preferences of early achievement for recruitment, politics on who takes which research scholar in some institutes/labs and male students' preference for male advisors, red tapism and a combination of gender and hierarchical culture among the male administrative staff, gendered assumptions in women's leadership abilities and in recruitment are some of the examples of practices and norms that create barriers for women scientists in rising in organizational hierarchy, obtaining recognition and in establishing a successful professional identity. Interpretation of incidents of discrimination is seen as unrelated to the formal system (equated with written rules) which keeps intact the 'rational' status of organizations.

The idea of women's primary domestic role gives rise to norms and practices that devalue women in public spaces leading to inequality for women in science. These include beliefs and practices reflecting the dual burden assumptions of male colleagues and biased treatment of pregnant employees. Work–life balance policies are inadequate (in alleviating dual burden on women) on the one hand, and buttress a masculine environment if availed by women because men are either not the targets of those policies or are not availed by men. The denial of gender inequality at the workplace precludes any discussion about gender within the organizations. Women's marginalization is best exemplified in perception of women as 'privileged'.

The chief dilemma of women scientists is how to position themselves as 'scientists' and not as 'women scientists' in context of the professed 'gender-neutral' workplace on the one hand and the gendered value system on the other. On the one hand, men's domination of science and science organizations construct gender in day-to-day practice of science. On the other hand, normative role expectations from women interfere with the acceptance of their professional status at the workplace. The middle-class notion of an ideal Indian woman conflicts with the idealization of a 'male model' in scientific research. Woman's devotion to family might be the expectation but it creates a perception of not being committed to research. A woman scientist's quality of research is often doubted (as in the statement that women's research is 'mediocre') and unlike in IT, the commitments of the academia/labs to D&I remains minimal. Some women are seen as compromising career for family. However, such compromises imply structural constraints and lack of social and institutional support.

The theory of critical mass assumes that increase in proportions of minority will positively impact their position within organizations. However, as this chapter shows, the problem is much more complex. Increase in critical mass is unlikely to change the gendered system, norms and practices. The professed dual burden on women is a narrative that distracts from the workplace inequality; the conflict between family and work roles is an issue of a masculine environment at the workplace and of practice of norms that devalue and thereby perpetuate women's lower position in science. Gender in scientific institutions needs to be tackled to create a level playing field for women. This forms the subject of Chapter 5.

NOTES

1. Narrated by Subha Tole on 12 December in the Indian Society for Developmental Biologists (InSDB) Session Meeting at IIT Kanpur (11–15 December). Available at http://www.devbioindia.org/docs/InSDB2018_Program_30112018.pdf (accessed on 8 August 2019).
2. Private sector is contributing about 38 per cent of gross expenditure on R&D in 2014–2015 and dominates drugs and pharma, and transportation (Ministry of Science and Technology 2017). The scientists in this study (Gupta 2017) are employed full time and the nature of their work disallows certain policies like work from home. Nevertheless, these organizations consciously promote worker-friendly culture through, for instance, family holidays, plush office space, high-quality lunch provision and freely available tea and coffee throughout the day.
3. Available at https://www.thehindubusinessline.com/economy/policy/govt-to-refund-employers-for-seven-weeks-of-maternity-leave-given-to-employees-wcd/article25506910.ece (accessed on 8 August 2019).
4. Available at https://labour.gov.in/sites/default/files/Maternity%20Benefit%20Amendment%20Act%2C2017%20.pdf (accessed on 8 August 2019).
5. Available at https://wayback.archive-it.org/5902/20150629194053/http://www.nsf.gov/statistics/nsf96311/5sidebr2.htm (accessed on 8 August 2019).

REFERENCES

Acker, Joan. 1990. 'Hierarchies, Jobs, Bodies: A Theory of Gendered Organizations'. *Gender & Society* 4 (2): 139–158.

———. 2006. 'Inequality Regimes: Gender, Class and Race in Organizations'. *Gender & Society* 20 (4): 441–464.

Aiston, Sarah Jane, and Jisun Jung. 2015. 'Women Academics and Research Productivity'. *An International Comparison, Gender and Education* 27 (3): 205–220.doi:10.1080/09540253.2015.1024617

Ananth, Sudarshan. 2014. 'Women Leaders in Indian science'. *Current Science* 107 (9): 1366. Available at https://www.currentscience.ac.in/Volumes/107/09/1366.pdf (accessed on 8 August 2019).

Belle, Deborah, Laurel Smith-Doerr, and Lauren M. O'Brien. 2014. 'Gendered Networks: Professional Connections of Science and Engineering Faculty'. In *Gender Transformation in the Academy (Advances in Gender Research, Volume 19)*, edited by V. Demos, C. W. Berheide, and M. T. Segal, 153–175. Bingley: Emerald Group Publishing Limited.

Belliappa, J. 2013. *Gender, Class and Reflexive Modernity in India*. Basingstoke: Palgrave Macmillan.

Bobbitt-Zeher, D. 2011. 'Gender Discrimination at Work'. *Gender & Society* 25 (6): 764–786.

Brumley, K. M. 2014. 'Now, We Have the Same Rights as Men to Keep Our Jobs': Gendered Perceptions of Opportunity and Obstacles in a Mexican Workplace'. *Gender, Work & Organization* 21 (3): 217–230.

Cabrera, S. F., and M. C. Thomas-Hunt. 2007. '"Street Cred" and the Executive Woman: The Effects of Gender Differences in Social Networks on Career Advancement'. Electronic version. Available at http://scholarship.sha.cornell.edu/articles/371 (accessed on 8 August 2019).

Campion, P., and W. Shrum. 2004. 'Gender and Science in Development: Women Scientists in Ghana, Kenya and India. Science'. *Technology and Human Values* 29 (4): 459–485.

Collins, Lynn H., Joan C. Chrisler, and Kathryn Quina, eds. 1998. *Career Strategies for Women in Academe: Arming Athena*. New Delhi: SAGE Publications.

Collinson D., and J. Hearn. 1996. 'Breaking the Silence: On Men, Masculinities and Managements'. In *Men as Managers, Managers as Men*, edited by D. L. Collinson and J. Hearn, 1–24. London: SAGE Publications.

Connell, R. W. 2000. *The Men and the Boys*. Berkeley, CA: University of California Press.

Didion, C. 2009. 'Women in Engineering—Gender Differences Report: An Overview'. The National Academies, Women in Science and Engineering Workshop Jefferson Lab, Newport News, VA, USA.

Dresselhaus, Mildred. 1986. 'Women Graduate Students'. *Physics Today* 39 (6): 74. Available at https://physicstoday.scitation.org/doi/10.1063/1.2815038 (accessed on 8 August 2019).

Eagly, Alice H., and Steven J. Karau. 2002. 'Role Congruity Theory of Prejudice towards Female Leaders'. *Psychological Review* 109 (3): 573–598.

Etzkowitz, H. 2007. 'The Athena Paradox: Bridging the Gender Gap in Science'. *Journal of Technology Management and Innovation* 2 (1): 1–3.

Etzkowitz, H., C. Kemelgor, and B. Uzzi. 2000. *Athena Unbound: The Advancement of Women in Science and Technology*. Cambridge: Cambridge University Press.

Fox, M. F., and C. Faver. 1985. 'Men, Women, and Publication Productivity among Social Work Academics'. *Sociological Q* 26 (4): 537–549.

Gangopadhyay, R., and B. Das. 2016, 25 October. 'DST WOS-A: The Scenario from Recipient's Perspective'. *Current Science* 111 (8). Available at https://www.currentscience.ac.in/Volumes/111/08/1307.pdf (accessed on 8 August 2019).

Grover, Shalini, Ellina Samantroy, and Nupur Dhingra Paiva. 2015. '"New India's" Inflexible Workforce—Caring is But Women's Works'. *Guest Post*. Available at https://kafila.org/2015/05/31/new-indias-inflexible-workforce-caring-is-but-womenswork-shalini-grover-ellina-samantroy-nupur-dhingra-paiva/ (accessed on 8 August 2019).

Gupta, B. M., Suresh Kumar, and B. S. Aggarwal. 1999. 'A Comparison of Productivity of Male and Female Scientists of CSIR'. *Scientometrics* 45 (2): 269–289. Available at http://link.springer.com/article/10.1007%2FBF02458437?LI=true#page-20 (accessed on 8 August 2019).

Gupta, Namrata. 2007. 'Indian Women in Doctoral Education in Science and Engineering: A Study of Informal Milieu at the Reputed Indian Institutes of Technology'. *Science Technology and Human Values* 32 (5): 507–533.

Gupta, Namrata. 2010. 'Doctoral Research Environment in an Indian Institute of Higher Learning in *Science and Technology*'. *Science, Technology and Society* 15 (1): 113–133.

———. 2013. 'Women in Scientific Research in Government and Industrial Laboratories: A Comparative Study of Work Environment and Socio-Cultural Milieu'. Report submitted to Indian Council of Social Science Research, vide Fellowship no. 2–11/10/S.Fel.

———. 2016. 'Perceptions of the Work Environment: The Issue of Gender in Indian Scientific Research Institutes'. *Indian Journal of Gender Studies* 23 (3): 437–466.

———. 2017. 'Gender Inequality in the Work Environment: A Study of Private Research Organizations in India'. *Equality, Diversity and Inclusion: An International Journal* 36 (3): 255–276.doi:10.1108/EDI-04-2016-0029

Gupta, Namrata, and Arun K. Sharma. 2002. 'Women Academic Scientists in India'. *Social Studies of Science* 32 (6): 901–915.

———. 2003. 'Gender Inequality in the Work Environment at Institutes of Higher Learning in Science and Technology in India'. *Work, Employment and Society* 17 (4): 597–616.

Hargens, L., J. C. McCann, and B. F. Reskin. 1978. 'Productivity and Reproductivity: Fertility and Professional Achievement among Research Scientists'. *Social Forces* 57: 154–163.

Hasan, S. A., Mahender Kumar Sharma, Sushila Khilnani, and R. Luthra. 2012. 'Research Productivity of Female Research Scholars and Their Migration Pattern in Pursuit of Higher Education and Research'. *Current Science* 103 (6): 611.

Heilman, M. E. 2012. 'Gender Stereotypes and Workplace Bias'. *Research in Organizational Behavior* 32: 113–135. Available at https://doi.org/10.1016/j.riob.2012.11.003 (accessed on 8 August 2019).

Heuer, Mark. 2006. 'The Influence of Indian National Culture on Organizations'. In *Management in India. Trends and Transition*, edited by Herbert J. Davis, Samir R. Chatterjee and Mark Heuer, Chapter 2. New Delhi: Response Books.

Holt, H., and S. Lewis. 2009. '"You Can Stand on Your Head and Still End Up with Lower Pay." Gliding Segregation and Gendered Work Practices in Danish "Family-Friendly" Workplaces'. *Gender, Work and Organization* 18: e202–e211.

Jayaraj, N. 2017, 11 February. 'Women Scientists in India: What We Learnt from a Year of Lab-Hopping across the Country'. *Firstpost*. Available at https://www.firstpost.com/living/women-scientists-in-india-what-we-learnt-from-a-year-of-lab-hopping-across-the-country-3274516.html (accessed on 8 August 2019).

Joseph, M., and A. Robinson. 2014. 'Policy: Free Indian Science'. *Nature* 508 (7494): 36–38. Available at https://www.nature.com/news/policy-free-indian-science-1.14956#/b2 (accessed on 8 August 2019).

Kanter, R. 1977. *Men and Women of the Corporation*. New York, NY: Basic Books.

Kawakami, C., J. B. White, and E. J. Langer. 2000. 'Mindful and Masculine: Freeing Women Leaders from the Constraints of Gender Roles'. *Journal of Social Issues* 56: 49–63. doi:10.1111/0022-4537.00151

Kelan, E. K. 2009. 'Gender Fatigue—The Ideological Dilemma of Gender Neutrality and Discrimination in Organizations'. *Canadian Journal of Administrative Sciences* 26 (3): 197–210.

———. 2010. 'Gender Logic and (Un)Doing Gender at Work'. *Gender, Work and Organization* 17 (2): 174–194.

Kondaiah, Bittu Karthik, Shalini Mahadev, and Maranatha Grace Tham Wahlang. 2017, 29 April. 'The Production of Science Bearing Gender, Caste and More'. *Economic & Political Weekly* 52 (17): 73–79. Available at https://www.epw. in/journal/2017/17?0=ip_login_no_cache%3D56c057e6d3286446ca90590 c3ac04118 (accessed on 8 August 2019).

Korvajärvi, P. 2011. 'Practicing Gender Neutrality in Organizations'. In *Handbook of Gender, Work and Organization*, edited by E. Jeanes, D. Knights and Y. M. Patricia, 230–243. Hoboken, NJ: Wiley-Blackwell.

Krishna, V. V. 2001. 'Reflections on the Changing Status of Academic Science in India'. *International Social Science Journal* 53 (168): 231–246.

Kumar, N. 2009. Gendered Equation in Science: An Organizational Aberration? In *Women and Science in India*, edited by Neelam Kumar, 13–30. New Delhi: Oxford University Press.

Kurup, Anitha, R. Maithreyi, B. Kantharaju, and Rohini Godbole. 2010. *Trained Scientific Women Power: How Much Are We Losing and Why?* IAS–NIAS Research Report. Available at http://eprints.nias.res.in/142/1/IAS-NIAS-Report.pdf (accessed on 8 August 2019).

Levinson, D. 1978. *The Seasons of a Man's Life.* New York, NY: Knopf.

Lewis, P., and L. Simpson. 2012. 'Kanter Revisited: Gender, Power and (In) Visibility'. *International Journal of Management Reviews* 14 (2): 141–158. Available at https://onlinelibrary.wiley.com/doi/full/10.1111/j.1468-2370.2011.00327.x (accessed on 8 August 2019).

Lewis, Suzan, and Anne Laure Humbert. 2010. '"Discourse or Reality?: "Work-Life Balance," Flexible Working Policies and the Gendered Organization, Equality, Diversity and Inclusion'. *An International Journal* 29 (3): 239–254. Available at https://doi.org/10.1108/02610151011102884023 (accessed on 8 August 2019).

Lewis, Suzan, Richenda Gambles, and Rhona Rapoport. 2007. 'The Constraints of a "Work-Life Balance" Approach: An International Perspective'. *The International Journal of Human Resource Management* 18 (3): 360–373. doi:10.1080/09585190601165577

Long, Scott J., and Mary F. Fox. 1995. 'Scientific Careers: Universalism and Particularism'. *Annual Review of Sociology* 21: 45–71.doi:10.1146/annurev. so.21.080195.000401.

Martin, Joanne. 1990. 'Deconstructing Organizational Taboos: The Suppression of Gender Conflict in Organizations'. *Organization Science* 1 (4): 339–359.

Masoodi, A. 2016, 19 April. 'Where are India's Female Scientists?' *Livemint.* Available at https://www.livemint.com/Politics/N0j16kL2ZAzk94ssOKoTdK/ Where-are-Indias-female-scientists.html (accessed on 8 August 2019).

McPherson, J. M., L. Smith-Lovin, and J. M. Cook. 2001. 'Birds of a Feather: Homophily in Social Networks'. *Annual Review of Sociology* 27: 415–444.

Merton, R. K. [1942]1973. 'The Normative Structure of Science'. In *The Sociology of Science*, edited by R. K. Merton, 267–278. Chicago, IL: University of Chicago Press.

Ministry of Human Resource Development. 2018. *AISHE Final Report 2017–2018*. New Delhi: Department of Higher Education, Government of India. Available at http://aishe.nic.in/aishe/reports (accessed on 8 August 2019).

Ministry of Science and Technology. 2017, December. *Research & Development Statistics at a Glance 2017–18*. New Delhi: Department of Science & Technology, Government of India. Available at http://www.nstmis-dst.org/statistics-Glance-2017-18-2.pdf (accessed on 8 August 2019).

Morley, L., and B. Crossouard. 2015. 'Women in Higher Education Leadership in South Asia: Rejection, Refusal, Reluctance, Revisioning'. Executive Summary. Centre for Higher Education and Research, University of Sussex. British Council. Available at https://www.britishcouncil.org/sites/default/files/women_in_higher_education_leadership_in_sa_-_executive_summary.pdf (accessed on 8 August 2019).

Mukhopadhyay, C. C., and S. Seymour. 1994. 'Introduction and Theoretical Overview'. In *Women, Education and Family Structure in India*, edited by C. C. Mukhopadhyay and S. Seymour. 1–33. Boulder, CO: Westview Press.

Nature. 2015, 14 May. 'A Nation with Ambition'. *Nature* 521: 125. Available at https://www.nature.com/news/a-nation-with-ambition-1.17520 (accessed on 8 August 2019).

OGD. 2012–2015. 'Scheme-Wise Extramural Research and Development Projects Approved Open Govt. Data'. Government of India. Available at https://data.gov.in/catalog/scheme-wise-extramural-research-and-development-projects-approved (accessed on 8 August 2019).

Padavic, I., R. Ely, and E. Reid. 2019. 'Explaining the Persistence of Gender Inequality: The Work–Family Narrative as a Social Defense against the 24/7 Work Culture'. *Administrative Science Quarterly*: 1–51. Available at https://doi.org/10.1177/0001839219832310 (accessed on 8 August 2019).

Palackal, A., M. Anderson, and B. Paige Miller. 2007. 'Internet Equaliser? Gender Stratification and Normative Circumvention in Science'. *Indian Journal of Gender Studies* 14 (2): 231–257.

Pandey, Kartikay. 2007. 'Nose-Diving Scientific Temper: A Clarion Call for Science Enthusiasts'. *Current Science* 92 (1): 7.

Patel, R., and M. J. C. Parmentier. 2005. 'The Persistence of Traditional Gender Roles in the Information Technology Sector: A Study of Female Engineers in India'. *Information Technologies and International Development* 2 (3): 29–46.

Radhakrishnan, Smitha. 2011. *Appropriately Indian: Gender and Culture in a New Transnational Class*. New Delhi: Orient Blackswan.

Rajadhyaksha, Ujvala. 2012. 'Work-Life Balance in South East Asia: The Indian Experience'. *South Asian Journal of Global Business Research* 1 (1): 108–127. Available at http://dx.doi.org/10.1108/20454451211207615 (accessed on 8 August 2019).

Rajadhyaksha, U., and S. Velgach. 2015. 'What Is a Better Predictor of Work–Family Conflict in India?—Gender or Gender Role Ideology'. In *Work and Personal Life Interface in the International Career Context*, edited by Liisa Makela and Vesaa Sutari, 71–93. Berlin: Springer.

Ramadoss, K., and U. Rajadhyaksha. 2012. 'Gender Differences in Commitment to Roles, Work–Family Conflict and Spousal Support'. *Journal of Social Sciences* 33 (2): 227–233.

Reskin, Barbara F. 1978. 'Sex Differentiation and the Social Organization of Science'. In *The Sociology of Science*, edited by Jerry Gaston, 6–37. San Francisco, CA: Jossey-Bass.

Ridgeway, C. L. 2009. 'Framed Before We Know It: How Gender Shapes Social Relations'. *Gender & Society* 23 (2): 145–160.

Ridgeway, C. L., and S. J. Correll. 2004. 'Unpacking the Gender System: A Theoretical Perspective on Gender Beliefs and Social Relations'. *Gender & Society* 18 (4): 510–531.

Roth, W. D., and G. Sonnert. 2011. 'The Costs and Benefits of "Red Tape": Antibureaucratic Structure and Gender Inequity in a Science Research Organization'. *Social Studies of Science* 41 (3): 385–409.

Sinha, J. B. P., and R. N. Kanungo. 1997. 'Context Sensitivity and Balancing in Indian Organizational Behaviour'. *International Journal of Psychology* 32 (2): 93–105.

Srivastava, Sanjay. 2018. 'Masculinity Studies and Feminism: Othering the Self, Engaging Theory'. In *Men and Feminism in India* (South Asia edition), edited by Romit Chowdhury and Zaid Al Baset, 35–49. Abingdon: Routledge.

Stack, S. 2004. 'Gender, Children and Research Productivity'. *Research in Higher Education* 45 (8): 891–920. Available at https://doi.org/10.1007/s11162-004-5953-z (accessed on 8 August 2019).

Subrahmanyan, Lalita. 2009. 'Women in Science in India. Has Feminism Passed Them By?' In *Women and Science in India*, edited by Neelam Kumar, 178–205. New Delhi: Oxford University Press.

Sur, Abha. 2009. 'Dispersed Radiance. Women Scientists in C. V. Raman's Laboratory'. In *Women and Science in India*, edited by Neelam Kumar, 98–136. New Delhi: Oxford University Press.

Thapan, Meenakshi. 2007. 'Adolescence, Embodiment and Gender Identity: Elite Women in a Changing Society'. In *Urban Women in Contemporary India: A Reader*, edited by Rehana Ghadially, 31–45. New Delhi: SAGE Publications.

Thite, T. 2017. Women in Indian Science—A Young PhD's Perspective. Available at https://thelifeofscience.com/2017/09/11/women-indian-science-young-phds-perspective/ (accessed on 8 August 2019).

Wennerås, C., and A. Wold. 1997. 'Nepotism and Sexism in Peer-Review'. *Nature* 387 (6631): 341–343.

Williams, C. L. 1992. 'The Glass Escalator: Hidden Advantages for Men in the "Female" Professions'. *Social Problems* 39: 253–267.

Xie, Y., and K. A. Shauman. 1998. 'Sex Differences in Research Productivity: New Evidence about an Old Puzzle'. *American Sociological Review* 63 (6): 847–870.

Undoing Gender-Based Inequality

> ... *progress towards gender equality will be slowed to the extent that efforts are focused exclusively on women ... that to be effective, expanding efforts to include men requires a broad vision.*
>
> — Padavic, Ely and Reid (2019: 43)

This chapter analyses the nature of the existing discourse, initiatives and policies encouraging women in S&T from higher education onwards. It focuses on the need for thinking at various levels: state, organizational and individual. It discusses the importance of men's participation in bringing change. Given the complexity of the issue, it is not possible either to cover all the problems or to suggest changes dealing with all the facets of the problems. Nevertheless, the present understanding of the issue makes it possible to present a perspective on the policies and suggest the required changes therein. It indicates the possible changes that could help in moving towards gender equality. The chapter points out the need for future research to capture various aspects of the problems faced by women in science.

WOMEN IN S&T EDUCATION: AFFIRMATIVE ACTION

As the previous chapters show, women's representation in science and engineering education does not lag behind the developed countries. On the contrary, a recent study (Stoet and Geary 2018) shows that gender gap in pursuit of STEM degrees rises with an increase in national gender equality. Finland, which excels in gender equality, has one of the world's largest gender gaps in college degrees in STEM fields, and Norway and Sweden, also leading in gender-equality rankings, are not any different (fewer than 25% of STEM graduates are women). Authors conclude that the liberal mores in these cultures, combined with smaller financial costs of foregoing a STEM path in developed countries discourage women to opt for careers in STEM. In less gender-equal countries, life quality pressures promote girls' and women's engagement with STEM subjects; a well-paying STEM career may appear to be an investment in a more secure future in less gender-equal countries.

The findings of Stoet and Geary (2018) applies to India to some extent. As seen in Chapters 1 and 2, women's engagement with S&T education is partly related to financial security. The other reason is patriarchal emphasis on women's marriage. High value attached among the urban middle classes to educated, earning brides and a better availability of 'suitable', high status, secure and higher paying jobs in the sector compared to others has prompted a growth of S&T education among women in India.

Further, women continue to be severely under-represented in the elite institutes of S&T such as the IITs at the UG level. Due to decline in the number of women admitted in the IITs and a gender imbalance, a committee headed by the Director of IIT Mandi, Professor Gonsalves, was set up in 2016 by the Joint Admission Board (JAB) of the IITs to make recommendations for increasing female enrolment in the IITs. This report confirmed the role of biases that limit access to coaching; that choices for women during counselling are based on gendered view of branches and proximity to home (JAB Sub-Committee 2017). The committee found that 1,400 women within the range of ranks finding admission did not join IITs and another 2,400 women qualified JEE (Advanced) but with lower ranks. One of the recommendations of this committee was supernumerary seats for women in its report in 2017. The central government decided to raise the number of women initially to 14 per cent from 2018 and ultimately to 20 per cent by 2020 in these institutes, with the intention to phase out the supernumerary seats by 2026. Since only those who qualify JEE (Mains) and then JEE (Advanced) will make it to the new merit list, merit is not being compromised in any major way. The cut-off for JEE (Advanced) will be irrespective of gender.

The system is fundamentally different from the quota system.[1] It creates two pools for any programme (e.g., EE at IIT Kanpur): gender-neutral pool and female-only pool; women will first compete in the female-only pool and then in the gender-neutral pool. Supernumerary seats for women are expected to decrease every year reaching zero in the next 5–8 years as the percentage of women reaches 20 per cent. The report says that the scheme is a flop if the women in gender-neutral pool do not increase over the next three years and should be discontinued. Among the long-term measures, the report recommends efforts to tap potential of girls from class 8 and counselling for parents, teachers and girls for encouraging girls to aim for top institutes.

However, by its very nature, raising number of seats for women creates quota in favour of women. While it will not affect the number of seats for men, as it is a supernumerary quota, the fact of some lower ranked women entering the IITs' UG programme compared to men remains applicable. Further, these provisions while differing from quota might well digress into quota. The caste quota for 'Scheduled Castes and Tribes' in the post-independence period was intended for only 10 years; however, reservations have continued to grow in terms of the number of castes included and the proportion of seats reserved. For instance, in another decision recently, government has introduced 10 per cent quota in education and jobs for the economically weaker upper castes. The politics of vote banks makes scrapping of reservations too hazardous for any government to risk.

Further, who is likely to benefit from the supernumerary seats for women? As mentioned in Chapter 1, the women who get through JEE are mostly from urban middle class and upper castes. Patriarchal structure impacts negatively the admission to expensive JEE coaching centres for women, and women in these centres are under-represented (Chapter 1). However, as a professor from IIT writes, all seats may not go to those women whose parents refused to send them to coaching (Sanghi 2017). Also, entry through supernumerary seats might dilute the assumption that women who enter are as meritorious as men, which in turn will affect the status of women in those institutes. Affirmative action has been criticized as 'a double-edged sword' that increases the numbers of women and minorities modestly but also denigrates them (Etzkowitz, Kemelgor and Uzzi 2000: 227); that it fails to address intersecting categories such as of class and urban–rural dimensions as in an African study where it led to an increase in number of women from a group that would have anyway gone to university (Onsongo 2009).

Nevertheless, the efforts being made to increase the proportion of girls are helpful from the point of view of utilizing human resources (bright women who clear JEE [Advanced]) and of gender equity. As seen in Chapter 2, a lack of critical mass fosters and reproduces masculinity in the IITs and the bastions of rationality appear to be infested with gendered practices. An increase in number of women in the IITs will help in creating a healthier environment.

The larger question is how to reduce the significance of coaching and thereby create a level playing field for all those appearing for the JEE, irrespective of caste, gender or economic status. To maintain the quality of students entering IITs, the IITs themselves conduct JEE (Advanced). However, in the present system, although the syllabus of JEE covers the syllabus of class XI and XII, the nature of questions in JEE requires superior knowledge due to tougher questions and extreme paucity of time to finish the question paper. Most questions combine various concepts of sciences and answering requires extreme preparedness, hence the need for coaching. The report of JAB itself admits the role of coaching in preparedness for JEE. Chapter 1 also shows that those who take coaching have a higher success rate in cracking the JEE than those who do not.

There has been much thinking within the IITs on the issue of reducing the need for coaching and the modifications to the JEE pattern continue to be made to achieve this objective. The Ministry of Human Resource Development has come up with an IIT preparation app and solved question papers of the last 50 years free of cost; it plans measures to reduce difficulty level of JEE by focussing on class XII syllabus; to release audio–video lectures among others.[2] At present, it is the faculty from sciences (PCM) in the IITs that usually set the questions for JEE (Advanced). Some faculty members from engineering could also be involved so as to avoid inclusion of highly complex questions from science and maths, and to include those relevant to both sciences and engineering. Also, there is an urgent need to check for the length and complexity level of the paper. The society highly covets seats in the IITs primarily due to a paucity of good quality institutes. Hence, to reduce competition for these seats, it is imperative, in the long run, to raise the quality of university education. Growth of quality jobs in diverse sectors will help to reduce pressure to study engineering.

WOMEN SCIENTISTS: DISCOURSE ON GENDER INEQUALITY

Enrolment of enough women in S&T is insufficient for ensuring sufficient women in careers. Increase in numbers of women at workplace does not imply gender equality at workplace as women continue to lag in representation in government sector academia and research institutes and are even fewer in higher positions.

One solution suggested worldwide for increase of representation is affirmative action. Affirmative action programmes have been followed in Sweden in case of students and professorships; in EU Horizon programmes for research funding, etc. In India, quota or reservation system as a solution to under-representation has been rejected by the women scientists unequivocally. Reviewing *Current Science* articles (*Current Science* being a leading scientific journal in India) on quotas for women scientists, Malhotra (2018) found in the 1990s itself that 'The quota system is seen as not being in the interest of women as it could be perceived as "patronizing" and could also lead to a "feeling of disgust" amongst women and "resentment" amongst men' (1,717). Moreover, problems persist not just at the entry level but at all stages of career. Fixing the percentage of women for various selection/promotion committees at policy and planning stages have been suggested due to the argument that women and men perceive women's problems differently (Kurup and Maithreyi 2011; Sinha and Sinha

2011). Research studies on quota in evaluation committees show that the success of such measures is mixed. The assumption behind such quota is that men tend to select men. While there are evidences of such gender homophily in selection of candidates for academic positions, some studies report the opposite (Checchi, Cicognani and Kulic 2015). Gender quotas have been introduced in selection boards of European countries such as Norway, Sweden, Finland and Spain where compulsory share for both genders is 40 per cent; this has resulted in limited success. Gender quota in evaluation committees is not sufficient to raise representation of women, nevertheless presence of women makes committee members more aware of gender issues (Wallon, Bendiscioli and Garfinkel 2015).

The thinking on gender in scientific research careers has picked up in the recent years, particularly after the NIAS report on women in science in 2004 which highlighted the low proportions of women scientists in elite institutes and fewer reward recipients among women. A study of articles in *Current Science* (Malhotra 2018) affirms the attention accorded to this issue as the number of articles on the subject rose to 16 in the period 2000–2009 from 5 in the previous decade. The women scientists themselves have taken the lead in visiblizing the marginalization of women in science through participation in panels (Inter-Academy Panel of Indian Academy of Science–INSA–NASI), workshops and creating exclusive website and Internet resources.[3] The global forums of women scientists (e.g., TWAS, AWIS) and subject-specific conferences and groups such as International Conference on Women in Physics, have provided platforms for women in science in India to voice their issues and understand country-specific and global parameters of their problems. In the last 15 years, the understanding of various problems faced by women scientists has grown due to the availability of data through survey-based reports sponsored by government and various science academies (e.g., INSA 2004; Kurup et al. 2010; Ministry of Science and Technology 2010; Niti Ayog 2017). Further, narratives of women scientists brought together by the social scientists (e.g., EPW 2017) and the women scientists (e.g., Godbole and Ramaswamy 2008), the media showcasing interviews with women scientists (https://thelifeofscience. com/) since 2016 and research-based studies of the social scientists have sharpened the understanding on the issue.[4]

The significance of the role of women scientists in Indian science and innovation is being increasingly recognized as evident from the 2013 Science, Technology and Innovation (STI) Policy of the government which professes 'gender parity' as one of its aims (Ministry of Science and Technology 2013). Schemes to encourage women scientists to re-enter career after break has been existent since 2002–2003 and now restructured under Knowledge Involvement in Research Advancement through Nurturing (KIRAN). Many advisory committees have women as members.

Various government initiatives that began from the first decade of the millennium have the following basic strands:

1. Doctoral and postdoctoral fellowships exclusively for women by various government departments and agencies (e.g., UGC, DBT, Science and Engineering Research Board [SERB], DST, etc.) to bring back women scientists after career break and encourage research among women scientists in universities and small research labs through extramural projects (e.g., WOS-A and WOS-B of DST; BioCARe of DBT).
2. Schemes to train women in IPR, encourage entrepreneurship (e.g., WOS-C; Bio-Tech Park in Chennai set up by DBT).
3. Awards for women scientists, for example, SERB Women Excellence Award for women scientists below 40 years of age to those who have received recognition from any one or more of the following national academies (involving research grant of ₹5 lakhs per annum for a period of 3 years once in lifetime).
4. Specific schemes to enable women scientists to achieve work-life balance (e.g., Mobility Scheme).
5. Women scientists in government sector are also beneficiaries of the generous government rules for paid maternity leave (26 weeks for two surviving children and 12 weeks thereafter) and childcare leave. The childcare leave (since 2008) can be granted to women employees having minor children below the age of 18 years for a maximum period of 2 years (i.e., 730 days) during their entire service, for taking care of up to two children. Since 2018, single males are also entitled to it.

6. Scheme for women scientists to collaborate abroad: Run jointly by DST and Indo-U.S. Science & Technology Forum (IUSSTF), Indo-U.S. Fellowship for Women in STEMM (Science, Technology, Engineering, Mathematics, and Medicine) is designed to provide opportunities to Indian women to undertake international collaborative research in premier institutions in the USA to enhance their research capacities and capabilities.

7. Efforts to upgrade women's universities through CURIE.

8. Setting up a standing committee for promoting WIS in 2016[5]; holding workshops, conferences, etc.

LIMITATIONS OF THE EXISTING DISCOURSE

While the government is making considerable efforts at improving women's representation in scientific research, a few limitations might be pointed out. There is a gap between the policy (usually well-intentioned) and its implementation. For instance, the woman scientist under WOS-A scheme, designated as, Principal Investigators (PIs) far from being integrated into the mainstream might face harassment from the staff of the agencies for the release of funds for their project (Gangopadhyay 2017). The claim of 30 per cent women getting permanent jobs in academia due to WOS-A scheme appears unsubstantiated by data (Gangopadhyay and Das 2016).

The philosophy underlying most policies seems to reproduce gendered notions. The gendered philosophy of 'separation of spheres' and that women are the centre of the family and are supposed to prioritize family over career is reproduced through policies. For example, a publication of DST-Centre for Policy Research (Tewari and Bhardwaj 2018: 13) states:

> WOS-C scheme aims to train women having qualifications in science/engineering/medicine or allied areas in the area of IPR and their management for a period of one year. The training will allow them to work from their homes *and thus maintain a good balance between professional and domestic demands.*

Similarly, Mobility Scheme, is aimed to provide an opportunity to women scientists who are facing difficulties in their present job due to relocation (marriage, transfer of husband to any other location within the country, attending ailing parents and accompanying children studying in different city) and is expected to act as filler while searching for other career options at a new place. The initiative intends to provide a harmonious environment during early phases of women scientists *where they would like to stay active in research in addition to attending and fulfilling other responsibilities in the domestic front.*[6]

Women scientists recognize the gendered nature of the policies aimed for their benefit. For instance, Godbole (2017), physicist at IISR, Bangalore, while acknowledging that the Women Scientist Scheme of DST has led to an increase in the fraction of women principle investigators from 11 per cent in 2001 to about 30 per cent in 2010, remarks:

> We have programmes to come back from a break, but not for minimizing/avoiding the breaks and their after effects…consider schemes like DISHA and KIRAN which are in place to help women scientists to relocate or redefine their careers and achieve career–family balance. Such schemes should be meant for couples, with either of the partners doing the relocation or the redefinition. (Godbole 2017: 672)

According to Vaidya (2017: 83), neuroscientist at TIFR:

> When you single out women as the sole caregivers, it fails to achieve the broader change that is needed to level the playing field. However, if maternity–paternity leave policies were discussed collectively as the best way to ensure that families can generate the required time to manage child-rearing and their work, it would send a different message.

That the childcare leave should be extended to men also was recommended in the Women in STEM workshop at New Delhi in 2015 by women scientists.[7] In one of the few gender-neutral measures, crèche facilities have been provided by the Maternity Benefit (Amendment) Act, 2017, for organizations with 50 or more employees; however, Crèche Guidelines framed in 2018 have been legislated by only a few states and how successfully they are implemented by the employers has yet to be seen.[8]

DST aims to increase the participation of women through gender mainstreaming (GM). On the DST website, it states: 'KIRAN

(Knowledge Involvement in Research Advancement through Nurturing) embraces women-exclusive schemes of DST with the mandate to bring gender parity in S&T through *gender mainstreaming*'. However, exclusive programmes for women do not constitute 'gender mainstreaming' and this strategy was not conceived with the aim to achieve parity in numbers. In fact, gender mainstreaming (GM) emerged worldwide because of the dissatisfaction with the strategies that focused on women (UN 2002: 9) and because there was

> recognition that inequality between women and men was a relational issue and that inequalities were not going to be resolved through a focus only on women. More attention needed to be brought to the relations between women and men ... there was a need to move away from 'women' as a target group, to gender equality as a development goal. (UN 2002: 9)

The UN defines GM as: '...the process of assessing the implications for women and men of any planned action, including legislation, policies or programmes, in all areas and at all levels'. That women's and men's concerns and experiences should be integral for any design, implementation, monitoring and evaluation of policies and programmes in all spheres; 'so that women and men benefit equally.... The ultimate goal is to achieve gender equality' (UN 2002: 1). Further, GM aims at altering structures, institutions and practices as dealt with later. Since 2005, the Government of India has adopted 'gender budgeting' at the levels of the planning, budget formulation and implementation processes. It is seen as a major instrument of GM. However, gender budgeting statement reflects women-specific schemes and pro-women schemes (MWCD 2015). Also, there remains a big gap between budgetary outlay and outcome due to non-utilization of the allocated funds. Gender commitments do not get translated into budgetary commitments in the absence of funds, functions and functionaries (Rudra 2018). The concept does not entail mere increased outlays for the women-centric programmes; rather, it demands financially effective decisions of the public sector based on the principles of gender equality and analysis of gender-differentiated impact of the earmarked public expenditure allocations (Rudra 2018).

Thinking on gender parity among the scientists and the administrators have at times resulted in measures that further segregate women and fail to create respect for them in the scientific community. For instance, Women's Science Congress (WSC) was inaugurated at the 99th Indian Science Congress (ISC) in 2012 to showcase contributions of women in S&T. ISC is held annually by the Indian Science Congress Association (since 1914, having at present membership of about 60,000 aiming to advance the cause of science),[9] whose executive committee includes Secretary, DST (GOI). ISC has had only four women presidents since its inception. The WSC, 'it is hoped, will help in breaking the myth that still persists that women are less suited to pursue science and encourage more women to pursue science' (ISC 2012: 1). However, the fact of holding a WSC, separate from ISC, shows that women lack opportunities for leadership and recognition in the mainstream scientific community. In a reiteration of the pre-independence argument that education of a woman educates a family, a former general president of the ISC said at the seventh edition of the WSC:

> Like Madam Curie and several others have shown, it is possible for women to contribute significantly in science and thereby improving our society, not only this but a child learns most from his or her mother.... She can share her experience and knowledge with her child. (Ashok 2018)

Women scientists have questioned the rationale for holding a separate WSC. According to them, while such a conference might generate networking among the younger women scientists, the separate sessions reek of gender inequality. Nobel Laureate David Gross pointed out that there was not a single woman who spoke at the inaugural ceremony of the ISC in 2016, which 'shows that there are not enough women in power. They did not even feel it necessary to include someone (female speaker)' (Basu 2016). The minister herself considered the separate sessions as a sign of prejudice and felt that it was not required (Basu 2016). The WSC in its seventh edition was held despite repeated calls from the women scientific community that it be scrapped (Ashok 2018).

While in the short run, the WSC might help to discuss the issues of women in science, promote networking and visibility for the young scientists, in the long run, this is not likely to promote gender equality. The WSC is expected to provide recognition to women scientists, but by holding WSC separately from ISC, it constructs the ISC as a congregation of men and thereby reproduces the notion of the scientist as 'male'. For women scientists, to be recognized as a 'scientist' and not as a 'woman scientist' requires integration with the mainstream scientific community.

Hence, the question that arises is how to view the problems of women scientists or what perspective to adopt so that women scientists can utilize their potential fully. This is discussed in the following sections.

CONCEPTUALIZING CHANGE

Broadly, the policy and decision-makers at present view gender inequality as an issue of a skewed ratio needed to be set right; second, gender inequality is seen as a social problem and issues in achieving work-life balance as women's problems and not as part of systemic inequality. Also, it is a top-down approach where women scientists become beneficiaries of the programmes handed down by the government. A holistic reform requires, on the one hand, encouraging discourse for reforms at the organizational/workplace level so that organizations and scientists therein could recognize the need for reforms and think of the measures and, on the other hand, overhaul of the institutions of science and education.

In most of the measures for gender equality, the aim is to enhance the representation of women scientists at all levels and forums. Indian policy towards women scientists professes the goal of 'gender parity', as stated in STI Policy 2013. It is reiterated in the SERB document on goals: 'Realising the importance of gender parity, ensure that appropriate programmes pro-actively have mechanism to encourage enhanced and equitable representation of woman scientists'.[10]

However, the way forward will depend on our philosophy which will also guide our approach. The question is should we aim for gender parity or gender equity or gender equality? Sociocultural norms construct inequalities based on biological differences. Hence, an enabling environment for women requires overcoming the specific obstacles that women face so as to enable a level playing field. These call for measures of 'gender equity'. Gender equity means fairness of treatment for men and women according to their respective needs. However, as European Institute for Gender Equality notes in its definition of 'gender equity'[11]:

> The term 'gender equity' has sometimes been used in a way that perpetuates stereotypes about women's role in society, suggesting that women should be treated 'fairly' in accordance with the roles that they carry out. This understanding risks perpetuating unequal gender relations and solidifying gender stereotypes that are detrimental to women. Therefore the term should be used with caution to ensure it is not masking a reluctance to speak more openly about discrimination and inequality.

Focusing on 'difference' tends to reinforce stereotypes. Gender equity cannot be a goal by itself. The goal is to achieve gender equality. Gender equality does not merely mean equality in numbers. It is not the same as gender parity. 'Gender parity' measures gender balance in a given situation and concerns 'relative equality in terms of numbers and proportions of women and men, girls and boys, and is often calculated as the ratio of female-to-male values for a given indicator'.[12] Gender equality, as aptly defined by the European Union, does not mean that women and men will become the same but that women's and men's rights, responsibilities and opportunities will not depend on whether they are born female or male. Gender equality implies that the interests, needs and priorities of both women and men are taken into consideration, thereby recognizing the diversity of different groups of women and men. Gender equality is not a women's issue but should concern and fully engage men as well as women. Equality between women and men is seen both as a human rights issue and as a precondition for, and indicator of, sustainable people-centred development.[13]

The obstacles for women scientists in the Indian context arise from a rigid dichotomy of public–private spheres, from a historic growth of science and its institutions and India's place in a developing world economy and research network, which have created science institutions and organizations as male-dominated and masculine. Hence, there is an urgent need for gender equity measures, but we also need to move forward towards gender equality targeting the structures and processes that create gender inequality.

Government policies help in addressing the issues of gender equity. However, more such initiatives need to be thought out. An excellent measure was suggested as far back as 2000 in a report[14]: that of relaxation of age for recruitment and to compete in open selection for a permanent job by 5 years; some of the measures suggested in this report have been incorporated such as post-doctoral fellowships/grants for women above 35 years and childcare leave.

Gender equity for a level playing field also requires greater sensitivity to women's issues during recruitment/promotions and hence the need to improve representation of women in such selection committees. However, merely improving representation is not likely to help unless systems generating inequality are targeted. Difference between gender equity and gender equality might be demonstrated through an example of networking. Creating women's networks, a gender equity measure, is immensely useful in creating mentorship and visibility. However, they have limitations. Such networks are unable to deal with exclusion of women from powerful networks which are usually male (Cabrera and Thomas-Hunt 2007). Gender-neutral networks could bring more equality between men and women in research (Checchi et al. 2015). The way forward that aims for gender equality would conceptualize making informal interactions and networking between the scientists within and outside an institute easier for both men and women (Gupta 2016). This and other areas of concern in moving towards gender equality are dealt with in the next section.

TOWARDS 'GENDER EQUALITY': CHIEF AREAS OF CONCERN

Moving towards gender equality requires consideration of organizational and institutional issues. Dealing with such issues requires measures of gender equity that take into account the specific needs of women; these measures have to be combined with those leading to gender equality and an integration of women scientists within the scientific community. Chief aspects that need consideration are: (a) interaction issues, (b) biased and wasteful organizational practices, (c) biological differences and (d) work-life balance structures.

Interaction Issues

Interaction is a potent forum in which the basic rules of the gender system are at play and cultural beliefs about men's competence are established (Ridgeway and Correll 2000). Also, such interactions create network of connections that are gender-neutral and could be helpful in moving up the academic career ladder. Given the significance of the culture of hierarchy and the lack of informal interaction between women scientists and their male colleagues which maintains masculine hegemony in the institutes, structural changes that reduce hierarchy and improve informal interaction could change the work climate. Large hierarchical structures are detrimental to gender equity climate (Ridgeway 2009; Smith-Doerr 2004). In a study on CSIR labs (Gupta 2016), one example of a possible model of change was found in a centre for interdisciplinary research that was set up in a CSIR lab in 2010. The building which houses the centre incorporates the construction style which is different from the traditional. Instead of offices arranged in a long dark corridor, it has a circular design which is more interaction-friendly. But more importantly, the group of scientists in this centre has formulated its own rules of management.

This centre at CSIR2 does not have an overarching HOD; it is headed by a collegium of five scientists, including two women scientists at the time of the study, who hold office for two years. The members of the centre have established a coffee club which meets once a week. The work environment here is perceived as quite positive and has an impact on gender relations. This positive environment is attributed to lesser hierarchy and greater space for informal interaction. For instance, Anamika (female, Scientist E1), when asked how she perceives gender equality at her workplace, said (Gupta 2016):

> Gender equality is [achieved] when people surrounding you perceive you as a colleague and not a 'woman colleague'.... Yes, it (gender equality) exists in my group. It's a collaborative and cooperative environment. People talk about their research, seniors are trying to be your mentor [she just joined about a year ago]; there is a Friday coffee club where I go, we discuss, debate. There is comfort in the work environment.

The centre has considerable internal collaboration and mutual interaction and has a robust output in terms of research productivity. However, it has miniscule impact on the entire institute and such centres are rare. Their positive role needs to be highlighted so that similar models can be established in other institutes as well.

Another initiative encouraging interaction existing in many parts of the world is that of 'mentoring'. Mentoring programmes (MPs) build on the idea of older, senior professionals sharing their experiences and networks with younger professionals in order to help them advance in their careers (Powell 2018). In India, MP usually implies interaction of the young women in science with the senior and established women professionals through workshops and seminars. The DST of the Government of India and the Science Academies conduct a series of mentoring workshops and surveys. They include mentorship and awareness workshops, addressing the student community, executives in industry or administrators in high-level institutions, etc. Indian Women and Mathematics (IWM) is a network of Indian mathematicians which through workshops and conferences (funding from National Board for Higher Mathematics) aims to raise awareness about current research in mathematics and provides opportunities to those in postgraduate studies or research, especially those in small towns, to meet other women mathematicians. Another example is the University of Baroda's intergenerational mentoring, wherein the senior faculty took time off to mentor young girls in a challenging cultural context where they were married off early (Kurup, Mathew and Singh 2017).

These mentorship and awareness workshops are extremely helpful in creating information about the opportunities and available resources for those aspiring for a career in scientific research and for tapping the potential in smaller cities. However, there is a lack of mentorship programmes within the academic/research system that aims at the mentoring of the young women scientists so as to enable them to use their potential fully and to rise in organizational hierarchy. For instance, in many US universities, new faculty members are assigned to those ahead of them (Etzkowitz et al. 2000). These seniors act as mentors introducing them to other faculty members, inviting them in social functions and give advice, tips and strategies which help in knowing policies and create a sense of what is required/expected of them. Compared to informal mentorship, formal MPs are a more transparent, formalized and egalitarian way of providing mentors (Powell 2018).

Organizational Reforms

Gendered practices, particularly work practices that are constrained by gendered images of competence and organized around gendered ideas of who is an 'ideal worker', can be inefficient organizational practices and unproductive for both men and women (Rapoport et al. 2002). The notion of an ideal worker and the male model of scientist that appreciates devotion of long hours to the lab/workplace are unrelated to the quantity and quality of the work performed. The gendered practices in our study also include (as detailed in Chapter 4) meetings without much agenda or urgency, bureaucratic red tape at lower levels, a lack of transparency and a hierarchical culture. Several issues that impact women (and men) also include unwillingness of some institutes to hire couples; lack of lateral recruitment in academia and age preferences. Rapoport et al. (2002) suggest a practical approach to bring about gender equality referred to as 'dual agenda'. This approach assumes that by making changes in work practices to enhance gender equality and through work-life integration, it is possible to enhance workplace performance and organizational effectiveness (Charlesworth and Baird 2007).

Organizational practices that construct dominant masculinity such as the long-hours work culture might be detrimental to the men desirous of a better work-life balance as shown in a study on private research labs indicating prevalence of multiple masculinities (Gupta 2017). Predominance of men in decision-making activities might actually be a dominance of senior powerful men that marginalize junior men as well. Similarly, not all men are likely to find it comfortable to network with seniors or powerful men in science for recognition.

Thus, measures to eliminate gender inequality are likely to improve the work climate for men also.

As noted in Chapter 4, committees for recruitments and promotions are known to ask gender-based questions. However, the system is not transparent; hence, it is difficult to say that there is gender bias in actual selections. Transparency in the system and accountability for evaluations could result in greater efficiency. As Ridgeway and Correll (2000) say:

> ...when evaluators are accountable for their assessments—in that they must be prepared to explain them to others—they look more closely at the information available to them and consider the impression their decisions will make. Both greater cognitive scrutiny and concern for appearances reduce the extent to which people rely on implicit stereotypes to form their judgments of others. (117)

Work–Life Balance

A lack of work-life balance structures is creating a debilitating impact on women scientists (and women professionals in general) as they consolidate the assumptions of dual burden on women. The structures are required not only for a better work–life balance for women and men but also for creating a socio-psychological climate in which it might be assumed by the recruiters and the seniors that women can take care of family (since the assumption that women are primary caregivers is not likely to change in the near future).

As Ramadoss and Rajadhyaksha (2012) remark, by itself, multiple roles are not stressful unless one finds it difficult to manage those roles. Studies find that families are rejecting the traditional gendered dichotomy of public–private sphere and that men and women in dual career families are committed to both work and family roles, although working women demonstrate greater egalitarian gender role ideology (GRI) than men (Rajadhyaksha and Velgach 2015). However, there is a structural lag, and policies and workplaces are changing at a much slower pace. In fact, men receive greater support from colleagues, bosses and extended family members than women because of the structural lag coupled with the traditional mindset that women do not need support (Ramadoss and Rajadhyaksha 2012). Increasingly, crèche is required not only for women and men professionals but also for doctoral, postdoctoral researchers and for those attending conferences. Other support structures could include age-based support for childcare, for instance, for preschool and school-going children, commuting facilities for scientists outside campuses, etc.

It is imperative that various provisions such as childcare leave are made available to men and that the structures (crèche) and family-related leaves are used by men also. Not only the organizational support for family roles is lacking but also, as indicated in Chapter 4, the available structures and policies are perceived to be facilities for women; and flexi-leave or the paternity leave is seldom availed by men justifying the masculine culture of long hours. Studies show that when organizational culture aggressively encourages employees to use family-friendly policies by tying executives' compensation to the usage and results of work/life programmes, employees take advantage of them (Ridgeway and Correl 2000). In Sweden, laws give parents 480 days per child which they can take at any time until the child is 8 years old. Both parents can share these days, *although 60 are allocated specifically to the father* (Abad-Santos 2013). Indian childcare leave is much more generous but is meant for women and single men as mentioned earlier.

Dealing with Biological Differences

India has one of the most generous paid maternity leave rules in the world. In the USA, lack of paid maternity leave is believed to be one of the reasons for lack of women in science (Abad-Santos 2013). Pregnancy is an obvious biological difference and logically should not entail a loss in terms of professional development.

Some enlightened suggestions and measures have been put forth lately to avoid professional loss resulting in this period. For instance, Ananth (2014) suggests that for women scientists taking maternity leave, 3/2 multiplicative factor to the work she completed during the period should be applied when considering evaluation. In a landmark initiative by IISC Council in its meeting held on 24 June 2017 vide resolution no. VII, resolved that

(i) a provision be made in the existing evaluation policy for tenure and promotion in the case of woman faculty member who undergoes maternity by sanctioning a benefit of additional one year for consideration for evaluation for promotion or tenure. (ii) This benefit will be limited to only two maternities in a woman's career.[15]

As shown earlier, the maternity leave in India is viewed as a loss to the workplace by colleagues and the bosses. This is evident in the government effort to compensate companies for the loss of part of the period (Chapter 5). However, in academia/research labs, it is difficult to compensate and counter the feeling (of colleagues) that women 'take off' after every few years.

INITIATIVES WORLDWIDE: TARGETING ORGANIZATIONS

World over several programmes have been afoot to enhance gender equality. This has resulted in improvements, although there is still much to be achieved (Shen 2013). There is much to learn from these initiatives and adapt them to our national context. For instance, similar to the Norwegian Gender Balance Project at the University of Agder aimed to address gender imbalance in professorships and leadership (Lund Forthcoming), it would be useful to provide counseling to women candidates for professorship through 'preliminary evaluation committee' to heighten their chances of promotion; and to establish search committees to invite talented women from non-elite institutes to apply for positions. Some other detailed examples are given in the following text.

Gender Mainstreaming

GM was endorsed at the World Conference on Women in Beijing in 1995 (UN 2002). This approach suggests that all legislation, policies and implementation should be assessed in terms of implications for women and men (UN 1997). GM aims at the structures of the organization, rather than targeting individual women as 'lacking' (and thus responsible for their own discriminated position). In practice, it requires all staff to have knowledge on how to consider gender equality in their everyday work practices (Eveline, Bacchi and Binns 2010:

241–242). It includes, for example, training for recruitment committees as a way to remove barriers to women gaining professorships (Winchester et al. 2006). It may result in a new governance structure that integrates all relevant strategic and operational actors and units, the establishment of transparent, structured and formalized procedures, etc.[16]

GM has been carried out in a variety of organizations from multilaterals to governments to small and large non-governmental organizations. Nevertheless, there are reviews suggesting many failures and few positives coming out of GM programmes. The failure of the strategy is owed mainly to the following: losing sight of transformative agenda in trying to make the approach palatable to the organizations, technical issues such as lack of integration of gender perspective and analysis in plans and monitoring, deep-seated biases and complex power structures and over-absorption in organizational dynamics of GM losing sight of the results achieved on the ground. However, it has brought indirect benefit through increasing the theorizing and understanding of the gendered nature of organizational practices, procedures, routines and cultures (Milward, Mukhopadhyay and Wong 2015).

ADVANCE Programme

In 2001, the NSF in the USA launched the ADVANCE programme to catalyze change that will transform academic environments in ways that enhance the participation and advancement of women in science and engineering. Prior to the NSF ADVANCE programme, most efforts at increasing the numbers of women faculty in academic STEM focused on 'fixing the women' (belief that women lack in skills or qualifications compared to men)—the ADVANCE programme put money and focus on 'fixing the institutions' (belief that the inequality is systemic) instead (Rosser 2004). The NSF awards support comprehensive programmes for institution-wide change. A seminal programme within the ADVANCE portfolio is the Institutional Transformation Grant, which provides large-scale, multi-year funding to institutions of higher education (IHEs) focused on fundamental organizational changes that should broaden participation of women and foster gender equity in STEM academic careers.[17]

The ADVANCE programme has invested over $315 million to support initiatives at more than 175 IHEs and STEM-related non-profit organizations since its inception (Furst-Holloway and Miner 2019). Some of the strategies used by the IHEs include increasing awareness of and reducing implicit gender bias among members of faculty search committee through workshops (after data collection at the institution); department-level climate change using the dual agenda approach; attempts to boost careers from associate to full professor through the development of a demographic database to track the gender distribution among faculty ranks over time, attempts to raise awareness and action through workshops, panel discussions and departmental meetings and policy changes such as clarifying post-tenure review; addressing issues of isolation by stimulating research collaborations through seed money and travel grants for women-led research project teams, interdisciplinary knowledge exchanges, cross-sector research showcases and an informal Research Café (Furst-Holloway and Miner 2019).

Athena SWAN/SAGE

Government and organizations have come together in carrying out initiatives for gender equity/equality through Athena SWAN (Scientific Women's Academic Network) charter in Great Britain and SAGE (Science in Australia Gender Equity) in Australia. These are evaluation/accreditation programmes where the institutes that sign the charter commit themselves to promoting and supporting gender equality for women. Such institutes apply for awards which have been linked to funding. For example, in 2011, the UK chief medical officer made it a requirement for academic departments applying for funding from the English National Institute for Health Research to hold the Athena SWAN silver award.

Reforming Institution of Science in India

There are other grounds for inequality apart from discriminatory structures in organizations. These include inequalities in institutions of science (grant agencies, award committees and scientific academies) and doctoral/postdoctoral education system.

Reforming the institutions of science implies creating an educational and research ecosystem that provides equal opportunities for all desirous of a career in S&T. This requires, first and foremost, strengthening of our universities and raising the quality of doctoral education. This necessitates greater research funding and structural changes in universities to encourage research. There is a need to think about greater encouragement to women in doctoral and postdoctoral research while reducing harassment (of men and women) during the programme. Women (and men) researchers would benefit from opportunities generated through greater collaboration between academic institutes and between academia and industry. Based on the analysis in the earlier chapters, an area for reform includes streamlining the methods for securing external funding. Systems of awards and recognition such as fellowship of academies that requires nomination by existing fellows and impart power to few who decide should be reworked to include practice of self-nomination and power to more than one independent committee (Gupta 2007).

There is also a need for data collection agency so that analysis could reveal and highlight the gaps in our understanding on the issues of women in science. Lack of data is a roadblock in understanding gender issues and thereby tackling them. Some suggestions on the data are: while we have enrolment figures for women in various degrees (UG, PG and PhD), we do not know how many women (and men) drop out at the national level. Hence, it is imperative to have data on this. The initiative of collecting data by MHRD through NIRF is very helpful for researchers in social sciences. However, the recent data by NIRF (2019) have actually omitted the information regarding the faculty strength in each institute and the gender-wise break-up of the strength.

Further, it will help to assess women's position in S&T in various institutes if the government could include in NIRF: numbers on women doctorates, postdoctorates; women faculty in science and engineering separately and gender disaggregated data of institutes on how many men and women are there at various positions in the organizational hierarchy. We need an autonomous body that can collate data from various sources, such as Census, NIRF and DST for the purpose of understanding various dimensions of S&T education and personnel.

Social Change as Enabler of Gender Equality

The Indian society exhibits continuity and change. As shown in the earlier chapters, the defining femininity of teens carries attributes of women as family oriented and sexually chaste typical of the middle-class families (Diwakar 2016). The son preference and differential socialization of boys and girls create male privilege and masculinity in society and institutions of education. Construction of self-assured masculinity is impeded due to inhibited interaction (Iyer 2014). These attributes translate into male entitlement and women's marginalization at public spaces.

However, the Indian social system is also undergoing dynamic change and with it the position of women is getting transformed. The implementation of neoliberal policies from the 1990s has brought considerable changes in the cultural practices of the Indian middle classes which appear to have affected women and gender relations (Fernandes 2006). For example, media portrayal of women indicates fewer restrictions on women's movements and dress (Dewey 2008); there is greater acceptability of women in public sphere; families headed by young couples displaying greater egalitarian attitudes are on the rise and dual earning couples are becoming increasingly common in urban India (Ramadoss and Rajadhyaksha 2012). This transitional milieu has raised the possibility of multiple masculinities and femininities, thus challenging the prevalent notions of masculinity at the research institutes. Younger men or those with working wives are more sympathetic to the dual burden concerns of women (Gupta 2016). While a woman's role in the family continues to be regarded as pivotal by the society, including by women scientists themselves, change is witnessed in terms of greater family support and a higher determination among women to pursue a career (Gupta 2016). Some men are desirous of a work-life balance and dislike the long-hours policy (Gupta 2017). It is also encouraging to note that men scientists are participating in the discourse on gender equality as shown in the following text.

Men as Feminists

Feminism is a philosophy that cannot be attributed to any particular sex. According to Encyclopaedia Britannica, feminism is the belief in the social, economic and political equality of the sexes. Since, historically, women in most cultures have been denied full rights, it is manifested as advocacy of women's rights and interests.

In India, the colonial period saw men emerge as the champion of women's rights before women themselves took up the cause. The social reformers of the age fought against the evils of the time such as Sati, purdah and for widow remarriage, women's education, etc. Gandhi played a major role in encouraging women to come out in protest against the British and thereby creating visibility for women in public spaces. The views of the reformers and nationalist might seem limited when judged by today's aspirations and values; nevertheless, they were radical for those times. While women had to fight hard for suffrage rights in Britain and the USA, the constitution-makers of India incorporated women's equal right to vote without any such protests/movements. However, such rights made little dent on the patrifocal ideology, particularly on the public–private dichotomy.

In the post-independence period, the dominant reaction of men to feminism in India has been one of opposition (Choudhary and Baset 2018). For instance, in academia, it has implied trivializing feminist concerns, theories and methodologies (Tellis 2000). However, since the 1990s, pro-feminist men's organizations have emerged to address violence against women; proliferation of NGOs has provided the 'conceptual infrastructure' necessary for such men's organizations (Choudhary and Baset 2018: 16). Two generations of men feminist scholars have been produced for whom feminism has been a major part of their formal intellectual training. Since the start of the millennium, there is a growing thinking on how men could also be a part of the solution; to engage with the policymakers to incorporate perspectives on masculinities in various gender-related initiatives in the country (Chatterji 2011).

For men, the task is to highlight the construction of maleness and thereby contribute to the understandings of gender (Srivastava 2018). The manner in which cultures of masculinity shape them and the suffering due to power differentials among men (due to differences in caste, class, caste, region) can potentially provide inroads into modes of thinking that oppose patriarchal power.

Studies on men scientists have been limited. But from the available evidence, since the beginning of the millennium, there has been a growing interest among the men scientists about the position of women. Malhotra (2018) notes more men participating in the discussion as shown by a significant increase in the proportion of articles authored by men in *Current Science*. Of the 23 articles between 2010 and October 2016, eight articles were with men as sole author/first author. An article, for instance, recognizes that 'the academic community has a skewed gender ratio, which gets worse when the focus shifts to leadership' (Ananth 2014: 1366); that one of the main reasons is the maternity leave which delays promotions and makes it harder to reach leadership positions; he suggests 3/2 formula referred to earlier. His other suggestions include allowing portion of research funds to be used for childcare, provision of crèche and qualified childcare workers and 30 per cent quota for women on governing boards of all institutions.

Research shows that there are some men who differ from the hegemonic viewpoint on the system's impact on women (Gupta 2016). While most men tend to deny that the system in terms of processes and practices creates barriers for women, a few consider the barriers as systemic, such as lack of acceptance of women in leadership positions and lack of godfathers (Gupta 2013: 41–69). Such men represent a version of masculinity, 'more open to equality with women' (Connell and Messerschmidt 2005: 853).

Society also seems to exhibit different ideas of dominant masculinities, different for workplace and home. This is apparent in the contradictions about role of men in a woman scientist's personal life and at the workplace. Most women scientists attribute their success in career to their father or husband; however, the workplace appears to let them down. For example, Aruna Dhathathreyan, Raman Research Fellowship awardee and Professor Emeritus Scientists at a CSIR lab (Central Leather Research Institute) writes in *Lilavati's Daughters* (Godbole and Ramaswamy 2008: 104): 'To be accepted as a scientist who happens to be a woman is still an uphill task.... A woman is expected to be docile and not ask too many questions'. However, Dhathathreyan attributes her survival in science to her husband, also a chemist, sharing in child-rearing. The dominant form of masculinity in the domestic sphere seems to be more egalitarian than at the workplace.

Women Scientists as Feminists

Subrahmanyan (1998) had felt that 'feminism has indeed passed these women by' (281); that while women scientists were not totally non-feminists, without their involvement in overall women's movement, their problems could not be solved. However, change is now visible among the women scientists as they are more willing to voice the discrimination faced at the public platforms, are integrated with the international platforms on women in science and are taking active interest in transforming their position in science than about 15 years ago. Women scientists are receiving greater attention from corridors of power as our government is increasingly recognizing the need to increase the participation of women scientists.

Unlike in the West, feminists in India do not see men as the chief protagonists (Chitnis 2005). Women scientists, even as they unite to highlight their position, do not posit men as the cause of an unequal work terrain. Their focus, and rightly so, is on creating a level playing field so as to be able to contribute fully to their profession. However, any change necessitates collaboration of both men and women. This, in turn, requires greater awareness and a will for radical changes in structures and practices, organizations and institutions to efficiently use human resources and a desire for a more just and humane society.

CRITICAL AREAS FOR RESEARCH

There are no easy solutions and to utilize the potential of women in S&T requires a combination of greater access to and improvement in the quality of higher education, creation and access to jobs, gender awareness and women empowerment. However, the primary requirement is a need for more scholars and a research network of social scientists working on women in S&T. For this, it will be helpful to have research centres in IITs and premier institutes of S&T apart from universities for an exclusive study of women in science. The findings of such centres/scholars should be in the public domain accessible to the policymakers. Specifically, studies are required urgently in the following areas and the methods that might be helpful for those are listed as follows:

1. Conducting study of recruitment and promotion procedures, experiments of the Ross–Macusin type to understand gender biases in selection. This will help to enlist support for finding solutions.
2. Conducting study of men and women Masters, doctoral and postdoctoral students regarding their career plans, higher studies abroad and bottlenecks. Longitudinal studies from Masters level in this regard would be very helpful. This will help to trace the weak links in the pipeline to faculty positions.
3. In-depth qualitative studies on organizational structures, processes and informal environment as creating barriers.
4. Social network analysis to understand the nature of exclusion from networks, facilitators or bottlenecks in collaboration for women.
5. Comprehensive statistical studies on research productivity and its relation with marriage, parenthood and age will help in understanding if men and women have different periods at which they produce maximum/minimum research.
6. Qualitative studies of scientists to understand the relative importance of research productivity, networking and visibility in construction of 'merit'.
7. Qualitative studies to understand if the present policies and programmes for women also create inroads into the male-dominated power structure and masculine culture in academia/government research labs.

8. Historical and descriptive studies on how does India's post-colonial structures of science and its third-world status impact women scientists in terms of opportunities for recruitment, promotion and research.

These and various other aspects pointed out in the book need to be further researched to understand the nature of issues and find solutions.

A FINAL WORD: DOES DISADVANTAGE FOR WOMEN IMPLY UNEARNED PRIVILEGE FOR MEN?

Studies on psychology of prejudice point out that discrimination and privilege are two sides of the same coin (Kite and Whitley 2016). Advantages associated with being a member of the privileged group accumulate and can have significant impact. These advantages are invisible and unearned. Those with privilege often become annoyed when confronted by the fact of their privilege as it seems to negate the hard work and their own efforts in their accomplishments (Ferber 2012). However, as Johnson (2006: 21) remarks in this context, existence of privilege does not mean that the person did not do a good job or does not deserve credit for it, rather it means that he/she is getting something that others are not, even though they are similar in every respect except for the social category to which they belong to. Hence, access to privilege does not determine outcomes but it is an asset that makes positive outcomes more likely.

Thus, stereotypes in society and masculinity in science privilege men and make their success more likely than women even though the latter may be similar in talent, ability and aspirations. Hence, the issue is not of men versus women, but of an unequal social, institutional and organizational system that creates disadvantages for women professionals in S&T.

NOTES

1. On quota: Creation and allocation of supernumerary seats for female candidates is fundamentally different from reservation of seats for female candidates. Please see https://josaa.nic.in/webinfocms/Handler/

FileHandler.ashx?i=File&ii=110&iii=Y (5); Supernumerary Seats for Females. Also see https://josaa.nic.in/webinfocms/Handler/FileHandler. ashx?i=File&ii=109&iii=Y (26; Business Rules; accessed on 9 August 2019).

2. Available at https://timesofindia.indiatimes.com/city/delhi/HRD-to-bring-IIT-preparation-app-to-curb-coaching-menace/articleshow/52326935.cms (accessed on 9 August 2019).

3. For instance, Professor Rohini Godbole (Physicist at IISc Bangalore) is an avid supporter of women pursuing careers in S&T, is the Chair of the Panel for Women in Science initiative of the Indian Academy of Sciences; member of the steering group of the DST for WIS. Along with Ram Ramaswamy, Godbole jointly edited *Lilavati's Daughters*, a collection of biographical essays on women scientists of India, which was published in the form of book by Indian Academy of Sciences in 2008. Available at http://rmgodbole.in/women-in-science/ (accessed on 9 August 2019).

   Shubha Tole is known to be vocal about the unique issues she has faced as a woman scientist. In 2009, as a member of a committee to reform the competitive grant system of the Department of Biotechnology, Government of India, she recommended an exclusive childcare allowance for women postdocs and PIs to encourage higher quality and consistency of childcare (Agrawal 2016; http://www.tarshi.net/inplainspeak/interview-shubha-tole-science-career/ [accessed on 9 August 2019]).

4. https://thelifeofscience.com/

5. Available at http://www.dst.gov.in/sites/default/files/Standing-Committee-OM-Composition.pdf (accessed on 9 August 2019).

6. Available at http://www.dst.gov.in/scientific-programmes/scientific-engineering-research/women-scientists-programs (accessed on 9 August 2019).

7. Available at https://www.britishcouncil.in/sites/default/files/report_-_women_in_stem.pdf (accessed on 9 August 2019).

8. Available at https://www.livelaw.in/law-firms/articles/national-guidelines-crches-maternity-benefit-act-142685 (accessed on 9 August 2019).

9. Available at http://sciencecongress.nic.in/pdf/Regulation_Bye_Laws_2012. pdf; Also, see regulations of ISCA at http://sciencecongress.nic.in/pdf/ Regulation_Bye_Laws_2012.pdf (accessed on 9 August 2019).

10. Available at http://serb.gov.in/pdfs/about_serb/Vision_Mission_Goal.pdf (accessed on 9 August 2019).

11. For definition of gender equity, see https://eige.europa.eu/thesaurus/ terms/1175 (accessed on 9 August 2019).

12. For definition of gender parity, see https://eige.europa.eu/rdc/thesaurus/ terms/1195 (accessed on 9 August 2019).

13. For definition of gender equality, see https://eige.europa.eu/rdc/thesaurus/ terms/1168 (accessed on 9 August 2019).

14. Available at http://psa.gov.in/sites/default/files/book/Scientific-Advisory-Committee-to-the-Cabinet-Report/#p=1 (accessed on 9 August 2019).

15. Available at https://www.iisc.ac.in/policy-on-extension-of-time-for-submission-of-reports-for-evaluation-for-tenure-and-promotion-in-the-case-of-women-faculty-members-who-have-undergone-maternity/ (accessed on 9 August 2019).
16. Available at https://eige.europa.eu/gender-mainstreaming/policy-areas/research (accessed on 9 August 2019).
17. Available at https://www.nsf.gov/funding/pgm_summ.jsp?pims_id=5383 (accessed on 9 August 2019).

REFERENCES

Abad-Santos, Alexander. 2013, 7 October. 'The First Step to Having More Women in Science Is Maternity Leave'. *The Atlantic.* Available at https://www.theatlantic.com/politics/archive/2013/10/first-step-having-more-women-science-maternity-leave/310246/ (accessed on 8 August 2019).

Agarwal, S. 2016. *Interview: Shubha Tole talks about tracks only women scientists navigate.* IndiaBioscience. Available at: https://indiabioscience.org/columns/opinion/interview-shubha-tole-talks-about-tracks-only-women-scientists-navigate

Ananth, Sudarshan. 2014. 'Women Leaders in Indian Science'. *Current Science* 107 (9): 1366. Available at https://www.currentscience.ac.in/Volumes/107/09/1366.pdf (accessed on 8 August 2019).

Ashok, S. 2018, 19 March. 'Few Women in Science, Fewer on Stage of Science Congress to Speak about It'. Available at https://indianexpress.com/article/india/few-women-in-science-fewer-on-stage-of-science-congress-to-speak-about-it-5102624/ (accessed on 8 August 2019).

Basu, Mihika. 2016, 5 January. 'Women's Science Congress Seeks Raison d'etre'. *Bangalore Mirror.* Available at https://bangaloremirror.indiatimes.com/news/state/hal-is-a-gift-from-govt-of-india-to-people-of-ktaka-pm-in-tumakuru/articleshow/50429840.cms (accessed on 8 August 2019).

Cabrera, S. F., and M. C. Thomas-Hunt. 2007. '"Street Cred" and the Executive Woman: The Effects of Gender Differences in Social Networks on Career Advancement'. Available at http://scholarship.sha.cornell.edu/articles/371 (accessed on 8 August 2019).

Chadha, Gita, Asha Achuthan, C. Shah, Sumathi Rao, J. Subramanian, G. Venkataraman, S. Ramdorai, B. K. Kondaiah, S. Mahadev, M. G. T. Wahlang, and Vidita A. Vaidya. 2017. 'Review of Women's Studies'. *Economic & Political Weekly* 52 (17): 33–86.

Charlesworth, Sara, and M. Baird. 2007. 'Getting Gender on the Agenda: The Tale of Two Organisations'. *Women in Management Review* 22 (5): 391–404. Available at https://doi.org/10.1108/09649420710761455 (accessed on 8 August 2019).

Chatterji, S. 2011. 'Back to Family, India Together'. Available at http://www.indiatogether.org/praajak-children (accessed on 8 August 2019).

Checchi, Daniele, Simona Cicognani and Nevena Kulic. 2015. 'Gender Quotas or Girls' Networks?' Towards an Understanding of Recruitment in the Research Profession in Italy'. Quaderni Working Paper DSE No. 1047. Available at https://ssrn.com/abstract=2707577 or http://dx.doi.org/10.2139/ssrn.2707577 (accessed on 8 August 2019).

Chitnis, S. 2005. *Feminism: Indian Ethos and Indian Convictions*. London; New York, NY: Zed Books Ltd.

Choudhary, R., and Z. A. Baset. 2018. 'Introduction'. In *Men and Feminism in India* (1st edition), edited by R. Choudhary and Z. A. Baset, 1–18. Abingdon: Routledge.

Connell, R. W., and James W. Messerschmidt. 2005. 'Hegemonic Masculinity: Rethinking the Concept'. *Gender and Society* 19 (6): 829–859.

Dewey, S. 2008. *Making Miss India Miss World: Constructing Gender, Power, and the Nation in Postliberalization India*. Syracuse, NY: Syracuse University Press.

Diwakar, Vaishali. 2016. '"It's Complicated": The Construction of Indian Middle-Class Teens in Social Media'. *Journal of Creative Communications* 11 (2): 161–182.

Etzkowitz, H., C. Kemelgor, and B. Uzzi. 2000. *Athena Unbound: The Advancement of Women in Science and Technology*. Cambridge: Cambridge University Press.

Eveline, J., C. Bacchi, and J. Binns. 2010. 'Gender Mainstreaming Versus Diversity Mainstreaming: Methodology as Emancipatory Politics'. In *Mainstreaming Politics: Gendering Practices and Feminist Theory*, edited by C. Bacchi and J. Eveline, 237–261. Adelaide: University of Adelaide Press.

Ferber, A. L. 2012. 'The Culture of Privilege: Color-Blindness, Postfeminism, and Christonormativity'. *Journal of Social Issues* 68 (1): 63–77.

Fernandes, L. 2006. *India's New Middle Class: Democratic Politics in An Era of Economic Reform*. Minneapolis, MN: University of Minnesota Press.

Furst-Holloway, Stacie, and K. Miner. 2019. 'ADVANCEing Women Faculty in STEM: Empirical Findings and Practical Recommendations from National Science Foundation ADVANCE Institutions'. *Equality, Diversity and Inclusion: An International Journal* 38 (2): 122–130. Available at https://doi.org/10.1108/EDI-03-2019-295 (accessed on 8 August 2019).

Gangopadhyay, R. 2017. *All these Happened to a Woman Scientist*. Available at https://www.researchgate.net/publication/317823465_All_these_happened_to_a_Women_Scientist (accessed on 8 August 2019).

Gangopadhyay, R., and B. Das. 2016, 25 October. 'DST WOS-A: The Scenario from Recipient's Perspective'. *Current Science* 111 (8). Available at https://www.currentscience.ac.in/Volumes/111/08/1307.pdf (accessed on 8 August 2019).

Godbole, R. 2017. 'Women in STEMM: Involve the Institutions!' *Current Science* 112 (4): 671.

Godbole, R., and R. Ramaswamy, eds. 2008. *Lilavati's Daughters: The Women Scientists of India*. Bangalore: Indian Academy of Sciences.

Gupta, Namrata. 2007. 'How Critical is Critical Mass? Implications of the Minority Status of Women in Science in India'. *Current Science* 93 (6): 766–768.

———. 2013. *Women in Scientific Research in Government and Industrial Laboratories: A Comparative Study of Work Environment and Socio-Cultural Milieu.* Report submitted to Indian Council of Social Science Research, vide Fellowship no. F.No. 2–11/10/S.Fel.

———. 2016. 'Perceptions of the Work Environment: The Issue of Gender in Indian Scientific Research Institutes'. *Indian Journal of Gender Studies* 23 (3): 437–466.

———. 2017. 'Gender Inequality in the Work Environment: A Study of Private Research Organizations in India'. *Equality, Diversity and Inclusion: An International Journal* 36 (3): 255–276.doi:10.1108/EDI-04-2016-0029.

Indian Academy of Sciences, National Academy of Sciences, and Indian National Science Academy. 2016. *Women in Science & Technology: A Vision Document.* Available at http://www.nasi.org.in/Report%20-%20Women%20in%20 Science%20&%20Technology%20-A%20Vision%20Document.pdf (accessed on 7 August 2019).

INSA. 2004. Science Career for Indian Women: An Examination of Indian Women's Access to and Retention in Scientific Careers. New Delhi: Indian National Science Academy. Available at https://www.ias.ac.in/public/ Resources/Initiatives/Women_in_Science/report.pdf (accessed on 8 August 2019).

ISC. 2012, 5–6 January. *First Women's Science Congress: Women in Science and Science for Women.* Bhubaneswar: KIIT University and NISER. Available at http://www.isc2012.com/pdf/women2.pdf (accessed on 8 August 2019).

Iyer, Padmini. 2014, 11 November. 'Negotiating Masculinities and Learning to "Be a Man" at School in New Delhi, India'. Paper Presented at the 2nd MenEngage Global Symposium, New Delhi, India. Available at http://sro. sussex.ac.uk/55744/1/Iyer_%282014%29_Negotiating_masculinities_and_ learning_to_%27be_a_man%27_at_school_in_Delhi.pdf (accessed on 8 August 2019).

JAB Sub-Committee. 2017, 14 June. *Highlights of the Recommendations of the JAB Sub-Committee for Increasing Female Enrolment in B.Tech. in IITs.* Available at http://students.iitmandi.ac.in/~tag/doc/Report_Highlights_JAB_SC_Female_ BTech_14Jun17.pdf (accessed on 8 August 2019).

Johnson, A. G. 2006. *Privilege, Power, and Difference,* 2nd edition. New York, NY: McGraw-Hill. Available at https://blogs.lanecc.edu/engaging-diversity/ wp-content/uploads/sites/76/2015/02/Privilege-Oppression-and-Difference. pdf (accessed on 8 August 2019).

Kite, Mary E., and Bernard E. Whitley, Jr. 2016. *Psychology of Prejudice and Discrimination,* 3rd Edition. New York, NY: Routledge.

Kurup, A., and R. Maithreyi. 2011. 'Beyond Family and Societal Attitudes to Retain Women in Science'. *Current Science* 100 (1): 43–48.

Kurup, Anitha, R. Maithreyi, B. Kantharaju, and Rohini Godbole. 2010. *Trained Scientific Women Power: How Much Are We Losing and Why?* IAS–NIAS Research Report. Available at http://eprints.nias.res.in/142/1/IAS-NIAS-Report.pdf (accessed on 8 August 2019).

Kurup, Anitha, L. Mathew, and T. Singh. 2017. 'Women in STEM Disciplines'. Meeting Report. *Current Science* 112 (10): 1986–1987. Available at https://www.currentscience.ac.in/Volumes/112/10/1986.pdf (accessed on 8 August 2019).

Lund, R. Forthcoming. 'Becoming a Professor Requires Saying No: Merging Equality and Quality Agendas in a Norwegian Gender Balance Project'. In *New Perspectives in Gender, Science and Innovation,* edited by Helen Lawton Smith, Colette Henry, Henry Etzkowitz and Alex Poulovassilis. Cheltenham, UK: Edward Elgar Publishing.

Malhotra, C. 2018. 'The Malaise of Under-Representation of Women in Science'. The Indian Story Current Science 115 (9): 1714–1723.

Milward, K., M. Mukhopadhyay, and Franz F. Wong. 2015. 'Gender Mainstreaming Critiques: Signposts or Dead Ends?' *IDS Bulletin* 46 (4): 75–81. Available at https://opendocs.ids.ac.uk/opendocs/bitstream/handle/123456789/7732/IDSB_46_4_10.1111-1759-5436.12160.pdf?sequence=1 (accessed on 8 August 2019).

Ministry of Science and Technology. 2010. *Evaluating and Enhancing Women's Participation in Scientific and Technological Research: The Indian Initiatives.* Available at https://www.ias.ac.in/public/Resources/Initiatives/Women_in_Science/taskforce_report.pdf (accessed on 8 August 2019).

———. 2013. *Science, Technology and Innovation Policy 2013.* New Delhi: Government of India. Available at http://www.dst.gov.in/st-system-india/science-and-technology-policy-2013 (accessed on 8 August 2019).

MWCD. 2015. *Budgeting for Gender Equity.* New Delhi: Government of India. Available at https://wcd.nic.in/gender-budgeting (accessed on 8 August 2019).

National Institutional Ranking Framework (NIRF). 2019. National Rankings 2019 and ARIIA 2019, MHRD. Available at: https://www.nirfindia.org/2019/Ranking2019.html

Niti Ayog. 2017. *Status of Women in Science among Select Institutions in India: Policy Implications.* Final Report. Kolkata: SSESS. Available at http://www.niti.gov.in/writereaddata/files/document_publication/Final_Report_Women_In_Science_SSESS.pdf (accessed on 8 August 2019).

Onsongo, J. 2009. 'Affirmative Action, Gender Equity and University Admissions. Kenya, Uganda and Tanzania'. *London Review of Education* 7 (1): 71–81. Available at http://sites.miis.edu/comparativeeducation/files/2013/01/Affirmative-Action-Kenya-Uganda-Tanzania.pdf (accessed on 8 August 2019).

Padavic, I., R. Ely, and E. Reid. 2019, 14 February. 'Explaining the Persistence of Gender Inequality: The Work–Family Narrative as a Social Defense against the 24/7 Work Culture'. *Administrative Science Quarterly* 1–51. Available at https://doi.org/10.1177/0001839219832310 (accessed on 8 August 2019).

Powell, Stina. 2018. 'Gender Equality in Academia. Intentions and Consequences'. *International Journal of Diversity in Organisations, Communities and Nations:* Annual Review 1 (18).doi:10.18848/1447-9532/CGP/v18i01/19-35

Rajadhyaksha, U., and S. Velgach. 2015. What Is a Better Predictor of Work–Family Conflict in India?—Gender or Gender Role Ideology. In *Work and Personal Life Interface in the International Career Context*, edited by Liisa Makela and Vesaa Sutari, 71–93. Berlin: Springer.

Ramadoss, K., and U. Rajadhyaksha. 2012. 'Gender Differences in Commitment to Roles, Work–Family Conflict and Social Support'. *Journal of Social Sciences* 33 (2): 227–233. Available at http://www.krepublishers.com/02-Journals/ JSS/JSS-33-0-000-12-Web/JSS-33-2-000-12-Abst-PDF/JSS-33-2-227-12-1289-Ramadoss-K/JSS-33-2-227-12-1289-Ramadoss-K-Tx[9].pdf (accessed on 8 August 2019).

Rapoport, R., L. Bailyn, J. Fletcher, and B. Pruitt. 2002. *Beyond Work–Family Balance: Advancing Gender Equity and Workplace Performance.* San Francisco, CA: Jossey-Bass.

Rhoton, Laura A. 2011. 'Distancing as a Gendered Barrier. Understanding Women Scientists' Gender Practices'. *Gender & Society* 25 (6): 696–716. Available at https://doi.org/10.1177/0891243211422717 (accessed on 8 August 2019).

Ridgeway, C. L. 2009. 'Framed Before We Know It: How Gender Shapes Social Relations'. *Gender & Society* 23 (2): 145–160.

Ridgeway, C. L., and S. J. Correll. 2000. 'Limiting Inequality through Interaction. Utopian Visions: Engaged Sociologies for the 21st Century'. *Contemporary Sociology* 29 (1): 110–120.

Rosser, S. 2004. *The Science Glass Ceiling: Academic Women Scientists and the Struggle to Succeed*, 50–57. New York, NY: Routledge.

Rudra, S. 2018, 10 August. 'Gender-Responsive Budgeting: A Task ahead for India's 15th Finance Commission'. ORF Occasional Paper. Available at https:// www.orfonline.org/research/gender-responsive-budgeting-a-task-ahead-for-indias-15th-finance-commission/ (accessed on 8 August 2019).

Sanghi, D. 2017, 17 April. 'Yes, the IITs Have a Gender Ratio Problem. Here's How to Fix It'. *The Wire*. Available at https://thewire.in/education/reservations-best-way-improve-gender-ratio-iits (accessed on 8 August 2019).

Shen, H. 2013. 'Inequality Quantified: Mind the Gender Gap'. *Nature*. Available at https://www.nature.com/news/inequality-quantified-mind-the-gender-gap-1.12550 (accessed on 8 August 2019).

Sinha, U. B., and D. Sinha. 2011. 'Are Indian Women Scientists Victims of the "Glass Ceiling"?' *Current Science* 100 (6): 837–840.

Smith-Doerr, Laurel. 2004. *Women's Work: Gender Equality vs. Hierarchy in the Life Sciences*. Boulder, CO: Lynne Rienner.

Srivastava, S. 2018. 'Masculinity Studies and Feminism: Othering the Self, Engaging Theory'. In *Men and Feminism in India* (1st edition), edited by R. Choudhary and Z. A Baset, 35–49. Abingdon: Routledge.

Stoet, G., and D. C. Geary. 2018. 'The Gender–Equality Paradox in Science, Technology, Engineering, and Mathematics Education'. *Psychological Science* 29 (4): 581–593.

Subrahmanyan, L. 1998. *Women Scientists in the Third World: The Indian Experience.* New Delhi: SAGE Publications.

Tellis, A. 2000. 'Resisting Feminism'. *Indian Journal of Gender Studies* 8 (1): 117–119.

Tewari, R., and M. Bhardwaj. 2018. *Mapping Patents and Research Publications of Higher Education Institutes and National R&D Laboratories of India.* Chandigarh: DST-Centre for Policy Research, Panjab University. Available at http://www.dst.gov.in/sites/default/files/FULL%20BOOK-Chandigarh.pdf (accessed on 8 August 2019).

UN. 1997. *Report of the Economic and Social Council for 1997.* New York, NY: United Nations. Available at http://www.un.org/documents/ga/docs/52/plenary/a52-3.htm (accessed on 8 August 2019).

———. 2002. 'Gender Mainstreaming'. An Overview. New York. NY: United Nations. Available at https://www.un.org/womenwatch/osagi/pdf/e65237.pdf (accessed on 8 August 2019).

Vaidya, Vidita A. 2017. 'Towards a Narrative of Gender in the Biological Sciences'. *Economic & Political Weekly* 52 (7): 83. Available at https://www.epw.in/author/vidita-vaidya-0?0=ip_login_no_cache%3Dc042279136a20d561724c5c0655c7939 (accessed on 8 August 2019).

Wallon, Gerlind, Sandra Bendiscioli, and Michele S. Garfinkel. 2015. *Exploring Quotas in Academia.* Available at https://www.embo.org/documents/science_policy/exploring_quotas.pdf (accessed on 8 August 2019).

Winchester, H., S. Lorenzo, L. Browning, and C. Chesterman. 2006. 'Academic Women's Promotions in Australian Universities'. *Employee Relations* 28 (6): 505–522.

INDEX

ABOUT THE AUTHOR

Namrata Gupta is a sociologist who works on women in science and engineering, with a focus on how the participation and rise of women scientists in academia and research laboratories is affected by the organizational aspects, patriarchal sociocultural norms and a lack of universalism in science. Her research also includes the study of women engineering students and relationship between gender and technology. She has published extensively with reputed journals of SAGE and other publishers. She has several publications to her credit in collaboration with renowned international researchers, such as those in the journals *Minerva* and *Cambridge Journal of International Affairs*, in the report 'Gender and Excellence in the Making' published by the European Union in 2004, and in the book *Handbook of Science and Technology Studies* published in 2007. She has been the recipient of several fellowships and grants from the Indian Council of Social Science Research (ICSSR). She has also been a member of the Associate Board of *Work, Employment and Society* from 2012 to 2017 and has been invited to international workshops including an NSF-funded workshop in the USA.

ABOUT THE AUTHOR

Namrata Gupta is a sociologist who works on women in science and engineering, with a focus on how the participation and rise of women scientists in academia and research laboratories is affected by the organizational aspects, patriarchal sociocultural norms and a lack of universalism in science. Her research also includes the study of women engineering students and relationship between gender and technology. She has published extensively with reputed journals of SAGE and other publishers. She has several publications to her credit in collaboration with renowned international researchers, such as those in the journals *Minerva* and *Cambridge Journal of International Affairs*, in the report 'Gender and Excellence in the Making' published by the European Union in 2004, and in the book *Handbook of Science and Technology Studies* published in 2007. She has been the recipient of several fellowships and grants from the Indian Council of Social Science Research (ICSSR). She has also been a member of the Associate Board of *Work, Employment and Society* from 2012 to 2017 and has been invited to international workshops including an NSF-funded workshop in the USA.